CineWorlding

CineWorlding

Scenes of Cinematic Research-Creation

Michael B. MacDonald

BLOOMSBURY ACADEMIC
NEW YORK • LONDON • OXFORD • NEW DELHI • SYDNEY

BLOOMSBURY ACADEMIC
Bloomsbury Publishing Inc
1385 Broadway, New York, NY 10018, USA
50 Bedford Square, London, WC1B 3DP, UK
29 Earlsfort Terrace, Dublin 2, Ireland

BLOOMSBURY, BLOOMSBURY ACADEMIC and the Diana logo are trademarks of
Bloomsbury Publishing Plc

First published in the United States of America 2023
Paperback edition published 2024

Copyright © Michael B. MacDonald, 2023

For legal purposes the Acknowledgements on p. viii constitute an extension of this copyright page.

Cover design: Louise Dugdale
Cover image: CSA-Printstock/Getty Images

All rights reserved. No part of this publication may be reproduced or transmitted in any form or by any means, electronic or mechanical, including photocopying, recording, or any information storage or retrieval system, without prior permission in writing from the publishers.

Bloomsbury Publishing Inc does not have any control over, or responsibility for, any third-party websites referred to or in this book. All internet addresses given in this book were correct at the time of going to press. The author and publisher regret any inconvenience caused if addresses have changed or sites have ceased to exist, but can accept no responsibility for any such changes.

Library of Congress Cataloguing-in-Publication Data

Names: MacDonald, Michael B., 1974- author.
Title: CineWorlding: scenes of cinematic research-creation / Michael B. MacDonald.
Description: [1.] | New York : Bloomsbury Academic, 2023. | Includes bibliographical references and index. | Summary: "Provides a methodology for the emerging area of screen production research and research-creation from a cine-ethnomusicological perspective"– Provided by publisher.
Identifiers: LCCN 2022028546 (print) | LCCN 2022028547 (ebook) | ISBN 9781501369391 (hardback) | ISBN 9781501369438 (paperback) | ISBN 9781501369407 (epub) | ISBN 9781501369414 (pdf) | ISBN 9781501369421 (ebook other)
Subjects: LCSH: Motion pictures–Philosophy. | Motion pictures and music.
Classification: LCC PN1995 .M226 2023 (print) | LCC PN1995 (ebook) | DDC 791.4301–dc23/eng/80880822
LC record available at https://lccn.loc.gov/2022028546
LC ebook record available at https://lccn.loc.gov/2022028547

ISBN: HB: 978-1-5013-6939-1
PB: 978-1-5013-6943-8
ePDF: 978-1-5013-6941-4
eBook: 978-1-5013-6940-7

Typeset by Deanta Global Publishing Services, Chennai, India

To find out more about our authors and books visit www.bloomsbury.com and sign up for our newsletters.

Concepts are exactly like sounds, colour or images, they are intensities which suit you or not. (Deleuze and Parnet 2007: 4)

Contents

Acknowledgements	viii
Introduction: A cinematic style of thought	1
1 CineWorlding with musics' undercommons	23
2 A worlding proposition for/from an alternate reality	49
3 *Living Flame of Love*: Creative practice research and practical musicology	75
4 Virtual and actual in posthumanography	97
5 Diagrammatic posthumanography of Margø's *In Between*	123
6 Bodying in intensive and extensive spaces: *John Wort Hannam Is a Poor Man*	147
7 *Quartet 2* and affect vectoring	173
8 Crystal image in cinematic research-creation: *Pimachihowan*	189
9 The crowd behind the lens, *WE'RE TOO LOUD*	211
10 *Elders' Room*: The opportunities and challenges of decoloniality	237
11 Activist minor cinema	259
Notes	267
Bibliography	284
Index	296

Acknowledgements

This book is a statement of where I am at the moment, in the middle of a developing cinematic research-creation practice. This middling is a singularity, but it is never alone. There are many people who are part of these cinematic research-creation investigations both in front and behind the camera, in the editing suite, audiences, lecture halls, and as editors, reviewers and readers of the following chapters. There have been so many rich discussions that it is impossible to credit everyone who has influenced cineworlding. Thank you to all of you who come out to independent films, to lectures, attend classes and ask questions, because you have no idea how your curiosity spurs a genesis of thinking-feeling, a proliferation of rooms of thought and joyful solidarity.

I am always amazed that people want to be in one of my films. I have so much gratitude for all of the time and attention, generosity and willingness to play together. None of the films nor any ideas in this book could possibly have taken form without you.

Andy Bennett and Paula Guerra and the KISMIF family have provided an exciting space to discuss these ideas, to think-feel and talk about how cinematic research methods can contribute something to making our cities and scenes more connected and resilient. I have had incredible experiences working with graduate students and researchers at the KISMIF Summer School, and with support from the European Union ERASMUS + program, I gave a series of lectures at the University of Porto in the summer of 2019, which turned out to be an important ecology for the germination of the ideas you are about to read. KISMIF provides an opportunity to connect with many artists, activists and academics and continues to have an enormous impact on my development as a research-creation practitioner.

It is one thing to think-feel the intensities that follow but it is quite another to make them concepts. I need to recognize Erin Manning for the generous hours of conversation and particularly the encouragement to use the experience of process directly, to allow the event to be the source of the concepts no matter how strange they sometimes appear at the beginning.

Thank you Sable Chan, for your introduction to the choral music scene and your careful reading and thoughtful questions. Thanks to Diana Pearson, for being part of all of these wild journeys. Your constant support while listening to ideas develop, your patience in reading drafts and your always helpful feedback (usually over drinks!) have opened so many rooms for new thoughts. And finally, to Barley for the constant breaks from writing and the reminder of the importance of cultivating more-than-human family.

I would also like to thank the MacEwan University Faculty of Fine Arts and Communications and recognize the valuable financial support from the Social Science Research Council of Canada (SSHRC), without which cinematic research-creation would perhaps only be an idea.

Introduction

A cinematic style of thought

How can new styles of thought be developed, knowing that style in philosophy is not decorative, but is rather a navigational tool that traces the force and movement of concepts?

(Braidotti 2019: 122)

As a relational matrix of humans and nonhumans, or 'a mode of existence' (Simondon 2016; Latour 2002), technology is at the heart of questions of mattering, and consequently at the heart of the political. And precisely because technology is about making connections, it 'matters which ones get made and unmade' (Haraway in Kunzru 1997); it matters whether those connections are aiming at the appropriation and commodification of the generative forces of human and nonhuman bodies for the demands of the political economy, or working towards the production of a more liveable future for everyone.

(Barla 2018)

In the third act of *Another Day at the Office* (2019), a career retrospective short film commissioned by Paris' Pompidou Centre, Richard Linklater sits in a psychologist's office inquiring about a potential ADHD diagnosis, but with no interest in pursuing therapy: 'I used to think that the arts were some kind of calling, but now I think it's just maybe . . . the right therapies for the right conditions.' In this quick retort, Linklater points to the overturning of a modernist aesthetic inheritance. Art is not about a calling, the work of genius or separate from living in the world, it is the 'right therapies for the right conditions'. This echoes Felix Guattari idea that 'art is not just the activity of established artists but of a whole subjective creativity' (1995: 91). Art making need not be defined by representation, form and narrative; it can be an emergence of a singularity within a world of vectoring forces, sensations and concepts. It can be, in other words, an ethico-aesthetic practice. For Guattari, the ethico-aesthetic is a particular kind of social therapy, not a singular therapy that works on a presumed unified subject, limited to patient and doctor, but as becoming of an ecological singularity, an assemblage: 'The assemblages of aesthetic desire and the operators of virtual ecologies are not entities which can be circumscribed within the logic of discursive sets ... one gets to know them not through representation but through affective contamination. They start to exist in you, in spite of you' (1995: 93). Perhaps the experience of creative practice, art's process, troubles inherited notions of agency and anthropocentricism. Linklater is an artist, his observations on art as therapy come from a practitioner and not an aesthetic theorist. Is art different as process, when its concepts sprout from within the ecology of creative practice? When you take seriously creative process as a location of research, many new kinds of nonhuman beings play decisive roles and require explanation. This highlights the ethical relations between human and nonhuman beings operating in ecologies and suggests that the therapeutic may be bound up with the emergence of new creative beings, and that its practice may be profoundly political. When a cinematic camera plays a decisive role in an emergence, it is also profoundly aesthetic.

In this very short and disarming film, Linklater brings together critical theoretical questions about spectacle, financialization and the market, situating his creative practice as an ethical practice that cannot help but circulate within flows of capital. And also a practice that cannot help but to make space for aesthetic practice and creative livingness. Even though Linklater is required to circulate within financial circuits, his creative practice is not defined by them, not reduced to an object of capital, and it can still be therapeutic. There is a feeling of a Brechtian dis-ease at the completion of the film, characteristic of Linklater's cinematic approach. The film concludes in a more or less celebratory *I am happy* way, but his happiness does not wipe out his concern about being able to make another movie. Will he remain forever stuck in capitalist pre-production meetings? His angst over the capitalist control of aesthetic production, the market jargon that he tries to avoid becoming snared by, his critical ruminations on spectacle, and ultimately humble realization of cinema as therapy is a good place to begin to think about cinematic research-creation process as being in potential for capture, critique and care.

We live in a time of previously unknown audiovisual potential. The emergence of the digital cinema ecosystem in 2009 has transformed communication. Cinema or audiovisual production has never been more accessible, but cinematic realism has paradoxically never seemed more complex and entwined with capital. As I write this introduction in summer 2022, Instagram has announced that it has moved away from being a still photo app and has reoriented itself to 'reels'. Audiovisual self-production has mutated as a consequence of social media and people have never been more comfortable thinking of themselves as brands. 'Media creators' produce themselves as content, not art, and produce themselves for an attention economy. The incredible possibility for media production and dissemination is, as Jacques Derrida and Bernard Stiegler point out, a *pharmakon*, both a poison and a cure. Audiovisual technics (the ability to read and write in digital cinema) has never been more accessible to the general public. The downside or poison is that capitalist self-production is, like Linklater's production company, deeply coded by the machinery of advanced platform capitalism. The technology is available for us all to know each other differently, more intimately and complexly, and what is emerging are echo chambers and division. The question that this book poses is how a digital cinematic poetic therapy might be realized from the context of ethnographic music studies. Cineworlding's take-away is that while ethnographic cinema has been committed to representation as a mark of its rigour, the new paradigm that research-creation offers is a way to rethink ethnography beyond representation, to think-feel creativity and becoming as rigorous in its own way, and to innovate models for digital creative education and experimental cinema-thinking. Ethnography is important; it is a kind of scholarly realism that can play a role in this emerging media scape, this technosphere. But not as it currently exists because it is too coded by humanism.

Following critical and engaged pedagogues like Paulo Freire and bell hooks, we know that education can be a place for community building and solidarity. The question becomes how might higher education become more than it is, to utilize an audiovisual technological production practice to open learning, self-inquiry, social inquiry, environmental inquiry, and to invent practices of *well-becoming*. After more than fifteen years as a scholarly filmmaker, I have had a variety of experiences that suggest to me that cinema production has much more to offer teaching and learning than what is currently understood. Cinema is often reduced to its films. But cinema production, the making of films, is rarely an area of sustained inquiry. I believe, as I will argue throughout this book, that cinema production, as Linklater suggests, is an ethico-aesthetic practice that has the potential to have positive impacts on teaching and learning in higher education. Centering creativity over representation moves us 'beyond the relations of actualized forces, virtual ecology will not simply attempt to preserve the endangered species of cultural life but equally to engender conditions for the creation and development of unprecedented formations of subjectivity that have never been seen and never felt' (Guattari 1995: 91). The development of research-creation, as it is called in Canada, or practice-based and art-based research elsewhere, is the key to this revitalized ethnographic and educational practice.

Research-creation occurs when research is applied to creative practice, and when creative practice becomes a site of research. The process is iterative, each term working on the other, and it leaves neither research nor creative practice unimpacted. There will always be at least four types of outcomes from cinematic research-creation: (a) a film, (b) reports on process, (c) a transformed filmmaker and (d) new and sometimes short-lived social groups. In my experience with cinematic research-creation, artistic process has become my main musicological and cinematic concern, sometimes leaning towards practical musicology, sometimes towards cinematic practice, sometimes philosophy. If my experience is representative, then a research-creation practitioner will be an artist-researcher and as a consequence they will be connected to the academy, an art world and a social world. In my case I move between the music industry, the film industry, the university and music communities in Canada, the United States and Portugal. I am never completely settled in any one location. As a filmmaker, I'm too much a musicologist, as an ethnomusicologist too much a filmmaker, as a researcher too much an artist. This instability is characteristic of the process that cinematic research-creation puts into motion. And at the same time, the instability leads to exciting possibilities for musicological and ethnomusicological research. Instability should not be read as inherently lacking in rigour; instead, rigor should be determined by the ability to stay with the complexity of process. Doing this requires the development of a process-based conceptual vocabulary.

At the beginning of my work in cinematic research-creation, I was looking for a way to think about cine-ethnomusicology from the perspective of cinematic production. Along the way, which is discussed in the pages that follow, I experienced much more than I expected. Cinematic research-creation continues some of what was started in ethnographic film but the emergence of the digital cinema ecosystem has changed more than just the cinematic medium; it brings ethnographic cinema and digital humanities together. Becoming a cinematic artist without relinquishing a researcher subjectivity poses all manner of questions. Asking what it means to think cinematically about music leads to recognizing the agency of the camera, of music, and brings posthumanism and process philosophy together. It proposes the possibility that cinema-thinking is a different type of thinking than book-thinking. This observation provokes deep questions about Western ideas of reason, rationality and universality and provokes political questions about knowledge and the psychic, social, technological and environmental ecologies that emerge with it. It also poses ethical questions about what one does with a technology capable of moving digital information at above two-thirds the speed of light. Holding on to both research and artist subjectivities provokes questions about multiplicity, searching questions about how many people are actually behind this lens, in this body, but also about the production of more subjectivities, more complexity in the relationality that the camera production process sets into motion. A multiplicity behind a lens, a multiplicity in front of the lens, all constantly embedded in complex ecologies of objects, practices, beings that are moving at different speeds, at different rhythms. Cinematic research-creation is complex because it is vibrational and productive, and perhaps significant for the same reason.

Take a music video, for instance, which is often reduced to its capitalist role as advisement for the music. When a music video is used in cinematic research-creation, music video production can be studied from a variety of angles of interest to music studies. It can be an ethnographic site where the production process provides insights into the relationships between music creators and audiovisual creators. Sociologically, the music video's circulation and reception can be studied to provide insight into question of spectatorship, fandom and industry. Musicologically, the becoming of music's audio-vision can be studied to understand the ways that music and musical audio-vision are entangled, how music becomes visualized and visuality becomes musicalized. Cinematic research-creation allows a perspective from behind the camera to explore auto-ethnographically the creative practice that seems to suggest that music's affects are vectored in rhythmic visual percepts, or in other words, the mixing of sound and visual perceptions that can be called *chromesthesia*. It can also provide access to the kinds of learning that are experienced by digital cinematic DIY artists, and the kinds of relationships that emerge from these creative practices. The exciting and challenging thing about cinematic research-creation is the complexity of its potential outcomes. And this is precisely what has made writing this book both exciting and difficult – cinematic research-creation troubles disciplinarity and language.

Following Felix Guattari's idea of the ethico-aesthetic paradigm, the creative practice occurs in an ecological system, contributing to it and drawing on it. I repeatedly discuss four ecologies (conceptual, social, technological, environmental) as an attempt to more precisely follow the flows of forces. These ecologies are only possible to treat separately in theory, in a kind of abstract process that writing allows. The ecologies always emerge as components of a singularity. When a music researcher makes a film with people, they form a singularity; they collectively emerge. This emergence draws upon these four ecologies to produce a complex node. How this node functions, the ethics of its practice in articulating itself can be considered a social therapeutic when it forms an emergent solidarity that benefits everything that makes it up. This emergent multi-bodied singularity is aesthetic, political and ethical. Calling it a node risks dissolving the complexity to a point, but it is useful momentarily for providing a sociological perspective. My work with KISMIF (*Keep It Simple, Make It Fast!*), an international DIY music and culture network curated by Paula Guerra and Andy Bennett, has emphasized to me the global emergence of these nodes and the ways these nodes hyperlink with each other through academic/practitioner/artist networks that are oriented to doing this kind of ethico-aesthetic work. KISMIF constantly deals with the three Cs of capture, critique and care. Making nodes is necessary critical and care-based work, just as recognizing that the nodes have a molecular component, are unique, made up of beings of different kinds and have ecological impacts on four registers. The cinematic research-creation node is productive, networked, more-than-human and part of cinematic research-creation.

Reporting on this productivity requires the development of a literary style that moves back and forth between four ecological registers. The artist-research can never be separated from the study, and each study, like each work of art, each node, each network of nodes, is specific, emergent and non-generalizable. This has proven to be challenging for readers who want to hang onto a scientific account of culture. But it is also important to remember that over the twentieth century, science has begun to learn to contend with complexity and emergence. What is scientific is to be true to the evidence even if it does not conform with or confirm previously held expectations. In this sense, cineworlding is indeed a scientific account of cinematic research-creation even if at times the shifting perspectives, the resistance to traditional Western ideas of agency, of subjectness, are complex, unstable, shifting and disconcerting.

Donna Haraway's *A Cyborg Manifesto* (1991) set this project in motion: 'So my cyborg myth is about transgressed boundaries, potent fusions, and dangerous possibilities which progressive people might explore as one part of needed political work' (154). The original plan for this work was in three parts. The first part was going to be written from the perspective of *cyborgrapher*, a cyborg-ethnographer who comes into consciousness in the middle of action. The cyborgrapher is part cinema camera, part hard drive, part immediate uplink to servers and audiovisual platforms, and part wetware. The cyborgrapher moves about the world making audio-vision for reasons that remain unclear. The second part of the work would have been theoretical analysis of audio-vision and ethnography, with part three dedicated to the observational documentary, music videos and improvisational fiction films (ethnofictions) that I have made over the last fifteen years.[1] However, this plan began to immediately run into problems. Conceptual tentacles began to reach out past the planned sections. The cyborgrapher needed theory, needed a discussion of specific film projects, and needed specific resources to position itself/ourselves. We (the cyborgrapher, theorist, artist) could not abide with the spitting of us up across three predetermined sections. Our process could not effectively be divided without these organizational separations doing damage to the reporting. We began to realize that what was organizing our thinking was an unhelpful desire to separate practice from theory from technique and all from sensing and world-emerging/worlding. Cineworlding would not abide separations. It was an ecotone, a space of ecological complexity where individual ecologies, digital cinema technology ecosystem, ethnographic research ecosystem, philosophy ecosystem, cinematic art ecosystem interfere/entangle/interpenetrate each other to produce a rich ecological zone where new complex beings proliferate. We found ourselves with these beings.

The language that I use across the book will at times feel personal, and it is necessarily so because it is impossible to separate one's body from the more-than-human flux of process and emergence in this research-creation ecotone. My literary approach is meant to be read as a report from a matrix/ecology. The matrix, for instance, is the process of practising cine-ethnomusicology where a camera-body interface began to sprout/emerge, not as a consequence of a distanced judgement on what a camera does, but first experienced as slight tremors in my thinking-feeling. I began to see-hear differently when I looked through a viewfinder and listened through headphones. At first I enjoyed it as an artist, but soon it began to trouble the researcher. It was as if the researcher was allowing this data to slip by unanalysed. Perhaps because the researcher, accustomed to ethnographic film, was used to thinking of the cinema camera as a passive recording device. But in this case the researcher began to contend with the camera's generative relationship with the artist. The artist-researcher began to see-hear in audio-vision. As this filmic process developed, the artist-researcher began to see cinematic futures – a virtual editing suite and virtual film screening – not because they intended to, but because these futures began to overlay onto the research-artist's seeing-hearing. But not only this. They began to see-hear pasts, visual images and sound-images that had the signature of other filmmakers from other places and times. It was as if these other filmmakers would come alive in the camera-body assemblage. The continuing of these 'hauntings' or emergences mixed complexly with audio-visionary future-pasts.

Rosi Braidotti writes: 'What happens to subjectivity in this complex field of forces and data flows? My argument is that it becomes an expanded relational self, engender by the cumulative effects of all these factors' (2013: 60). The 'expanded relational self', a posthuman subject is complex 'because it is interconnected with changing what counts as "we" – the subjects of thinking and of knowledge' (2019: 131). Braidotti's naming of the *posthuman condition* is a dual recognition that 'we' are posthuman and post-anthropocentric. The 'we' is defined as 'We-Are-(All)-In-This-Together-But-We-Are-Not-One-And-The-Same (Braidotti 2019: 52–5). The post in both instances does not mean 'after' Humanism; it signals a critical intervention into the construction of the Human as Man, what bell hooks has called *Imperialist white-supremacist capitalist patriarchy*. Posthuman also signals a return to the externalities of the Human, what has been Othered by the Human, namely racial, ethnic and classed Others, nature and technology. This overlaps with post-anthropocentricism. This requires, according to Braidotti, 'to reinscribe posthuman bodies into radical relationality, including webs of power relations at the social, psychic, ecological and micro-biological or cellular levels. The post-anthropocentrism of our science and our globalized and technologically mediated times makes it urgent to work towards 'a new techno-scientific democracy' (Haraway 1997: 95)' (Braidotti 2013: 102). This is complex work, especially for the humanities, because it requires an 'understanding of ourselves as a species, and not just of a culture or polity. Secondly, it demands accountability for the disastrous planetary consequence of our species' supremacy and the violent rule of the sovereign Anthropos. Most people with an education in the Humanities and the Social sciences are neither accustomed nor trained to think in term of species' (2019: 10). While philosophical posthumanism critiques the Anthropos, ethnography is dealing with ongoing coloniality and post-coloniality and the Dēmos: Ethnos. To join with posthumanism, it seems that not only does ethnomusicology need to deconstruct its commitment to the Ethnos but also to its commitment to the Anthropos. Ethnomusicology and cine-ethnomusicology could look at the posthuman condition with fear, but it is also possible to approach it with affirmative enthusiasm and invention. My proposal in CineWorlding is for the development of *posthumanography* as a way forward. For all of the philosophical richness of posthumanism as it currently exists, I think *ethnography* (rethought as *posthumanography*) still has a major role to play in documenting and sharing emerging posthuman inventiveness. *CineWorlding: Scenes in Cinematic Research-Creation* is an attempt to respond to the posthuman condition with a cinematic posthumanographic research-creation method called cineworlding.

The challenge with *posthumanography* is that it does not occur at one interface nor even on one continuum. For instance, ethnography might find itself on the natureculture continuum in its practice. But upon closer inspection, the ethnographer finds themselves, through their use of technology, on a technoculture continuum as well. My original construction of the cyborgrapher suffered from this, positioning the cyborgrapher somewhere on the technoculture continuum and the theorist on the natureculture continuum. But I soon realized that the cyborgrapher emerges in process, existing in an ecotone of natureculture and technoculture. Further, as I attempted to write the cyborgrapher into existence, I began to realize that its singularity was never separate from my theoretical and artistic singularities. This required bringing Guattari's *three ecologies*, together with Deleuze's cinema books, Deleuze and Guattari's work on *What Is Philosophy?*, and Brian Massumi and Erin Manning's activist philosophy, together with Braidotti and Bernard Stiegler. Stiegler contributed a three-book study on *Technics and Time* which contributes technics to Braidotti's posthumanism. *Posthumanography* seemed to emerge when this theoretical ecology was allowed to participate in digital cinematic practice.

This book is written for those of us who look-listen through an audio-enabled camera and see-feel a world overflowing with forces and movements of all kinds and who then feel compelled to share. To be compelled to make films is to be drawn into a *relational matrix of humans and nonhumans*. I still remember the feeling of being drawn into my parents Super8 camera. The simple world of my childhood kitchen was broken open when I looked through the viewfinder, I was entertained by the play of light spilling through the window. I was drawn into the curves and lines, light and shadow. It was not a different perception of the kitchen that I inspected as part of a determined whole, but instead each zone between light and shadow, each line or curve, emerged as percepts that affected me for a duration that had with it a quality of felt intensity, an affect. The duration of looking was a duration of feeling, not inspection. I did not feel separated from the space, separated by the technology. Instead, I felt closer to a world that was not invisible, it was there and familiar, but vibrated my perception anew. A virtual world unlocked by the camera lens. I felt the force of light, its affects emerging as my body submerged into it, the camera, my body, kitchen, light and duration all together as a singularity. Perhaps it was this event that drew me, much later, into filmmaking. It is certainly this ongoing experience and my need to make sense of it and to share it, that is the inspiration for my inquiry into cinematic research-creation and ultimately this book.

Some years later, I would have the same experience with a microphone and headphones. The sound-images of an environment reawakened a feeling of the virtual. The viewfinder and microphone acted on me. Recording technologies have played a central role in my creative and now academic life. These technologies have always felt as if they are extensions of my body. These technologies do not create an artificial world, they bring out the virtualities that are swarming there. I have secretly felt myself to be a creative cyborg and was liberated by Rosi Braidotti's *The Posthuman* and Bernard Stiegler's *Technics and Time*. I no longer feel like I have to hide my posthuman-ness because I realized that it was not a private fantasy; it is a feeling of confluence with audiovisual technics. Understanding posthuman creative practice has become central to my theoretical project, *cineworlding*. Braidotti, however, does not look through a camera and Stiegler does not make films. Cineworlding is an posthumanographic inquiry into these philosophical ideas, a space to test them out and perhaps to build on them and challenge them. When I look-listen through a camera-microphone technological assemblage, continue this experience into the editing suite, and then onto a big screen with a group of people, I feel beauty and possibility. I do accept that I am by nature optimistic. But it feels like beauty, optimism and poetry[2] are indeed necessary if for no other reason that they are life-affirming and provide a space to explore capture, critique and care. The affirmation of life must be oriented to all life not just human life. Cinema is a way for me to witness the poetry of ecological life across the conceptual, social, technological and environmental ecologies. Can the practice of cinema production help us cultivate an ecological therapeutic for living?

Plan for the book

I began making films in the early 2000s by compulsion. I had long felt drawn to cinema but lacked access to the technology. During my PhD, I purchased a small camera and began making films. More than a decade later, I began to feel that my cinema work had much to contribute to my scholarship, but I had a challenge finding models that resonated with me. I read ethnographic film literature but found there little about what happens when you look through the lens. I also dove into film studies and enjoyed enormously the approaches to film analysis, but once again the film was already made. Filmmaking literature, and there is a lot of it, focuses on cinematic production techniques and was enormously valuable for my developing techniques but did not get me closer to theorizing what was happening in my process, in my technological entanglements, nor was there models of critique.

I was struck by a seemingly simple question: what holds filming, editing, screening and audience filmmaker Question & Answer together? How do they cohere as a social and cultural practice? And further, why is it that this practice has played such a minor role in my academic training and never as part of a class that was not already framed as a film production class. Is making a film so much less valuable than writing a paper? It is certainly not less accessible. I tried coming up with all kinds of structural answers and metaphysical answers but they were all disappointing in one way or another. I began to think that perhaps there is much more going on in this process than the available literature covered. And that perhaps, if I could begin to explain the academic value of digital cinema then I could convince my fellow faculty to accept cinematic work from students.

Research-creation was developing and I was introduced to Erin Manning and Brian Massumi, who shared a fondness for process thinking. From them I began to realize that there is a great deal happening in the details of my practice, body-technology assemblage, and that I could focus my attention on questions that pertained precisely to the relation between bodying and cinema practice as they in-fold each other. They helped me pose obvious questions. For instance, how do I know when to hit record? Is this a decision that I make?, a triggering from the camera?, a meeting place of forces?

My approach to *CineWorlding: Scenes of Cinematic Research-Creation* begins with my films. All of the films discussed in this book are freely available at www.cineworlding.org. In the opening chapters, I begin to think about neo-materialist worlding within research-creation and sketch out a cinematic empiricism that is rich with virtualities. In Chapter 3, I follow the creation of a choral music work from four notes heard on a late-night movie through to its staging as a 45-minute artistic reflection on the beauty of spirituality. This film allowed me to think about how music works to vector beauty affects through bodies. Chapter 4 surveys a number of films and thinks about Deleuze's virtuality and actuality. In Chapter 5, we begin to think about posthuman subjectivity a topic that we return to in Chapters 8, 9 and 10. In Chapter 5, we see how the cinema allows a collection of bodily intensities to emerge onto the screen's extensive space. In Chapter 8, music playing in the intensive space of the filmmakers body emerges on screen, where in Chapters 9 and 10 we complicate the body of the filmmaker showing it to be a crowd behind the lens, a crowd that is potentially composed by as yet unrecognized colonial forces.

In preparation for the mixing of theory and practice that is the basis of the book, I have included three workshops that you can do to help set the stage for your reading. You can use these exercises with your class or do them on your own. I have found that the type of posthuman thinking that emerges in cineworlding's posthumanography is best approached when it is already grounded in the experience of cinematic production. My theoretical propositions in this book come out of cinematic practice, problems posed in the act of thinking about filmmaking. The challenge in the planning and writing of the book is how to put these posthuman experiences into words. Students often chafe at the posthuman language that I employ until they ground themselves in cinema production. Once they do this, they often begin to see-feel the need for the sometimes strange terminology and turn of phrase. When we find ourselves lost for a term to explain the experience, concepts fill the gap. Concepts are not made to distance us from the world but to bring us closer. Creating concepts is not something magical or something that requires special abilities to notice; it is just that we are often not provided the time to attune ourselves to our affective relationships with technology. So as an offer, I include the following three short reflections on central concepts that appear throughout the book. This operates as a kind of definitions section, but the definitions are affective and produced in your body more than they are conceptual. This may help orient you to the content that we will be exploring and elaborating throughout *CineWorlding*.

Cineworlding's affective technicity

Reading:
Deleuze, Gilles and Felix Guattari. 1994. 'Percept, Affect, and Concept'. In *What Is Philosophy?* New York: Columbia University Press.

Reflection on percepts and affects

Using a camera, whether it is your cell phone or a digital cinema camera, invites you into cinema-thinking. This invitation does not need to be taken up. For some there is resonance, an intuition that there is something that can be experienced beyond perception. For others, there is no resonance. If you resonate with look-listening to the world through this technology, and are inspired into worlding the world in cinema, then there is already a seed of a new kind of thinking taking root in your body: cinema-thinking.

Cinema-thinking is compositional doing-making, images that take shape by working with blocks of sensation in duration. The camera equipment is a materiality (lens, sensor, controls, camera-body, memory, light and editing equipment) that makes cinema possible, but does not define it, but it does begin a process. This materiality is to filmmaking what a brush and paint is to painting. This is the plane of materiality. In cinema-thinking, the plane of materiality enframes the world and through this act of doing-making moves towards a plane of composition, in the doing-making of the film. This is not a one-way voyage and does not stop as long as you are developing your cinema-thinking. The plane of compositions also informs the plane of materiality, as you will see in the next exercise. They are in dynamic relations and between them and through them emerges new kinds of thinking, that begin to produce refrains, territorialities, monuments of percepts and affects.

As we will see in the first exercise, the recognition of thinking between these planes is an event. Why come up with fancy names? Because Deleuze and Guattari are trying to show that there is a process of movement-thinking in making-doing, that the technology of art is not art, that the beings of percepts and affects are forces in the world. They want to do this so that we can see that cinema-thinking IS thinking, and a different form of thinking from conceptual thinking.

This is an important starting place because it begins an invitation to think across difference. Cinema-thinking is already starting to think difference, and to see that it is a thinking that is not human alone, or better, more-than-human.

This opens a productive space to decolonize, not through negative critique alone, but using a power of positive critique to open a space to think about thinking.

This positive critique is important for universities and school in that the practice of cinema-thinking enacts a positive critique of the literary culture of learning. There is more and different kinds of thinking, and cinema-thinking begins to open a door to thinking about thinking. These different forms of thinking can live together, but as is often the case, cinema-thinking is reduced, in the eyes of the academy, to a technical practice. The technical practice is seen to be a craft, and a craft is seen to be of a lower level of thinking from philosophy or science. *CineWorlding* is learning to think thinking differently, to put thinking with percepts and affects on the same level as thinking with concepts. This is a positive critique that will help us move towards decolonizing knowledge.

Assignment one: Cinema-thinking[3]

There is not one place to begin, but one has to begin. The camera on your phone as it is or enabled with an app (Filmic Pro, for instance – to help unlock the potential of the phone's camera) is enough. But if you have a digital cinema camera or any camera for that matter, go and grab it. Make sure that you are recoding audio and I would suggest you wear earphones. I want you to think percepts and affects as you produce them with the materiality of this equipment. The first assignment is simple.

1. Use your camera app as it is and point it at something close and then far away. Do this a few times paying attention to the time it takes for the camera to refocus. There are a number of events here – the event of focus, the event of finding focus, the event of focus again. Record this process. Watch it. Put it away for a day or so. Watch it again. Finally, write about the difference between recording it and watching it later. The difference is what we are looking for. This is another event.
2. Take your camera and record whatever you want for any amount of time. Leave it for a day or so and then look back at it. Write about the experience of time in the shot. This is called time pressure.
3. Think about where you grew up. Pay attention to the texture of the space, the closeness or openness, the colours, intensities, rhythms, timbres. Take your camera and begin to collect visual images and audio images that feel like these percepts and affects. Try to avoid direct references – like a

black-and-white photo of a street. Instead, think about the percepts and affects. Write about the process.

Reading:
Manning, Erin. 2016. 'Artfulness'. In *The Minor Gesture*. Durham: Duke University Press.

Reflection on artfulness

Most of the artists I have known who have remained engaged in practice over time do so because it is an important or perhaps defining part of their life practice. A life practice is the development of systems of techniques for existence, a dedication to the development of these techniques into an expressive regime of relationality. This expressive and existential regime is complex and to reduce it to a sound object or visual object erases the livingness that resonates through the world setting into motion thinking-feeling of all sorts. This dedication to resonance, to existential thinking-feeling, is precisely what Manning means when she refuses the object-centred idea of art (the object) and defines art as a way, art as practice. The way is oriented to learning and 'acts as a bridge towards new processes, new pathways' (2016: 47). What guides the development of these techniques into a fully developed technicity? Intuition, Manning says, 'both gets a process on its way and acts as the decisive turn within experience that activates a productive opening within time's durational folds' (2016: 47). What does intuition work on, where does its energy come from and what directionality does it service?

In his book *The Fold*, Gilles Deleuze considers Leibniz's critique of Descartes' thinking about the relationship between the mind in the body. He quotes Leibniz who wrote, 'I must have a body . . . because an obscure object lives in me' (1992: 97). He goes on to say that the body does not explain the mind that 'the depths of the mind are dark', but that this mind, though dark, possess a 'clear and distinct zone of expression'; it is as if 'the depths were made by an infinity of tiny folds endlessly furling and unfurling in every direction' (98). Deleuze goes on to say that these folds are microperceptions of the world and are 'minute, obscure, confused perceptions that make up our macroperceptions' (99). Manning's intuition resonates with the energy of the folds, the learning of the mind's body and the body's mind as it worlds the world. Artfulness is worlding and 'intuition crafts the operative problem' (Manning 2016: 47). Intuition is not therefore a surface practice, it is not unthinking instinct, but working at the level of microperceptions, it is the thinking that is not yet conscious thinking, macroperceptions. Intuition moves across the plane of materiality unfolding a 'clear and distinct zone of expression' drawing the body-lens-microphone assemblage across the surface of the world, chasing energetic flows that flit at the corners of thinking-feeling. Folding and unfolding the world into the body's mind, establishing zones of expression folded into one's developing technicity. Just as we move from the plane of material to the plane of composition with the camera, so too do we move from the plane of material to the plane of composition with the editing software. Intuition guides the way.

Microperceptions that inform intuition and guide the development of the shot will be unfolded on the timeline of the editing software. The timeline becomes the starting point for the next operative problem, for the play of intuition. This play is complex. Walter Murch, the celebrated editor, points out in his classic *In the Blink of an Eye* that a scene made up of only twenty-five shots can be edited approximately in 39,999,999,999,999,999,999,999,999 different ways.' This level of complexity cannot be thought. It is beyond comprehension and the only way to move forward into this kind of complexity is by intuition. There is no best edit, or perfect edit, there is only your edit, the particular organization that gives your thoughts shape in duration. The proposition is then: what is your edit? It is the edit that resonates in you. Not the you that is trying to make something that looks like someone else's work, but the you that feels for the microperceptions in your work, the percepts and affects that allow the emergence of the plane of composition, thinking in time.

Assignment two: Cinema-thinking with the editor

There is not one place to begin, but one has to begin. Manning uses the term 'technicity' drawing from Gilbert Simondon's philosophy. By technicity Simondon means 'a way in which technical objects exist in the world',[4] which proposes a way of thinking of the human-editor relationship, but also the camera-editor, shot-editor, film-editor relationships. There are machine-machine relations just as surely as there are human-machine-world relations. This means that an editor is not a static thing but an ecology that you are entering. As you use the editing software, you will notice that the software will begin to work on you as well. You will consider your shots differently, your settings, your approach. The editor will work through you while you work through the editor. This is what Manning is getting at when she writes that artfulness is a 'rigorous process that consists in pushing technique to its limit, revealing its technicity. Technicity: the outdoing of technique that make the more-than of experience felt' (2016: 50).

1. The editor is not just a tool to cut clips together; it is a compositional space. Take your camera (your phone with or without the app) and shoot a number of random shots. Try to be as intentionally random as you can be (which may in itself be difficult)! Next, choose a piece of music. To try to stay with randomness use the number 1 pop hit on the day you were born. Put a clip of the music on the audio track and then begin to put your shots together. This is a montage exercise. Pay attention to the kinds of 'sense' that begins to emerge. Write about it.
2. Repeat the first exercise with the number 1 R&B or country or hip-hop (etc.) hit on the day you were born.
3. Continuity editing is the technique of putting shots next to one another to convey movement through space and time. Film a friend walking and disappearing around a corner. Stay far enough away that your friend disappears. Now go somewhere else not connected to this particular street. And film your friend walking and taking another corner. Then film them walking up to a door somewhere else. Put these all together on your timeline. Consider the worlding that you have created.
    a. Using your phone as an audio recorder, record footsteps, bird sounds, traffic noise, whatever and put these together on the timeline.
    b. Put it away for a day or so and then come back and watch it.
    c. Write about it.
4. Time pressure shot is a long single shot that brings forward the feeling of time. Take a time pressure shot.
    a. Put it on your timeline both with and without music.
    b. Come back the next day and watch it.
    c. Write about what you feel.

Reading:

Deleuze, Gilles and Felix Guattari. 1987. '1837: Of the Refrain'. In *A Thousand Plateaus*, 310–23. New York: Columbia University Press.

Reflection on the diagram between the plane of material and plane of composition

The plane of material and plane of composition need to begin somewhere, to generate the process where the material of the universe presents itself to machine-perception, to a process that Deleuze calls an 'image of thought'. The image of thought is the thinking of thinking. It is a set of techniques and practices that we recognize as thinking. In the last reflection, we followed Leibniz's critique of Descartes. Where for Descartes, thinking presented itself as self-evident. But we might ask of him, how did you recognize thinking? How did you know what was happening is called thinking? And that you can write it down so that we can also recognize the thinking-of-thought. There is a smuggling in of an 'image of thought', that Deleuze through Leibniz identifies. Leibniz characterized dark and mysterious processes in the body, generating both a thinking body and an embodied mind. But the process, thinking, is not self-evident unless we already recognize what thinking is. This observation, that thinking is not self-evident but requires an 'image of thought' to identify, presents an opportunity to think thinking differently. Machine-perception is broad enough to include the kinds of thinking that audiovisual machines generate through our engagement with them. In cinema there are two that we are interested in, audio-thinking and visual-thinking. In contemporary cameras they are conjoined into sync sound, audio-vision. Between the planes of material and composition operates an abstract machine, a diagram. It is the diagram that enacts a force onto the plane of material drawing it into the plane of composition. The application of force is the diagram. Diagrams, as Deleuze and Guattari point out, have proper names and dates. For the time being think of it as a style. The signature way an artist realizes a shot. It is the way that you make a shot, it is the feeling of seeing like an artist you admire and want to copy. The moment I framed a shot like Werner Herzog or Les Blank, or Agnes Varda was also the moment that I understood the diagram. Herzog, Blank, Varda are diagrams that live in my body; they are the names of aesthetic forces that come alive in the act of making a shot. Till I make the shot I did not realize they lived in me, but in the act of composing they came alive.

Audio-vision starts up when we jump in with intension and begin to survey the world. A filmmaker is someone who gets swept away in the potentials of audio-vision, where the perceptual world in transformed: 'Every milieu is vibratory, in other words, a block of space-time constituted by the periodic repetition of the component' (313). The vibratory potentiality of the world is the plane of material for the filmmaker. The rhythms of the world, world music, present potential refrains that constitute the plane of materials and it is intuition about the force of refrains that initiates a new 'image of thought', that of cinema-thinking.

Cinema-thinking is the machine that operates between the plane of material and the plane of composition; it is the organization of these techniques (focus, movement, pan, colour temperature etc.) that acts on the plane of materials transcoding the images of perception into the plane of material, transcoding the plane of materials into the plane of composition, transcoding the plane of composition into the plane of materials for the editor. We then gather these compositions, which we call shots, into a folder. The shots can be individual shots that operate on a single vector, or can be a collection of shots of the same image, taking different perspectives, different approaches to the same image, producing a multisided (or multi-eyed) image. This collection of images produces a refrain that presents itself virtually, that you can move around an image in perception looking at it from various angles, and in cinema this exploration can be extended using audio-vision to include not only the percept of the image but its affects (colouring, sound, sound art, music).

When we move to the timeline assemblage, we begin by taking these coded images and produce a new relation between them on the editor. They become decoded and their relations produce new codes: 'Every milieu is coded, a code being defined by periodic repetition: but each code is in a perpetual state of transcoding or transduction' (313). There are a variety of ways that these repetitions may be experienced. It can be the repetition of content, of framing, colouring, focus, movement, grain, pixel, depth, intensity, timbre, pitch or any other. Light and sound are vibrations and anything that is experienced is already in repetition, already forming a milieu, a refrain. A short burst of sound, or of colour is already a repetition of vibration whether it is light waves or sound waves. The repetition is rhythm, the rhythm is a refrain, the refrain gets coded and transcoded by ears, by microphones, by eyes, by camera lenses and the processors in the sensor, in the viewfinder, in the editor.

Artfulness is in intuition but also in the practice of intuition, its development into cinema-thinking. It is through the practice of cinema-thinking, in the experience of what happens with the camera that the image of thought of cinema-thinking emerges. I can describe in words an experience of cinema-thinking, in the event that produced a refrain that acts as a germ of an idea that stretches out and calls together a variety of forces, linking to other events, moving the force of perception across the curves and undulations of the world, but it will never simulate cinema-thinking. Cinema-thinking will only happen as machine-thinking, whether you are operating a camera, working with an editing software, or watching blocs of sensations in duration as you become entangled in audio-vision. But it is only in the process of being inside this entanglement, this milieu, that will allow the forces of cinema-thinking to emerge from the shadows of the body's mind and mind's body.

So why bother to write this at all? Because I believe that our familiarity with cinema-thinking has been coded as not-thinking. It has been coded as entertainment and its image of thought has remained unarticulated. Artists do not need to articulate cinema-thinking, though many have. And it is in serious deliberation of the interviews, lecture, and Q&As with people like Les Blank, Fellini, Herzog, Wenders, Varda, while also reading Deleuze, Guattari and Manning, that I have begun to realize the potential of writing about cinematic research-creation. There is a political significance to recognizing cinema-thinking. It opens up the possibility of recognizing a new image of thought in the university, which has perpetuated a single way of thinking, a neurotypicality, a belief that there is only one image of thought and it is self-evident, European and dominant. Cinema-thinking presents an image of thought much closer to us than most books, in the palm of our hands, streaming audio-vision for many, many more hours a day than most of us read. And we seem to know very little about it as a form of thinking. If my hunch is correct, it is because we have recognized the camera as an entertainment machine and have written it off. But I do not believe that a machine is coded to be anything but a machine, a tool that can be used to do any kind of work. I want to encourage us to start thinking about the machine of cinema as a new image of thought, opening us into the exciting world of cinematic research-creation. If we can begin to recognize cinema-thinking as thinking, we can then explore what thinking in audio-vision can enable, thinking-in-process, in duration, in vibration, in-act. And when we can begin to do this, we can also collectively expand our collective minds to recognize other forms of thinking, other images of thought, ultimately and hopefully, transforming the university to become more that it has been and concerned with the more-than-human.

Assignment three: Refrain in the grain/pixel/colour/sound

1. Take a series of shots of the same image but change the colour temperature each time by small increments. Put them on the time line and match the colours.
2. Record a collection of sounds, put them in an audio folder on your computer. Create an audio bin in the media tab and in the edit tab create a short musical piece with these clips of audio. Listen to the refrain that you produce and allow it to tell you what to film (chromesthesia – more on this later). Go collect those images and see what you come up with.
3. Take a series of shots that have no relationship to each other. Take clips of music and put the clips together on the timeline. Colour each clip expressively ignoring what is possible in reality, draw out the colour intensities from the music (intensive space).

1

CineWorlding with musics' undercommons

To be in but not of – this is the path of the subversive intellectual in the modern university.

(Harney and Moten 2013: 26)

Decoloniality, enclosure and the commons

The question of decoloniality is being posed everywhere in music and sound studies. It has become a central concern for music students who have created influential Facebook groups and social media accounts to push for institutional change. Scholars are also making significant contributions. Philip Ewel's 'white racial frame' in music theory (2020) developed into a popular video essay by Adam Neely, Dylan Robinson's Hungry Listening (2020), critical discussion about decolonializing of music history (Walker 2020) and music studies (Attas and Walker 2019; Tan 2021) are all making contributions. As I write this, there are job postings seeking to establish much-needed faculty and student diversity in music departments and schools in Canada and the United States. Diversity based on identity is necessary, important and long past due. But this will not transform the university alone, will not rid it of its coloniality. The North American university is increasingly corporatizing no longer ashamed of its complicity with capitalism, to job preparation, to work-integrated learning and the expansion of student debt. In music and sound studies, the expansion of legitimate subjects in the conservatory is illustration of its commitment to decoloniality, but it can also be characterized as an incursion into the musical commons.

Stefano Harney and Fred Moten in *The Undercommons: Fugitive Planning & Black Study* (2013) begin their thinking of coloniality and the university by way of Hollywood's 'upside down way that the make-believe media portrays colonial settlements . . . the settler is portrayed as surrounded by "natives," inverting, in Michael Parenti's view, the role of aggressor so that colonialism is made to look like self-defense' (2013: 17). The settler's fort is indeed surrounded by 'the common beyond and beneath-the before and before-enclosure' (2013: 17). The so-called self-defence of settlement is the process of the enclosure of the before of the commons. The common social life attempts to continue un-surveilled, undocumented and creative in the commons, outside the walls of settlement. The settler 'having settled for politics, arms himself in the name of civilization while critique initiates the self-defense of those of us who see hostility in the civil union of settlement and enclosure' (2013: 18). Beyond settlement and enclosure is the life of the commons, the creative practices of living together, of making and inventing all of that which matters to us in the moment. Critique is self-defence, the development of ways of bringing to sight both the commons and the strategies of settlement's enclosure. The commons is the creative life that is full of potentialities, of change and of livingness. It is the place where creativity happens where it can, in basements, in common spaces. And in these places of the creative commons there are no permanent institutions – rules are made on the spot to match the games that will be played for as long as they need to be. There is knowledge of the university settlement, its walls, towers, functionaries and guards. They are easy to see. The settlements forays into the commons enact enclosures: 'in the clear, critical light of day, illusory administrators whisper of our need for institutions, and all institutions are political, and all politics is correctional, so it seems we need correctional institutions in the common, settling it, correcting us. But we won't stand corrected' (2013: 20). The university as museum, its ethnographic collections, archives, geographical maps, historical surveys all enclosures. Its disciplinary societies, memberships, conferences, research centres all enclosures. Ethnographers wander out of the university to map the commons, making content for the settlement whether a city block or continent away, mapping the commons continues.

And yet the university is a place of refuge. It is a place where fugitive artist-thinkers can find a place to make work sheltered from capitalisms transformation of art into content.[1] Where scholar-artists can find spaces to meet with newer learners to plot and scheme for a new future, invent new way of working and new ways of living together.[2] But it must be remembered that it is 'not a place of enlightenment' (2013: 26). Its so-called enlightenment is the correctional order of settlement, not the exploration of what human life means. A 'fugitive' (26) social order is plotting against the disciplinary fuelled by dreams of what tools and techniques are necessary to build collective decolonial futurity. There seem to be at least two approaches to decoloniality, one that centres the concern with diversifying the university, and a second fugitive 'undercommons of the enlightenment' (26): to be in, but not of the university (26). This second decoloniality does not concern itself with the politics of disciplinarity but only how to nurture what Harney and Moten call the beyond of teaching: 'not finishing oneself, not passing, not completing; it's about allowing subjectivity to be unlawfully overcome by others, a radical passion and possibility such that one becomes unfit for subjection, because one does not possess the kind of agency that can hold the regularly forces of subjecthood, and one cannot initiate the auto-interpellative torque that biopower subjection requires and rewards' (2013: 26). The beyond of teaching for the undercommons of the enlightenment is a working definition for this second model of decoloniality. *CineWorlding: Scenes of Research-Creation* works through the consequences of an emerging practice of cinematic research-creation as a toolset for decoloniality. Thinking in cinema unsettles the who and the what of enlightenment thinking that still too often constitutes the humanities. It attempts to open towards the more-than-human of the Earth and technology simultaneously. Cineworlding is cinema-thinking as the ecology of practices (Stengers 2005):

> An ecology of practices does not have any ambition to describe practices 'as they are'; it resists the master word of a progress that would justify their destruction. It aims at the construction of new 'practical identities' for practices, that is, new possibilities for them to be present, or in other words to connect. It thus does not approach practices as they are – physics as we know it, for instance – but as they may become. Maybe we can then speak again about some sort of progress, but, as Brian Massumi puts it, it would be a progress brought about by a 'social technology of belonging', addressed to the many diverging practices and their practitioners as such, not a progress linked to any kind of Truth, to any contrast between the old 'belonging' man and the 'new man', or the modern man. (186)

A cinematic ecology of practice is a practice that thinks in movement, image, duration, colour, sound, sonic texture and with force of diagrams towards worldings. Each work is both research and creation, a study of becoming, of thinking-feeling, a demonstration of what a technological body can do and how conceptual, social, technological and environmental ecologies emerge from practice. Does cineworlding contribute to the well-becoming of these ecologies? In the making of the work, cinematic technologies 'unlawfully' overcome the subject called researcher and artist, and the force of becoming in the cinematic works resists easy definition as either research or cinematic art making it unfit for either disciplinarity or capitalism.

Techniques of fugitivity and musics' undercommons

Indeed I have taken refuge in the university. I began to think about the social role of cinema when I was still a professional musician and activist. The films that I wanted to make, both its subjects and contents, were not fit for the marketplace. As an artist-activist, I did not have access to the kinds of financial support that research makes possible nor the time and money to invest in the kind of work I wanted to see. I took a gamble that a university research path would provide me with the infrastructure I would need to make the work that I felt was required. Isn't that what university is for? I believed, and still do, that cinematic creative practice, what I call cinematic research-creation, was an approach that could reverse the polarity between the university-as-settlement and music-worlds-as-commons. My strategy required that I learn how to succeed in the university as a critical activist-scholar and to develop a cinematic way of doing creative research. It has taken many years to develop my approach and to figure out a way to articulate it. This book is the beginning of the second, articulating phase of this project. This film work exists in a tension between doing critical work inside the university as an act of decoloniality, fraught with the constant risk of falling into disciplinarity. Cineworlding does not seek to construct a discipline of cinematic research-creation nor a cinematic methodology. Instead, the film work attempts to bring the worlding practices of the commons into the university, not as data, or archival document, but as anarchival[3] disruptor. I am trying to disrupt two things: the 'documentation paradigm' (Norton 2021), and the 'image of thought' of the humanities that gives the documentation paradigm its sense and value. If the humanities were oriented to decolonial posthumanist futurity instead of colonial mapping and categorizing then ethnography could be about mobilizing ecological strategies for living that respond to pressing needs.

The films that I will discuss are made in partnership with the artist in the musical commons with whom I work. The films exist in a space between critical digital humanities scholarship, audiovisual ethnography, ethnomusicology and art films. This is a space that allows the film to have value for the artists I work with so that they can utilize them as they wish. The films are also a form of scholarship that can be used in classrooms to share models of learning and living music in the commons so as to unsettle the conservatory image of thought that too often reduces music to a cycle of training and testing. Music's existential artfulness is, in my experience, dulled by this endless cycle of conservatory training. While at the same time university-trained musicians export a colonial difference into the commons, oftentimes seeing their literacy as the mark of civilization. It is my hope that the films operate a kind of critical pedagogy by drawing music student into an existential situation with the musicking of the commons. In doing so, I hope that the musical commons come alive to music students who innovate on ways to join the musical commons, to find strategies to connect and make community beyond the walls of the conservatory, and to build friendships and connections to artfulness in the commons. To world themselves into music worlds that operate differently and in so doing become allied to the causes of the musical commons. And to utilize their skills and access to make contributions to the commons, to build more equitable creative spaces, to help open access to music's existential potency. Which is also to say, allied to an active role in decolonial futurity.

What can a posthuman body do?

The motivation for *CineWorlding: Scenes of Cinematic Research-Creation* come as a consequence of the worldings in the music commons that occupied me in the first phase of my creative life. When I returned to the university at 30, it was not a surprise that I would once again have to world myself to the university. I was about to learn, as Moten and Harney had already, that what counts as thinking in the university has a kind of mindblindness to the thinking-feeling outside itself. What I expected on my return to university was a space for critical theorizing about, as Spinoza asked, what a body can do. But what I found was not that. Instead, there was a constant assertion, though unnamed and unaddressed, of what a body was, and as a consequence what music was. Meaning was limited to signification, not the slippages and excess of posthuman poetry. Music history was treated as a linear progression, musical expression as geographical and political. The reasons for musical change were found outside of music in the political realm, music and identity were foundation. But none of this resonated with me and my experiences.

In my creative life as a musician, music's meaning was its force. Its meaningfulness was its ability to affect the players, the audiences. Composition began with the ability to be affected by sound and to affect sound. It was the exploration of the gap, the interface, the interstices[4] between my body and the body of my instrument. It was the exploration of the double-sidedness of what Deleuze and Guattari called content and expression and the ways these were diagrammed (grabbed by the middle) in different musics. The way I would play the piano or bass, but also the way the piano and bass would play through me. The way the force of my fingers would release a sonic force from the instrument and the way that force seemed to shape what would come next. The give-and-take across a bridge of material affects, the relationality in the music. The bodying (flesh body-technological body) as a kind of forming of the abstract machine of interaction, the interstices between body and machine body, the edges of the encounters. Play a note on your instrument. Now slow it down so that you think speculatively about what forces are coming together at your point of contact, all that rushes towards your fingers (the material history of this instrument, this kind of instrument, this song, this music, this kind of music, the material history of music) and what rushes towards the note (your physical body, your history, schooling, history of education, human histories of musicking). It was also an exploration of the ways that subjectivity was overrun by the organization of contents, expression and concepts. The way a piano player in a gospel band learns how to move a force through one's body into the piano in ways different from classical music, jazz or country. It was about the rhythm, tone, attack, phrase, accent and silence. It was learning that even in the silence of a moment, a force is released.

My most transformative musical moment was silence. I was directing a seventy-voice gospel choir with a seven-piece R&B band. We were playing a sold-out concert to 1,400 people and I lifted my hand to hold a moment of silence on an upbeat. A silence that filled the hall burned through my body. The silence was a growing force. The interstices between musical movements in a piece emanated powerfully through the bodies in the hall. The silence was not empty; it was a preaccleration[5] building to a feverish level so that when my hand dropped, we all entered together into a release that brought the audience to its feet. This is musical meaning that is not a definition. Definitions are enclosures. Music is about learning how to body-worlding, to borrow an idea from Brian Massumi and Erin Manning that I will return to later: to biogram. Music was about the diagram of the rock band, gospel choir, country band, jazz band and flamenco ensemble. It was the way that the plane of material of gospel music would move into the plane of composition and the way the Spirit arrived as a force that moved through us all. It was that moment in flamenco when we all connected with each other, and with our audience, when the guttural shout announced the arrival of Duende, the spirit of flamenco. Meaning is the force that announced arrival. The late-night moments in the country band where in a strange town the dancing audience will press close to the stage and the bass player stood on the sound system to get closer to them. It was the interstices between audience and band where the force of the event made the air quiver with attraction. These events are what is meaningful in music. Meaning is a force, not a collection of words attempting to signify. When the words attempt to replace the force, coloniality is active. When the explanation for music reaches to politics, the settlement is enclosing music into itself, cutting off the wildness of the commons.

So if words enclose the commons, why do I write this book? Because I am an optimist and I believe that the music studies and the humanities can be different than they are. That it can be allied with the commons, that is to say, with futurity. I have plenty of reasons to think this and have had plenty of experiences with activist academics that have shown me how to be a fugitive, to write about force without trying to capture it. None of my examples are perfect nor is my method, but decoloniality cannot be too precious. Reading Deleuze and Guattari, Massumi, Manning, Moten and Harney and others. Speaking with researchers around the world, with graduate students, with undergraduate students seeking refuge and a place to theorize difference in their lives and communities. I am convinced that the refuge of the university can be a place to develop the techniques of fugitivity called decoloniality.

My experience has been difficult and full of setbacks and resistance. At my dissertation in 2010, I presented a short five-minute video of my festival research that, I thought, illustrated the character of the festival machines we would be discussing. I titled my dissertation 'Back to the Garden', as an homage to Joni Mitchell song, and used the song for what might be described as a research-creation music video. At the time I thought of it as an opening presentation but did not recognize that it was a research-creation video. At the conclusion of the music video, the chair of the defence committee instructed everyone that the video content could not be included in the discussion, that functionally, the committee had to forget their experience. There was no mechanism for a defence to include audiovisual content. I was stunned. I should have probably prepared myself for what came later. After a spirited defence of my theory that music festivals are an assemblage of machines that produce territories, the external examiner, a well-known American ethnomusicologist remarked that this was not ethnomusicology. At the time I took this very personally and as a criticism. I wanted very much to be included as an ethnomusicologist. Now looking back, perhaps I should have taken his remark to be prescient.

Thinking in the humanities is consistently portrayed as the rational cognitive reflective processing activity of an individual self-aware subject at a distance; modernity/coloniality's volition-intentionality-agency triad (Manning 2016: 6). Research and art were separated and seemed to have little to say to each other. Thinking was reserved for an individual pre-existing stable and 'normal' unit of wetware that excludes thinking as force that happens across the more-than-human. Normative thinking in the humanities produces an exclusive neurotypicality, an aesthetics of truth, and by way of apathy, helplessness or neglect, contributes, with little resistance, to the expansion of cognitive capitalism and 'neuro-totalitarianism' (Berardi 2018: 64–6). This makes the thinking-feeling of worldings in the commons functionally invisible. The humanities collects modes of thinking – not to share ways of thinking together in the commons, or of doing-thinking differently by asking what can a body do – in order to collect, identify and enclose them. This is the ongoingness of enclosure of the commons. Humanities thinking is somehow inoculated against thinking infections that could be picked up from where its functionaries (and I include myself here) travel. The professional university supports and upholds a neurotypicality which 'stages the encounter with life in such a way as to exclude what cannot fit within its order' (Manning 2016: 4). There can be little doubt in the definition of the university-as-settlement. There is overwhelming evidence of collected worldings, yet little evidence that music education has changed since the nineteenth-century conservatory. The fugitive decolonial work is a creative critical intervention into humanities thinking in partnership with the musical commons. It is about getting infected by worldings and helping to multiply productive ecological variants. It requires a critical theoretical investigation into more-than-human thinking. But this comes with a warning from Harney and Moten. Critique is a radiation; it is what Bernard Stiegler and Derrida call pharmakon, radiation as both a cure and a poison. This critique is not meant to replace my film work, or explain my film work, I write in order to upset the Human, to report from my studio what I think the posthuman body can do. To risk the radiation of critique, there needs to be a reason. The risk with critique, the poison, is that it can cut us off from the livingness we are attempting to amplify. This book is not needed by those who make movies or make music. They already know what they are doing. This book is written for researchers and students who are looking for a fugitive practice inside the university. For those research-creation practitioners and students who need to copy and paste a critique of the Human. Steal my work. Make it work.[6]

Research-creation proposition

After a first career as a touring musician, I returned to university. In the ten years between leaving my undergrad and beginning graduate studies, a tremendous change was taking place in the humanities in Canada: the emergence of research-creation. Around me were PhD students in philosophy, literature, visual art and media studies who were launching experiments in thinking resonant with artfulness. My own studies in ethnomusicology, however, remained unchanged from the way my supervisors, and, perhaps, their supervisors, had been trained. If there was any innovation in my programme, innovations in ethnographic practice since Writing Cultures, it was not evident.[7] There seemed to be no struggle with ethnography as process, where 'forms of order are partially dominant, and partially frustrated. Order is never complete; frustration is never complete' (Whitehead 1966: 87). We did not consider that 'standardization of method creates a culture of surveillance. So intent on following proscribed methods, we see researchers replicate the same ideas rather than develop something new' (Gullion 2018: 31). Some ethnographic methods texts even go so far as to dismiss the challenges posed by integrated world capitalism and ignore challenges to humanism posed by process philosophy like Whitehead, Bergson, Deleuze and Guattari, critical race theorists like Franz Fanon and bell hooks, anti-humanists like Foucault, feminist posthumanists like Braidotti and postcolonial theorists like Walter Mignolo, who all in their own ways challenge the humanist foundations of ethnography. Even in the face of all of this, one popular method text from 2010 states: 'There is no real difference or special significance required in the consideration of multi-sited ethnography. It's not the paradigm shift it is some time represented to be' (Madden 2010: 53) asserting that an ethnographic field is a combination of geographic space, social space, and the mental construct of the ethnographer (Madden 2010: 54). One can easily see in this the recurrent binary between human and society/human and environment that is an inheritance of humanism's 'nature/culture division [that] has created problems not just in our ability to gain knowledge, but is also a major factor in the inordinate suffering in/of the world' (Guillon 2018: 149). By constituting the relationship between human metal construct and the environment, it separates out the conceptual, social and technological from environmental ecologies. This separation is useful for maintaining the 'objectivity' of scientism, but does nothing to advance social science and the humanities. We simply cannot ignore the volition-intentionality-agency triad of modernity/coloniality (whiteness), or the ecology of practices of science and technology studies because it is inconvenient, nor can we ignore the fact that 'language cannot fully describe movement. Movement does not give itself over to the order of language, any more than it surrenders itself integrally to visible form. The orders of experience are incommensurable' (Manning and Massumi 2014: 41). In the face of these challenges, it is necessary to imagine new ways of doing audiovisual music and sound studies that may risk incomprehensibility by ethnographers, humanities scholars and social scientists alike.[8]

While research-creation was developing, music studies remained somehow separate from its intellectual experimentation and burgeoning transdisciplinarity. Perhaps it was because there had already been a long practice of anthropological cinema in ethnomusicology, or because unlike these other disciplines music was already hemisphere between creatives in music performance and scholars in the musicologies. Art making had its place. The humanities scholarship in music and sound studies had its accepted forms of documentation.[9] It was not until I was asked directly if my little films were art or research that I blurted out that they were art. But a moment later, I said unthinking (but was it the thinking of intuition?) that they might be research too. It was the first moment of thinking this thought. These little films might be research! Immediately I was notified that if they were research that I had breached research ethics and that I was going to have to meet with the chair of the music programme to discuss my infraction. Not much of a celebration for having a new thought. I was stunned and a little hurt. But it did underline a transformational, and perhaps deviant, practice. If I was getting in trouble instead of being laughed off, perhaps this was something significant.

Dirtbag artfulness[10]

While I was learning ethnographic film techniques,[11] I began making experimental films and music videos for my own enjoyment and creativity.

I did not at first consider these research, nor did anyone else. They were art, but not the type of art that was done in the fine arts. I've always thought about my practice as dirtbag artfulness, in the best possible way. It certainly did not occur to me to reach out to the Digital Humanities or Fine Art Department with my experimental music videos. They were experimental music videos and hardly worth getting too excited about. My creative practice was always oriented by a DIY process, had an always present NoWave style that is probably a consequences of my love of doing it all by myself or in very small teams of friends. I love anarchist relational art that is more oriented to process than product. The process is always present on the surface of the medium, always feels a little bit outsider, a freedom that I find full of life at the edge of capacity and articulation. Instead of seeing this art as having a lack of polish and craft, I prefer to think of its nonconformity as having the 'shape of enthusiasm' (Manning 2013: 184–203). My dirtbag artfulness is oriented to 'an intensity of the withness of expressibility, activates a process, that takes the shape of enthusiasm, a kind of Spinozist joy of the betweenness of experience. An enthusiasm with life in the making' (Manning 2013: 185). Manning, reflecting on Autistic perception, is both critical of neurotypicality and committed to the decoloniality of thinking-feeling and connects the 'shape of enthusiasm' to activist philosophy: 'the in-act of worldings yet to come, in the tremulous ecological resonance of the elastic almost where movement moves and life lives' (Manning 2013: 185). Perhaps the immediacy and energy of my dirtbag artfulness had more to teach me than I had first thought. As I develop cineworlding throughout this book, the films and my process embraces a dirtbag artfulness that I want to celebrate. I am not interested in creating a formal DIY aesthetics for cineworlding but, instead, to open space for 'the undercommons of the enlightenment' (Harney and Moten 2013: 26). To embrace dirtbag artfulness, a move inspired by Syilx and Tsilhqot'in playwright Kim Senklip Harvey, is to queer my location in the academy, making space for me and others to become more than whatever colonial researchers have been. To embrace dirtbag is to operate a 'generalized queering that would take a "bad" word and transform it even further. A majority established these words as categories and binary oppositions that control the ways a social body thinks of its milieu. They have to be disconnected from the group in which they were imprisoned' (Conley 2009: 30). Dirtbag has long been a way limiting inclusion, enforcing class and race-based hierarchies, and policing expression.

Research-creation

Years later I would read Owen Chapman's 'Research-Creation: Intervention, Analysis and "Family Resemblances"' (2012), where I would learn, with just a little jealousy, that while I was getting reprimanded at a leading Canadian university, the soon-to-be Dr Chapman was innovating in this thing called 'research-creation'. This was what I had been seeing happening in other humanities areas! Research-creation! That's what it's called. Chapman explained that research-creation was an 'emergent category' in university research that was related in some ways to practice-based research and art-based research in other countries. That it could claim creative interventions by the likes of Walter Benjamin, Marshall McLuhan, Donna Haraway and Roland Barthes as some of its earliest practitioners. In the early 2000s, a variety of Canadian universities began to include research-creation as a kind of interdisciplinarity that found its way into the rubrics of the national research funding agency, the Social Science and Humanities Research Council of Canada. But as Erin Manning and Brian Massumi have pointed out, research-creation was established 'without a strong concept of how creative practice and theoretical research interpenetrate' (2014: 88). It is one thing to suggest the application of a form of creative practice and a form of research, an interdisciplinary approach where both disciplines retain their territorial status and definition of knowledge. It is also not enough to recognize that creativity has always been a form of research and that research is creative, this does little to engage with the politics of knowledge production. There are approved forms of creative practice included in the university and, therefore, into research and creative practice. The emergence of research-creation does not in itself do anything to disturb the neurotypicality that characterizes approved models of thinking and research outcomes:

> it is urgent to turn away from the notion that it is the human agent, the intentional, volitional subject, who determines what comes to be. It is urgent to turn away from the central tenet of neurotypicality, the wide-ranging belief that there is an independence of thought and being attributable above all to the human, a better-than-ness accorded to our neurology (a neurology, it must be said, that reeks of whiteness, and classism). Neurotypicality, as a central but generally unspoken identity politics, frames our idea of which lives are worth fighting for, which lives are worth educating, which lives are worth living, and which lives are worth saving. (2016: 3)

For Manning and Massumi, research-creation is an opportunity to rethink thinking, to question the volition-intentionality-agency triad (2016: 6), to ask what it means to think and who and what is admitted into thinking. This opens a political project that highlights neurotypicality as unspoken whiteness and hidden classicism in its methods and methodologies, in the very foundations of how thinking is conceived in the humanities. Dirtbag artfulness became for me a way into research-creation.

The little experimental films grew into larger and more complex cinematic propositions. As the films reached more audiences (at the time of this writing they have been screened at more than fifty international film festivals and many universities), I began to take my cinematic work more seriously. While I was focusing on developing my cinematic research-creation practice, I began to meet scholars working in audiovisual ethnomusicology or cine-ethnomusicology. My dirtbag artfulness began to take on a different character, it began to feel like an intervention into scholarly thinking-feeling, a queering of what it means to think. I began to think differently about each project, moving from filmmaker to cinematic research-creation practitioner. I began to come into contact with scholars like Stevance and Lacasse, who patiently assured me that my work was indeed research-creation. At a practice-based research summit, I was fortunate to meet Erin Manning, who, with Brian Massumi, would radically change the direction of my research-creation practice. Manning patiently helped me dig deeper into my films, offering a way of thinking my films that were full of the minor gesture (Manning 2016). And while I had been reading Deleuze and Guattari for many years, Manning and Massumi's work has helped me to see the centrality of the virtual in Deleuze and Guattari's thinking, and the politico-aesthetics of research-creation which has also been deepened by Natalie Loveless's important intervention into research-creation. *Cineworlding: scenes of cinematic research-creation* seeks to offer a diagrammatic approach to cinematic research-creation that will encourage scholars, students, musicians, artists, filmmakers to meet and invent ways of thinking-feeling together with the digital cinema ecosystem. I think of this offer as a Cineworlding proposition.

Thinking in cinema

Thinking in cinema is thinking with the more-than-human and beyond neurotypicality. Learning to consider cinema-thinking as more than the 'documentation paradigm' (Norton 2021: 123), more than entertainment,[12] and more than a text will open space for innovations in thinking the humanities, critique the still too prevalent Kantian notion of thinking at a distance from life, and in proposing relational thinking hopes to contribute to a fugitive decoloniality. The question of what cinema-thinking is is related to its valuing. Cinema-thinking is not a matter of allowing audiovisual technology into music and sound studies, but instead, to articulate a fugitive image of thought for the humanities, to think the more-than-human world with the more-than-human thinking of audio-vision, oriented to inventing a diversity of research-creation approaches and institutional systems needed to value them.[13]

Felix Guattari challenges the idea that what thinks is an individual unit of self-aware reflective wetware:

> it is not sufficient to think in order to be, as Descartes declares, since all sorts of other ways of existing have already established themselves outside consciousness, while any mode of thought that desperately tries to gain a hold on itself merely turns round and round like a mad spinning top, without ever attaching itself to the real territories of existence; which, for their part, drift in relation to each other like tectonic plates under continents. Rather than speak of the 'subject', we should perhaps speak of components of subjectification. (2000: 35–6)

So instead of an individual, Guattari proposes an event where an 'interiority establishes itself at the crossroads of multiple components, each relatively autonomous in relation to the other, and, if need be, in open conflict' (2000: 36). Antonio Damasio, from a neuroscience perspective, quite clearly illustrates that thinking-feeling is an evolutionary phenomena that has developed over evolutionary time and is built upon an archaeology of thinking-feeling evident deep in the past and is shared with single cell organisms and cultures, and at every scale of life in between.

Cinematic research-creation as a critical pedagogy in music education

I now teach in one of a small number of music programmes in North America with a music degree in jazz and contemporary popular music. Our programme has teachers and administrators committed to equity, diversity, inclusion and accessibility. But even in this context, where we are not directly participating in the conservation of Western Art Music, the master works of great men still informs the development of students. The canon is different but a canon still remains and the thinking about what music is, how it should be taught, and how to value student outcomes remains little changed from the European conservatory. There clearly needs to be more than the inclusion of formerly excluded repertoire. The hope is that including scholars who have been systematically marginalized will make a transformative impact. I have no doubt that these scholars will. But it should not be left up to new often previously marginalized faculty to carry the responsibility for systematic change. The 'image of thought' of modernity/coloniality needs to be addressed by those who have benefitted from it the most. Whiteness' modernity/coloniality needs to be dismantled by those for whom it directly benefits, by those it has produced. As Walter Mignolo has taught, modernity/coloniality has been quite successful and included into itself the 'Others' it has created. We can see this in the institutionalization of 'traditional' and formerly 'primitive' music whose repertoires and practitioners have been invited into music schools but rarely into musicology. Ethnomusicology's prefix (ethnos) is evidence of this and so too is the inclusion of traditional and popular music. Walter Mignolo calls this the colonial difference. It is ethnomusicology but not musicology, popular music but not musicology. Hypermodernity/neocoloniality is transforming universities so as to include value matrices of capitalism in the definition of popular music as the successful artists of the popular music industry, and includes the previously anti-capitalist DIY movements into itself just the same without disturbing its colonial image of thought. There needs to be a decoloniality within music studies that seeks to confront directly the modernity/coloniality image of thought that remains far too present. I grew up in DIY music cultures and now watch music students under the baton playing punk music. The sounds of music can be deterritorialized from their cultural practices and reterritorialized into modernity/coloniality. This is the machinery of whiteness, and it must be deconstructed by those who have become the inheritors of whiteness. It is time for a fugitive disruption in this machinery, to throw wrenches into the machine. These tools will be conceptual, and throughout the book, I am attempting to identify tools for the job.

Stevance and Lacasse suggest that research-creation as interdiscipline is a way for musicology and music performance, the university heritage and the conservatory heritage, to engage with each together. As Erin Manning points out in regards to the hyphen between research-creation, it is not enough for a research method to be attached to an art practice. The hyphen needs to act as an operator that changes what we understand both terms to mean. In the case of music and sound studies, how does musicology-music performance operate on each other to change each other? And where does this change take place? My proposal in this book is that the change is not in repertoire alone but at the level of what Gilles Deleuze and Felix Guattari call the diagram. The diagram is a critical tool to understand how systems of control are operationalized. For the time being, let me define the diagram as an abstract machinic that operates at an interface. In practical terms, the interface comprised of the body of the musician, repertoire, pedagogy, the body of the instrument, university and capitalist systems of value. The diagram is the abstract machine that operates between these bodies and on each of them.

On the diagram

Bonta and Protevi describe the diagram as 'the outline of the traits of expression of an abstract machine' (2004: 79). The diagram is a way of thinking about the compositional power of intensity which

> is immanent to matter and to events, to mind and to body and to every level of bifurcation composing them and which they compose. Thus it also cannot but be experienced, in effect – in the proliferation of levels of organization it ceaselessly gives rise to, generates and regenerates, at every suspended moment. (Massumi 2002: 33)

The diagram is a way of thinking about emergence (Massumi 2002: 32), organization that is the 'spontaneous production of a level of reality having its own rules of formation and order of connection' (Massumi 2002: 32). In an early film I made with Dr Guillaume Tardiff called *The Genius of the Violin* (2012), we brought two musicians who played fiddle and one musician who played violin and created a situation for them to play each other's repertoire. Each player struggled with the others repertoire and you can see it in their bodies and hear it in their playing. What is it that we can see-hear? It is the virtuality of the diagram in audio-vision (Chion 2019). The interstices between the physicality of an awkward body next to a flowing body in the visual-image and sound of two violin/fiddle lines in open conflict in the music, the audio-image. But it is important to note here that awkward is a value statement relative to what is already accepted as known by the viewer. So it seems the diagrams are entwined with value. The events that emerged in cinematic research-creation began to pose a diagrammatic problematic. As Deleuze points out, and will be discussed in the following, the diagram has a name and a date. It is called by proper names like Beethoven, Duke Ellington, Beyoncé. The conservatory is a machinic assemblage that operates by way of installing diagrams. But is there a diversity of diagrams or a capitalist diagram that has enclosed these names, institutionalized their repertoire and installed a diagram that equates musicality with reproduction of the hits as determined by systems of capitalist value? Wouldn't a Duke Ellington or Beyoncé diagram engage with what is cool in the musical commons at the moment and produce original music to contribute back to the building of the commons? The surround of the music school settlement should be teaming with sonic innovation, underground connections, artistic partnerships in the beyond of teaching. But is it? In my experience it is rarely the case. I think the question of decoloniality as the undercommons of the enlightenment is partially a diagrammatic question since the diagram is a question of how bodies are able to do thinking-feeling-doing together, and the definition of what together means.

For the past fifteen years of working in cinematic research-creation, I have begun to confront the diagrammatic in music education. It began with my own process of beginning to take my cinematic work seriously, not just as dirtbag artfulness but as research-creation. I began incorporating cinematic research-creation projects into my developing musicology stream. As the only full-time musicology in my programme, I have the benefit of working with student cohorts throughout their programme. Originally, I saw my job as introducing students to the wide world of musicology. Even though my intention was to make musicology useful for these students, there always seemed to be a gap between what I am trying to do and their developing performance, audio recording and composition practice. Each semester I would try ways to bridge this gap, to try to bring more and more performances into the musicology classroom. But still there was a gap. I began to notice a consistency. Perhaps I could characterize it as difficulty of thinking-feeling their practices of their areas of interest. They were increasingly proficient in their technical abilities (techne), but their think-feeling (episteme) was not developing at the same pace, or maybe not at all. From my perspective, this was taking a toll on their creativity and in some cases their mental health. I began to wonder what was happening. As the research-creation projects became more and more about their creative practice students would default to a 'documentation paradigm' (Norton 2021), making films about what an individual musician did technically, but not about their creative practice, not about their creative thinking. If research-creation is going to contribute to decoloniality at music schools then we need tools to think about how creativity and artfulness is done. If, as I suggest and will discuss in the following, music schools install diagrams, how might research-creation be oriented to a deep exploration of the formation of diagrams and how might music students, and perhaps students across the humanities, be encouraged to innovate on the diagrammatic. The diagram is a question of thinking-feeling and becoming. If diagrams are captured by modernity/coloniality, by hypermodernity/neocoloniality, then innovating on the diagrammatic may contribute to decoloniality from within the modernity/coloniality as fugitive thinking and the beyond teaching for the undercommons of the enlightenment.

Hacking machinic relations in music studies

Characterizing the relation between art and philosophy, Gregg Lambert wrote: 'This is the picture that I will employ to portray the relationship between philosophy (the creation of concepts) and the domain of nonphilosophy (art, literature, and cinema) as components of a larger machine that are assembled together in order to work, occasionally to produce something called thinking' (Lambert 2012: 20). These machinic relations are not reserved for technological, metal or plastic machines alone, but point to all sorts of production: semiotic production, territorial production, unconscious production, artistic production, conceptual production and environmental production. For Deleuze and Guattari, abstract machines are theoretical, but real, and think the flow of time, of space-time and causality. Machinic relationality challenges structuralist ideas and provide a new image of thought to work against casual dogmatisms that still too often structure thinking. How might the idea of machinic unconscious, for instance, be useful in understanding common words in music school. Take inspiration. Music students and faculty alike regularly speak of tapping 'into a flow of inspiration', a Platonic unconscious, inspiration as 'a gift from mystery', a Christian unconscious, inspiration as 'the spirit of the age', a post-Kantian unconscious. These are more than ideas about inspiration, they structure student's artfulness. The consequence is that inspiration is thought to have magical qualities separated from the livingness of the intuition in the act of creative thinking-feeling-doing. As topics for inquiry, inspiration and creativity are given short thrift, are often passed over in curriculum and left unthought even though the abstract machine/diagram of intuition-creation is the very foundations of the problem of art making. To pose the problem of art making is to articulate the artistic problematic that needs to be examined. For Erin Manning, 'intuition is a key to a process' and is 'allied to the creation of a problem [where] the artful comes to expression' (Manning 2016: 14). A machinic paradigm treats inspiration as the in-folding of an abstract machine, a diagram, that is central to the creation of a plane of material that 'ascends irresistibly and invades the plane of composition of the sensations themselves to the point of being part of them or indiscernible from them' (Deleuze and Guattari 1994: 166). To say that unconscious is machinic is to recognize that it is conceptual: 'why stick this label of "machinic unconscious" onto it? simply to stress that it is populated not only with images and words, but also with all kinds of machinism that lead it to produce and reproduce these images and words' (2011: 10). Music history is also a collection of diagrams, not a stable structure, or a linear causality. The names of master artists, the way these artists sound, the repertoire they produced, the modes of learning that have been enshrined in curriculum, in methods of practice and rehearsal are diagrams. Students are conceptually and physically produced to reproduce these diagrams, the interfaces of mind, body, instrument technology, sound technology, stage, audience, educational institution and economic structure. History is not an inert subject of study but an institutionally valued collection of diagrams that populate possible student becomings. Do music students learn to navigate diagrams or are they judged by their ability to be disciplined into a select group of privileged diagrams of 'creativity'? Is music school a theatre for trying on diagrams and a place to learn techniques for diagrammatic escape, or a disciplinary institution trapping bodies in diagrams? A thinking society or a control society?

The machinic foregrounds and makes material the actions that continually reproduce social structures, not as idealism but existential dramaturgies at the heart of the very act of living. These machinic relations are not component parts of a pre-existing structure, but instead operate to produce autopoietic self-producing components (individuals, groups, institutions) by way of diagrams/abstract machines in order for process 'to take on a new light: causalities will no longer function in a single direction, and it will no longer be allowed for us to affirm that "everything is a foregone conclusion"' (2011: 11). Machinic relations can open space for thinking thinking-feeling differently, but they can also close space. Opening space for thinking means to overcome thinking at a Kantian distance and post-Kantian spirit to engage machinically in the act of creative livingness and through invention, active in the production of a more-than-human futurity. To focus thinking on the abstract machine of art making is to open artistic thinking and art pedagogy to the virtual futurity that is being produced in the present, to recognize the ethical and political dimensions of art making, community making, society making, to recognize the forces of conceptual, social, technological, environmental ecologies and to get beyond the volition-intentionality-agency triad.

Thinking-feeling and becoming operate at the crossroads of multiple components. In *What Is Philosophy*? (1994), Gilles Deleuze and Felix Guattari discuss philosophical, scientific and artistic thinking as diagrammatic practices at a crossroads. Thinking in three modes. They are not presented hierarchically. Each mode has affordances of expression that deal in a particular way with what they identify as their existential contents. Thinking does not start on itself but brings content to expression somehow, and this somehow is what counts. By 1966, writes Lambert, Foucault already began to recognize 'the final exhaustion of the last vestiges of "Humanism" belonging to the previous tradition of philosophy after Kant' (2012: 11). I believe that for scholarly nonphilosophy in music and sound studies, the end of the post-Kantian image of thought causes a break in the relations between philosophy, science and humanities. The humanities remains in many areas committed to conserving a post-Kantian image of thought, perhaps even unaware of the image of thought maintained by that model of thinking (is there a post-Kantian unconscious deep in curriculum of music education?). Critical race studies, decoloniality, feminism and indigenous thinking have been influential in critiquing the practices of disciplines, critiquing post-Kantian models. My initiation into the critique of post-Kantian philosophy began at the conclusion of an interview with Mi'kmaq elder Joel Denny, who said:

> I know what you think you are doing. But you do know that we don't need you. We don't need your scholarship. We already know what we're doing with our traditions. You are here because you have lost something in your own tradition. If you can figure out what it is that you have lost, you wouldn't need to come talk to me about my traditions, because you will already know the answer.

What is it that I am looking for in my own tradition? Is it an image of thought that connects me to the life of the planet? A way to make art that is oriented towards a decolonial future? An image of thought that can help me leave whiteness behind? A philosophy of immanence through which to practice my cinematic-thinking? Perhaps the key is to explore the creative possibilities of the diagram.

Immanence and the Fire Lesson

The central scene of my film *Pimachihowan* (Chapter 7) shows Little Red River Cree Nation chief Conroy Sewepagaham building a fire. David Lertzman asks, 'Can you tell us about Pimachihowan?' and Conroy responds while in the act of building the fire: 'I'm doing it now'. He goes on to say that nothing starts on its own, echoing for me, or more precisely, refraining Erin Manning and Brian Massumi's observations that thought does not start on its own and that it operates in the minor gesture, the in-folding of the in-act in the event. The event of the Fire Lesson brings living, thinking-feeling together in worlding. This poses a question of what it means to think the in-act of fire building. This is a move away from post-Kantian idealism. The in-act of worlding is a thinking-feeling with livingness, what Deleuze calls immanence. Deleuze and Guattari write that 'the plane of immanence is not a concept that is or can be thought but rather the image of thought, the image of thought that gives itself of what it means to think, to make us of thought, to find ones bearings in thought' (1994: 37). Livingness is movement and change in duration as Erin Manning shows in Relationscapes, where there is an 'emphasis on the immanence of the movement moving: how movement can be felt before it actualizes . . . how thought becomes concept is parallel to how duration becomes experiential space-time' (2013: 6). For Sewepagaham it is the becoming-fire, the preacceleration into the body-wood-lighter assemblage that is the eventness of thinking Pimachihowan, thinking with the more-than-human earth and more-than-human technology of fire making. The event of the Fire Lesson, like the event of art, orders the world but not by ideological function but by diagram. It operates within an order and seeks more. Not just to confirm a structure that was there before and will remain, thus creating stillness in thought, but instead, to find in movement a little space for creativity 'a little bit of chaos released back into our idea of Order' (Lambert 2012: 187). The diagramming of a world by the Fire Lesson is worlding.

The Fire Lesson occurred, as will be discussed in the Pimachihowan chapter, for the camera. It was not planned in advance with the film team, only Sewepagaham knew about the Fire Lesson. Lertzman and the film team followed Sewepagaham into the forest. The Fire Lesson was both a worlding practice and produced as a consequence of the presence of the cinema camera a cineworlding, a series of images made up of a block of audio-vision where bodies collecting wood in a forest's open space become content or cinematic material and a warm fire to sit around, an expression and a cinematic composition. It is at this moment at the apex of the Fire Lesson where the affects of the Fire Lesson impact me later in the editing suite and music gifted to the film from Sewepagaham's father feels the most appropriate. What are the affects that cause thought to move into music? That makes the soundtrack make audiovisual meaning (as force). In the movement of the bodies in-folding, the fire event there is

> the feeling of seeing [that] the abstract line of the event is a vision-effect. It is an effect of the event-triggering tension . . . it expresses that differential in an abstract perception of the dynamic unity of the event, as you feel you saw it with your eyes, or perhaps eyed it with feeling. In other words, the dynamic form of the event is perceptually felt, not so much 'in' vision as with vision or through vision: as a vision-effect. It is a lived abstraction: an effective virtual vision of the shape of the event, including in its arc the unseen dimensions of its immediate past and immediate future. (Massumi 2011: 17)

The event of making the fire is the doing of Pimachihowan, it is a diagram, a concept on the plane of immanence, both a way of worlding and a block of audio-vision in cineworlding. A Nehiyawak (Cree) Tea dance is a sound-image that is the thinking-feeling of the event, the perceptually felt with vision, a vision-effect, a sound-effect. The diagram 'is a word that activist philosophy uses to name a speculative-pragmatic procedure for navigating this complexity of experience's passing, taking special aim on the "critical" moments. These are the junctures where one moment of experience's passing passes into another, informing it of (in-forming it with) the potential to become again: technique of existence' (Massumi 2013: 25). Speculative in the sense that it is about inventing and imagining, pragmatic in that it is about doing. Cinema-thinking beyond the documentary paradigm is audio-vision's speculative-pragmatics. This is the starting place for cineworlding's research-creation proposition.

Cineworlding's images: Visual-images, sonic-images

Perhaps the most significant obstacle to cinema-thinking is to overcome the common thinking about the image. It is understandable that the cinematic, the audiovisual image has a dubious place in Humanism. It is here perhaps that Plato's *Allegory of the Cave* is still so impactful. Isn't the cinema exactly the shimmering shadows on the wall that Plato warned us about. And isn't the role of the thinker to escape from this world of illusion in order to reach the truth of the world. Steven Feld remarked about scholarly film that its task is to disentangle that which is scholarly from that which is entertainment (Feld 1976). Any discussion of scholarly film seems to take for granted the observational documentary mode as the de facto scholarly approach to filmmaking. The music video and fiction film are obviously entertainments. But why is this so obvious? Perhaps as mockumentary and reality TV have made clear there is an audiovisual aesthetics of truth. While it has become commonly utilized by the entertainment industry scholarly cinema still pretends this aesthetics of truth do not exist.

Chromesthesia

Catherine Russell (1999) has pointed out that experimental film and ethnographic film have been kept distant from each other providing little opportunity for art practice and research in audio-vision to mix. Cinematic research-creation provides an opportunity to rethink this division. In my own audiovisual work, I move between music videos, observational documentary and fiction film but am always doing research-creation. I have been critiqued many times for mixing music video aesthetics inside observational documentary films as if one was pure. Responses to these 'too artsy' sections suggest to me a discomfort with artful audio-vision and a need to discipline audio-vision's aesthetics to ensure it is scholarly and trustworthy. I believe this discomfort points to the perceived 'risky nature' of the image, its perceived potential to undermine scholarship, its impurity. But is human perception of the world, our empirical observations, what we see when we watch observational documentary? Do we perceive the world on a flat plane of reality, what I call an ethnographic plane of correspondence? Or is our perception of the world always cut through with virtualities that populate our perception, dancing shadows that point to the synesthetic or perhaps more precisely chromesthetic affects of the world. The ethnographic plane of correspondence, evidenced in the documentation paradigm, has no space for virtuality and affects, for chromesthesia. Chromesthesia, the entanglement of audio and visual perception, where sound makes thought move with image and colour intensities or vice versa. Chromesthesia gives sound intensity agency in creativity, opens thinking to pre-signifying intensities and a-signifying virtualities, exploding the volition-intentionality-agency triad and the ethnographic plane of correspondence. The observational documentary production process, its filming and editing, is a diagram that suppresses the theorizing of chromesthesia. Is this scholarly? I believe that it is an aesthetic practice that performs scholarship as an aesthetics of truth and limits empiricism to only what is acceptable. This is the ongoing power of Humanism, the diagram of the Human, whiteness not empiricism.

The screen

When I introduce virtuality in a class situation, I always begin by asking students to consider how often their mind has 'wandered' during a lecture. How often they are 'lost in thought'. Both of these notions carry with them a negative connotation. But lecturers, teachers and entertainers know very well that look. When there is more going on behind the eyes than what is going on in perception. There is no flat ethnographic plane of correspondence, there is a playfulness of virtualities in the audiovisual field of perception. If we want to claim a radical empiricism in our audiovisual work then it will have to take account for not only the disciplined ethnographic plane of correspondence but also the dancing virtualities that Plato told us were illusions. These illusions, visual-images and sound-images, tell us something important about experience and in my filmmaking I regularly use music video techniques because this is the 'uncanny feeling' of the semblance (Massumi 2011) the virtualities of audio-vision, the jumps in thought that make connections beyond the conceptual, audiovisual approximations of the affects that are mixed with the precepts of perception. We do not just see-hear the world as a flat plane but are constantly mixing it with other kinds of images. So it is necessary to consider the relation between the visual-image, sound-image and consciousness.

The relation between the image and consciousness is, as Paola Marrati illustrates, a central problematic for early twentieth-century philosophy:

> The two great projects for reviving philosophy at the beginning of the twentieth century – Bergson's and Husserl's – had the same point of departure: the necessity of filling the gap between consciousness and its images, on the one side, and the world and its things, on the other, and thus abandoning the dispute between idealism and materialism in order to rebuild philosophy on a ground closer to experience. (2008: 29)

The major difference between Bergson and Husserl can be characterized by thinking consciousness as light. For Husserl, consciousness is always consciousness of something. The thing appears when the light of consciousness is poured on it. The idea that consciousness is light is biblical. God gave light to the world. For Bergson, on the other hand, the universe is light and matter already:

> In an opposite move from phenomenology which makes consciousness a light that shines on things Bergson sees light reflecting everywhere, it is light that draws the subject. Recognizing luminosity in the universe reverses the long held western belief that it is God or consciousness that is the source of light in a dark universe. Consciousness become an 'opacity that allows light to be revealed'. (Marrati 2008: 32)

Bergson's universe is a material universe but not a mechanistic one made up of image and movement, image and matter (movement-image and flowing-matter are the same), an 'infinite universe, on which closed systems are made and unmade, defined by Deleuze as a block of space-time or a plane of immanence' (Marrati 2008: 30). The image is an image of matter and matter is the other side of the image. The movement of the image is the movement of matter; the movement of matter is the movement of the image. The way an image responds to another image characterizes what kind of matter it is:

> In the plane of immanence, light propagates itself in all directions, and movement-images, blocs of space-time, are figures of light in which rigid bodies are not yet formed. There is no eye to which such images can appear because light encounters neither obstacle nor screen to reflect it. But the notion of appearing in itself is no longer enigmatic: one now understand that 'the eye is in things, in luminous images themselves,' to use Deleuze's words, or, as Bergson puts it, that 'photography, if there is photography, is already taken, already developed, at the very heart of things, and at all the points in space'. (Marrati 2008: 31)

Deleuze sees Bergson's universe as a metacinema because it gives rise to 'living images and to everything that our ordinary perception sees and names: actions, affects, bodies' (Marrati 2008: 32–3). For Deleuze, the screen is not a place of illusion but a membrane of thinking, a meeting place of external and internal images the

> identity of the world and brain, does not form a whole, but rather a limit, a membrane which puts an outside and an inside in contact, makes them present

to each other, confronts them or makes them clash. The inside is psychology, the past, involution, a whole psychology of depths which excavate the brain. The outside is the cosmology of galaxies, the future, evolution, a whole supernatural which makes the world explode. (Deleuze 1989: 206)

In cinematic research-creation, the screen allows the projection of my/our cinematic-thinking in a public venue, to invite others to participate and discuss my cinematic-thinking. When the cinematic screen becomes a membrane for the projection of a coherence that is the consequence of cinematic research-creation, which is another way of saying the coherence of thinking images, the artistic film says something about perception. It then is possible to see that Bergson and Deleuze's ideas of the image provide a way of thinking about perception as

> nothing other than the effects of the black screen, light reflected by a living image, and the brain, also an image, is nothing other than an interval between an action and a reaction. Rather than making the brain the mysterious receptacle of images, Bergson makes it one image among others on a plane of immanence that contains only light-matter and time. (Marrati 2008: 34)

Deleuze's Bergsonism provides the first step to thinking cinematic research-creation beyond the documentation paradigm. It challenges a long history of doubt about the status of the image and the image's relation to illusion.

Afraid of the image?

Thinking the audiovisual image and its relation to audio-vision in a predominantly audiovisual culture characterized by systems of control, advertising, marketing and the industrialization of audio-vision brings out the political and ethical dimensions of cinematic research-creation. The fate of audio-vision's concepts, the thinking of audio-vision should not be left to entertainment streaming platforms and social media advertising. Decolonial struggles have widely identified capitalism as a site where the expansion of systems of coloniality perpetuate. If cinematic production is left to marketing and capitalist entertainments because of an ancient and unconsidered (unconscious?) fear of the image, then the humanities is ceding the dominant mode of communication to capitalism and its expanding coloniality. Re-thinking the image with Bergson and Deleuze provides Cineworlding a way to make a contribution to decoloniality in the humanities.

2

A worlding proposition for/from an alternate reality

The 'Ave' was busy as usual as I made my way home from the voting station. Lines of cars lit softly by a late-afternoon sun in a sky much less cloudy than my thoughts. At first it was just a repetitive obsessive yelling, as common as the rumble of cars and police sirens in north central Edmonton. Pink Floyd's *The Wall* began playing in my mind as the yelling took form: 'We don't need no Education!!' A shock to thought. On election day, a person across the street standing precariously on top of a bus-stop bench is obsessively yelling 'We don't need no Education!!'. The shock, a nooshock (Deleuze 1989: 156), inaugurates a circuit of thinking-feeling-composing with intensive audio-vision (Chion 2019). *The Wall*'s unfolding begins as an intensity that is hard to distinguish from the rhythmics of the city, rhythmics of the body and rhythmics of thought. The city becomes a scene, chaotic vibrating energies emerging into rhythmic form. The nooshock of obsessive yelling set music playing intensively in my body while virtual images began moving across my visual perception, chromesthesia. The music film was already playing in my mind when I took notice. There were already intensive sounds, colours, movements and images that flickered across my perceptual field, my (is it my possession or a blurred boundary between self and world?) audiovisual attention becoming more attuned to, and obsessed with, tiny rhythmic details of the environment as my body was falling already into entrainment with the intensive music. My body was not still; it was becoming. Body is not the right word here; it was a body-becoming: bodying. Microperceptions were already in action when I began to notice what was happening. At first I was just enjoying it without it even rising to the level of a signified enjoyment. Because I try to teach this mode of awareness as an audiovisual practice, I began to take note of the details. Is there a kind of cinematic-thinking machine waiting in my body? Something that works between my boding and the environment? Is there a machine, a collection of techniques, waiting to be put to work? And what is this machine waiting to work on?

These conceptual questions flicker and recede as my awareness moves to proprioception, entertained by the body playing with the world. A series of cinematic shots emerge as I feel the rush of my metabolism kick in time to the thrum of the deep groove of the song. There was no reflective moment when I thought to myself that I should make a film. There was only the smallest interstices between the event of troubled walking and the event of grooving to *The Wall*, and the event of in-forming cinematic chromesthetics. In-forming instead of the too casual taking shape in my imagination. The latter would rush to hide the complexity of this thinking-feeling-becoming in audio-vision and the ecology of the city's rhythmics. It would hide the event of the music in my body, an affect that starts up a compositional practice that is like a hallucinatory vision stretched over the screen of immediate perceptions of the city surrounding me. My field of vision multiplied beyond 'natural' perception expanded by audio-vision, actual and virtual images superimposed[1] in a holographic entertainment[2] of the world. The play of entertainment attenuates consciousness of a self, a thinning of consciousness that feels like a splitting up a single self into a multiplicity, proprioception's feeling for the body's self-enjoyment stretched out into the city's vibrations, layered with virtual images related to *The Wall* in different ways. These moments I remember, new interpretations of things I just saw transformed into cinematic images, all of this becoming-body, becoming-music and becoming-city.

This holographic superimposition, waking vision, is fed through cinematographic framing techniques and filtered through virtual lens choices and virtual colouring. Microperceptions and fleeting feelings dash like sensual comets across an intensive screen of present-ness. The experience of self-division, watching the unfolding of techniques in one's own body, rather than composing, decentres the notion of authorship and perhaps even personhood in the humanist mode. The in-folding of story, the textures and timbres of virtual shots, virtual montage or virtual series, as they assert themselves in a transgressive tumble of virtuality-actuality-world. An attenuated consciousness vibrates the hyphen between seeing-hearing, creating-receiving, thinking-feeling, mind-body, imagination-memory. The vibrating hyphen is the Greek *enotikon*, the root symbol for both the hyphen and the musical slur, the musical technique for tying two or more notes together. The vibrating enotikon marks both the relation and distance between two terms, it marks the impact of each term on the other, but also the distance between the terms.[3] It is an interstices, a gap, a creative space of emergence, where something in excess of the terms may emerge from its relationality. It is, as Leonard Cohen wrote, the crack in everything that lets the light in.

In praise of undisciplined thinking

The richness of the above description may obscure the fact that this it is a very 'normal' experience. It is a description of being 'lost in thought'. How many times in a week does this play of imagination, memory, sensation, feeling and thinking occur? I could not possibly say. For me, like most people probably, being lost in thought is common and entertaining. The practice is commonly treated as unimportant or worse, a bad habit of undisciplined thinking. It lacks the significant results/outcomes, the 'value' of paying attention to the here and now. A utilitarian value. Perhaps it is called 'lost' because it is another way of describing a kind of thinking that does not have obvious capitalist value. But what if we see this pejorative description of lost as disciplinary, as too much tied up with imperialist-white supremacist-capitalist-patriarch, as bell hooks would call it. What if we took these 'lost' moments very seriously for what they seem to be, the expression of an existential creative relationality entertained by the world. Why is it that the word thinking is reserved for sober and sombre distant reflection? The disciplined consciously organized and focused application of a mental faculty on an object and for a predetermined result, entrainment not entertainment (Manning 2016: 81). How does entrainment compare to the joyfully exuberant and playful entertainment that seems to gush from the hyphen, the vibrating enotikon, between body-world. What if, just for a moment, we would invert the privilege between entertainment and entrainment, revoking the dismissive 'lost' from 'lost in thought' and instead highlighting and emphasizing, perhaps even cultivating entertainment as the play of worldmaking. This would give entertainment a central role in understanding the world and this understanding would be in motion (just like the world!), it would be worlding.

Polyversity: An alternate reality

I do like science fiction very much and think its lessons deserve a more central place in the humanities. Sci-fi helps orient thinking into the future, to see the future in the present. The act of playing potential futures out virtually. Sci-fi is a kind of simulator.

So let us use this technology, this simulator. Imagine a world where Heraclitus' flux was embraced over Plato's forms. Instead of ridding the cave of its shadows, the dancing images would be seen as worlding. These worlding philosophers would not see their calling as discovering a sunny outside of the cave, an objective privileged perspective on unchanging reality hidden behind the illusions of the world. But instead, they would be practising the joyfulness of worlding, making situational braids resonating with the vibratory livingness of the world in this moment and in this place. In this sci-fi alternate reality, the vibrating enotikon is world-becoming and its practice is worlding first principle. Instead of the habit of seeing the words on each side of the hyphen, they look for opportunities to hyphenate. Each hyphen is an activator of new kinds of thinking: thinking-feeling.

A relational enlightenment

In this alternate reality, the Enlightenment was not dedicated to determining the uniqueness of humans in the world, but instead to worlding human with more-than-human life more-than-human technology into relationality that recognized constant change, constant becoming. Thinking-feeling was nurtured, its practice dedicated to developing an ever-increasing relationality, becoming-with ecology, worlding-biosphere. In this alternative timeline, perhaps, a machinic process ontology emerged as dominant. The flux of heterogeneous universes coming into expression through interaction. Flux, understood as constant flows, were machined in the production of livingness. Machining is not reserved for technological machines, because machining is the origin of the universe. Technology in machining's extension. Technology is not set in distant alterity to human; it predates modern humans. Technological machines played a key role in the sympoiesis of *Homo sapiens*. Fire technology, tool technology, communication technology, decorative technology, ritual technology pre-existed *Homo sapiens* by many millennia (Stiegler 1998).

Thinking-feeling was a mutation even older than *Homo sapiens*. It was a mutation of the earth that developed upon ever-increasing complexity over evolutionary time, mutated into brains and minds (Damasio 2018). Human beings were not the first to think, to make, to create. The earth thinks and provides the architecture for thinking-feeling. From bacteria to artificial intelligence, consciousness mutates. Homo sapiens did not begin fully formed in a garden of Eden, invented by a god, but in the processual universes, worldings of bio-techno-eco-creativity. Creativity is machinic operations on flows of difference that produce difference. Ears did not create sound but evolved as a capacity to hear in a world full of sound. Hearing complexifies sound (language and music), by creating circuits with minds and metabolisms. Eyes do not exist to critically reflect on light alone, but evolved in a world bathed in light and further complexifies light and colour (plastic arts and cinema). The brain was not created to behold the world, but is an evolving machine to organize and supervise complex biological machinery (organs), to make sense of visual-images, skin-images, scent-images and sound-images. The human mind emerged as the human organism mutated technically. It found ways of transforming the earth into tools and then organizing these tools into ecologies of practices that have a style. Let us call any particular organization of an ecology of practices a diagram. Hunting diagrams produced enough bioavailable protein to advance brain complexity. Humans travelled great distances over millennia. Degrees of whiteness emerged in Europe and Asia not as a pregiven, but in a machinic relationality with the light of the biosphere. A consequence of a reduction of sunlight and a reduced need to protect bodily machinery against UV radiation. Bodily change as a consequence of a changed relationality to light. The environment is not external to our body, its traces are in our bodies.

Machinic process

Machinic operation is physical, singular and unique as well as diagrammatic and abstract. Machinery operates on flows and flows of flows. Machines work on content to bring it to expression. Eyes work on reflected light, ears on reflected sound to construct a physical world in which the organism lives. Reflected light, not the object, is what touches the eyes. We live in a world of images that are matter and matter that are images as Bergson explains. Reflected light is a content that is worked on by an organism to bring that image-matter into expression. There is a gap between content and expression where this work is done, and this is the diagram, the abstract machine. This work is an application of a force (Massumi 1992) that is the machinic operation. The diagram allows the image to emerge as the coming together of content and expression. Diagramming is process, the way force affects. Content is made up of virtualities that give expression its potentiality. These characteristics are universes. As Massumi explains, for a woodworker, the characteristics of a piece of wood holds virtualities that are recognized. The particular way the wood feels and the way the grains run. These are forms of content that express a universe of virtual characteristics. This is the right piece of wood to realize this object. The object that the wood worker is trying to realize is its form of expression. The diagram is the way the wood worker applies the force needed to realize the form of expression of their choosing, by recognizing already that a content expresses a useful form of content. The diagram is the force that transforms content into expression. This force is shaped by the virtualities of the form of expression. But it is also shaped by how the wood will respond. The wood also has a force.

Music machines

For a musician, each vibrating object has a potentiality to become content, to populate a plane of material for music making. A musical act, before it is an act, is already musical. Its perpetration already transforms a vibrating world into a plane of material, the sources of music. Its diagrams, the way force is applied to content for expression, are part of a constellation inside incorporeal universes of music. Music is an incorporeal universe, an always-expanding abstract constellation of diagrams that exist virtually. The instruments are technological bodies that are vibrating with possibility, waiting to rejoin a refrain. Every machinic act on sound can produce refrains, an abstract machine that produces a node in space-time that draws in content from regions of the incorporeal universe to work on sound matter in a process that territorializes bodies and their environments. In short, worlding instead of humanism. In this alternate reality, art is not an object, a stable category for reflection, is not reduced to entertainment-as-detached reflection. Using and innovating on musical diagrams is an aesthetico-political[4] practice. Diagramming is the refraining of a world, constantly becoming, worlding.

Polyversity

Worlding took many forms as its medium of composition and sharing, and sharing was understood as becoming-with. The media form mattered, as each form has its own characteristics and ecology of practices. Worlding swelled its practices and topics with an understanding of becoming-in-relations at every scale of existence from the quantum to the cosmic. The polyversity was established as a network of nodes with a mission to cultivate and share worlding practices, theorizing and curating a diversity of worlds: polyverse. Instead of separating out objects for analysis, worlding became oriented to building greater and more complex webs of futuring. Its storylines would matter, because it matters what stories story the world (Haraway). Worlding is the emergent processes of coming into relation, becoming-with the living worlds. Its stories accompanied a person's journey through life, ritualized their perspectives, contributed to multilinear heterogenous genealogies across species. Worlding did not separate knowledge making into a caste of makers serving audiences because it was each person's existential practice. Worlding was worlding-the-world. Worlding was the relationality of the present-future-past assemblage, knowledgeable that worlding does not begin on its own nor is separable from a future-becoming.

Worlding study in the Polyversity

Worlding is a study practice that seeks to diagram eco-social-subjectivities. The production of subjectivity is 'the ensemble of conditions which render possible the emergence of individual and/or collective instances of self-referential existential territories, adjacent, or in a delimiting relation, to an alterity that is itself subjective' (Guattari 1995: 9). Music is not an object for study, but is a component of a diagram. Music is incorporeal universes of sound and value that have proper names which label a diagram. These diagrams are used by human social life to form collective assemblages of enunciation. These collective assemblages of enunciation are also self-referential and mutating. Music is a sympoietic operation; it is a becoming-with subjectivities in time-space that makes connections across time-space. These collective subjectivities have ecological opportunities and consequences. Ecology is understood as the operation of organisms (at all scales) with their environment, itself constituted by actualities (the now) and virtualities (pastness and futureness as potentials). Study at the polyversity is oriented to a futurity of life, dedicated to creation and inquiry of eco-social-subjectivity diagrams. An existential economics where 'A Life' (Deleuze) is the guiding principle of all inquiry.

Let us stay in this alternate reality and imagine the kind of study that it could promote for the person who has Pink Floyd's *The Wall* currently playing in their mind.

Worlding *The Wall* at the Polyversity: A case study

This person is a practitioner of cinematic worlding. For their own reasons, which they cannot really articulate very clearly (but are constantly exploring), they are drawn to cineworlding music. They find themselves caught up in music's resonant webs of sensuousness and have found themselves produced by its flows. They enjoy and become entertained easily by musics' refrains and are called to share them cinematically. Each film becomes an opportunity to experience the music-world entanglement, a developing compositional-existential practice, 'a way' of living artfully (Manning 2016: 46–65). Neither cinema nor music is a topic for worlding; it is a medium of cineworlding. Music is not the sound of being connected to the world, it is the connection. Cinema is not looking at the world but a practice of making worlds. Cineworlding music uses audio-vision as the medium to in-fold the intensities of music's connections so that others may also experience these unique virtual-actual in-foldings of intensiveness and be encouraged to think-feel their own relationality and meaning.

Chromesthesia

Let us return to the street. Before *The Wall* becomes a music field emanating from memory, it is first an 'obsessive' refrain (Guattari 2011: 119). Obsessive because it is looped by the yeller, with the first line repeated over and over again. The relationship between the obsessive refrain and the walkers auditory memory is crucial here because it is a central question of what constitutes a sound field and a music field, and then their roles in cinematic composition. While it is common to think of a sound field as an intensive emanation of sound particles moving through space-time, it is an empirical fact that music fields also emerge from memory, itself the crystallization of previous events.[5] The machinic operation in this case is a process that connects the obsessive refrain to a constellation of music field memories that exist as a unified memory field and that carry a multiplicity of time-space references that occur as virtual visual field experiences. What I mean here is that the music field as remembered, occupies only one perceptual track so to speak. It partially fills auditory perception, taking central place. It is heard along with the intensive sound field where a body is immersed. But this music field is not unitary, its layers of experience are intensive and extensive that can contribute shifting images that appear as signifying and asignifying visual percepts and concurrent virtual visual sensory flows: audio-vision. The sensory flow (perception) itself is not unaffected. Perception begins to take on a different quality, the world as experienced moves from 'normal' perception to artistic perception, becoming a plane of material emerging, by way of a forming diagram, into a virtual plane of composition. In this sense, even the most abstract music videos can be seen as the actualization of the virtualities within living perception.

These fields are not separate from affects and intensive space. The event of its remembering is expressed as both auditory memory and affects, thinking-feeling. A sound field affects the body on its skin affecting intensive space from within. It shares, it seems, in Massumi's description, 'a rustle at the periphery of vision (audiation in this case) that draws the gaze towards it. In every shift of attention, there is an interruption, a momentary cut in the mode of onward deployment of life. The cut can pass unnoticed, striking imperceptibly, with only its effects entering conscious awareness as they unroll' (2015: 53). Instead of gaze, perhaps, we might think of these as microperceptions of audiation. When the feeling is experienced as one's own, you 'recognize it as a content of your life, an emotional episode in your personal history. But in the instant of the affective hit, there is no content yet. All there is is the affective quality, coinciding with the feeling of the interruption, with the kind of felt transition' (2015: 54). It is in this transition that cineworlding begins to take shape, a practice of entangling perception and proprioception in an intersensory virtual audiovisual chromesthesia. Chromesthesia is an entanglement of a body with a visual field and a sound field, it is audio-vision beyond the volition-intentionality-agency triad of humanism. This audio-vision is not necessarily fully formed images but instead an in-folding of virtualities that play across visual perception where colour, shape and movement intensities are taking shape. It could be said that chromesthesia is an intensive diagram that connects audio-visions percepts and affects.

A film begins to take shape

I see the figure of the walker at the same time as I feel my body bodying. I am entertained by cars zipping by, the general vibratory sounds of the city, entertained by my footfalls lining up with the kickdrum thrumming my auditory memory. This is the vibrating enotikon. Intensities. The practice of worlding means taking seriously these elusive events, to prepare attention for the complexity of this vibratory swelling, and to recognize in this the emergence of a plane of material. The emergence of the plane of material is a shift from the entertainment of the world into a thinking-feeling-creating space where ecological intensive entertainments become chromesthesia. The meta-recording procedure begins with intensive space, a practice of logging away in memory the traces of a compositional audio-vision event as they take shape. Developing this practice requires a deep immersion into the virtualities that populate the world-bodying relationality, allowing consciousness to drift, subjectivity to dissolve enough to make room for multiple superimposed or holographic co-current locational realities. This is perhaps why Federico Fellini, a filmmaker for whom virtuality is present to a high degree, remarked that for him LSD was not very impactful as 'artists are already frequent travelers between the conscious and unconscious mind'.[6] Perhaps audio-vision composition might be existential journaling about intensive psycho-travel? A kind of journal entry that is not predicated on language but on movement, colour, sound and affect: *chromesthesia*.

Chromesthesia helps us think about intensive space and its entanglements with perception, virtuality and audio-vision. It is also important to remember the bodying that is also occurring on another channel that is entangled with the production of subjectivity. There is a joyful becoming of the walker, its bodying, that is the mutual entanglements of audio-vision, the obsessive refrain, and the city. These flows are in-folded into an assemblage of enunciation. This assemblage of enunciation has an existential function to 'establish a system of repetition, of intensive insistence, polarized between a territorialized Existential territory and deterritorialized incorporeal Universes' (Guattari 1995: 26). The obsessive refrain provided a flow, an opportunity for the walker to deterritorialize a single sentence (we don't need no education) attaching this sentence to incorporeal universes of music and cinema. A deterritorialization that territorializes the walker through a 'system of repetition' which is not a repetition of sameness but the uniqueness of this existential event. Its intensive insistence that territorializes the thinking-feeling walker as a unique living entity in this moment. Just as the clips of the world and memory are deterritorialized into an emerging compositional practice, a thinking-feeling creativity that is another facet of its intensive insistence. To diagram this process is to enact worlding, to make a film of this process is cineworlding. It is not to be distant from it, to observe it, but to be involved in the diagramming of a collective assemblage of enunciation.[7]

The scriptwriter: Another subjectivity comments

From the mirco-conscious process (intensive space), a new subjectivity emerges that I call the scriptwriter. The scriptwriter emerges from the in-folding of intensities and cinematic techniques and begins to machine intensities, the harmonics of the series, each scene piling on images adding harmonics to audio-vision. The previous process does not arrest at the arrival of the scriptwriter, the holographic entertainment continues in all of its throbbing glory. There is a division in consciousness perhaps, a division quite like cell development, a division as complexity where the emergence of the scriptwriter becomes a consequence of the attunement towards the entertainment and the already embodied techniques of cinema production.

The scriptwriter begins to work on scenes in series. The shots do not emerge from nowhere but instead grow from the intensities of their connections. It is as if the shots grow out from the intensities of the series so that the shot is the connector or pathway of the intensity. Shots do not exist independently of each other and the shots themselves are, in an important way, emerging from a prelinguistic, pre-semiotic intensive space. What this means is that the interstices between the shots is where the energy of the composition still resonates even as the intensities cool into extensive forms (moving images). The description of the shots functions as a type of conduits which uses descriptive language meant to be treated as a shorthand for the intensities that cannot be captured by language.

Scriptwriting is just like music composition in that the intensities should not be explicated but provided provisionally. The score is not the music. The composer provides a kind of map for engaging with the intensities of musical potential and the performers draw out the intensities implicit in the map. The script becomes a plane of material that will be worked on, a creative force that works on the score, bringing the intensive-potential buried in the score into the world. But before the script can become a plane of material, it must do its machinic work. The script is a diagram and operates in the same way as a music score, the music is not in the notes but in the relations of the notes-in-series. The intensity of the script is not in the words, it is in the intensive-potential between the words, between the shots. The body's intensive-potential, the intensity of becoming-*The Wall* that is penned so that the filmmaker self, which will come back to this scene, will have access to this event. From the plane of material to the script plane of composition which then becomes the plane of material for the cinematic plane of composition.

Thinking the intensive-potential of the becoming-body in the city, and then the becoming-body in the film enacts a worlding of the world that is music. The becoming-body in the city is a worlding of the world that is becoming-*The Wall*. The cinematic process worlds cinematically the worlding of the world. Continuing the process of becoming into cinema-thinking. This process is called cineworlding music.

The script writer takes over the narrative.

Tagline: On Election Day

What is the consequence of hearing a ragged musical reference? This short film, *On Election Day*, follows the bodily transformation and technological travel of a musical event that begins with an obsessively yelled line of a Pink Floyd song on election day and ends with a living room dance party for one. Beware what you listen to, it just may make your day better.

Title: On Election Day

Fade in:

Ext. sunny afternoon, outside an urban voting station

White male – presenting middle-aged man walks out of the voting station. He takes a moment to exhale, attempting to release tension. It fails.

                                                                                                        Cut to:

Ext. sunny afternoon, election day, busy city street

He stares at the sidewalk with hands in his jean jacket pocket, his body is tight with tension. Regular impression marks his thick greying beard from a long day of wearing a mask. On the other side of the street, a young person in a white hoodie and loose-fitted blue jeans with black sneakers stands up on a bus-stop bench. They raise their hands in the air and begin repetitively shouting at the world.

                                                                                                        Cut to:

Ext. sunny afternoon, bus stop busy urban street

Shouter
WE DON'T NEED NO EDUCATION!!
WE DON'T NEED NO EDUCATION!!

Music: Pink Floyd *The Wall*

Cut to:

Ext. sunny afternoon, election day, busy city street

As the shouting continues, the walker, without looking up, changes their posture and their pace. A slight grin crosses the walker's face as the walker steps in time with the music. The music continues.

Ext. sunny afternoon, quiet inner-city neighbourhood street.
    A collection of election signs dot the front lawn of a quiet street.

Cut to:

Ext. sunny afternoon, election day, busy city street
    Feet walking to the beat of the music.

Cut to:

Ext. sunny afternoon, outside a small town baseball field

A high fence separates a small group of young people from music concert. A small town rock band walks by the group ushered into the backstage of the concert. One of them wears a Pink Floyd t-shirt. The group tries to get in with the band but are stopped by security.

Cut to:

Ext. sunny afternoon, election day, busy city street

Walker looks up smiling, walking with a much freer gait, grooves to the music.

Cut to:

Int. music store.

A young girl takes a guitar off the wall and plugs it into an amp. The store manager, a young man in his twenties, watches from a distance. The young girl tries and tries to play in time with the soundtrack.

Cut to:

Ext. sunny afternoon, election day, busy city street

Walker takes a left turn down a street and walks towards a small house. Opens a small metal gate and keeping time with the music skips up the stairs and into the house.

Cut to:

Int. small house.
A small record player is opened and a vinyl copy of Pink Floyd's *The Wall* is placed on the turn table. The needle drops and the small living room is filled with the sound of the record. The walker plays air guitar, shakes his head at himself and walks out of the room.

Fade to black.

The scriptwriter concedes the narrative

Cineworlding practice in an alternative reality

With the film scenes sketched out, the next stage of cineworlding music would be to gather together equipment and someone to play the multiple parts and begin the cinematic process. Locations, rehearsing, filming, sound recording, editing, colouring, mastering and delivering the content. In each step of the cineworlding process, the worlding student would meet and discuss approaches with more senior cineworlders. Their conversations would be about what is learned about the world through the process of cinematic production. Less concerned with the filmic outcome because it will emerge from a dedication to cinematic process (no new film can come unless this film comes first). The film will eventually happen because there is a relationality with an audience that continues the cineworlding process. But the audience, though virtually always there, is not the priority. The priority is to use the cinematic process to follow the lines of entanglements, to puzzle and marvel at thinking-feeling the world, the sharing that is stimulated by the world, the activation of a matrix of perception-imagination-memory-sensation. The production process is the situation that has to first happen so that the worlder can be immersed in the matrix. All worlders know this as the second principle: nothing starts on its own. Worlding does not start from a blank slate but instead from entertainment of the world.

In the discussions with senior worlders, the junior realizes that this short film draws together the rhythms of the city, its movements and intensities through their body. The nooshock instigates a series characterized not by static images but a series of intensities that fold into the body: collective enunciation of subjectivity. The in-folding is the vibrating enotikon that is the becoming of living, the thinking-feeling of sympoiesis, becoming-together. This is the third principle: in-folding is living. Cineworlding is thinking as in-folding. Music is not an addition to the urban scene but instead is the becoming-rhythmics that is always at potential. The vibrating enotikon expresses virtual folding of space-time into the coordinates of space-time of every becoming-body.

Audio-vision

Though it is common in film composition to consider music an addition to the film image, cineworlders know that there is no rule that says this is the only way film is composed. As Michel Chion notes when speaking of the music video:

> its (music video) only constraint being to synch up audio and video at certain points to solder the image to the music: this way the image can move around at will in time and space. In the limit case of the music video, there is no audiovisual scene to speak of, that is, no scene anchored in a coherent spatiotemporal continuum. (2019: 80)

One of the characteristics of music is its ability to enact time-space origami, it does this by in-folding time-space through the production of what Deleuze and Guattari call a refrain. The refrain territorializes time-space but not in a straightforward way. In our little film *On Election Day*, the refrain works on the body's feltness to itself, and in-folds visual images into the refrain. To treat these images casually as representational content would be an error.

Developing techniques

Cineworlding does not look to 'read' its films because any act that abstracts movement and duration from cinema transforms it. Stopping the movement abstracts the event and draws it out of experience: 'Experience is (in) movement. Anything that stands still – an object, a form, a being – is an abstraction from experience' (Manning 2016: 47). This abstraction threatens to cut movement and time out of cinema, and since as the great Russian filmmaker Andrei Tarkovski said, cinema is sculpting with time, liquidating time and movement from analysis transforms cinema into something else. Cinema is movement-in-time. Cineworlders are constantly after ways of thinking movement-images and time-images. And what of the audience? What does the audience do when watching cinema? Cineworlders do not consider cinematic spectatorship to be still, to be disciplined, to be empty. But instead already dancing with thinking-feeling where cinema has the opportunity to provide a new refrain that may make a collective thinking-feeling possible. It is not collective as the enacting of the same but collective-as-difference, dancing a body's unique expression of thinking-feeling in time with the rhythm of others thinking-feeling, to recognize that thinking-feeling is not isolated in the body. Cineworlding is not interested in analysis for its own sake but instead is interested in developing techniques that can inspire more ethical and diverse worldings.

Audio-vision is more than the addition of images to music, or music to images, it is a relational practice that can be as differently tuned as each living moment. The forth principle: worlding is as unique and diverse as a breath. It is a dynamic process and not a technical fact. Composition is paying attention to in-folding, following and then cineworlding its virtualities. These becomings populate a script that later will be out-folded with a series of cinematic techniques, in-folded again into a film, so as to be out-folded through media, and once again in-folded by spectators. The response of spectators shapes the effectiveness of techniques and introduces questions of value. There are events that characterize each of the phases of cineworlding. Cineworlding is not about making a film but about using creativity to practice becoming-cinema and to follow the transformations through each in-folding and out-folding. The goal of thinking-feeling cineworlding is not to provide rules for how worlding practices must happen, but instead to live a practice, an artful way of becoming-with the world. It is to become with the vibrating enotikon, because as the fifth principle states: learning to stand still requires accepting constant movement. And just as the body is composed of more than its metabolism, thinking-feeling is being composed by faculties and technologies, cineworlding is a 'connection machine' (Manning 2009: 24). Cineworlding is the rhythms of the city that become a plane of material, where techniques allow a plane of composition to emerge. Cineworlding is about developing audiovisual compositional practices, diagrams: 'the conjunctive force that in-gathers an artwork's intensity' (Manning

2009: 124). The diagram works at the interstices between the plane of material and plane of composition. A becoming-body is a type of diagram: a biogram.

The walker biograms three times

In *On Election Day*, the action in the film is the becoming-body of the walker. There are three events in the film. The body-tense, the body-grooving and the body-dancing. The music is a new rhythm, altering the becoming-body of the walker and multiplying the visual field with scenes, each with a rhythm that adds, scene by scene, new rhythmic qualities, like pigments of rhythmic colour. But let us not move past this moment too quickly.

Erin Manning reminds us that 'walking is all about taking the next step. Walking is never one-off: the momentum of the last step feeds the advance into the next one' (2009: 49). The momentum of walking has a groove, a set of spatiotemporal displacements that is about a duration between steps, the walker's rhythm. The rhythmic momentum is a signature of the walker, a signature in movement that has two kind of qualities that run through each other. The first quality is the feeling of walking, is the body's proprioception of balance, tempo and rhythm. The second is the body's physical interaction with the world, that we 'walk with, as well as within, the environment perceived relationally' (Manning 2009: 49). The space between the steps is not empty space but the space of movement. To focus too closely on the contact of foot to ground does not tell us much about changes in preacceleration. Is the swing of a walker the consequence of the footfall or the differential preacceleration that moves into each step? The swing, the gait, the signature is to begin to think walking as a coming-into-form, 'to conceive of taking form itself' (Manning 2009: 5). To conceive of taking form, as Manning suggests, requires a language of movement 'that foregrounds incipience rather than displacement' (Manning 2009: 5). Preacceleration 'refers to the vital force of movements taking form. It is the feeling of movements in-gathering, a welling that propels the directionality of how movement moves' (Manning 2009: 6). The walker's signature, their swing, is a quality of a body-becoming movement: bodying.

The walker's exhalation in the opening of the film establishes a space-time as well as a its texture. Though the walker stands still, there is movement. The body breathes, attempting to release strain. When the body begins to walk down the street, the strain is not gone. The shoulders and the gait carry the strain from the unsatisfactory exhalation moments before, it is a series. There are two kinds of movement that occurs in the scene, the body moving across space and the camera moving through space. The camera 'walks' with the walker and movement is not the breaking up of space into divisible units, the steps are not making divisions, 'movement is indivisible' (Manning 2009: 127). The walker-camera assemblage creates movement as tension.

There is no 'music' yet in a traditional Western sense; the music has yet to begin. But there is sound-as-music in the R. Murray Shaffer and John Cage sense. We are listening to an urban soundworld and moving with its rhythms. The walker is not a subject distinct from a background, the walker and the city is movement: bodying. When *The Wall* begins, it is not the introduction of music, but a cut that emanates from inside the walker. No one else in the profilmic world hears *The Wall* (though perhaps the yeller does!). The music is not the background for the body, but is the body-becoming: bodying. The event is the release of tension in the body that is the transformation of the textural rhythms of movement. This is an art of movement, a worlding of a body-becoming: bodying. The composition of a body-becoming is the biogram:

> The biogram must not be thought as an image of the body. It is always deterritorialized. It holds nothing. It is a principle of conjugation, of consistency. It creates a texture before it coagulates into a form. Better to say that the becoming-body 'biograms'. To biogram is to create a virtual resonance that expresses the conjuction between series that prolong what a body can do. Not what movement is, but what movement can do. (Manning 2009: 126)

Cineworlding shares with ethnography an interest in whole bodies and whole acts (Heider 2006: 114). It marks a confluence between cinematic neorealism and ethnography. It also marks a confluence between neorealism and social science and humanities research. The place where research and creativity meet. It is not really a place though, but processes. It is a process where music studies experiences the event of *The Wall*, and also, where art experiences the event. I am careful to not say, the same event, or the same body. Ethnography tends to function on an ethnographic plane of correspondence, where coordinates of physical time-space are mapped onto a body. For Heider, the whole body is the whole physical body. But a body is far more than this, a body is 'pure plastic rhythm . . . a body that resists predefinition in terms of subjectivity or identity, a body that is involved in a reciprocal reaching-towards that in-gathers the world even as it worlds' (Manning 2009: 6). The body is bodying through its becoming which 'are rhythms of speed and slowness, rhythms alive in the nuances of movement moving' (Manning 2009: 124). The body-becoming, its bodying is its worlding.

The whole act for Heider is the whole visible act occurring on an ethnographic plane of consistency. But like the definition of the whole body, it falls short of being whole. Bodying reaches across time-space in imagination, memory, sensation which are all mixed-up in perception and its action. There is no divisibility, acts do not occur as discrete actions, there is no clear present where the ethnographic present can occur: 'the biogram works in a strange paradox of time' (Manning 2009: 125). This is not a mystification of living, it is the opposite, it is an embrace of what everyone knows. We do not exist in a rational flat time-space. Our minds 'wander' and 'get lost' though in polite society we pretend not to notice. We all know that we are constantly in-folding pastness and futurity into this 'moment'. Federico Fellini was very precise with his neorealism. In 8½, the protagonist is unable to make a film and, in his frustration, constantly in-folds time-space, building a world that is joyfully unstable, and a bodying that is so full of brimming instability that Fellini biograms the director's bodying as a carnival.

For cineworlding, whole acts are not simple physical manipulations in a flat time-space, but the creation of complexly folded time-space, rich in virtuality, and movement. The biogram 'carries the movement of the event even before the event has expressed itself as such. The biogram cannot represent anything because it has no pregiven form. It creates out of the plane of consistency that it preempts. It is diagrammatic because it has not yet determined its function' (Manning 2009: 125). The biogram is diagrammatic, not a technique exactly, but an emergent outcome of techniques that allow bodying to emerge in the plane of composition.

Research-creation as the realization of this alternate reality?

Let us now return still vibrating with the buzz of this alternate reality and ask if cinematic research-creation, what I am calling cineworlding, is not indeed a step towards this process-oriented alter reality. Cineworlding is a meeting place between research and creation. Or more precisely the vibrating enotikon between research-creation that is the energy where preconcert talks, interviews, research papers, books, films, interviews, scripts, lectures issue forth. The hyphen between research-creation is not a simple punctuation mark; it represents a complex form of thinking-cinema, thinking-movement, thinking-form, thinking-music.

Research-creation is a category in Canadian scholarship that does not come out of nowhere. It has 'family resemblances' (Chapman and Sawchuck 2012) with practice-based research and art-based research. It emerged in the 1990s as an ongoing consequence of interdisciplinarity, the reorganization of knowledge production and is, according to Stevance and Lacasse, 'the nerve-center of this transformation' (2018: 23) in the arts and humanities. For them research-creation in music studies might focus on training music performers in research methods and having musicologists work more closely with performance faculty and their students on projects. Music departments are a complex blend of two different histories. The music conservatory and the research university. This hybrid dimension of the music school has not produced a seamless fusion, but has fault lines that sometimes can result in organizational division in programmes. In my own professional practice, however, where I am the sole musicologists in a university programme full of performers, music theorists, composers and recording studio professionals, research-creation is a way for me to meet students where they are as artists and to interest them in thinking deeply about their developing creative process. Research-creation helps students develop an orientation to study-in-practice, to process as artfullness. For Harney and Moten, study is

> what you do with other people. It's talking and walking around with other people, working, dancing, suffering, some irreducible convergence of all three held under the name of speculative practice. The notion of a rehearsal – being in a kind of workshop, playing in a band, in an jam session, or old men sitting on a porch, or people working together in a factory – there are these various modes of activity. The point of calling it 'study is to mark that the incessant and irreversible intellectuality of these activities is already present'. (2013: 109–10)

Orienting art practice away from an exclusive focus on the production of an art object and towards study as process, something that research-creation can contribute, can reframe what happens in the rehearsal space. It can help students recognize that this space is where study occurs and that through study music education can be reoriented to bodying and futurity.

This is not to say that research-creation is not without challenges and opportunities of many kinds. As Chapman and Sawchuck have noted: 'methodological and epistemological challenge to the argumentative form(s) that have typified much academic scholarship. In research-creation approaches, the theoretical, technical, and creative aspects of a research project are pursued in tandem, and quite often, scholarly form and decorum are broached and breeched in the name of experimentation' (2012: 6). But these discussions are quite a long way from the worlding practices that I have been so far suggesting. Research-creation is not liberatory in and of itself, it is as likely to remain entrenched in 'scholarly form and decorum' as it is to do much-needed decolonial work. To get there, it is necessary to pose the question of 'what we do in the academy and for whom' (Loveless 2020: 224–5). Worlding in my alternate reality did not address the university, but a polyversity, because for me the form and shape of the university is not a forgone conclusion.[8]

For Loveless, social justice movements are foundational to research-creation's practice. Loveless writes: 'I work with research-creation, first and foremost, as an intervention into the contemporary university landscape, one that is interdisciplinary and centres feminist, queer, decolonial, and critical race theory interventions while working committedly across practice/theory lines' (2020: 225). Erin Manning's research-creation engages Harney and Moten's 'study' (Manning 2016: 27), where study is not owned by the university, by institutions. Study is about a commitment to radical love, solidarity, existential becoming: 'we prepare now for what will come by entering into study. Study, a mode of thinking with others separate from the thinking that the institution requires of you' (Harney and Moten 2013: 11). In study we can hear bell hook's urging to recognize that all communities have aesthetics (study) even though they may be rarely written about in books (1990).

Study does not happen only in a university and by researchers, study happens in a community of people. The absence of the university in my alternate reality is perhaps utopian, but also perhaps orienting. If research-creation as study is to be queer, feminist, decolonial then perhaps it is a little anti-institutional, not by way of institutional critique but through a decolonial engagement with the commons: study as worlding. Cineworlding, my orientation to the practice of creative enthusiasm, for decolonial alterity did not start on its own. In fact, my interest in the potentialities of alternate realities is a consequence of my introduction to study 'in the undercommons' (Harney and Moten 2013: 26), not by a university professor but by a security guard at a Tim Hortons at 2 am.

Sci-fi study in the undercommons

It was a hot summer night. After many days of backshift, it is impossible to sleep regular hours, so on my day off I had taken up a practice of late-night reading at a twenty-four-hour coffee shop. I had a favourite seat in the back corner, the furthest seat away from the door and the bathroom. It was the least likely place to be interrupted by people passing. After a couple of weeks of this routine, I caught the attention of the security guard who remembered me and walked over. A burley man that in an animation of the scene would have been a security bear. Before saying anything he just looked. I had no idea why I had caught his attention, and it made me uneasy. He asked me about what I was reading. Surprised, I stumbled over my words and showed him the book cover. He nodded thoughtfully and asked if I had noticed the group that in previous weeks had been gathering at the large round table. I replied that I had. In fact, it would have been hard to miss, a large gathering of late-night rowdy people drinking coffee in a cloud of cigarette smoke. In the previous two weeks, they had been the only other people in the coffee shop and had paid me absolutely no attention.

The security bear explained that he organized a late-night book club once a week on the quietest night, tonight. It is always open to people but that they only read sci-fi novels and preferred obscure and local authors. If I was interested, he said, I would be more than welcome to join them. He explained that they share books and discuss them. I thanked him for the offer but quietly felt uncomfortable with the idea of joining a much older group of people at 2 am to discuss books I had never heard of. But that was the way I was at eighteen. An unfortunate insecurity that I was soon to get over.

The book club was in full fury soon after 2 am. I kept my head down pretending to be focused. In reality, I was listening to their conversations and peeking at their rowdy ritual. He caught my eye though, after all he was a security guard. He called me over using a voice that provided little choice. I closed my book, picked up my coffee and awkwardly ambled across the café. I sat in an empty stool between two enthusiastic readers who immediately started peppering me with questions. I knew absolutely none of their references. They laughed at me good-naturedly and one handed me a novel written by a Nova Scotia author. I still remember the enthusiasm of my time spent reading that book. I read in all of my spare time. On breaks during work, in the morning sun with hands still smelling of rotting produce. The dark green smudge on page edges that marked a trail through the yellowing softback novel. The plot of the book is secondary, though still memorable. Its story is entwined with the enthusiasm of the group, the fatigue of working backshifts, and the intellectual joy in studying together. Through the kindness and generosity of a security guard, I was introduced to joyful study. A 2 am sci-fi reading group at a Tim Horton's coffee shop might not sound like the start of a scholarly project, but perhaps that is a problem in its own right. Why should it not be an appropriate start for an anarchist worlding project? Wasn't the security guard my professor practising what Harney and Moten call 'the beyond of teaching' where 'it's about allowing subjectivity to be unlawfully overcome by others, a radical passion and passivity such that one becomes unfit for subjection, because one does not possess the kind of agency that can hold the regulatory forces of subjecthood, and one cannot initiate the auto-interpellative torque that biopower subjection requires and rewards' (2013: 28). Transformative teaching and learning occurred in this coffee shop such that almost thirty years later I still resonate with those lessons. Why should study be owned by educational institutions? This experience imprinted itself on me and continues to reverberate through my developing practice.

It has taken time to come back to this lesson. The biopower of the university is strong and so too are the needs to pass if one wants to dedicate one's life to professional study. The struggle to 'be in but not of' the university is a real struggle. In a public lecture at the University of Alberta, Walter Mignolo described institutional decoloniality as a practice that can happen in the corner of a lecture hall among a handful of people. Decoloniality is not a fact, not a state, but a practice. To practice decoloniality is difficult work that is fraught with wrong turns. I once believed that lecturing about critical theory was a practice of decoloniality until after a particularly dark lecture, I returned to my office and with a marker scribbled the word 'Critique', crossed it out, and underneath wrote 'Enthusiasm'. ~~Critique~~ Enthusiasm. Such little words, for such a big epistemological project.

Conclusion: Cineworlding as decolonial futurity?

To read sci-fi in a community group is to be worlding. It is a practice of study that inspires curiosity, engages thinking-feel, opens up questions about the world, and builds community solidarity. ~~Critique~~ Enthusiasm was the beginning for me of a practice to rethink my relationship to critical theory. It was many years later before I read Erin Manning who introduced me to Harney and Moten who helped me make sense of the seed of transformation buried in that note:

> To distance oneself professionally through critique, is this not the most active consent to privatize the social individual? The undercommons might by

contrast be understood as wary of critique, weary of it, and at the same time dedicated to the collectivity of its future, the collectivity that may come to be its future. The undercommons in some ways tries to escape from critique and its degradation as university-consciousness and self-consciousness about university-consciousness. (Harney and Moten 2013: 38)

In research-creation, I am attempting to develop decolonial practice through enthusiastic and alternative worlding. Cinema is the medium of this project and cineworlding is the name I pin my hopes upon. The alternate reality that I used as a platform to launch this project is one that I believe in. It is not merely a fictional situating but a way of thinking my way out of the power structures of disciplinarity, the hegemony of critique. Since completing my PhD in 2010, I have been trying to make sense of where I fit. As Erin Manning lovingly pointed out in an earlier draft of a chapter included in this book, I sometime write as if there is a spectre peering over my shoulder. That spectre is my desire to live up to the expectations of a discipline, to perform intellectualism. It is perhaps easy to retort that a discipline is not a thing, but only a group of people. But if it were as simple as that, decoloniality would be an easy task. It is not. Coloniality is a diagram, it is in my body, a collective assemblage of enunciation, a haunting, a psychosis, a monster (Chapter 11). Decoloniality is a practice to exorcise those conceptual personae and institutional practices (diagrams) that peer over my shoulder and induce me into coloniality. As a settler Canadian living and working as part of an occupying force, finding a way out means creating solidarity but it also means creating an alternative modality for study. Indigenization is important work. But settlers need also do the work to decolonize Western thought.

To do this, I engage with the possibilities of research-creation. It is a political act. I am not interested in situating cineworlding within any discipline and follow Erin Manning's insistence that research-creation is *not* a method, does not require institutions and is oriented to study. Each chapter in this book begins life as an engagement with a film I have made since 2008. Some films are music videos and some are documentaries. There are other films that are docufictions and improvisational fiction films. A discussion of these films will have to wait for a future book project.[9] In cineworlding, the type of film does not matter. What I hope to show is that cinema can produce, like the coffee shop reading group did, a collective situation for study. In each film project I will discuss, I will present more and more layers of cineworlding, with more conceptual development. My hope is that readers will be inspired to try cinematic research-creation. The new and unfamiliar terms are included to try to break free of modernity/coloniality. Often these terms are complex, like worlding, chromesthesia, diagram, bodying, intensive space, decoloniality. I will come back to them over and over again in different situations. I ask the readers patience if at times these concepts seem fuzzy. My understanding of these concepts is quite holographic and it requires different approaches to secrete layers of the conceptual hologram. It is interesting to note that these terms, though awkward at times, open up new ways of seeing-hearing-feeling-conceptualizing worlding. I believe that in worlding, there is something that we possibly all see-hear but that rarely gets included in scholarly discourse. So the terms are meant to be tools to sketch out audio-vision's practice and are not meant to be concepts that reside only on the page. This is a book about practice and each chapter is a diagram that I have developed for myself. I am not asking you to import any of these diagrams into your practice. Quite the contrary. I hope that reading this book will be liberating, will set you off on your own journey to develop your own techniques, your own community of study.

Finally, if cineworlding can be recognized as legitimate knowledge production, which is my goal with this book, then we can say that it is possible to expand scholarly ways of knowing and approaches to study. If we can do that over the course of this book, then it is possible to begin to experiment with our institutions, programmes, classes, curriculum and pedagogy. I just need to find five or six people willing to gather in the corner of a university room to begin to practice decoloniality together. If we can do that. Then we have begun.

3

Living Flame of Love

Creative practice research and practical musicology

Cine-ethnomusicological trouble

The auditorium was hot. Dinner had run late and since it was the first day of the working group meeting in Lisbon, we had trouble finding a place to eat quickly. Just half a block off a side street we found an Italian restaurant, had a quick pizza and glass of beer and headed back to the screening. It was the first time I've screened a new work for a room full of ethnomusicologists, and I was expecting to get into some trouble with the film. I was told that this second meeting of the International Working Group on Audiovisual Ethnomusicology was going to continue its scientific orientation to ethnomusicological film, and that my film, *WE'RE TOO LOUD*: an ecomusicological love story, was perhaps not the kind of film that was going to be embraced easily. So, my walk back to the university theatre was mixed with dread and anticipation.

The film began with only a short introduction and the first person walked out about twenty minutes into the screening. They were followed by others. The worst possible outcome was happening. I kept telling myself that I was prepared for this. The film had already been accepted to be screened in an art house cinema in Edmonton in the fall, so it had already achieved the outcome I had hoped. I can handle fellow ethnomusicologists walking out because the film will be screened for a wider public. But it still hurt. The film ended and the question period began with the simple question, 'Why do you consider this an ethnographic film?'

It wasn't the question, but the tone. Heavy with the footsteps of fleeing colleagues, the tone was accusation; the tone was disciplinary. And the questioner, lifted up on the shoulders of bodies no longer in the room, levels the charge without saying it: this is not ethnography. The anthropological judge holding disciplinary court. And of course, it's this person elected to read the charge, the anthropologist whose films on traditional African music are funded by colonial institutions, who frames and records beautifully with expensive gear, who avoids explaining the musician's Disneyland T-shirt, who gorgeously maintains tradition and keeps modernity and the market economy of traditional music just off screen (though at times I think I can hear the rumbling of the FedEx truck delivering those DVDs).

The critical floodgates open, my head begins to fill with responses, my mouth opens and out comes a trickle. The backpressure mounts as I feebly explain why an ethnographic film about a second generation 'back-to-the-lander' rock musician struggling with gentrification needs to be an appropriate subject in contemporary ethnomusicological work. The evening winds down. It's really hot in here. We spill out onto the street in what feels to me as two camps. Those who still need an explanation, and those, mostly students, who are frustrated by old ways of working, and the spectre of a scientific anthropology that continues to haunt ethnographic film practice, even as we insist that it does not. The Q&A is the evidence.

Practical cine-musicology

The goal for *WE'RE TOO LOUD* was very practical. The film was meant to provide community members with an opportunity to consider the difficulties of young artists working on the island. It was also a second film in what is emerging as a series of case study films to understand the survival of DIY musicians in global capitalism. Owen Chapman suggests that art-based research, practice research, and research-creation have 'family resemblances'. But of course resemblances do not mean that they are the same. Each orientation offers a slightly different perspective on the question of what research-creation can contribute to music studies. In the last two chapters, we began to explore the concept of the refrain, territorialization and the in-folding of cinematic research-creation as a mode of compositional audio-vision. The notion of transversality is useful here and means the intersecting of different topologies. Artful writing working transversally through ethnography, and ethnographic writing operating transversally through art making.[1] Transversality is key to my practice of research-creation and extends the concept of the enotikon from the previous chapter. It is not just a link, but a musical slur, and in the operation of the musical slur, transversality is operationalized.[2] Transversality means that art practice and ethnography, in this case, work through each other, transdisciplinarily, and in the process change the operation of both terms. Transversality does not determine the outcomes of the research-creation methodology; instead, it should be seen as a proposition for the practitioner to attempt clarity of the ways in which both ethnographic practice and art practice are changed by working on each other. This idea will be more fully explored in a later chapter when we begin to think about subjectivation in research-creation. But for the moment, it is necessary to reflect on what happens when ethnographic film and research-creation operate through each other transversally, neither remains the same. And in my experience, the outcomes may not be obvious to ethnographers. In a discussion of "*WE'RE TOO LOUD*" and "*Living Flame of Love*", I intend to show the way that this transversal research-creation approach resonates with Simon Zagorksi-Thomas's suggestion for a practical musicology (2022) while maintaining a commitment to artfulness. Artfulness is not a way of dressing up the documentary but instead investigates subjectivity, a topic that ethnography has long been troubled by. I want to suggest that research-creation studies of process subjectivity can only be done through art and that will never become subservient to observational documentary methods. My thoughts on this are not theoretical alone but come from experiences I have lived as a professional musician before becoming an ethnomusicologist. So it is to my academic pre-history that I must first turn.

Practical films from a grounded perspective

I was a professional musician before coming to academia. During my time in the music industry, I worked as a performer, audio recording engineer, retail manager of a folk music store, booking agent, music manager, choral conductor, private teacher, home-schooling association music teacher, sound technician and event production manager. Over a period of more than ten years, I travelled across North American in diverse ensembles playing in a country band, a flamenco group, and even acted in a musical dinner theatre. Between these road gigs, I had a wide variety of other employment. I enrolled into higher education, specifically ethnomusicology, to attempt to understand the social consequences of a specific technological transformation: the mp3.

In 2003, I was a retail manager of the Ottawa Folklore Centre. It was one of the few folklore centres left in Canada. In the 1970s, a number of these centres opened across the country inspired by the NYC Folklore Centre. They established a kind of unofficial network for folk and roots musicians. I was a customer of the Ottawa and Halifax Folklore Centres while I was on the road in the 1990s and in 2000 when I relocated to Ottawa, Ontario, after a sudden departure from a touring band that I had been with for three years, I found myself working there. Over the next four years, I would learn about the history of the Folklore Centres and their place in the music industry of folk and roots music in North America. But the industry was changing very quickly.

One of the fascinating things about the Folklore Centre was its boosterism of folk and roots music. It was dedicated to hiring musicians, developing teachers, supporting luthiers and connecting musicians and music lovers with the instruments, equipment and artists that would inspire them. As a consequence of this we would regularly host events. Over the years, we produced an important collection of original recordings. We began to think about what we could do with them. One suggestion was to put mp3s of the recordings online, perhaps even sell them. The owner of the Folklore Centre at the time said: 'No one will buy music online'. Wow. That was in 2003. The iPod, iTunes and now streaming platforms have changed all of that in a radically short amount of time.

Just two years later, the flamenco ensemble I was then playing with received a fan email from Japan thanking us for our recent album. The email's author enthusiastically stated that they liked the album so much they had made ten copies for their friends. Wonderful, our music was being shared in a country it was never released in, and we were making absolutely no money for it. Our oil heat had just run out and as if this email was a sign, ten copies at 20 Canadian dollars each was exactly how much money we needed to fill the oil tank. We spent the next three days sleeping under all the clothes we owned so as not to freeze to death. I decided the next week that I needed to understand what was going on with this industry.

The next September I began graduate school. My experiences over the next decade highlighted for me that there is a massive gap between university and the music industry. It is a gap that is kept in place by a complex of arguments about the need to preserve thinking from industry, to not succumb to the neoliberal agenda, a mountain of critical theory that promotes the horrors of capitalism, and the preciousness of free creativity. The complex thing about this is that I agree with just about all of it one way or another. But I think there is a way to maintain criticality while also partnering with musicians trying to understand the technological and economic processes that shape and reshape their lives.

What can a machinic assemblage do?

There is a rich body of theory and practice that recognizes the value of cinema for doing research. Just as Spinoza famously asked 'what can a body do', we might ask the same of cinema: 'what can a cinema camera do'. It seems to me that asking about the camera is to ask about the machinic assemblage of cinema-thinking. It is to ask what a body can do in a register open to what Bernard Stiegler calls technics. Even the surveillance camera, the most dehumanized mode of audiovisual capture extends audio-vision outside of the body. I am not bothered by the suggestion that technology dehumanizes, because I read these concerns with the dissolution of an already problematic and oftentimes romantic anthropocentrism. Vertov's *kinopravda* (cinema truth) is an offer to develop a posthuman cinematic philosophy, machine-thinking assemblages that stretch out beyond the human mind, asking what the posthuman body can do.

This is the central refrain that will be worked out across this book in these 'scenes of research-creation'. I want to forestall a common critique about philosophical research-creation that it is somehow distant to practice because of its sometimes challenging vocabulary. Let us take Deleuze and Guattari's Body without Organs (BwO), for instance. Musicians are very comfortable with machinic assemblages though do not often notice. Let us take just one example: pianist. This is a posthuman identity. A pianist is comprised of a human body and a technological body. Pianist is an abstract machine (the diagram of style and rep) that operates at the interstices of these two bodies and folds these bodies into one identity. The practice of the pianist is to ask: What can this posthuman body do?

My questions about cinematic research-creation asks precisely the same question and transversally to the BwO we call pianist. The pianist is a machinic assemblage, just a very familiar one. It seems to me that this posthuman is already the heart of music studies (how many programmes require all students to become this machinic assemblage?). Asking what the audiovisually enabled body can do for music studies is linked to what the piano-enabled body can do. Performers regularly audio record and audiovisually record their performances for later study, thus extending their BwO and incorporating second-order cybernetic learning. This practice recognizes variation in perception of time-space while in the process of performing. The recordings provide the performer an opportunity to critically reflect on the difference between the immediate experience and the later reception. Philosophically, there is already the acceptance of the variations of subjectivity at the heart of music pedagogy, or second-order cybernetic principles in music pedagogy. What if performers were taught to do auto-ethnography? This practical exercise would become research-creation. These research outcomes would take on a new life as practice theory, extending studies into performance psychology and development. These studies could lead to artist-centred innovations in pedagogy and a deeper understanding of the development of techniques and contribute to an understanding of art-based human-machine interfaces,[3] working against the division between episteme and techne (theory performance split) that is still at the heart of music studies. The door to research-creation is to ask: What can a music machinic assemblage do?

Transversal art-ethnography of process: On refrains

The music machine deterritorializes a refrain and 'music submits the refrain to this special treatment of the diagonal or transversal, it uproots the refrain from its territoriality. Music is a creative, active operation that consists in deterritorializing the refrain. Whereas the refrain is essentially territorial, territorializing or reterritorializing, music makes it a deterritorialized content for a deterritorializing form of expression' (Deleuze and Guattari 1987: 300). In this way, we might see Christopher Small's description of the music 'ritual' in musicking as a reterritorializing of the refrain by the Western art music assemblage that includes composers, orchestras, audiences, conservatories, history, architecture, ticket sales, advertising, cleaners and the like.[4] These reterritorializing musical refrains have proper names that include Beethoven, Mozart, Cage and so on. But these are not bodies alone, but bodies without organs, machinic assemblages and diagrams. This does not do damage to Small's proposition that musicking is a process, but suggests that Small was only looking at one part of the machinic assemblages. Deleuze and Guattari warn that music is not a refrain but a sound machine that lays hold of the refrain and deterritorializes it. They insist that 'it is not really known when music begins ... but music exists because the refrain/rhythm exists also, because music takes up the refrain, lays hold of it as a content in a form of expression, because it forms a block with it in order to take it somewhere else' (1987: 300). The refrain is territorializing, it is 'crafted from rhythm (horizontal axis) and melody (vertical axis), drawn from chaotic and cosmic forces, and essential to the establishment of a home or abode. Any body, possessing a refrain, can use this refrain as protection as that body wonders out' (Bonta and Proveti 2004: 133). It is an in-folding of content into a time-space coordinates that resonates with virtuality. Cineworlding music can make a contribution to a study of the refrain by extending this focus on process. Cine-ethnomusicology can develop as a practical musicology working with local music cultures, not to document them alone, to abstract their musical practices for others to enjoy, but to help community members develop their musical practice beyond the notes, to understand the consequences of grasping hold of the refrain, of machining sound within capitalist systems of control.

Machinic assemblages as process

There is a second consequence of recognizing the machinic assemblages as process and not structure, and this pertains to the cultural studies of music and pop music studies. This is particularly important for those who critique Western art music for its colonial ideology, or make blanket critical and dismissive statements about capitalism. The problem with ideology, as Brian Massumi has illustrated, is that it relies on the idea that people have become duped by a particular programme, an ideology, and that what is required of critical theory is to show that the ideology is nothing but a lie constructed by elites. Ideology is based on the idea of society as a structure thoroughly infused with ideas that work against the best interests of most of the people of that society and that 'mechanism of power defend and reproduce that structure. The structure is an organized whole composed of parts that have specific functions and occupy determinate positions within that whole. The relations among the parts have a coherence dictated by the structure of the whole they compose and whose general interest they serve' (2015: 84). But process is different. Process moves not from the top down but the bottom up. Living systems are constructed by interactions that produce higher-order entities that are different than what they produce. The higher-order entities are assemblages constructed by machinic processes (molecules, cells, bodies, cultures etc.). These machinic processes are not closed to the outside, the way a structure is; they emerge sympoietically with their environment. Process is ecological. Following processes makes evident the interaction of organism-environment.

If we consider Small's description of the symphony concert as structure, where is its ecology, its process, its machinic inputs and outputs and emergences? There is no ecology because it is an abstract structure, an abstract map of the symphony concert.

Unfortunately, it is musicking in name only. Consider the smallest example that Small mentions: the people who clean the concert hall. In a structural description of the symphony concert, these cleaners appear but do not act. In comparison, in WE'RE TOO LOUD the crisis that sets the film in motion is the question of whether the community hall was cleaned properly. The lack of cleaning, a tiny aspect of the concert assemblage that deserves no description or study in musicking, is enough to shut down Breagan Smith's entire music season. His ensemble is characterized as unprofessional and deemed to be a risk by the board of directors who supervise the hall rentals. For Smith, the broken mop similarly illustrates the lack of capacity of the hall management to take their agreement seriously and he is reluctant to take responsibility for the state of the hall the morning after his concert. This may seem like a strange point of conflict, and in itself the conflict is not important, except to illustrate the machinic assemblage of the concert 'ritual'. It is not so much a ritual as Small suggests but a machinic assemblage that relies on the functioning of all of the machines that make it up.

The malfunction or misfunction of a machine within the assemblage produces semiotics that signify back onto the musical act. Breagan Smith and the Good Times are signified as a risk by management, but from the perspective of the band they were risky because of their musical sound. The dirty floor (was it dirty?) of the community hall is a machinic signification that gets territorialized onto Smith's ensemble. A structural description of musicking does not provide a theory that can explain how this can occur. Using a process approach informed by machinic assemblages can help to explain how a broken mop and a dirty floor semiotize machinically. The dirty floor is deterritorialized, it is no longer just the scent of beer on a floor, but becomes something else. It is reterritorialized as unprofessional and as a breach of contract. The breach leads to the cancellation of the rest of Smith's summer performances putting his existential gamble of island life in jeopardy. For Smith, however, the response to the dirty floor is deterritorialized and reterritorialized as a critique of the music his ensemble plays. He is being policed, he believes, because the island culture is being gentrified. Its newly powerful summer residents live a different life than the full-time community, have different ideas of cleanliness, different levels of understanding about all-ages community events and the place of alcohol. A smell of old beer in a morning yoga class, understandably terrible, plays a significant role in the operation of a music scene. This is not something that would ever be accounting for in abstract structural schematics. Perhaps, this is a great example of truth being stranger than fiction.

Cinematic machining

Deleuze and Guattari suggest that ecological process is always territorial. Territoriality in process means that there is constant deterritoriality and reterritoriality. The machinic assemblage is always in process, always machining. Machinic process allows us to not only ask questions about what constituted the musical assemblage (this would be enough to make it valuable) but also what happens when a cinematic body joins an assemblage. It is not just a question of the growth of the assemblage on the ethnographic plane of correspondence, the immediate territoriality, but also how the cinematic work is a machine that will deterritorialize this process, deterritorialize it from the ethnographic plane of correspondence and the ways this mobile audiovisual block will be reterritorialized elsewhere. When a question is posed about the disruption that a cinema camera produces, it misses the point that processes of deterritoriality are already in operation. There is an added deterritoriality, but not an imposition of deterritoriality. The 'imposition of deterritoriality' presupposes a natural state of social practice in advance of the arrival of the cinema camera. But this is an illusion. There is no natural state, only machinic states of deterritorialization and reterritorialization. A process orientation to practical musicology will set aside Humanist myths, its organic naturalism, to see that the organic is machinic!

Living Flame of Love: A machinic case study

Where does *Living Flame of Love* begin? Is it the friendship between Pro Coro Canada director Michael Zaugg, Halifax-based choral composer Peter Togni, and Toronto-based accordionist Joseph Petric? Perhaps it begins with Pro Coro Canada's commitment to performing original Canadian choral works? As one of only five professional choirs in Canada and as a requirement of the national funding bodies to which it responds, there is an encouragement for this practice. Though Pro Coro committed to the world premiere of the work, they did not commission it. Joseph Petric, an internationally known accordionist, has been committed to convincing the world of the possibilities of the accordion as a concert instrument. To do that, works that take the accordion seriously need to be commissioned. Petric reached out to Togni to commission a choral work that featured the accordion as a solo instrument. Why Togni? As a choral composer and long-time host of a choral music radio show on the Canadian Broadcast

Corporation, Togni is a nationally known composer. There is no single reason for this trio to form a group, even if Togni and Zaugg both hold Swiss passports. Even before the first notes of *Living Flame of Love* are put to paper, there is already a rhizome that connects the founding of Pro Coro, to the history of the accordion, to the founding of the national broadcaster, to the formation and application of cultural policy that guides funding decisions and that provides an opportunity for the connection of the creative practice of these three music professionals. Where then to begin the film? As Deleuze and Guattari have often noted, when you are presented with a rhizome it does not matter where one enters, so just pick.

Section one

Peter Togni's beauty

The film opens with an abstract shot dominated by an orange glow with slightly vibrating globules of colour. The voice of Peter Togni introduces the film, and using possessive language identifies himself as a composer:

> I think I was watching an old movie. Maybe it was a fragment of what I heard in there. I was this chord that kept coming back to me and it was kind of the beginning of the whole piece was these three notes (plays sustained notes) and then this note (plays note). So you play those together (chord). And it just appeared. And I like to think it's a conversation I am having with the almighty . . . in music.

There are aspects of this description that are important to highlight, as they set the diagrammatic machine of the film into motion. The first, as was said in the last chapter and repeated by Deleuze and Guattari in this chapter, that it is impossible to say where music begins. A fragment of 'some old movie' sets off an obsessive refrain for Togni, a refrain made up of four notes that were deterritorialized from an unnamed TV movie score. But these notes were not deterritorialized by accident or chance alone they were motivated already by Petric's commission of Togni to produce a work for accordion, harp and choir. Togni's engagement with these notes was motivated by the commission and converted his perception of these notes into a plane of material, a deterritorialized block of sound. Finally, Togni's voice remains an 'abstract faciality which speaks at the heart of speech, dressing up subjective black holes, masking semiotic collapses, deploying personalogical structures of power' (Guattari 2011: 76). Before Tongni's face it shows the machinic assemblage of faciality beginning its work, territorializing the abstract orange screen, the four-note refrain, and the landscape music refrain that is about to emerge that will reterritorialize Togni's voice as a block of landscape music into faciality. The potential meaninglessness of the abstract orange screen, a semiotic black hole, is kept at bay by the machinery of signification. The orange screen is facialized by Togni's voice, even if it is only as some composer, some choral composer somewhere. Even this is enough to make this moment meaningful. The faciality machine, a Guattarian machine is not a priori but 'itself is produced by its production' (Guattari 2011: 31). It begins the assemblage of enunciation for both *Living Flame of Love* and for Peter Togni, a process that will continue to secrete layers of meaning around both, drawing all action and all actors into the *Living Flame of Love*-Peter Togni machine. The operation of these machines works at the interstices of ethnography and art practice, the hyphen between research-creation. Following the faciality-landscapity machine, playing with its relation to the diagrammatic machine of the choral score with the proper name *Living Flame of Love*, charts an alternative pathway through audiovisual ethnography. Not one of direct presentation or identification, but one that plays with the machinic processes of production in order to elucidate them, their relations to meaning production, and ultimately to delve into the potentialities of digital cinema for knowledge creation and the uniqueness of cinema-thinking for music studies.

Very quickly Togni moves from these first three notes to the fourth and then plays the chord. The notes are reterritorialized as a chord cluster, begin to act as a refrain, and then almost immediately they are deterritorialized again and reterritorialized as a conversation with the almighty in music. Between the plane of material (content) and the plane of composition (expression) (Guattari 2011: 41–3; Deleuze and Guattari 1994: 163–99) there is a diagrammatic machine called choral composition. Guattari explains that

> it is neither at the level of formal unites of content nor at the level of distinctive elementary traits that we will be able to seize the resources of semiotic creativity, but at the pragmatic level of the assemblages of enunciation and at the level of molecular matters of expressions and the abstract machines that these materials bring into play. (Guattari 2011: 43)

Togni's TV listening opened onto a compositional plane, a territory, which opened up into a becoming-spiritual. From commission to TV, to piano, to God. *Living Flame of Love* becomes a diagrammatic machine (a becoming-score) that allows Togni to connect to his creator and this spiritual practice.

This practice does not start on itself. It is supported by a Petric's commission. There is no clear causal connection between these operators, their connection was produced by Togni's diagrammatic machinism, his compositional practice and his spiritual practice working transversally through each other. But it is also reversible. These factors also allow the abstract machine to operate. It does not matter to Togni that his sound-prayer began life as deterritorialized sound particles from an old movie score. Nor does the professional practice of writing for commission taint his spiritual journey in music. These do not feature in at all to his explanation. Composition and spirituality work through each other, the appearance of the refrain (does it appear or is it produced?) is the diagram for *Living Flame of Love*. It is the diagrammatic machine that will draw in instrumentalists, choirsters, conductor, audience and filmmaker. So it is here that the film begins. With this short description of this four-note prayer that the operator of *Living Flame of Love* begins its work, becoming-score, becoming-recording, becoming-world premiere is used in the sound track, becoming-film as the camera is high above the prairie shaking on the autumn winds that cut across the land.

Aerial cinematography as deterritorialization

I had never shot digital cinema from a plane before. A pilot friend asked if I would like to go flying with him. Of course I took him up on the offer and took my camera. I had originally planned to use the footage for the opening of a short film that would open with this footage and then have the main character looking up at a plane flying overhead. To move perspective from the sky to the earth. But when I began to edit *Living Flame of Love*, I realized that this footage, filmed some six months earlier would be an excellent place to begin.

Living Flame of Love opens with harp and accordion, and a prairie landscape. We have yet to see Toni's face, heard only his voice, and just as Togni reterritorialized the four notes so do does the film reterritorialize Togni's voice and music as material. The spirituality that becomes central to the film is a particular kind of prayer, one that is contemplative but will not, as Togni says, 'lull you to sleep'. To prepare viewers for Togni's contemplative mood, the opening of the film was designed to take its time, to produce an event that would work on the kind of contemplation that Togni had described to me, and that I had experienced with him on a few occasions. I had aerial footage as material, how might I compose with this for affect. Werner Herzog's aerial footage is often used to produce just this kind of dreamlike contemplation. Using the music as a guide, I edited the footage to correspond with shifts in the compositional structure. Each new assemblage of voices was edited with a new durational shots of flying towards, and then over, Edmonton's city centre. The tremor of the little place, the coming-ness of night, the new glow of city lights, and eventually the long slow contemplative shot of the orange-red glow of sunset that connects to the opening abstract orange glow, to produce a refrain.

The assertion of spirituality mixes with the aerial contemplation of the landscape and the opening of *Living Flame of Love*. Togni's voice and music are deterritorialized and reterritorialized on the transforming landscape around Edmonton. This is a practice of landscapity (Deleuze and Guattari 1987: 172–3). A territoriality of spirituality in the meditation on duration and change of the landscape-face-music assemblage. The deterritorialized block of sound territorialized by the deterritorialized visual block of aerial photography territorializes spiritual reflection to offer a viewer an invitation to experience an affective stirring, affects of spiritual reflection and a line of flight that moves beyond the cinema. This is the transversality of art practice and ethnography.

Refrain, temporalization and micropolitics

To characterize the durational aerial photography as a landscape shot, however, misses the point. The shots are not static, are not stabilized by a tripod nor by any form of digital stabilization in postproduction. Instead, the landscape shivers and bounces carrying the energy of the autumn winds that buffeted the small plane on this October day on the western prairie. In the last chapter, we spent some time reflecting on the refrain as the rhythmics of the body and the rhythmics of the city and the usefulness of the biogram as a non-textual strategy for bodying. In this scene, the landscape-face-music assemblage produces a refrain that carries with it a tempo, duration and movement that does not move in the body's normal time. It also does not move in contemporary cinema's normal perceptual time. There are no fast cuts, no action to speak of. Duration becomes the subject of the shot, duration becoming visible. Durations visibility is not the goal of the shot, the artistic goal is not to say 'Look see, time is passing,' the time-image shot opens onto other horizons, makes other connections. These connections are not semiotic; however, this shot does not demand that the viewer makes this or that connection, the 'direct time-image is the phantom which has always haunted the cinema' (Deleuze 1989: 41). It is not about 'meaning', so to speak, but instead opens a space for an alter-temporalization.

The duration of the landscape music assemblage territorializes a relationship between buffetted plane and ground in order to open up the potential for the viewer to no longer think about what is on the screen, but to allow this image to territorialize a refrain. The refrain deterritorialize the 'intimate temporality' (Guattari 2011: 109) of the viewer, to confront the media-produced capitalist temporalities that occur at high speeds and characterized by a liquidation of the possibility of escaping the screen. Fast cuts require high degrees of concentration that keep the viewer 'engaged', or perhaps controlled. Slow cuts and long durations that characterize the time-image encourage the viewer to escape on their own lines of flight: 'this [time] image is virtual, in opposition to the actuality of the movement-image. But, if virtual is opposed to actual, it is not opposed to real, far from it' (Deleuze 1989: 41). Temporalization is not apolitical, but micropolitical: 'both capitalist refrains and faciality traits must be classified among the collective micropolitical infrastructure responsible for arranging our most intimate temporalization and modeling our relationship to landscape and the living world' (Guattari 2011: 109). Opening *Living Flame of Love* with this scene is a micropolitical act that seeks to deterritorialize the viewers' capitalist refrain, and reterritorialize viewers in their own contemplative, or what Peter Togni will characterize as a, spiritual refrain.

After the cinematic pass over the city reaches a crescendo and its most complex rhythms a downward, dark tremulous glissando on the harp brings the first section to stillness. The choir meditates on the words 'Oh Living Fame of Love', that grow in mood and colour as the camera focuses on a smooth aerial view of the orange glow of the setting sun. The orange glow, setting sun and, in the conclusion, the single candle refrain the alter-temporalization of spirituality that is the diagrammatic assemblage of *Living Flame of Love*. Such a great leap from four notes in an old movie score to the contemplation of spirituality, a conversation with the almighty through the production of a refrain that is capable of reterritorializing intimate temporalities. But what is the process of getting from the four notes to the concert assemblage?

White wall and black hole at the piano: The music icons painted in audio-vision

When finally Peter Togni is seen, he is seated at a grand piano in an old Halifax, Nova Scotia church, playing through sections of the score that was just heard in its full choral and instrumental realization. We are placed back at the beginning somehow moving backwards in time from the previous scene. Togni's face is partly lit, its environment shows part of his face and we lose part of his face and body to the darkness of the shadows. This is the contrast cinema shares with faciality: 'In film, the close-up of the face can be said to have two poles: make the face reflect light or, on the contrary emphasize its shadows to the point of engulfing it "in pitiless darkness"' (Deleuze and Guattari 1987: 168). The white screen of the face reflects light and is open for viewing and signification. It is a screen upon which the viewer projects as much as the light of a film projector reflects off of a screen, or a digital screen lights up the faces of viewers. Peter Tongi is not only given but becomes open, perhaps more mysterious in his particularity. But perhaps it could be said another way. The face emerges from the blackhole that was abstraction before it was landscapity, before it was sunset and spirituality: 'the face, at least the concrete face, vaguely begins to take shape on the white wall. It vaguely begins to appear in the black hole' (Deleuze and Guattari 1987: 168). Togni's face, however, does not bring the mystery to a conclusion. His face just proposes new questions. His face dispels only partially the abstract faciality of a composer replacing it with a face that is this composer, a composer in particular, a composer composed by significance and subjectivity: 'Significance is never without a white wall upon which it inscribes its signs and redundancies. Subjectification is never without a black hole in which it lodges its consciousness, passion, and redundancies' (Deleuze and Guattari 1987: 167). The close-up, its faciality, opens the filmic exploration into Peter Togni's subjectivation, the productive engagement with mystery that is Togni's becoming. It is in his eyes, in the quiet rumble of his talking voice. The comfortable proximity to the screen (to the lens and filmmaker it implies) and his near-whispering ruminations on music, painting and beauty that he shares almost secretly with the viewer.

Beauty affect vectoring

Beauty, Togni says, is 'influenced by order, and boundaries. But the most beautiful thing about beauty to me is freedom. And freedom to make choices. And finding something within yourself that you didn't know. Or it might resonate with something in yourself that you might feel are really dark . . . but you need them in order to journey'. For Tongi, beauty is not about tranquillity and peace, it enlivens and energizes, and 'doesn't put you to sleep'. Sleep here is both literal and figurative. He is interested in a compositional machine that mobilizes an affect that is beautiful, but also at times that is complex and difficult. The refrain for Togni, its four notes, are used to produce choral figures which for the composer are musical icons that keep appearing. They are musical audio-vision: 'musical painting in my mind' that are 'romantic and beautiful and then splinter off to become a little bit ambiguous'. The score is a diagram of sound paintings, audio-vision already and a machine for becoming-spiritual. The score deterritorializes icons, religious paintings of beauty meant for contemplation. He works to reterritorialize them as sound icons. Using choral and instrumental compositional techniques, Togni reterritorializes the affects of contemplation and beauty. Doesn't this suggest that Togni thinks about beauty as an affective assemblage that moves by vectoring, that uses consciousness, painting, poetry, composition, score, instruments, audiences as its medium?

> In a Deleuzian ontology one must emphasize that the regularities displayed by the different possible trajectories are a consequence of the singularities that shape the vector field . . . each possible sequence of states, each possible history, is generated by following at each point of the trajectory the directions specified by the vector field, and any regularities of propensities exhibited by the trajectories should indeed be ascribed to the topological accidents or singularity of the field of directions . . . singularities preside over the genesis of the trajectories. (DeLanda 2002: 27)

Scoring is diagrammatic, the emergence of an abstract machinic that will allow the conductor, instrumentalists, choristers and audience to engage in reterritorialization in a variety of ways. The score is a node, the territorialization of a Peter Togni diagram. Thinking in vectors allows us to look at these nodes that are both singularities and continuities. Vectors plot a course through which sound is machined as percept and affect, the score is not what holds beauty; it is instead a reterritorializing of deterritorialized aesthetic affects. To approach beauty as affect-vector allows us to tracks its affects by plotting points in a temporal grid. It's taking fleeting form in its in-folding along duration. But it also requires that we do not shut down analysis at any one point and claim that point as determinate. The beauty affect-vector continues moving through spacetime and is perhaps never determinate or even singular – which may frustrate Kantians. Beauty affect vectors does not require an event (Deleuze 1993: 86–93), they create events that are its in-folding, stimulates a receptivity for its prehension (Deleuze 1993: 88), its self-enjoyment (Deleuze 1993: 89) and individuality. All aspects of the pathway – here I am thinking of the conductor and choristers – may or may not open to the spiritual register that motivates Togni. But does that matter? If a chorister is not moved by the beauty affects does it limit its continued vectoring? The machinic assemblage of enunciation with the proper name *Living Flame of Love* does not determine how it is received, but perhaps the beauty affects can pass through bodies that still carry the affects that Togni is also an in-folding conduit for. It is important to see Togni not as the creator of the affects, he is himself a pathway, an in-folding machine that deterritorializes the beauty affect and reterritorializes in the diagrammatic assemblage of the scoring. Togni is a point in the vector field not its origin. Significance and subjectification, the white wall and black hole, do not determine the future, are not inscribed with unitary meaning, but like all machinic processes open onto an indeterminate futurity.

Section two

Pro Coro sound machines

The diagram moves in four directions from Togni to Michael Zaugg, artistic director and conductor for Pro Coro Canada, to Joseph Petric, accordionist and the artist who commissioned the piece, to harpist Nora Bumanis and to myself as filmmaker. The two instrumentalists will later meet with Togni and Zaugg to work over the score. As the instrumentalist do their preliminary work, Zaugg works on the score in private. He begins at the piano working on the diagram. There is a great deal of virtuality that occurs in this preliminary phase, that is another diagram, no longer that of the composer diagram, rich with the virtuality of sound icons, but now a diagram rich with the virtuality of Pro Coro Canada's voices.

Zaugg's diagram operates like an hourglass, wide at both ends and narrow in the middle. Width is equated with generality and narrowness with particularity. The bottom of the hourglass begins with the contextualization of the score. It includes study into the text, a poem composed by St John of the Cross, an important sixteenth-century Spanish Catholic priest and writer. For Zaugg, it is not only a matter of reading the poem but of trying to understand the aesthetic sensibility of the text, its cultural environment, the architecture of sixteenth-century Spain, the painters, the cultural and ecological environment. Zaugg seeks out the virtualities entangled with the poetry, to come in contact with what it carries. Doesn't this sound, once again, as if the musicians believe that art carries an aesthetic load, the poem is a carrier of affects that can be infectious if the receiving sensibility can be tuned to the proper temporal frequency. Perhaps it is necessary to think of the refrain not only through territoriality but the process of territorialization as infection. Zaugg works to become infected with the signifiance and subjectivity of the St John of the Cross' refrain.

First sound machine

This suggests that Michael Zaugg's first task is to transform his aesthetic subjectivity, to make it pliable so as to be connectable to St John of the Cross' aesthetic sensibility, his particular temporal vibrations. Zaugg engages in quiet study to do this, producing a virtual sixteenth-century Spain and allowing this to guide his reading of the poetic text. Once this process has begun, he then works to tune into Peter Togni's temporal aesthetic vibrations. This requires becoming familiar with Togni's earlier works, their progressions, their character, so that he might find the resonance between the sixteenth-century catholic mystical poet and the twenty-first-century Canadian choral composer. This is not the work, as Kant would have it, of disinterested reflection, but instead, working with a malleable aesthetic sensibility, modulating one's aesthetic sensibility looking for the moments of resonance where the poetic texts and musical texts make the notes vibrate with sense. Why, for instance, are there four poetic stanzas yet five musical movements; how do the four stanzas translate? Then each movement, each line, each melody, each sound, each word. Zaugg moves closer to the centre of the hourglass and in the process brings in the virtuality of Pro Coro's sound.

Second sound machine

For Zaugg, Pro Coro exists as a virtuality, a 'sound chip' that has each voice in the ensemble. While he reads the score, a virtual 'image of sound' is produced in his musical imagination. The notes of the score are deterritorialized and reterritorialized through a matrix of the virtual choiristers and the affective assemblage of his research. The sonorous faciality-landscapity of St John of the Cross in sixteenth-century Spain, the sonorous faciality of Peter Togni, and each of the sonorous facialities of the Pro Coro assemblage. Rich in virtuality, Zaugg begins to work through each note and phrase, playing with, as he describes, faders assigned to each voice, as if, as a choral director his job is to process the sound potentialities of each choir member to realize the virtuality of the choral score. As he works through each sound-word, he completes a circuit back to his body, the conductor's body. His body becomes a machine that will hook up to the diagram of the score and the bodies that make up Pro Coro. When it is time for rehearsal, Zaugg's job is to communicate the virtualities he has experienced and to be open to the actuality of the singers on that day and the environment they are singing in. The score-choir-conductor-venue assemblage is a machinic apparatus that will bring a dense cloud of sonorous virtuality into actuality, moving the beauty vector through their assemblage into the collective assemblage of the audience.

Third sound machine

The potentialities of Togni and Zaugg's temporal aesthetic subjective modelling would be wasted if the audience was not equally prepared. The audience arrives fresh from their own lifeworlds complete with all of the thoughts and stresses of their own lives. The concert hall, in this case a church venue, will do some of the work to prepare their bodies for the experience of spiritual beauty, but not all of it. Not only does Zaugg prepare the choir for the score but he also spends time thinking about the audience. Zaugg knows the audiences for Pro Coro, he carries a virtuality of them just as he carries a virtuality of the choir. He prepares notes for publication, questions for the composer, notes for introduction. The collective subjectivity of the audience must be modulated as well. The conductor's job is to work with the temporal rhythms of the venue in ways that will prepare the rhythms of the audience to be open to the virtualities of the performance. These affective events will only connect if the audience is attuned. Just as Zaugg prepared his own subjectivity to connect with the score, so too will he prepare the audience's subjectivities so that they can 'tune in' to the refrain, to be open to the events that are about to occur. Will they be moved, refrained?

Conclusion: Cineworlding as practical musicology

In the last chapter, a horizon for cineworlding was suggested, a working in the undercommons of the enlightenment, where cinema-thinking can contribute to knowing about the world. In this chapter, it is proposed that cineworlding *Living Flame of Love* expands the approach that Christopher Small took in musicking, to take machinic process seriously. Following the pathways of choral music lead us to have to consider territorialities, virtualities, actualities, subjectivities and aesthetic vectors. It is not simply a matter of sketching out a structure of a music event. The cinema camera brought faces, bodies, histories and events together that was sometimes art and sometimes ethnography. This study brings us outside or underneath official description of art music resonating with the love of artfulness as the way. It also proposes that we can do this by undertaking cineworlding that asks what a machinic assemblage can do.

Cineworlding the choral music assemblage allows us to see the work that happens along this path. It provides would-be composers and conductors a deeper understanding of the work that world-class professionals do behind the scenes. The film brings us closer to the concert process and the writing draws out even further what is hinted at but perhaps cannot be shown. This film can be a valuable learning tool for professional musicians and music students. Cineworlding is, therefore, a practical musicology.

The analysis stopped with the preparation of an audience. Does music continue to move as a vector through the audience and through the medium of cinema? This question will be examined in Chapter 7. This chapter expanded the cineworlding vocabulary to include a considerable use of the concept of subjectivity, but with little preparation for the reader. The next chapter will spend time discussing the virtual and actual in cineworlding before spending two chapters thinking about subjectivation of those in front of the camera, and in Chapters 9 and 10, subjectivation behind the camera. Across the chapter we moved from the concept of faciality-landscapity to the white wall and black hole, to subjectivity, temporal resonance and the refrain. We also began to see the ways that the conductor modulated their aesthetic sensibilities to resonate with the score, to become an operator of beauty. These concepts were used to explain the complex virtualities that composer and conductor utilize in their professional practice.

In the fourth and fifth chapters, we will ask questions about using the cinema camera to fall into the black hole of subjectivity. We will see that the black hole is not something that dissolves all information, but is more like a portal that opens up subjectivity that uses faciality as a white wall, a screen upon which subjectivities can proliferate. The white wall and back hole are shown to not be a binary but a fractal, where the black hole projects a version of itself on the white wall that always contains a black hole, that projects itself on the white wall that always contains a black hole. Cineworlding, bringing research-creation together by the vibrating enotikon, provides a space for art and ethnography to work transversally upon each other. This transdisciplinarity will provide a way to approach subjectivity study, to explore whether subjectivity is equitable with identity, as a unified object, or as a teaming multiplicity, a subjective assemblage.

4

Virtual and actual in posthumanography

What one should Learn from Artists. What means have we for making things beautiful, attractive, and desirable, when they are not so? And I suppose they are never so in themselves! We have here something to learn from physicians, when, for example, they dilute what is bitter, or put wine and sugar into their mixing bowl; but we have still more to learn from artists, who in fact, are continually concerned in devising such inventions and artifices. To withdraw from things until one no longer sees much of them, until one has even to see things into them, in order to see them at all or to view them from the side, and as in a frame or to place them so that they partly disguise themselves and only permit of perspective views or to look at them through coloured glasses, or in the light of the sunset or to furnish them with a surface or skin which is not fully transparent: we should learn all this from artists, and moreover be wiser than they. For this fine power of theirs usually ceases with them where art ceases and life begins; we, however, want to be the poets of our lives, and first of all in the smallest and most commonplace matters.
        Nietzsche, What one should learn from artists, 299, *The Gay Science*.

Cineworlding and posthumanography

Cineworlding grows from the middle. It is the middle of science, social science and art, the middle of seeker and sought, the middle of fact and fiction, the middle of vision and hearing, the middle of experiencing, recording, sharing. Posthumanography might be the most optimistic, beautiful and life-affirming of the social science methods. It is also the most demanding of everyone involved. It is an art of becoming, not a science of discovery, and its ethical challenges arises from its gravity, it permits no one a way out of a collective becoming. Its ethics are therefore about the future, a future built on knowing differently. It is an art-science of transpositions (Braidotti 2006) that I call cinema-thinking.

Just as description is central to written ethnography, cinema-thinking is central to audiovisual posthumanography. These two transpositions (ethnographic monograph and cineworlding) are 'two incomplete but at times complementary systems' (MacDougall 2006: 51). The value of an ethnography is conventionally determined by its ability to represent the culture of a people in a place. But is this interest in representation, this practice of documentation of musical acts, the only approach? And is recursive thinking about ethnography more than reflecting on the location of the ethnographer? I believe so. I am instead interested in forwarding a discussion of the machinic assemblage (Deleuze and Guattari 1983, 1987), the posthumanographer and the described world growing out from a location on the earth, reshaped (misshaped?), by its technologies, its techne (Foucault 1988: 24). If we want an ethnographic project to be more than the ordering of fixed images of the world, to be about exploring multiplicities, diverse ways of living collectively that lead to richer psychological, social, technological and environmentally connected lives, then we need to make this our explicit focus. And I believe this starts with an expansion of our theoretical frameworks.

Cineworlding should perhaps stand alongside Deleuze's movement-image and time-image as orientations to cinematic production. An analysis of the entire production process defines cineworlding, not just a relationship to the screen. The screen is re-articulated as a continuation of flows of sensation, flowing through the cinematic posthumanographer. This requires that we go beyond auteur theory, beyond screen studies, beyond screen production studies, and beyond current humanist ethnographic theory to develop posthumanographic methods that bring all of this theory and practice together in a transdisciplinary conversation.

Posthumanography recognizes that these parts of the process are already all together in becomings where 'every actual surrounds itself with a cloud of virtual images. The cloud is composed of a series of more or less extensive coexisting circuits, along which the virtual images are distributed, and around which they run' (Deleuze 2007: 148). Becoming, at any scale (body, person, family, community, society, technological system, environment) is comprised of relations of 'clouds' of virtual around a becoming actual, it is processes of actualization, and is therefore at the core of a posthumanographic project inquiring, in this case, after cineworlding music. Cineworlding music – a hypothesis that music is an emergent property; an expression of relations that are vectored through cinema – is based on a process ontology that explicitly requires the development of research methodologies to study relational processes. Posthumanography is a mapping of becoming-together and requires a radical shift in ontology and, therefore, research practice. Deleuze usefully proposes both a complex theory of just such a process ontology *and* perhaps, more importantly, for audiovisual ethnomusicology, a theory of cinema. As I will spell out in this chapter, Deleuze saw cinema as thinking, not a metaphor of thought, but thought itself.

A Deleuzian process ontology provides an original starting point for cineworlding, a new phase of ethnographic film, posthumanographic cinema made possible by the emergence of the digital cinema ecosystem. As such, we are free to re-evaluate audiovisual ethnography's founding orientations. We no longer need to frame ethnography within the anthropological project. What will we do with this freedom? I believe the first step is to re-evaluate what we think we know about cineworlding, so that we do not miss a moment of methodological openness to medianatures. It is time to be radical and to heed Deleuze's warning from Nietzsche that 'some values are born old and from the time of their birth exhibit their conformity, their conformism, their inability to upset any established order' (Deleuze 2001: 81). The emergence of anthropocene and capitalocene (Haraway 2016: 79–83) and its dominant cultural machine, what I have called elsewhere predatory anthropocene (MacDonald 2016a,b) suggests a requirement to re-evaluate the ethnographic project in the era of 'geo-hydro-solar-bio-techno-politics' (Protevi 2018: 175–8). To ask what is posthumanography with a digital cinema camera, or what is ethnography with a notepad, does not get us closer to what we need to understand or teach our students. What we need to know is what does it mean to think beyond the human in communion and on the earth that prepares the way to a more egalitarian futurity? What does it mean to think and report art-science, to think and report cineworlding? It is, I believe, to become, as Nietzsche suggested, the 'poets of our lives'.

We live in a society dominated by the screen, but how does the frame, shot and montage work in cineworlding? And since both anthropology and film studies have separated out the ethnographic, the visual and the audio into separate discussions where do we begin to bring these modalities together with posthumanism? Film studies has felt itself to be, perhaps, unqualified to deal with sound, while anthropological film has always oriented itself towards the ocular. Perhaps it is the historical and independent development of visual processes and sound processes, or the mechanical realities of the sound track being under the visual tracks. Or perhaps, the division of labour between directors of photography, cinematographers, sound recordists, composers and audio mixers. But there is no reason for us to accept any of these things, nor is it necessary for us to import this separation into our work. As good empiricists, we see-hear our frame, it is an audiovisual frame that is already a multiplicity, and needs to be understood in this way. The phenomenological experience of the see-hear frame that spills out over its edges is evident. It is not experience that is getting in our way, but an incorrect or outmoded epistemology.

Along the way it is necessary to reflect on some older notions that have remained alive in ethnographic film, like Karl Heider's suggestion of the 'distortions'(1976: 87) introduced into an ethnographic account by way of the production process. Though David MacDougall critiqued both Heider and Jay Ruby for their 'reverence for scientific method' (2006: 266), I do find some inspiration in Heider's observation that ethnographic filmmakers have particular 'methodological conventions for reaching the truth' (1976: 10). While I agree with MacDougall that their positivist assumptions about the truth are problematic, I am persuaded by their arguments that a discussion of method is important. I also wonder what is meant by science in this debate, surely it is not the twentieth-century science of complexity. Benjamin Harbert's 'American Music Documentary' (2018) pointed to this lack of convention in cine-ethnomusicology. Responding to this need requires an involved discussion on cineworlding techniques, and perhaps an opportunity to reflect more deeply on the development of these techniques in a systematic way that will make it easier for debate. This leaves us at the very beginning of a brand new practice with a mandate to bridge ethnographic cinema, music studies and sound studies together with posthumanism. My suggestion is to begin with a re-evaluation of the three founding parts of cinema: frame, shot, montage and to entangle these with flows of sound, and the human and nonhuman flows we encounter in our experience in the world. I propose an organizational model a triptych of three assemblages (territorial, production and screen). Doing this will draw out the multiplicities of virtual and actual within and beyond the frame, the emergence of space-time in the shot (*complex emergent temporalities* that I will deal with more deeply in my next book *Free Radicals*), and the emergence of indirect and direct images of time in montage. Taken together I propose to call this cineworlding.

Posthumanographer

I, like the world, am more full of virtual than of actual. I, because I am becoming all that I experience in the virtual and actual, am a subject of the cineworlding research. I am not a researcher all the time. I am filled with virtual filmmakers as well as virtual ethnographers. I have read them and watched them. As I theorize them, I am becoming them. There is a Feld, a Small, a Turino, a Baily, a Qureshi. There are also filmmakers; I have seen their frames, shots and montages. There is a Jean Rouch, an Agnes Varda, a Godard, a Michel Brault, a Werner Herzog. I feel them all sitting and waiting, sometimes patiently, sometimes not. Something happens, I have a sensation I do not quite understand. They begin to argue about how to proceed, what to say, what to shoot, how to frame. They look for traditional music, sometimes for wildness, some others look for reality, while others don't believe in such a thing as truth. An unknown is presented to me and I feel them emerging, they are each a way of thinking, and together we begin to think differently, look, listen and feel differently. The virtual and actual emerge together. We begin to chase after those feelings, the excitement and all of those virtualities emerge in complex constellations that I have difficulty untangling. We make decisions about a story, a microphone, we frame sound-images, we argue, we frame some more. We take shots, long shots, short shots. We begin to place shots next to each other. New ideas emerge in audiovisual intensities. We begin to colour our shots and try to re-feel that energy. What is that colour I am feeling in that sound-image, what is its intensity? It is almost that, but not quite. Yes, that's it. That was the colour I was feeling at that moment, that is the colour of that feeling I am feeling now. That is the colour I want the audience to feel, that audience that sits patiently in my mind cinema, those who always first see my films. Three moments of time at the same time, actualities, virtualities all connected to each other.

When I began using a digital camera to think ethnographically, my thoughts began to change, my way of looking transformed, my way of listening changed, my relationship to what I saw was no longer for ethnographic description, but was cineworlding. Cineworlding is a cinematic flux-image, a multiplicity, what Deleuze called a crystal image, the in-itself of the sensation, connected to the memory of the immediate past, and the becoming of the future. The crystal image 'concerns the temporal dimensions of the actual with its virtual' (Deamer 2016: 145–6). For Deleuze, the virtual are realms of potential that are not opposed to real, but opposed to actual. The virtual is real, but not actual. Cineworlding is real, and it is built up from a complex of virtual-actual relations. Cineworlding is a posthumanography of duration that allows new ways of thinking musicking. It is a posthumanography that allows us to pay attention to the affordances of audiovisual moving sound-images, what Deleuze calls movement-images, time-images, perception-image, action-image, affect-image. The camera is not just a technology to record, it is a new way of thinking posthumanographically that requires us to account for clouds of virtualities, thinking about the roles of time, space, duration, percept and affect in cineworlding. Deleuze argues powerfully that cinema is not an artificiality, it is a way of thinking. And he does not mean that as a metaphor, Deleuze means, as I will explore next, that cinema IS thinking.

Cineworlding 01: My body, sensations, our bodies in *Quartet 2* (2010)

I began to use a video camera in graduate school while studying with Federico Spinetti, a student of John Baily. Federico employed me as a research assistant which meant that I learned how to be his camera operator. I responded quickly to this new role enjoying learning how to work with new cameras and new editing technologies. I was soon making short experimental films on my own. I became particularly interested in the meeting place of ethnography and experimental film (Russell 1999) and the use of archival or found footage in ethnography, what Catherine Russell has recently called archiveology (2018).

Quartet 2 (2010) was made for a graduate student conference where I worked with a composition student, Dan Brophy, to visualize musical themes. Our approach required me to explore the Deleuzian and posthuman literature around affect and non-representational aesthetics. As we worked through the musical tensions, and I attempted to explain back to the composer my analysis of what I was hearing, something like a visual imagination that I had not yet explored awakened in me. While my body felt the music, I was struggling and 'stammering'. I wanted to share this experience with other people. But what is this experience of stammering? It is certainly a process of thinking the ellipse, of trying to understand, a reaching out for clarity. But it is not resolution. And what does it mean to think non-representational thinking-as-process, an experience that finds its force in duration not primarily signification.

Deleuze speaking about painting and sensation says that 'sensation is in the body, and not in the air. Sensation is what is painted. What is painted on the canvas is the body, not insofar as it is represented as an object, but insofar as it is experienced as sustaining this sensation' (Deleuze 2003: 32). I was interested in composing this sensation of 'stammering' in film. I was not interested in representing *Quartet 2*, I was producing a posthumanography of my listening. But I was not looking to represent posthumanography but instead to provide the viewer with an opportunity to live the sensations that occurred as part of thinking. And as we worked through what to call these sensations, we struggled with words for the thinking-feeling of an openness that struggles against closure, the feeling of the tug, the intensity of resistance against a black hole of cadential closure that calls us (as melody lines, as harmonies) to our end. What is the name for our desire to complete a phrase, complete a closure, to finish a scale? What does it mean to resolve, and why is it so important? Why are we so emotionally committed to the end?

I was having multiple competing experiences. I was both making deep musicological observations while at the same time exclaiming wild excited slogans: 'resolution is the end! It is death!', 'life is the tension between beginning and end!', and 'independence is resisting completion!'. But filming a bunch of slogans was not going to communicate my experience to anyone, no matter how affirmatively Nietzschean they were or presumed to be. I realized that fulfilling my project meant wandering into the middle of art-science, making a realization I would later read in Deleuze: 'There's no question of difficulty or understanding: concepts are exactly like sounds, colour or images, they are intensities which suit you or not, which are acceptable or aren't acceptable' (Deleuze and Parnet 2007: 4). I set about producing a list of intensities and began experimenting with how to produce them in film. The list was a process of time-stamping, so to speak, my bodily responses to Brophy's work. From this process, I began to identify my affective durations which would always complexify as I took notes, lines of flight emerging from flows, musical flows, visual flows, affective flows. Complex dreamlike images piled one-on-top of the other, space closed in, black closed in on white, white closed in on black, lines closed in on lines, thick textured lines of paint, and bodies, and shadows, and notes, and space. The result was a thirteen-minute experimental film that many viewers take as a music video for classical music. I find this association important and worth further exploration which I will undertake in a chapter on *Quartet 2* as refrain.

Where does this type of non-representation ethnography fit in our developing cine-ethnographic practice? I agree with David MacDougall when he says that if we were to re-invent visual anthropology, we would come up with a different set of questions than the history of written anthropology has put forward. We, those of us who are building cine-ethnomusicology, should take heed of these words and think deeply about the types of questions that we are forwarding and ask whether or not representational ethnographies are the best and only use of digital cinema. Posthumanography and cineworlding are my suggestions for where to locate music studies after feminist posthumanism and process philosophy.

To even begin speaking more about posing posthumanographic questions requires the development of a richer language that helps us overcome the binary of representational and non-representational ethnographies, to get in the middle place of art-science. We do have a good place to start as there has been some important introductory work on 'untangling' social science cinema from popular forms (Feld 1976), on the troubles of representation (Titon 1992), on the affordances of forms of media in ethnography (Baily 2009), approaches to camera movements in ethnography (Zemp 1988), or the still challenging postcolonial critique of ethnography (Rony 1996; MacDougall 1998; Grimshaw 2001). All of these approaches, however, treat the ethnographer, the field, the technology as distinct and untroubled units of analysis. I have already shown how an art-science approach to ethnography entangles the body of ethnographer and field, camera, editing suite, screen, and audience together in a series of chains of sensations, transpositions. At the screening of *Quartet 2*, I saw the bodies of fellow student respond in ways that resonated with my initial experiences and my editorial strategy, and this proved for me the posthuman case of the entanglement of body, subjectivities, technologies along complex vectors of sensations. The screen supported bodily sensations. Sensations are real. Sensations are actual. But not everything that happens on the screen is actual. In my next significant film, I wanted to investigate the complexity of virtual and actual.

Cineworlding 02: Frame and shot, virtual and actual in *Round Dance and Media* (2013)

Round Dance and Media began as a cinematic study of music in an emerging Indigenous political movement called Idle No More.[1] I blended approaches from music video aesthetics with experimental found footage films to produce a seven-minute film. While making the film I realized that my thinking about frame, shot and montage needed to be updated to include new technical process allowed by YouTube, digital video and digital video editing.

I was also challenged to think about the politics of representation in political movements and I wanted to include within the film the symbolic politics that are enacted in contemporary media. Media, perhaps especially so-called progressive media, present themselves as informed. But as the short film makes clear, the images that Idle No More protesters use and the images that new media used to describe these round dance events were often vastly different from the round dance that I attended and filmed. The music from the round dance organized at the University of Alberta on 13 January 2013 holds the entire film together in the way a music video does. I will use this film as an opportunity to unfold a theory of the cineworlding that starts with the sound frame.

Digital cinema works like film did before it, often at twenty-four frames per second. The frame is, therefore, carried over from film production as the starting point of cinematography. In digital recording, the frame also has an audio component. The frame is not the first digital image recorded on your machine; it is the relationship that you and the audiovisual camera have to the flow of experiences occurring around you, recognized on your skin, and in you. A frame is an actualization, it is also an abstraction, and a technological object. The frame is often conceptualized as a cutting, but I want to challenge this, and suggest that it is a joining (deterritorialization and territorialization), a multiplication of reality, the experience of the actual and the productions of the virtuals that mark the emergence of the posthumanographer.

Earlier, I recalled my entanglements with those who live in me, the names of ethnomusicologists and filmmakers whose ideas, images, habits of thinking have shaped and continue to shape my own. This was the beginning of the frame, a beginning that shapes my interests as a posthuman-musicologist and filmmaker surely as it shapes the finer details of where I position and point my camera. The camera is already a mode of thinking before it is pointed. The frame is already a multiplicity and worth a good deal of reflection. Deleuze writes that framing is 'the determination of a closed system, a relatively closed system which includes everything which is present in the image' (1986: 12, emphasis added). The frame, therefore, is comprised of subset and relations between objects, as well as the system that is built with the posthumanographer, and through the posthumanographer to other sets of relations. The frame of the cineworlding film, perhaps because of its hidden complexities, has left a great deal unexplored. Deleuze further suggests that the relations between objects in the frame are also related by way of depth of field, or their relation between objects in focus or out of focus. Light and shadow are also important elements of the frame. Objects in more light bring increased information to the viewer than objects in less light, but it also makes it more important, more mysterious. The angle at which the camera frames informs the relations between viewer and system creates another circuit. Is our perspective forced to look down on an object, or to look up at an object? Then there is, finally, the 'out-of-field' (Deleuze 1986: 15) which refers to that 'which is neither seen nor understood, but is nevertheless perfectly present' (Deleuze 1986: 16). Every frame has an out-of-field that is immediately present. And if it were reframed to include more, this new frame would also have an immediately present out-of-field that was related to the frame. These connections are part of the frame, and therefore the posthuman-musicologist is not only composing the frame but both the frame and the out-of-field.

Deleuze brings Bergson together with Peirce to illustrate why for him cinema is an 'image of thought'. Where Turino (2014) argued that Peircean thought might be a core theory for phenomenological ethnomusicology, I might expand on that and suggest that it is also a core theory for cineworlding. Taking Peirce's Firstness (affects), Secondness (percept) and Thirdness (concepts) to the frame – out-of-field relation provides a vehicle by which we can further multiply the system that is being produced by the layers so far unfolded (objects, relations, depth of field, light, angle, out-of-field). If we take the frame first, we can see that while Secondness relates to the images as presented, Thirdness opens out onto representations, and Firstness brings the viewer into direct, non-representational engagement with the frame. And this is a really important moment in cineworlding that is worth some reflection because it is a form of posthuman data which will be folded back into the film later in the process.

It is necessary to make a short digression to introduce Bergson into this conversation even before we get to the montage where Bergson's contribution becomes most obvious. Deleuze wrote his first major work on Bergson in 1966 and then expanded this close reading with the two cinema books. Deleuze returns to Bergson to work out the role of duration in reality. Bergson illustrates how difficult it is to think duration by illustrating how cinema is like thought itself. Deleuze picks up on this as the starting point of his cinema books. Both Bergson and Deleuze are concerned that Western thought is built on a belief in an incorrect way of seeing the world, as a world of discrete objects. Bergson argues that this way of seeing the world is a consequence of human thought as it developed since at least the Greeks. The film frame is a consequence of

Western thought, not just technology. This is a habit of thought that separates the world into objects. Bergson sees the film shot (a collection of frames) as the reinsertion of duration into thought, as if duration is a consequence. This illustrates the backward nature of Western thinking that duration is an addition, instead of the fundamental reality of the cosmos. It is as if 'cinema exposes, from the outside, so to speak, the most distinctive operation of human perception and intellect . . . of decomposing every single becoming into a series of stable elements that are like snapshots or immobile sections and then, after the fact, adding an abstract movement' (Marrati 2008: 9–10). Immersed in a universe of becoming, it is necessary for a living organism to separate out snapshots of reality, to separate out what is important for the organism in order to make life decisions: 'the habit of taking instantaneous and immobile snapshots of the becoming of reality, and of retaining only what interests us in them in order to act quickly slips towards a "natural metaphysics" lodged in language but also already lodged in the sense and the intellect' (Marrati 2008: 10). While these snap shots are how we think, the error occurs when we mistake our object orientation to the world as how the world works. The world is not composed of parts, these parts are a reduction that is required in order to think. The world is composed of becomings and it is our quest to get over incorrect abstractions that are a consequence, not of the world, but of our thinking. Reduction and representation is a useful map, but it has come to replace the territory, which is becoming. When stable images replace the instability of becoming, when the frame becomes the reality instead of a framing of a moment of becoming, when change becomes an abstraction instead of a fundamental component of becoming, our epistemology is backwards. We have separated ourselves from the earth with the making of our maps of the earth. For Bergson, the cinema is the mechanism of ordinary knowledge, a cinematographic mechanism of thought 'as though we had always made cinema without realizing it' (Marrati 2008: 11). This orientation may help us move past a discourse of cinema as an artificiality that introduces problems into ethnography. Instead, by following this process thesis, we may be able to see cinema as a modelling of thought, not as an artificiality that is introducing aberrations into thought. Cinema then becomes a meta-analysis of thought itself, and cineworlding, a technique of posthuman thinking. Through this we dissolve the episteme and techne division that separates pen and paper ethnography (episteme) from audiovisual ethnographic production (techne). We can instead see in both the blend of thinking and technology.

In Round Dance and Media (2013), I began to develop a montage technique to draw out semiotic entanglements in thinking representation. The environment is identified in the very first shot but without context. The first shot is a large open snowy path at the edge of what may be a field ringed with building and large trees. In the distance people walk past snow-topped outside tables, as rays of the sun peek into the top of the frame. It is a deterritorialized shot of a university campus. The mechanical sounds of a handheld microphone intrude on the shot introducing a space between what we see and action that is unfolding somewhere in the out-of-field. The second shot is a wide shot of a Nehiyaw elder standing on the steps of a university building holding a smoking container. The elder explains to the group gathered that he will ask 'for the spirits to join us', the sound of a squirrel chirping in the out-of-field draws his focus for a moment illustrating two kinds of out-of-field that are being drawn into the shot. The elder then explains the ritual that is about to happen in preparation for everyone present to join 'this great movement called Idle No More'. When the elder speaks these words they are echoed, but more loudly, by a news reporter introducing the montage technique that I utilize for the rest of the short film. The broadcaster[2] was framed by another video feed that shows other virtual Idle No More gatherings. The fourth shot is of the elder holding the smudge bowl as people cleanse themselves with the sacred smoke. A short montage follows this section where everyone who was gathered start to move somewhere in a procession, shot after shot the montage builds up an image of who is taking part, we see a group of people, of men and women, carrying hand drums, and one young man wearing a red shirt emblazoned in big white letters IDLE NO MORE. A single hand drum sounds from the out-of-field and soon other voices and drums join the pulse, cheers and whoops and the camera begins to move roughly, a single singer's voice heard thinly again from the out-of-field, and more singers join in. A short shot of a small group of drummers and singers framed by the shoulders of onlookers in the foreground and framed by a large number of people beginning to hold hands in the background. The developing of this shot is interrupted by more news footage, this time a news report that tracks the development of the movement across the country with interviews of the Idle No More founders and a discussion of the use of Twitter and independently made marketing content that is helping get the message not just across Canada but around the world. The rest of the short film develops the same way introducing different media outlets' coverage against the regular pulse of the Idle No More in the snowy field.

This short film helps to move our conversation from that of the frame to the shot and the montage. For Deleuze, the shot 'is movement considered from this dual point of view: the translation of the parts of a set which spread out in space, the change of a whole which is transformed in duration' (1986: 20). This change in space and duration has two faces: one pointing towards the frame and the other pointing towards the montage. This is another in between that on the one hand engages in the transformations of relations of objects in space and duration that became stopped as an image of thought in the frame. The relations inside and outside the frame, the closed system, start up (are joined) in the shot, and communicate their system relations through movement and duration. The shot is, therefore, not just more than the frame, it is different because of what emerges from the transformations of objects in space and its unfolding in duration. As Deleuze says of duration in Bergsonism:

> It is a case of a 'transition,' of a 'change,' a becoming, but it is a becoming that endures, a change that is substance itself. The reader will note that Bergson has no difficulty in reconciling the two fundamental characteristics of duration; continuity and heterogeneity. However, defined in this way, duration is not merely lived experience; it is also experience enlarged or even gone beyond; it is already a condition of experience. For experience always gives us a composite of space and duration. Pure duration offers us a succession that is purely internal, without exteriority; space, an exteriority without succession (in effect, this is the memory of the past; the recollection of what has happened in space would already imply a mind that endures). The two combine, and into this combination space introduces the forms of its extrinsic discontinuous 'sections,' while duration contributes an internal succession that is both heterogeneous and continuous. (Deleuze 1991: 37)

In the cinema books, Deleuze brings together Peircean semiotics, because of its forking out through Thirdness (representation) to both consciousness and society, and in Firstness (affect) and Secondness (percept) of living beings. Peirce provides a model of semiosis that contains a complex out-of-field that is pre-personal (affect), personal (experience) and post-personal (society) which Deleuze sees as a way of explaining complex folding and unfolding. And from Bergson he is able to give Peirce speed, to move semiosis, frame by frame, and to provide an empiricism of space and duration, that through cinema, sheds light on thinking-feeling. Once again, cinema is not an artificiality but is instead a laboratory for thinking about thinking. Cinema is thought, and through this analysis we can engage with the challenges of representation, of consciousness, of thinking about the contributions of changes in space and of duration, of space-time, of affect. Bergson argued:

> Consciousness is the body in duration. The body is in time: the body is not only in the spatial present of the now, but in the time of its past – all its past – oriented towards its future. Pure memory as a function of the brain is a spontaneous flow of energy which encounters the external world, the perception of which causes a break in that flow for the production of memory-images, affect and action in the now. (Deamer 2016: 11)

Deleuze builds this into a theory of the virtual that does not make a distinction between the actual as real and the virtual as fake, but instead of the actual and the virtual together 'entwined to the point where we can no longer tell which is which' (Rushton 2012: 89). In *Round Dance and Media*, the real of cineworlding (actual) is mixed with the virtual of the found footage, the real of the news broadcasts, and the virtual of its images, the real of its reporters experiences, and the virtual of their recordings as the film unfolds before the various intended subjects of the news on TV, news on YouTube, news inside my example.

Here we get to the core feature of Deleuzian film theory for cineworlding, Deleuze's complex theory of the virtual. This theory requires all of the previous discussion, the image of thought, the frame, the shot, time-space in order to make the following claim: the actual and the virtual is a collapsed binary that opens new approaches for cineworlding, and may lay the foundation for an original posthumanographic theory. The relationships between the virtual and the actual are a consequence of semiosis in space-time. Let us take the most basic (and perhaps abstract) example. The posthumanographer points their camera at a music performer. The posthumanographer is experiencing the present moment, this is the actual (a). This moment recedes into the past and becomes a memory, a retention of the sensations of the actual that are used to make sense of its musical unfolding, becoming a virtual (v). Because the present experience of sensation (a) and the immediate past sensations (v) are required to make 'sense' of this moment there is a necessary connection, an experience of space-time, experienced as a connection between the actual of the immediate experience over a lived duration, experienced as the distance between memory and the sensations of immediate experience (a-v) (sic. the vibrating enotikon). As Redner explains, 'sensation is fundamentally a conservation or retention of vibrations, a contraction of vibrations that takes place in a contemplative soul, not through action, but a pure passion, a contemplation that conserves the preceding in the following' (2011: 38). We might then recognize this as a becoming of audiovisualization, an audiovisual pathic thinking-feeling of music culture.

Now, with this observation in place, a posthumanographer's experience of the immediate present (a) is already entwined with the soon-to-be immediate past (v), and the framing for the shot (v1), and the potential montage (v2), which will be experienced by a virtual audience (v3). Four images, at least, are possible in any cineworlding shot (frame). But before we can do this, we should consider the role of montage and the unfolding of what I propose to call the cineworlding triptych.

Cineworlding 03: The territorial assemblage in *Megamorphosis* (2016)

As a posthumanographer, I am interested in theorizing what I am doing, not only with a camera – as if the technical operations are alone enough – but to state it from a posthuman perspective, what happens in the territorial flux (what used to be called the ethnographic field). An ethnographer does not simply enter into a field with a camera, instead there is an emergence of posthuman subjectivities emerging from the middle, from the flows. I believe it is the recording and sharing – becoming a node in a vector field – music's territorializing of complex flows that we are after in cineworlding. This suggests, as Heraclitus long ago recognizes, that life/reality is a process, in flux, constantly changing, moves us from an ethnographic field[3] with its suggestion of an unchanging nature into a territorial flux, territorializing.

Territorializing is a flux, a process ontology. I propose that we view this (first-order) process of the cineworlding as a folding of three posthuman assemblages: (a) the human-more-than human assemblage, territorializing flux that has traditionally been called the field [territorial assemblage], (b) the camera-ethnographer-editor assemblage [production assemblage] that has mostly escaped analysis with only a few important exceptions (Zemp 1988; Titon 1992; Baily 2009), and the (c) screen-viewer assemblage [screen assemblage], which dominates film studies and is benefitting from sound studies (Chion 2019). This first-order series allows us to analyse the heterogeneous elements that compose each assemblage. A benefit of this assemblage approach is that it invites a second-order analysis of relationships, or transpositions (Braidotti), between each of the three assemblages that compose the chain. So that we can both reflect on the steps of the process, but also study the relationships of flows into the cineworlding machine (three assemblages), and out of it (the film's vectoring mapped across nodes of further territorializing fluxes). It seems to me that first-order and second-order operation and analysis is what makes the difference between cineworlding and related disciplines like screen production (documentary and narrative) and film studies.

The cineworlding assemblage is composed of a heterogenous flux. Once duration is added to this process, we can begin to theorize the processes of an experienced posthumanographer aware of what is to come with these three assemblages, and to see this is as a technologically extensive consciousness entangling or submerging into flows. There is little written about this experience but it has been hinted at by Dzigo Vertov's kino-eye and kino-ear (camera-eye, camera-ear), Jean Rouch's cinetrance (Bogue 2003: 154; Rouch 2003: 93–4) and Werner Herzog's ecstatic truth (Ames 2012; Prager 2007). These different filmmakers suggest a similar thing, that there is something that emerges from the process of disturbance, the act of bringing a camera into a territorial flux. I thought for a long time that the disturbance is something artificial, like an interview subject getting too dressed up (more on this in Chapter 8), but it is a disturbance of thought, a sympoiesis, a cybernetic folding, an ouroboros. It is the emergence of awareness of the virtualities implicit in thought.

Megamorphosis (2016) is the first instance of my burgeoning posthuman awareness of the film as an image of thought in musicking. The film opens with a recording of a song that is going to be produced during the filming process. But not only that, the film follows the release of my book *Remix and Lifehack in Hiphop* (2016), which was a five-year ethnographic study with members of the Edmonton hip-hop community about the process of informal learning in popular music. Building on the approach to montage that I develop in Round Dance and Media, the film unfolds in three parts. The first part, filmed second, is the unfolding of a community drop-in cypher called Cypher5. It uses a two-camera setup, one camera shooting from a tripod outside the circle, and a handheld camera roughly navigating its way around the cipher. The second part, filmed first, is featured members of the cypher answering the question: 'Who is more powerful, your hip-hop self or your civilian self?' The question was posed by the circle facilitator Andre Hamilton, who is featured in the longest section of the documentary-style montage which provides the out-of-field of the urban circle some historic and locational substance.⁴

I have begun to build the territorial assemblage in the previous section and have suggested that it is made up of a territorial flux in time-space which then is broken up, or deterritorialized, so as to be conceptualized. This is the first phase of the process of thought. And as is well known by now, when these space-time flows are broken up, knowledge – the founding premise of the enlightenment project – slips into control and surveillance, the 'variety of visual metaphors (diagrams, grids, maps, etc.) serve to objectify knowledge. Both history and agency are denied to those now under the scrutiny of the ethnographer's eye' (Grimshaw 2001: 67). Powerful models of resistance have been developed by anthropological filmmakers like Jean Rouch and David and Judith MacDougall. David MacDougall has argued, building on a criticism forwarded by Steven Feld, that ethnographers should place greater attention 'to the interplay of tactile, sonic and visual senses' (MacDougall 2006: 60) and to get there requires filmmakers 'pay closer attention not only to the special properties of film but also to how films can better reflect their own experience of seeing' (MacDougall 2006: 60). The structure and flow of *Megamorphosis* was written collectively with the community of Hiphoppas. The opening montage follows the group gathering outside a community centre at night and making their way into the hall. The music that opens the film and accompanies this montage was written collectively by the group, and its recording is featured in the main body of the film and fades out into the sound of the group meeting, to return for the opening credits. The circle is interrupted by cutaways. The first one begins at six minutes, where facilitator Andre Hamilton (aka Dre Pharoh) discusses the unusual prevalence of pyramids in his part of Edmonton. After a quick tour of these icons, he brings us to the backyard of the community housing project where he grew up and showed us the back step that was his first stage. Before cutting back to the circle, we watch and listen to Pharoh reflect on the continuities between this space and the importance that it has played in his life, and in the circle that he is now facilitating many years later.

The territorial assemblage in *Megamorphosis* is multilayered. It includes the relationship between Pharoh and I, which has been discussed in great length elsewhere (MacDonald 2016a) as well as new material never discussed in the other works. We hear Pharoh's own words, hear him spit and have the experience of him giving directions, compliments, critiques and eventually watch him orchestrate the recording that opens and closes the short film. The relationship with the rest of the members of the circle had developed over the years of doing the first ethnographic work so that the film project was a fairly obvious development, but the first time that the circle really understood a part of what I was doing. The work of the territorial assemblage in this case is in line with the posthuman re-orientation away from traditional theories of collective action, that in music fall under the heading of genre, towards an ethnography of becoming, 'a micro-political register composed of heterogeneous collectivities in complex processes of composition and co-emergence' (Bignall and Braidotti 2019: 10). This micropolitical register can be found in youth studies and popular music studies. It is built up with territorial accounts of music making that is beyond that of the mainstream industry, but is none-the-less informed by it. It is also community music making but separate from that discussed in traditional music and classical music scholarship, though I think there is much more that can be learned from ignoring the genre specifications and taking a closer look at the processes of music production and the value becoming plays for the well-being and well-becoming of community. In this regard, I believe it is necessary to draw out the territorial assemblage for the content of the relationships and their relation to the out-of-field, without importing those virtualities generated by the codification of genre.

Posthumanography is an unquestionably important feature of the cineworlding and how the filming is undertaken is not at all straightforward. For instance, from the perspective of the drop-in circle, the editorial cutaways become a form of memory, a virtuality that is in relationship to the actuality of the circle. And each of these recording sessions has an actual-virtual relationship as described in the previous section. Each filming is both an actual-virtual with the future virtual for both the filmmaker and the Hiphoppa. Each Hiphoppa attempts to disentangle their virtualities in relation to the actuality that is being filmed, but the camera produces new kinds of becomings (something I will explore more directly in the chapter on Margø). And knowing that the cutaways were filmed a week before the circle adds another dimension. For each of the performers their reflections on their hip-hop name and the civilian name may or may not intersect with their cypher performance. But for the viewer, the reflection, because of editorial choices, entwine directly with their performance and shape the viewing of the cineworlding in a particular way. To help navigate these different relationships, I will explore the mobility of virtual-actual relationships through the production and screen assemblages to further illustrate the multiplicity of the cineworlding.

Cineworlding 04: The screen production assemblage in *Unspittable* (2019)

Unspittable marks the beginning of a different type of screen production that no longer draws from observational documentary and instead draws from fiction or at least neorealism/ethnofiction which will be the subject of my next book *Free Radicals*. After screening *Megamorphosis* to a variety of audiences, I began to realize that the documentary approach allows for a particular kind of knowing and sharing. Even my attempts to stretch the format resulted in a film that did not quite get into the experiences of Hiphoppas in the city. For *Unspittable*, I turned to the ethnographic fiction (ethnofiction) pioneered by Jean Rouch. As I will discuss next, I struggled to realize the film, and this struggle led me to thinking about the organization of film narrative, or lack of narrative. I was drawn to neorealism, new wave and nowave films and felt a deep connection with their approaches but perhaps not the content exactly. I could see a similarity between Rouch and the new wave but there were also significant differences. The distance in the literature certainly did not help, and this is something I hope to rectify in the future. There was something similar between Rouch's approach and Godard's, Varda's, and Wender's approaches, an open-endedness, a present-ness that drew memory, affect and modes of thought into the films. Deleuze's differentiation between movement-image films and time-image films helps me understand what I was experiencing. And the notion of the cineworlding emerged with my struggling over differences between Rouch, Godard and Varda. Before I get into *Unspittable*, a few words are needed to sketch out what a time-image film is all about.

Time-image films

Deleuze's cinema books are organized by two types of images: the movement-image and the time-image. His contribution is twofold; he provides a systemization of thinking about two different kinds of cinema that emerged from the beginning of cinema to the 1980s. Those that follow the now-standard situation-action-situation form (S-A-S) and the variant of this, the action-situation-action form (A-S-A). Deleuze calls these types of films movement-image films because they depend on, or create, a narrative arc that moves step-by-step towards resolution. Over the course of the development of the movement-image film, an indirect image of time emerges. Deleuze's preoccupation with time comes from his reading of Bergson, and in his cinema books he is interested to show how cinema produces images of thought. Deleuze claims that cinema realizes Bergson's writing about time in *Matter and Memory*. These books are not written just because Deleuze was a cinephile (though he clearly was); instead he is interested to show the ways thought occurs outside of the human mind. He is complexifying Bateson's cybernetic nesting of minds, and wants to show the ways cinema, what I will later call the screen assemblage, thinks. Time-image films are dependent on what Deleuze calls a direct image of time. The time-image film corresponds with neorealism, the new wave, new Hollywood and the new German cinema. These films do not move towards conclusion; in fact they make thought about duration, which is fundamentally open-ended. Deleuze remarks that the time-image liberates thought from the mechanization of the movement-image films (from the necessities of linearity and resolution). It would have been interesting for Deleuze to grapple with the music video, but this is something that we are required to do. Memory is an important aspect of time-image films, what Bergson called pure sensation. Time-image films 'chart the various journeys of their characters in terms of their insertions into sheets of past, their attempts to plunge into and relive the past' (Rushton 2012: 146). The time-image film allowed me to explore the consequences of live performance in hip-hop, getting beyond superficial ideas of the genre that allowed me to do cineworlding, not about hip-hop, but about the young people who are making it, and the families, communities, and environments that are becoming. The film moved beyond ethnography into cineworlding, an existential dramaturgy about music making in urban life.

Unspittable as cineworlding

I have known Amplify (Andrew Cardinal), the leader of Unspittable, since he was thirteen years old. He was the most junior member of an Indigenous hip-hop collective called RAW Nation with whom I first began the cineworlding project. Because I had already conducted many years of research with the Edmonton hip-hop community, published a book, and had made two films (*Megamorphosis* 2016; *Letters to Attawapiskat* 2016), I was well known inside part of the community. This notoriety provided me the necessary trust with members of the community. Unfortunately, my work with RAW Nation would not develop into anything because of the challenges the collective had staying together. Amplify, however, was one member of the collective who was working very hard to be recognized as an independent artist. I connected with him and he informed me that he had just put together a new group, Unspittable. I asked him about making a film with the group and he agreed to give it a shot.

We met for coffee with the three members and I explained the premise of ethnographic fiction, Jean Rouch, his work with students to make La Pyramide Humaine (1961) and that I wanted to make a film like this about making hip-hop in Edmonton. All of the members of the group were amused with the idea generally, and specifically about being in a film. They agreed to do it while also admitting that they still had little idea what the film would look like. I asked that they go home and write their individual stories and how they ended up connecting as friends and artists. The idea was that at our next meeting we would begin to sort out the scenes that we would need.

At the next meeting they arrived with a flow chart that provided the group's general timeline, their connections, interconnections and connections to other groups around the city. They identified the day the three of them met, that Amplify and Repression (aka Charles Woodman) had met previously as members of local groups. Repression had met Niko Krev (Colton Krevenchuk) in the city and were spending time together and that Repression wanted to introduce the other two. They explained that after a short phone call one morning, Repression invited Amplify over to his house and that Amplify agreed because he was excited to share a new beat he had just finished producing.

We decided that this was a great place to start and so I recruited a member of Cypher5, David Chung, and taught him how to work as a sound recordist. The idea was that David, as a member of the community, would not upset the environment and would easily fit into the situation. Further, it was a great opportunity to provide free professional training to an engaged member of the community. This approach worked very well and the three of us (Amplify, David, and myself) met at Amplify's house to begin filming. The situation was very simple. Amplify wakes up in the late morning and calls Repression about the new track. He is invited over and meets Niko. Then the three of them spit to the new track that Amplify had just made. Voila, Unspittable is formed. We spent the day improvising the two scenes and I went home with a few of their recorded track and put together a long cut of a scene that was eventually included as a flashback in the final film.

Over the course of shooting Unspittable, which took approximately two and a half years, we followed this same approach. Discussing scenes that we wanted to include, locations we wanted to explore, musical performances that would be important. Over the course of the entire production process, we attempted to find a narrative that would hold the film together. But as the months and then years went by, it became increasingly difficult to build a narrative out of the situations. The ethnographic discussions slowly moved towards a different kind of discussion, one that was about the finished film, not just the content: What is it that holds these sections together and how can we communicate the passage of time that has occurred? These discussions allowed us to reflect on the ethnographic project as a collective event, and the film, a container that allows something of a totality to emerge from the experience. This is when I began to think about the production as an assemblage, and assemblage that I call the production assemblage.

The screen production process has been little discussed (see Baily 2009), and it seems to me that it is in this assemblage where some of our greatest research findings may emerge. One of the struggles of discussing the production assemblage has been the resistance to art production as a form of scholarship. The art-science that I am proposing was difficult to articulate even five years ago. But today there are two growing streams of support, research-creation in Canada and screen production research in Australia.

Sophie Stevance and Serge Lacasses define research-creation as a collaborative interdiscipline. They argue that research-creation gets over the 'ontological misunderstanding' (Stevance and Lacasse 2018: 5) of the separation of performance/art production from humanities, social science and science research methods. Though this separation is particularly 'heated' in music studies (performance from musicology) (Stevance and Lacasse 2018: 7), it is not unique to music, and is seen in further divisions between screen production and research, or at a higher level, what has been called the two-culture problem, the divide between science and social science methods, or even at a higher level again, between Western and Indigenous ways of knowing. Stevance's definition of research-creation requires creative works to utilize identifiable research methodology as process, like ethnography, for instance. Stevance and Lacasse see research-creation as the 'combination of any research methods and any creative process' (2018: 124) that leads to the creation of a project where 'research will lead to a creative output that could not have existed without the research' (125) and should lead to the production of 'both scholarly and creative outputs' (126). In my experience, however, research-creation is not as simple as bringing art methods and research methods together. As has become obvious by now, the vibrating enotikon has produced the need to create new art-research concepts cineworlding, territorial flux, posthumanography, four ecologies, three assemblages and so on. Locating cineworlding as research-creation helps overcome some of the long-standing confusion about film process, production and outcomes, that is the ethnographic research discussed separately, but in relation with, the filming, editing and screening of the film.

To further clarify the use value of cinema, in particular, as a research method is the emergent Australian model of screen production research (Batty and Kerrigan 2018) described by practitioners as a 'patchwork of methodological approaches' (25) organized around a principle of 'an interactive process of practice and reflection by a researcher who is also the screen practitioner, and a theoretical perspective that informs the overall research' (Kerrigan et al. 2015: 13). One of the major contributions of screen production research is the implicit recognition of the methodological relationship between filmmaking and screenwriting as research methods (Batty and Kerrigan 2018). These models provide some direction on how to approach the production assemblage, seeing it as both the technical processes of making a film married with a potential recognition that 'each era thinks itself by producing its particular image of thought' (Rodowick 1997: 7). Deleuze's cinema books as well as his work with Guattari point to the increasing impact that audiovisual culture is having on or collective image of thought. We are, everywhere, deeply engaged in an audiovisual culture, a culture of the screen and yet here we are in music studies only learning how to deal with this reality. If, as Deleuze says, that cinema shows an image of thought then attending to the techniques of the production assemblage allows us to draw out our more-than-human consciousness of musicking. Of course, I am writing from the perspective of posthumanographer who does everything themselves, engaged completely in every transposition, in every assemblage. The outcomes of analysis of the screen production assemblage require me to think about thinking. It is not a mechanical and technical process to turn shots into a film, it is a mode of thought. To explicate this, I will turn my attention to the making of *Unspittable* as a time-image film.

In the territorial assemblage I sketched out a particular relationship between actual and virtual that looked like this: v AV v v. The actual was the experience and there was the virtual of the immediate past, and the two future virtuals. Now that we are engaging with the screen production assemblage our actual was the first virtual, so now the chart looks like this: v v av v. The actual-virtual of every shot, the virtual that was the actual-virtual of the territorial flux along with the virtual of the immediate past which is now the second virtual past. There is now one future virtual and that is the direction that all of the work in the production assemblage is oriented towards (or vectoring), it is the realization of the screen assemblage that occurs when future audiences become entangled with the film (a further node for the vectoring of concepts, percepts and affects). Perhaps it seems evident that from the perspective of the finished film the actual-virtual relationships of the screen assemblage would be: v v v av. And while this seems to be fairly logical as a chart, the reality is different. When you watch *Unspittable*, the actual-virtual relations within the film are generated by the montage, so that memory emerges from the editing of the film illustrating that 'memory is never finished with, it keeps reappearing, it keeps coming back, it keeps reinventing itself' (Rushton 2012: 146). The live performance section provides the actual and each montage emerges as Amplify's memory. As Rushton has remarked summarizing Deleuze:

> in the time-image, there is no longer merely confusion between the real and the imaginary 'in someone's head'; instead, the indiscernibility between the real and the imaginary, the present and the past, the actual and the virtual, becomes an objective 'fact' . . . when this occurs, what was virtual now becomes actual while what was actual correlatively becomes virtual: the actual and virtual become entwined to the point where we can no longer tell which is which. (Rushton 2012: 89)

Conclusions: The screen assemblage and cineworlding

I began making ethnographic fiction films (ethnofiction) because of research findings. It took learning about Jean Rouch's ethnofiction projects before I began to feel marginally justified for making fiction. I have come to realize that my hesitations and self-censoring are obstacles to good research and in this chapter I wanted to begin to present a much-needed justification for other scholars who may find themselves in my position. This chapter will be expanded in an upcoming book *Free Radicals & Posthumanography's Poetics: Improvising, Anarchiving, and Minor Cinema*, which will focus on the blending of documentary and fiction filmmaking in cineworlding the opportunities of 'cinematic realism' for the study of emergent cultural temporalities. There seems to be a large divide between research film and narrative fiction, a divide that is more a sign of discourse than of methodological significance perhaps. There is also a very large literature in film studies that we can draw from to help us develop a better understanding of our approach to the screen assemblage. Fiction is believed by some to be the sure sign of entertainment films and not social science films. But is this distinction defensible? From Plato to Nietzsche, fiction has played an important role in communicating research findings. Recently, the anthropologist Michael Jackson has made complex arguments for the telling of stories as *Existential Anthropology*. And while I could rely on these arguments, I think I would miss the particularities of cinema, and the methodological rewards of a deep analysis of cinema. To be frank, it is difficult to 'disentangle' (Feld 1976: 293) the films of Jean Rouch (ethnography) and Agnes Varda (cinéma vérité). But if we are going to establish cineworlding as a practice of cinematic research-creation, this is something we need to grapple with, instead of simply ignoring the challenge. A useful starting point in this process is to sketch out the cineworlding process that includes where the territorial flux meets cinema production, and the role of screening, and to try to understand 'cinematic realism' as the poetry of philosophical lives. Cineworlding will surely have a relationship with the communities filmed. It would be interesting to follow these vectors, to understand the value of the film for the communities where the films were made and the ways these films enter other territorial fluxes. It seems to me that there is a potentially rich area of analysis in the connecting of neorealism and new wave film studies literature, anthropological film literature on Jean Rouch (ethnofiction), sound studies and film music studies. The screen assemblage will require all of this for a starting point, and will also require reception studies of cineworlding films made up of diverse audience. But this exploration will need to wait for *Free Radicals & Posthumanography's Poetics*. There is much more that needs to be said about the basics of cineworlding before moving beyond the three assemblages.

·

5

Diagrammatic posthumanography of Margø's *In Between*

Diagramming is the procedure of abstraction that is not concerned with reducing the world to an aggregate of objects but, quite the opposite, when it is attending to their genesis.

– Massumi 2011: 14–15

In the last chapters, I have made the argument for a need to decolonize the Human not through critique alone but in the creation of a posthuman image of thought. This posthuman image of thought proposes bodying as a diagram of thinking-feeling-becoming with the environment and technology. Cineworlding is a way of study oriented to embracing the posthuman that moves beyond humanism's *volition-intentionality-agency triad* (Manning 2016: 6). This triad is based on the belief that humanness is exclusively defined as a 'normal' universalized operation of a single rational Human (*read as* whiteness). In the process of creating the Human, a tremendous number of Others were produced. Racialized Others for certain, but also more-than-human, technological and environmental Others. Humanist economics, for instance, externalized nature. It does not count environmental impacts in its value system which has led, as is now clear, to massive ecological destruction on a global scale where economic expenditure for clean-up can be counted as a contribution to GDP. What is externalized by modernity/coloniality matters. Racism is the consequence of the externalization of non-white sociality, and white supremacy is the fight to maintain this externalization. Technology has also been externalized. The impacts of the externalization of technology are not yet clear though, as Bernard Stigler has warned in *The Age of Disruption: Technology and Madness in Computational Capitalism* (2019), there is emerging a 'short-circuiting of the whole process of adjustment between the technical system and the social system' (195). Humanism provides little room for difference. To critique the universal it needs to be said that cineworlding is not for everyone, I write for those who look through a viewfinder and see-hear-think-feel resonantly. It is a manner of being in the flux of worlding oriented by a practice of audiovisual study. I write for these posthumanographers for whom this vocabulary may help you begin to understand your entanglements. I also write to increase the value of these cinematic diagrams in order to expand what it means to think and produce knowledge. Diversifying the university, to become a multiversity, a polyversity, is a posthuman challenge.[1]

In the process of writing this book, I have become more and more aware of the lack of concepts available to discuss cinematic or multimodal 'literacy'. Literacy means the capability to read and write, but it also means to have generalized capacity. Is it possible to say technological literacy, or technoliteracy? In short yes. But the ideas of reading and writing technology imports ideas from humanist literacy into cinema-thinking. It must be recognized that literacy is a capacity built on the volition-intentionality-agency triad. The individual expression of literate agency. It is difficult to write together, to co-author, to multi-author. Audio-vision by comparison is a collective, community process. It is a different modality and we need concepts that recognize and value its uniqueness. We also need to confront literacy's colonial difference. Compare the different connotations of these two pairs of statements: I am technical, I am literate; I teach at technical school, I teach at university. The bias against technicity as unthinking or less than thinking is interwoven with humanism. It is the expression of the colonial difference as a consequence of the externalization of technics. As a consequence, students in the school where I teach regularly complain that my curriculum includes instruction in audio-vision. They ask, 'what does audio-visuality have to do with music studies?' as they peer over their laptop screens or phones, faces bathed in the flickering glow of audio-vision.

Episteme-techne

'Technicity' is capability with *techne*, the root word of technology and technique. In the humanities, it is kept distant from 'episteme', the root word of epistemology. Epistemology is philosophy and knowledge, technicity is the ability to work with tools and technology (technics). While technics IS knowledge, it is not given equivalent status with conceptual knowledge. I am proposing the cultivation of conceptual-technical knowledge in cinema production that emerges from posthuman ecologies of assemblages.[2] These assemblages of enunciation challenge the primacy of the volition-intentionality-agency triad. Assemblages, as has been explored in previous chapters, are emergent sympoietic multiplicities. The assemblage recognizes that as a starting point technics is not an artificial addition to the Human, but technics *is* human. More specifically posthuman, not as after the human, but that the human has always been an assemblage of technics. Posthuman is post-anthropocentrism.[3] From the role that the technics of fire and hunting played in the emergence of *Homo sapiens*, the recognition that the human is a diagram between animal bodies and natural environment, to the role technics plays in extending memory and communication in smartphones, the human has always been posthuman, always emerging from the ecotone of conceptual, social, technological, environmental ecologies.

Concepts and vocabulary for cinematic technicity and posthuman ecology are necessary. And so too is it necessary to recognize that this different kind of knowing, research-creation's nonphilosophy, has equal value. Not better or worse, just different. In this sense research-creation is not new, but corrective and *potentially* decolonial. Posthuman research-creation starts from the 'assumption that the cyborgs are the dominant social and cultural formation that are active throughout the social fabric, with many economic and political implications' and that 'technological mediation is central to a new vision of posthuman subjectivity and that it provides the grounding for new ethical claims' (Braidotti 2013: 90). As disability studies has noted, 'the "normal" body is itself the consequence of a set of discourses and has always been enmeshed with prosthetic technologies, institutions and networks . . . there is no "natural" body in this interpretation' (Nayar 2014: 106). A posthuman proposition for the twenty-first century recognizes that 'technological civilization has led to the emergence of an increasingly independent world of images which absorbs ever more attention and energy, and is governed increasingly by its own rules' (Böhme 2012: 123) leading to a 'technification of perception' (Böhme 2012: 125). Cineworlding embraces cinematic research-creation in order to contribute posthumanography. But posthuman and the Ethnos are in conflict. The Ethnos is already othered by the Dēmos, the often invisible and assumed colonial Human standard. If there ever was a Dēmos, it has collapsed. The Ethnos has been shown to be a product of the colonial difference. There needs to be a decolonial alternative for the humanist ethnographic author. So it seems to me counterproductive to sneak the Ethnos back in. To underline this shift in worldview, I will continue to use the term introduced in the last chapter, 'posthumanography'.[4] In the last two chapters, we began to see that this posthuman world view begins in a world of light, images, movement, duration, assemblages and technics. Cineworlding is not a world of fixed, independent, immutable, organic, authentic human subjects, but a flux of worlding.

Posthumanography of Margø's *In Between*

Cassidy Margolis called out of the blue. She learned about my music video work from a sound engineer at a local recording studio. I had been thinking about the role of music videos in music and sound studies for some time and was wondering specifically about how to deal with the thorny question of subjectivity and subjectivation. While music studies and cultural studies are really good at handling identity and culture, subjectivity is less often discussed. It seemed to me that music video production might indeed be a good cineworlding model for just this kind of work. This is what I was thinking when Cassidy called.

We decided to meet at a local bar where we were both comfortable. She had sent me her upcoming single *In Between* and we had talked on the phone about her artistic identity Margø. I had done the kind of homework that I always do in preparation for meeting an artist to discuss a music video concept. I had listened to her new track and made notes about what emerged *chromesthetically* as I listened. Chromesthesia is the recognition that musical sounds generate colours, textures, images and movements for the listener. It is a kind of synesthesia, a working cooperatively of the senses. When I listen to music, I respond chromesthetically. Perhaps this is why I gravitated to cinema? The track did not inspire me to individually author a collection of images, the musical track is a sound field that generated in me (vectored) chromesthetic perception. The concept of chromesthesia recognizes the emergence of an assemblage, the becoming-with the audio track and the in-folding of visual-images that will in time vector intensities through the in-folding of the music video. These images are not formed necessarily, nor are they necessarily recognizable images yet. I have always been suspicious of the idea of a free imagination because my creativity was always relational, diagrammatic. My creative practice was always in relation with something, whether it was a musical instrument, pencil, paint brush or camera. Chromesthesia orients us to this relationality, to the formation of the assemblage and the music video that sympoietically emerges. Sympoiesis is a collective creation, a becoming-with.

I looked-listened to Margø's online content and past tracks. I returned again the next day after re-reading my notes to see which ideas resonated and which continued to develop. These ideas are not so much concepts at this point but are moving images, colours, and textures. It is a chromesthetic form of thinking where sounds produce visualizations. The visualizations are not quite fully formed yet, they are more impressions operating in intensive space than extensive images, feelings-in-thought not yet concepts. But it is enough for me to start figuring out search words to begin to put together a collection of images to bring to the meeting.

In Between was suggestive. There was nothing about it that was unified, it felt as if multiple personalities were converging in the track. Cassidy had given no indication in our phone call about this kind of complexity. Perhaps I was projecting onto the track my desire to explore a variety of images. The more I listened to the track, the more the subjectivities multiplied and forced their way to the surface. Not only were they multiple, but they were also not harmonious. There was a dark conflict happening in the song both lyrically and texturally. Before the meeting I put together a collection of sketches and images for myself and then worked out from these how to organize a conceptual pitch. This is always the most nerve-wracking as it is quite exposing to come to a meeting with an artist with your interpretation of their work. But this is precisely what the music video director does. This is the work. As a posthumanographer, however, it is quite a different process. The ethnographer, especially in the observational documentary mode, sits back and blends in. There is no opportunity for that when pitching a music video concept. It is helpful to have a clear artistic statement when you arrive at the meeting. This concept revolved around four different faces: a demon, a jazz singer, a hooded figure and a narrator. Four different faces of the one artist Margø. It is not simply that Cassidy has taken on another name, but that this name is the proper name of an assemblage of faces. Not an individual, but a multiplicity. The cinema camera may help these faces come into the world.

Faciality in music videos

The body proliferates in critical literature. There are returns to the body, an emphasis on the body, the place of the body in scholarship. With all of the discussion of the body, however, there is far less discussion of faciality. Deleuze and Guattari write that 'signifiance is never without a white wall upon which it inscribes its signs and redundancies. Subjectification is never without a black hole in which it lodge its consciousness, passion, and redundancies' (1987: 167). The 'white wall/black hole system' is a face, but it is not a white face. The face is constituted by white light that is always in relation to the black hole of shadows. In cinema everything is in a relation between light and shadow. The face signifies and is read, it is a screen. It is a special type of screen that reflects light and its reflection plays a role in social coding. The eyes, however, operate in the other direction, they always move inward, drawing awareness to something behind the screen. It is remarkable that in the history of ethnographic film, there is no theory of faciality that I am aware of.[5] Couldn't it be said that faciality is the nexus, the crossing point, of individuality and culture? The constantly morphing biocultural screen that confirms, challenges or confuses that which is spoken. The affirmative statement spoken with defiant eyes, the kind invitation accompanied by a menacing deadness. Faciality is central to semiosis but so far it takes little pride of place in ethnographic scholarship. Faciality is connected to subjectivation, the game of signification played out by every social media user's thumbnail, so many Instagram photos, so many government identity cards. The face is treated culturally as some kind of proof of identity but the eyes are left out; they are left to be scanned by machines. Machines can read the retina like a thumbprint. The retina is an identity marker that can be trusted but the retina is already not the eye. The eye is the gateway to the soul, the proof of an intensive interiority.

Music videos show us that we are much more aware of the expansiveness and complexity of subjectivation than is evident in most cultural theory. A generally accepted pushback perhaps is that music videos are entertainments, cultural products and not theory? And while this is perhaps true, why should music videos not be a technological-assisted study of subjectivation? Do music videos need to be seen only as products of popular music? This was my initial question when I began to make music videos as an ethnomusicologist. In the beginning, I was hesitant to even consider my music videos to be anything more than experimental audiovisual art. Slowly, however, music videos began to suggest more and more. Cineworlding music videos add to the growing area of music video studies that sees in the music video much more than an audiovisual delivery system for popular music.[6] However, questions about the entanglements of music and music video production – what is the visual track doing – are often skirted by the more common cultural studies approach focused on cultural analysis that attends to its signifying as a cultural product. Cineworlding approaches music video as a diagram that in-folds audio recording, image recording technologies, theatre, poetry, painting, dance, photography, experimental films and why not posthumanography? The music video might be something that is neither music nor film itself, something that grooves as an assemblage of enunciation. Second, while psychoanalytic analysis of music videos has been successful, borrowed from film studies, does this not also suggest a technological or machinic unconscious (Guattari 2011) with the cross-fertilization of popular music studies, philosophy, psychology and ethnography? If the music video is a machine for audiovisualizing the unconscious, as psychoanalytic film theory would suggest, then it is also its production, a psycho-production. Attending to faciality in Margø's *In Between* opens up space for thinking about music video as a machine for extending subjectivity outside the human body, its move from intensive to extensive space, from desire to image, from complex intensities to compound identities, its bodying. The music video becomes a theatre for posthumanography.

Music video as schizoanalysis

It would be naïve to insist that music videos are not made for an audience. Of course they always have an audience in mind. But it is often ignored that the artist produces that audience, draws individuals into a collective becoming-with the creative work. The familiar critique goes that because the music video is made for an audience to advertise a song that it is not a work of art on its own, but a commercial enterprise. In my mind this argument is simply reductive and the worst kind of Marxist thinking that performs radical-ness when it is simply contrarian and anti-popular. It is the kind of argument that is persuasive until it is not, like Adorno's critique of jazz and Hollywood films, that in time shows itself to be conservative, technophobic and regressive. I did not learn about the great radical philosophical writers from a university classroom. I learned their names and their texts from a *Rage against the Machine* photo insert. I did not learn about my posthuman body in a classroom, but on a dance floor as deep electronic pulses produced a vibrating many-headed organism that psychologically and socially changed each of its molecular components (each of its bodies submerged into the collective bodying of electronic dance music). The audience is part of the assemblage: audiovisual production, a virtual ensemble, a people yet to come. It is not simply a matter of entertaining a group of people but instead it is assembling them, calling them into becoming, through their willing embrace of popular media. A much more complex dynamic that is too often simplified with visions of manipulative entertainers, or entertainment companies shelling out cheap thrills for suggestible audiences. Posthumanography seeks to understanding the enthusiastic world of the undercommons, the minor aesthetic movements that reach for nutrients through the dense cover of the global capitalist technosphere.

It seems that ethnographic film has been scared off by these critiques. Though the mission of ethnographic film is to document culture, it has so far reserved itself to observational documentary aesthetics and the documentation paradigm. This is fine of course but it must be said that this self-imposed prohibition against the full use of cinematic production techniques falls far short of dealing with culture as it is lived in late modernity. As Adam Curtis has shown in his *The Century the Self*, corporations have utilized psychoanalysis and then brain science to prepare consumers for capitalism. Consumers are not facts but biological productions, every brand produces a people yet to come. In this way, capitalism overcomes the social and cultural restraints that Freud theorized. Franco 'Bifo' Berardi in *The Third Unconscious* (2021) provides a cartography of three periods of the unconscious. Freud described a repressive unconscious, a disciplinarity that prepares for biopower (Foucault), and produces neurosis. Deleuze and Guattari characterized capitalism as a producer of delirium, of schizophrenic productivity, and the unconscious as a theatre constantly producing new works. Berardi concerns himself with what he characterizes as the third unconscious, what is emerging now in the context of ecological destruction, viral infection and economic collapse.

Schizoanalysis is a mode of analysis that seeks to understand what Felix Guattari calls *The Machinic Unconscious* (2011). It is not an unconscious populated by archetypes, myths and legends but one that is productive and machinic. The unconscious, for Deleuze and Guattari, is not unified; instead it is schizophrenic and constantly mutating. The mutations are the outputs of desiring machines. Machines, not in the technological sense, but in the machinic sense of something that operates on flows. The machinic is not a metaphor for Deleuze and Guattari, they theorize the body as a collection, an assemblage of machines. A body is not in this view a unified thing, but is instead a machinic assemblage that is becoming in the world: its becoming is an enunciation. So the body is a machinic assemblage of enunciation, and audiovisual faciality is a means by which bodying can multiply itself upon a screen.

Collective assemblages of enunciation, their capture or autonomy

The value of this view for music and sound studies is that it is possible then to think of machinic assemblages of enunciation at very different scales. The hierarchization of culture and subcultures (what is it a sub of, and are there sub, sub, sub cultures) is no longer a theoretical or methodological problem. Nor is ideology and mediation the only way to theorize culture production.[7] In fact, instead of trying to understand how ideology seeps into a citizen through processes of repression, we can follow another path, that is, how does desire (intensive space) get machined to produce collective assemblages of enunciation (extensive space), and then, how are these assemblages captured (capitalism) or defended by practices oriented to the creation and maintenance of autonomous zones (minor).

A further value of this approach is that it no longer presents a distinction between media, technology and bodies. A machinic collective assemblage of enunciation can easily accommodate the presence of old and new media machines quite easily, seeing humans, not as a special preserve but as an expanding machinic assemblage. Critical theory can move away from its patriarchal orientation to dispensing cultural truth and demystifying culture from the armchair and instead do cultural research from within the mess of machinic processes.

Finally, how does one do this? That perhaps is the most interesting question. Cineworlding is one possible technique for this posthumanographic practice, where the practice of making audiovisual media is the research space. Digital cinema production provides very interesting machinic processes where digital production of music videos constitutes a theatre-laboratory. This is why research-creation is so significant for cineworlding. It is not a matter of becoming an artist because art production is better than social science or humanities studies, but instead, it is about making art so as to better and more closely and carefully do cultural research from within the mess of the collective assemblage of enunciation, to participate in the process of the production of proper names of a particular culture or cultural group. To finally throw out the arm chair and join in.

Co-composition

I arrived at the bar a little early to settle my nerves. I had worked on my artistic statement, rolling around the ideas about subjectivation, of faciality, of the four subjects that I felt I could feel in *In Between*. Cassidy arrived and sat down. We spent a little time chatting about music, about the studio. We discussed her career and her successes with her singles and her excitement about this upcoming single. Then when we both relaxed a little bit, we transitioned to the music video. She sat expectantly and my nervousness returned. I took a breath and launched into the idea. I began by saying that I felt like there were multiple and conflicting people in the song. That one of them was a kind of demon that looked something like Die Antwoord's Yoladi from their *I Fink Ur Freeky* music video, a fantasy lounge singer that looks a little too much like a cross between a Disney automaton and a Stepford wife as lounge singer, and a hooded phantom that taunts a narrator. Inspired by Zizek's Lacanian reading of horror films, the demon lives in a basement. There were still some pieces that did not quite fit together but that I would like to figure it out together if this concept resonated with her.

Cassidy did not even take a breath before launching into the ways that this interpretation lines up with exactly what she had been thinking about the song. She discussed the recording process, the textures, the synth parts and her concept for Margø. The character of Margø was precisely conflicted or at least complex where there is often a dark synth character mixed with a lighter pop sensibility. The multiple personalities are indeed in conflict but finding space inside each other and sharing space. Over the course of the conversation we put the rest of the pieces together. The narrator and hooded figure chase each other ultimately ending up revealing that the hooded figure IS the narrator and the demon. We agreed to move ahead with the production and that we would work together on the video piece by piece. Margø was interested in seeing the visual-images that I had put together and I set out to find a location for the lounge singer and she found a make-up artist, alien contact lenses and a basement location. We were becoming a team and the video's concept and realization was a collective effort from beginning to end.

Intimacy

I have long been uncomfortable with these common ethnographic words: subject, informant, interlocutor, participant. The scientific language produces a distancing effect and hides the 'intimate entanglements' (Latimer and Gomez 2019) of the work. Margot Weiss suggests in *Intimate Encounters: Queer Entanglements in Ethnographic Fieldwork* that it is necessary to 'explore the intimacies of the fieldwork encounter' to attend to the 'queer entanglements, connections, and intimacies that exceed identitarian frames' (2020: 1356). *CineWorlding: Scenes in Cinematic Research-Creation* is a call to think-feel the intimate entanglements of perception with machinic-perception, the machinic-thinking of cinematic research-creation and its intimacies with the worldings to which we attend. The relationality that I am calling to attention is thick with possibilities and under-researched relations. We are used to thinking about the relationality between fieldworker and field, but much less so between human-becoming-fieldworker assemblage, fieldworker-camera assemblage, fieldworker-camera-field assemblage, fieldworker-camera-field-film assemblage and fieldworker-camera-field-film-audience assemblage. These assemblages contain a richness of intimacies but perhaps as Weiss has observed, intimacy has been reduced to possessive sexuality, preserved for the human and that in opening a view of intimacy beyond sex allows us to see the 'unexpected connections and a density of relationality: entanglements that are too often obscured by taken-for-granted ways of knowing and categorizing' (Weiss 2020: 1357). The multiple assemblages in cineworlding seem strange to write but only because they are so common, and so often unthought. It is not only possible to have intimacy with technology, but for that technology to encourage intimacy with the more-than-human world, and perhaps by way of intimacy to care. Care for the way technology is utilized, care for the human and more-than-human relationalities that need to be cultivated in order to respond to colonization, white supremacy, mass extinction, ecological degradation, global warming, digital disruption and rapidly growing inequality. Intimacy is not a magic cure, but a reorientation of the humanities from the goal of individual enlightenment to intimacy with the affective field of more-than-human relationality.

What interests me about cinematic research-creation is the processes of machinic-thinking that unfolds in the action of creating a film, and the thinking-feeling of coming-to-awareness of the environment of the action unfolding. The drama of cineworlding is attuned to what Erin Manning calls the minor gesture: 'the minor gesture often goes by unperceived, its improvisational threads of variability overlooked, despite their being in our midst. There is no question that the minor is precarious' (2016: 2). The drama of cineworlding, for me, is working with the precarity of intimacy, the worlding together of improvisational threads of living, and the intimacy of cineworlding, of attuning cinematic perception or audio-vision to the 'dance of attention' (Manning 2016: 193). The dance of attention for Manning is not human attention but 'field attention – the event's attention to its own development, its own concrescence' (2016: 193). Intimacy is event in its own right. The gravitational field of attraction, its warm affects of care, of valuing.

Technology is often considered to be distancing and dehumanizing. Heidegger was quick to point out the negative impacts of technological framing. This belief is so commonly shared that it has reached the point of common sense. But for a filmmaker, the viewfinder and headphones of the digital cinema camera do not push me out of the world but, on the contrary, it is technology that allows me to attend more closely to the affects of an event's becoming. To become, as I will discuss in the next chapter, more intimately aware of the intensive space operating within extensive space. It is not a conceptual attention alone, but more of a thinking-in-feeling or feeling-in-audio-vision that directs my attention this way or that way through a field. Taking intimacy as a concept means to highlight the feeling in thinking, our thinking-feeling. There is also a second activist reason to theorize intimacy in cineworlding, to orient research-creation, as Natalie Loveless has, towards a feminist, queer, critical race theory, decolonial care of human and more-than-human worldings.

Writing about this intimacy allows me to think conceptually through what I call below the Spinoza-Bergson-Vertov proposition. I am aware that it is a risky move to name a proposition after three white European men. But I think there is potential value in engaging with a branch of European philosophy that has been thinking against the volition-intentionality-agency triad. Especially because this proposition is not a platform for certainty. But instead works towards a dissolution of all that is taken for granted in Western thinking. This proposition proposes posthuman process with bodying, camera-ing, image-ing, worlding:

> What makes us so certain that thinking is not in-the-moving, or in-the-feeling; and what makes us so certain that we can define a body in time and space as a separate and individual entity? These are old Cartesian categories, the first putting thought in the mind, out of the body; the second placing the body outside of its relation the world. (Manning 2016: 189)

Cineworlding is not a methodology or method but a way of thinking-feeling the in-act of research-creation where art works on research and research works on art.

A preacceleration towards REC

Consider the event of hitting the rec. button on a camera. There is a building intensity that triggers the push of the button. Preacceleration is a way of naming this building intensity. The event is the push of the button. Before the button is pushed, there is a change in the worlding, a thickening of experience, an uncanny feeling of something happening. This experience of the intensive space between the preacceleration and the event is the minor gesture. There is an affective stirring that brings out the feeling of being on a precipice of something significant, something in-folding. This significance is a feeling, a stirring in your camera-microphone-body-social-environmental assemblage. This is the before of the shot. It is a very significant territory for any aspiring filmmaker. Perhaps the most significant technique for working in cinema is how to become aware of this potential moment's becoming (documentary) or how to create this moment (fiction/music video). When to hit record requires a development of your attention to the energy of in-folding, the becoming of an event. Attending to the feeling of the minor gesture is a way of paying attention to the moment *before* you *know* it is the moment to hit record. What is this pre-knowing? This is an obviously important moment. Without it there is no film. But there is very little theoretical attention to this moment. Most analysis of ethnographic film thinks about what happens after this moment. I recognize the feeling of preacceleration as intimacy. In the building of this cinematic intimacy, the contents of worldings are transformed from a plane of material to a plane of composition (Deleuze and Guattari 1994). The plane of material (what you are looking at and listening to through the camera) takes on a different potential, it is becoming filmic, it becomes the plane of composition. Between the plane of material and the plane of composition is a threshold, a gap, an interstice. It is this interstice where the dance of attention is a field effect of the worlding-cineworlding assemblage. When you hit record is not universal. It is a space of action that is stylistic. And because it is stylistic it is specific to one's body. This is the diagram. It is my particular, and your particular, style. Your *agencement*. It is a complex assemblage of equipment, bodies, concepts and feelings that take a particular signature form. Across all of my films you can see my agencement. No matter what the subject or location, my films have a look. I am becoming diagram. It is more than a point of view; it is a texture and character. This is my agencement, my diagram. So thinking about the diagram is a way of opening up a space for investigation into cinematic research-creation that is not auto-ethnographic, it is not about me, but about me becoming machinic. This requires posthumanography.

Margø's monstrous faciality

The video opens with a preacceleration. A series of shots that will show up later in the video, different faces of Margø. Each face is interrupted by a digital glitch. The glitch is a refrain in the video. It is not symbolic or metaphorical, it is a glitch. The glitch is an error. It is a kind of breakdown. But in this video the breakdown is its act of addition. Each face adds up to Margø. No one is dominant. The glitch is something that Cassidy absolutely required. I created the glitch layer by layer but it was Cassidy who gave it its shape. Together we created the glitch refrain.

This co-authorship continued and extended. While I provided Cassidy with sketches of the characters, it was her work with a make-up artist that realized the monster, the glamourous monstrous cabaret singer, the hooded figure and Cassidy. Each face is a facet of Margø. The video camera and editing assemblage combine to produce a Margø that cannot exist without the screen. The music video provides a machine to make live the intensive energies that were circulating in the song. In the same way that the recording studio provided a machine for the making sonic of the bodily intensities that would become 'In Between'. Each technological step make these intensive beings more solid and in doing so externalized a world.

Together with the make-up artist, Cassidy created the monster that haunts everything in the music video world. It has bug eyes, white skin, is both alien and familiar. Its dead eyes and screaming vocals embody the white screen-black hole paradigm. The white screen is an opportunity to project horror onto Margø's body and the black hole of the monstrous eyes swallows all of the white. These eyes are nothing but black holes and they draw irrepressibly towards monstrous darkness.

Spinoza-Bergson-Vertov proposition

To think bodies, movement, duration and technologies in the event, I propose a proposition of the Spinoza-Bergson-Vertov proposition. This provided for me an avenue for thinking about my cinematic research-creation practice. It helped me recognize that cinema has the capacity to ask questions about what bodies and image can do together. It also helped me to think about the intimacies within and between assemblages. This is a different starting point than ethnographic cinema in the sense that instead of looking for functions of culture, as a social scientist would, we are asking a properly posthuman questions: (a) about the potentialities of bodies and technobodies in movement before a film is made, (b) while a film is being made, (c) following the transformation of organic worldings into digital cineworlding, (d) and finally, the way worldings of pixels and digital audio affect organic acoustic worldings.

Cinematic-thinking corrects 'our inherent tendency to use visual, spatial imagery to speak about time, and hence to think of bodies as entities distinct from their movements. But movement is inseparable from that which moves, and as soon as we speak of a thing as distinct from its action we reinstate a division between movement and the moving entity' (Bogue 2003: 19). We have seen that 'the diagram as techniques of existence is a way of informing the next occasion of these potentials of self-formation' (Massumi 2013: 15), and in the self-formation we see events folding and unfolding providing the opportunity for self-formation within the four ecologies. This is a study of movement and becoming, not of being. This requires thinking culture, not as a stable entity but instead as existential dramaturgy and art as a way of perceiving:

> All of this suggests a way of bringing art and 'natural' perception together while still having a way of distinguishing them. In art, we see life dynamics 'with and through' actual form. Or rather, we always see relationally and processually in this way, but art makes us see that we see this way. It is the technique of making vitality affect felt. Of making an explicit experience of what otherwise slips behind the flow of action and is only implicitly felt. Of making the imperceptible appear. In everyday perception, the same thing occurs. There is an artfulness in every experience. Art and everyday perception are in continuity with one another. But in everyday experience, the emphasis is different. It is all a question of emphasis, an economy of foregrounding and backgrounding of dimensions of experience that always occur together and absolutely need each other. Art foregrounds the dynamic, ongoingly relational pole. Everyday experience foreground the object-oriented, action-reaction, instrumental pole. (Massumi 2013: 45)

According to Deleuze, Spinoza defines a body in two ways. First, as being 'composed of an infinite number of particles; it is the relations of motion and rest, of speeds and slowness between particles, that define a body, the individuality of a body' (1988: 123). The body in this example can be any body not just a human body. It is the body of a horse, a tick, a human in Deleuze's discussion. This discussion of the body is not limited by the skin either. There is no reason to limit, as Vertov proposes, to think of the body as being terminated at the limits of the skin: 'We affirm the kino-eye, discovering within the chaos of movement the result of the kino-eye's own movement; we affirm the kino-eye with its own dimensions of time and space, growing in strength and potential to the point of self-affirmation' (Vertov 1984: 16). The phone that is so close to you is Vertov's kino-eye (camera-eye), with its optics, memory, network and connections, these are part of the technobody's becoming in technoculture. There is no clear distinction between natural and artificial, between organic and technological, we are natureculture-technoculture. It is necessary to consider bodies at various scales, to see them move, to produce fields, to follow Vertov down a 'path [that] leads to the creation of a fresh perception of the world' (1984: 18), a worlding. Movement and becoming is fundament to the becoming-body at any scale, to a body's participation in worlding as it affects and is affected by other bodies, Spinoza's second observation: 'a body affects other bodies, or is affected by other bodies; it is this capacity for affecting and being affected that also defines a body in its individuality' (Deleuze 1988: 123). Affecting and affection occurs in the event:

> By making everything an event, by emphasizing that there is nothing outside of or beyond the event, the aim is to create an account of experience that requires no omnipresence. The event is where experience actualizes. Experience here is in the tense of life-living, not human life per se, but the more-than human: life at the interstices of experience in the ecology of practices. From this vantage point of an ecology of practices, it is urgent to turn away from the notion that it is the human agent, the intentional, volitional subject, who determines what comes to be. It is urgent to turn away from the central tenet of neurotypicality, the wide-ranging belief that there is an independence of thought and being attributable above all to the human, a better-than-ness accorded to our neurology (a neurology, it must be said, that reeks of whiteness, and classism). Neurotypicality, as a central but generally unspoken identity politics, frames our idea of which lives are worth fighting for, which lives are worth educating, which lives are worth living, and which lives are worth saving. (Manning 2016: 3)

In cinema, a shot is an event and a movement-image. Audio-vision is not a point but is chromesthetic eventness: 'the enveloping of color and illumination in one another extends through the senses, each one bearing and indicating all. Mutually enfolding. A many-dimensioned virtual whole of feeling I enfolded in every actual appearance in any given sense mode. Synesthesia. A color, smell, or touch is an emergent limitation of the synesthetic fold: its differentiation' (Massumi 2013: 88). Movement-images are assembled into montage and a film. The screen on the camera, in the editing room, and in the theatre, phone, tablet, or monitor 'constitutes the development of the plane of immanence: "the brain is a screen" in the sense that it is a filter that extracts itself from chaos. This screen is a form of relation, of interchange, of mutual synthesis between the brain and the universe' (Flaxman 2000: 16). The shot, like the edit, and the screening are diagrammatic. The diagram is the interface between the audio-enabled camera and operator, and the worlding which this machinic-thinking field assemblage are self-recognizing and self-enjoying. The diagram is the abstract machine that is actualized in the moment of hitting record, selecting and cutting shots in the editing suite, the affects of the screening. The shot is swimming in virtualities, as is continually explored throughout the book. Affected by the abstract line of the event emerging the filmmaker see-hears the interface between this virtuality and the virtuality of the future film in the editing suite and the future film on screen. The territorial assemblage, full of virtuality-actuality, is content for the coming expression of what will come in the production and screen assemblages. These are not linear stages but are coming interfaces, a plane of material and a plane of composition that are becoming. Unlike the usual approach to filmmaking dictated by filmmaking primers that urge the filmmaker to have a story, research-creation must be open to the drama appearing: 'Sometimes at the culmination of the experience, the drama appears for itself. It is *seen*. Not actually, if that means corresponding to a sense impression striking the body's visual apparatus. Actually: as in *in act*. This appearing of the drama of an experience's self-enjoyment in the act is the semblance' (Massumi 2013: 17). Brian Massumi calls the embeddedness of the virtual in perception, its livingness, *semblance*. He writes that 'semblance is another way of saying "the experience of a virtual reality". Which is to say: "the experiential reality of the virtual." The virtual is abstract event potential. Semblance is the manner in which the virtual *actually appears*' (Massumi 2013: 15–16). 'Semblance' is a term first suggested by Suzanne Langer as the thinking-feeling event of perception. Semblance is the event of the virtual in perception. It feels different to see a semblance: 'there is the slight uncanny sense of feeling sight see the invisible' (Massumi 2013: 44). It is uncanny because 'when a semblance is "seen," it is virtually seen. However else could the virtual actually appear – if not *as* virtual? Seeing a semblance is having a virtual vision. It is a seeing-through to the virtual in an event of lived abstraction' (Massumi 2013: 18). A scholarship of semblance and event requires a scholarship of the virtual and an ethics of creativity: 'The aesthetic-political production of novelty is the excess invention of experiential *forms of life*' (Massumi 2013: 18). Cinematic production, moving from the shot to the editing desk, is a way to join with Langer, Massumi, and Manning:

> 'montage provokes a complete change in perspective: the image is no longer only in tune with moving things, it extracts and autonomizes the movement of these things, in order to link them to other movements, of the same things or different ones . . . in one instance, movement is subordinated to its parts; in another it subordinates them to itself in order to enter into an assemblage with other movements. The concept of the "movement-image" is thus inseparable from a multiplicity' (Zourabichvili 2012: 144).

Cineworlding is a proposition for a way of doing cinematic posthumanities scholarship.

Seeing (virtually) the hooded monster on the sofa

Margø is a multiplicity. Cinema production and the music video form provides a space for the visualization of each of Margø's textures present in her song *In Between*. This is unquestionably a music video made for entertainment but it is also an opportunity to think through subjectivity in contemporary life. It is quite clear, from what I have heard and read in reviews, that audiences understand that Margø is dealing with demons. Their interpretations of how she does that and what the end of the video means may be in conflict with each other but isn't this conflict and opportunity for audiences to discuss with each other their feelings and ideas about subjectivity, even if perhaps they do not have the language for it.

In the second verse of the song, the most Cassidy looking of all of the Margø faces sits on a sofa looking directly at the audience. She is constantly distracted by a hooded image, who we later learn is a version of the monster from the opening. The hooded image does not quite reach fully into extensive space when it is introduced. It exists halfway between intensive and extensive space. This in-between is the *In Between* of the song in my mind. It is not so much a concept as it is an experience of the space between. Perhaps it is the preacceleration, perhaps it is the minor gesture. In this way, the music video becomes a form of scholarship that uses images, colours, movement, to visualize something that is outside language. In this way, cinematic research-creation opens up previously inaccessible ways of thinking-feeling research. *In Between* is a diagram of Margø-Cassidy and can do something in 4 minutes and 12 seconds that cannot be done so complexly, in such a short time, any other way. But it is not just about the efficiency of the lesson, but the affective impact of it as well. The music video form is a potent vehicle for diagrammatic thinking.

Diagrammatic thinking

Perhaps, the way we think about thinking has further implications for thinking about art. For the humanities, art education has since the nineteenth century been oriented around the appreciation of master works of a culture. In this model, there are authorized models of expression that students learn to replicate in their journey to become musicians and artists. Too often musicians and artists do not consider their expressive, creative work to be *thinking-in-action*. A division exists in modernity/coloniality between thinking and expression. A division between thinking as episteme and doing as techne. But practice-based research, art-based research and research-creation are posing a challenge to this. Artfulness is thinking, and research is creativity. While many will readily agree to this if you take the next step and ask what kind of thinking is suggested by artfulness, how does one develop this mode of thinking and teaching artfulness, evaluating artfulness? These simple questions reveal a gap. What is this way of doing-thinking that is artfulness? Is this something artists should be thinking about or should this be left to professional philosophers? I propose that Fine Arts lacks an 'image of thought' for the thinking-feeling of artfulness. Professional philosophy has much to offer, but so too does our experience in the making of art. Let us take advice from bell hooks who recognized in *Yearnings* (1990) that aesthetic theory outside of modernity/coloniality is rarely written in books. Let us collectively articulate models of thinking-feeling that emerge from the study of diagrams! This lack of doing our own philosophy has unintended consequences, limits artfulness to disciplinary categories, further entrenches disciplinary silos, where conservatories dominate music education and rarely make space for artfulness-futurity. The humanities is the proper noun for the dominant agencement in the modern/colonial university. The humanities is a worlding practice, an agencement that provides what can be thought and makes it difficult to think what is outside of itself, its nonthought. More-than-human intimacy can be theory. Intimacy is diagrammatic in that it has a shape and style, an agencement, perhaps it is time to explore and theorize the intimacy of our relationalities.

The diagrammatic is a way of thinking-feeling-doing sound/music/art. Deleuze and Guattari write that:

> 'The diagrammatic or abstract machine does not function to represent, even something real, but rather constructs a real that is yet to come, a new type of reality ... abstract machines thus have proper names (as well as dates), which of course designate not persons or subjects but matters and functions. The name of a musician or scientist is used in the same way as a painter's name designates a color, nuance, tone, or intensity: it is always a question of a conjunction of Matter and Function. The double deterritorialization of the voice and the instrument is marked by a Wagner abstract machine, a Webern abstract machine, etc' (1987: 142).

If thinking is an image of thought, a diagram on the plane of immanence, and meaning is the event of force fields, is it not possible to construct another image of thought just as rich as the textual one that philosophy and science have constructed? Music and sound studies can investigate its diagrammatic functions to construct our own image of thought.[8] When artists work artfully, they utilize a plane of content and convert that content into expression. The way of doing this, of making the content into expression, is the diagram.

The diagram and biogram operate between content and expression, where there is an interface, a gap or interstices. The diagram works at the interstices of the forces of contents and expression. Contents work on expression. Expression works on content. There are two edges. The diagram is the abstract machine operating at the interface, the edges of forces. Between these two edges are 'a set of abstract relations between abstract points a "diagram" of a vectorial field ... form of expression and form of content fuse into the form of the encounter itself' (Massumi 1992: 14). The relation between an image of thought and the diagrammatic is interesting for cinematic-thinking and music-thinking because, as I discuss throughout the book, it offers ways to think the many facets of decoloniality. Artfulness functions by way of the diagrammatic, the abstract machine, and this way of thinking creativity may allow us to get beyond Western thinking (read neurotypical, classicist, patriarchal, white-supremacist) which continues to limit music scholarship and the humanities. The diagrammatic may, therefore, provide a way of inquiring after the event of artistic-doing promoting an ethico-aesthetic paradigm for artistic research and teaching. Perhaps it is time for music schools to start inventing more ethical and artful futures. This will begin when our music programmes become places where we get involved in the production of futurity, inventing diagrams, and not only conservatory, installing diagrams.

The diagram operates at the interface between content and expression and the form of content and the form of expression. The interstice is a gap but it is not empty, nor is it a void. It bubbles with virtuality. The four ecologies (conceptual, social, technological, environmental), rich with forces, does not get reduced by any kind of dialectic or mediation: 'The main point to be derived from this is that relation in activist philosophical sense is *not connective*' (Massumi 2013: 21). Massumi proposes, from Whitehead the relation-of-nonrelation:

> if we apply this concept of the relation-of-nonrelation to what occurs between occasions of experience, we are led to treat the experiences themselves as differentials. The consequence is that occasions of experience *cannot be said to actually connect to each other*. They may be said to 'come together' only in the sense of being mutually enveloped in a more encompassing event of change-taking-place that expresses their differential in the dynamic form of its own extra-being. (Massumi 2013: 21)

The event is composed but 'to compose, we must deal with the "constituent parts" – contributory factors of activity-in great detail. But the more detail with which we grasp them, the more apt they are to fade into a remoteness where they recede into nonrelation. Yet they may also advance into new experiential dimensions, forwarding experience into new directions for composition' (Massumi 2013: 25). Philosophers, scientists and artists all operate to compose potential and speculative worldings. Cineworlding's speculative-pragmatics operates diagrammatically to think about the interface of worlding and cineworlding in the development of audio-vision. It is fundamentally involved in thinking the faculty of audio-vision as machinic-thinking. A machinic sense. Since Deleuze, it has been noted that 'the problem of the virtual is indissociable from the question of the *abstract composition of the senses*, in excess of their actual exercise' (Massumi 2013: 18). Cineworlding is centrally concerned about posing questions in the humanities without presupposing what it is that is asking them. Speculative-pragmatic ideas like the diagram and chromesthesia invites thinking-feeling of the abstract composition of the senses. Audio-vision is a sense! Just a more-than-human one.

Between contents and expression there is a meeting of forces, contents have forces, expressions have forces: 'meaning is an encounter between force fields. More specifically, it is the "essence" (diagram, abstract machine) of that encounter' (Massumi 1992: 33). The encounter is an event that occurs in action. Philosophy deals with concept and conceptual personae, the characters that do the thinking in text. As Lambert points out, 'It is difficult to say exactly when the book became the dominant form of philosophical expression, but it is essentially related to the rise of the novel in literature at the beginning of the nineteenth century. In the book, the event of thinking was reconstitute as a narrative adventure, with a narrator and different characters' (Lambert 2012: 46). Philosophy's encounter with nonphilosophy, in this case literature, led to the privileging of an image of thought, an image of thought that is often unthought. I have long been asking why is it that the technology of print is taken for granted as a transmission of knowledge. It has widely acknowledged limits. It moves linearly, is prone to generalization and abstraction, and in my lifetime has become only one mode of communication among many audio and audiovisual modalities. But text still dominates the humanities. But does this need to be so? Obviously, I am not going to say that text should be abandoned for cinema, as each does its own work. What I believe is essential that space be made for a speculative-pragmatics of cinema-thinking in the Humanities. And that scholars take this space to practice and report on the more-than-human thinking that digital cinema offers, diagrams on the plane of immanence as a new image of thought.

Conclusion: Cinematic research-creation's twin dramas

The drama in research-creation is always double. The drama that will be carried through the films becoming and the drama of the research-creation practitioner's practice, the posthumanographer.[9] These are not strictly separated of course but work through each other. There is, however, a fork where the film moves in one direction for audiences and the scholarly writing moves in another direction for different audiences. While they move in different directions, these are also not strictly separated as the films are folded into this book, and the observations that emerge for me as I write this are folded back into my body, highlighting for me the developing diagram. Film and writing are not in conflict but are the forking of experience through different medium. Cineworlding benefits from both in my opinion. When cinema-thinking is applied to the posthumanities, the cinematic production process becomes a laboratory for 'a machine assemblage of movement-images [that] is thus not just any film, but an experimental film: a film that experiments on its owns conditions' (Zourabichvili 2000: 142). Francois Zourabichvili identifies the following as a key sentence from the movement-image to focus Deleuze's Bergsonian engagement with cinema: 'The material universe, the plane of immanence, is *the machine assemblage of movement-images*' (2000: 142). The experience of the machinic assemblage is 'a kind of perception *of* the event of perception *in* the perception. We experience a vitality affect vision itself' (Massumi 2013: 44). There is a preacceleration, minor gesture and event of a shot, of an edit, of a scene. There is also the processes of difference that chain these events together, where the virtuality of the shot, both its pastness and futurity, is felt vectoring in the editing suite, and vectoring again at every screening but differently in every body. Cinematic research-creation is a diagrammatic scholarship of movement, event, vectors, duration, time, affect, immanence. Its form must not be dictated by documentary conventions because the form does not determine its ability to think-feel meaning: 'meaning is not a presence, but an experience. Meaning is an effect of signification that does not belong to nature, but only exists in consciousness: a floating composition of neurological flows, of bodily and psychological matter that take a form. Friendship is the condition for the experience – the existence – of meaning' (Berardi 2018: 145). There is, therefore, always an ethical dimension of worlding, as worlding must always consider its affects, virtualities, futurities immanent in each event.

6

Bodying in intensive and extensive spaces
John Wort Hannam Is a Poor Man

Cineworlding is intimacy. Intimacy, not as sexuality, though it does carry some of those affective and transformative tones, but as an affective attunement to relationality coming into form. Intimacy is also not defined by proximity, as my students remind me after screening a film. Undoubtedly, a group of students will remark on the feeling of being voyeuristic. What is the source of this felt voyeurism, and what kind of limits does it point to in learning and maybe in society? Is this feeling of voyeurism a resistance to the affective embrace of life's in-folding? There is comfort in extensive space. Intimacy in cineworlding is, I believe, an indication of the presence of intensive space in cinema-thinking. Manuel DeLanda notes that one of the main contributions of Gilles Deleuze's philosophy are two pairs of concepts: virtual and actual, and intensive space and extensive space. As we have discussed already, the virtual and actual are not binaries but work through each other. Extensive and intensive have the same relationship as DeLanda notes: 'human beings not only inhabit extensive spaces, they themselves are extensive spaces. Generalizing this to include mental phenomena would involve defining psychological intensities (not only grief, joy, love, hate but also beliefs and desires which also come in different intensities) as well as the corresponding extensities'. Making reference to 'far from equilibrium thermodynamics', DeLanda is interested philosophically in the question of how bodies emerge from nonstable intensive space, going so far as to say that only in this 'zone of intensity can we witness the birth of extensity and its identity-defining frontiers'. The relationship between intensive and extensive space proposes

> new concepts where we can define the sense in which the metric space we inhabit emerges from a nonmetric continuum through a cascade of broken symmetries. The idea would be to view this genesis not as an abstract mathematical process

but as a concrete physical process in which an undifferentiated *intensive space* (that is, a space defined by continuous intensive properties) progressively differentiates, eventually giving rise to *extensive structure* (discontinuous structures with definite metric properties). (DeLanda 2002: 18)

Extensive coordinates emerge in a process of differentiation from intensive space. Musical examples are helpful here as intensive space and extensive space are important and familiar contributors to music.

Let us start with a plucked string or a blown pipe. The body of the instrument oscillates at a number of nodes. Each node's vibration organizes air molecules into waves that travel through space based on their energy potential. There are a variety of harmonics produced at each node and eventually as waves cross over each other, standing waves are produced. The pitch that is heard is the fundamental frequency but there are harmonics that contribute unequally to the timbre of the instrument. Pitch is the emergence of extensive space in a process of differentiating from an intensive space of vibrational nodes, organized air molecules, standing waves and harmonics. As everyone who has ever purchased an instrument knows, there is a selection process that unquestionable has to do with tone. The differences between instruments have to do with the qualities of materials used. These materials have capacities that the luthier knows how to pay attention to. Wood for a sound board has virtualities that can be seen, felt and heard in the wood before it is actualized as a soundboard. The differences between the tone of two guitars, for instance, have to do with the tonal qualities of the pitch. We can think of these differences as pointing to the intensive space from which the extensive space of tonal quality emerges. The wood's virtuality for the luthier is its capacity to affect intensive space.

Thinking horizontally, sit at a piano and play a C and then a C#. Listen to the space between the two pitches. Now sing the C and slowly glissando up to C#, and then down. Continue this practice slowing the rise and fall of the glissando each time. If you are anything like me you will likely have to check the pitch a number of times because the space between the two notes seems to grow each time you slow down the glissando. This is the intensive space between the extensive space of the two notes. The point here is not to then throw up your hands and say 'notes are random', but instead to feel the emerging of the C# from the intensive space. The pull of the gravity of coming into form of the C#. You can also do this exercise with any major scale, stopping on the 7th tone and gliss into the octave. The virtual forms of the scale act on the intensive space. You can feel the gravitational pull towards the octave. Let us define intimacy as this feeling of gravitational pull enacted by its coming into form, or as Mickey Hart's website[1] reads: 'In the beginning there was noise. Noise begat rhythm. First light, then sound. And rhythm begat everything else. We were born in noise, in chaos. The first sound in the universe was pure noise. The Big Bang.' The relationality of chaos and form opens thinking beyond a platonic universe of universal form and towards a universe of flux, creativity, change and becoming. As notes become territorialized in extensive space, they carry with them the virtualities of the harmonics, the extensive nodes of the harmonic overtone series, virtual relations that become actual harmony. This is not to fall into a structuralist position to then say that the diatonic scale and harmony are therefore fundamental or natural, but to recognize instead that there is an abstract machine that works on intensive space, territorializing intensive space to produce extensive space. There is a relationality and process, there is also virtuality. There are many ways that intensive space can be organized, the key is to recognize that its organization is not ideal, not ordained, magical or without foundation. It is not a platonic form, but instead extensive space is innovation and habit. Intimacy is a way of thinking about what it means to feel for the draw or heat of in-folding. Attuning to intimacy, to the gravitational force field, we can perhaps feel for the universe's intimacy with itself, and feeling for the more-than-human intimacy of the world.

I want to propose that cinematic research-creation is particularly well suited for an investigation of posthuman intimacy. Where a document treats forms as ontologically self-evident, cinema operates best when it deals with coming-to-form of extensive space. It opens up a way to investigate the extensive space without losing access to intensive space. My interest in intensive space is a consequence of experiences in making films. Often the decision to hit record is not conceptual but a feeling of atmospheric thickening, the affect of the intimacy of gathering form. It creates a kind of fuzzy-headed feeling like I am being pulled out of, or kicked out of recognizable space-time, and an intensity within experiences that begins to work on my perception, semblance, the uncanny feeling of the becoming seen of virtualities. This can happen with or without a camera. It has happened without a camera nearly all of my life and it was perhaps what drew me to cinema, the desire to make this the centre of my practice and to learn more about it. Semblance is a way of thinking about my art practice and the reason why I wanted to move my art practice into research-creation. To think-feel the thickening of experience. It feels like it has some directionality, that it is leading somewhere but in the flow of it the form is not yet known, nor is its temporal pull clear, the past is drawn together just as surely as the future potential. With camera in hand, the feeling of in-folding is the event of recording.

It is conventional in ethnography to focus attention on the event that came into form, from within the obviousness of its formation. And this is valuable to do. But it is also possible, from the safe location within the event, to turn around (imaginatively), put your back against the certainty of the form, and consider the flowing intensities coming into form of intensive space, and theorize. If we use the intensive space within music as a guide for our thinking in cinematic research-creation, we can see, as DeLanda explained in other terms, that there are spatial questions that need to be asked, that may form the basis of ways of doing posthumanography. Not a search for forms, but the development of techniques to attune attention to the coming into form.

In this chapter, I want to draw attention to intensive space, the intimacies in bodying that populate the extensive space of the cineworlding proposition. Intimacy[2] should not be reserved for humans. Before we consider intensive spaces in the bodying of *John Wort Hannam Is Poor Man* (JWH) let us first do some queering of the documentation paradigm by considering the becoming of more-than-human extensive spaces and how they point to intensive space: chromesthesia, bodying and anarchive.

Queering the documentary paradigm

At the core of the documentary paradigm is a model of thinking and valuing forms. This model carries with it at least two colonial threats. The first is it imposes a subject-object binary on the world, confirming the volition-intentionality-agency triad (Manning 2016: 6) that treats the more-than-human of the environment and technology as externalities. The second, as Dylan Robinson has pointed out in *Hungry Listening* (2020), supports modernity/coloniality's operation of collection and storage, stealing from the peripheries to create value in the centre. How else might we understand the treatment of audiovisual recording, rather than as documents for later analysis, a transcription of events. This perspective misses the interstices between shots, the virtualities that populate the shots in the movement-image and the time pressure that is created when we endure a long shot, the direct perception of time in the time-image. Treating shots as documents cuts out the virtualities of the out-of-field of the shot, and the audio field of the recording. It makes invisible the compositional practice, audio-vision's chromesthesia, the becoming-cinema of the plane of expression and the cinematic technologies involved in its expression. As a consequence of all of this reduction there is little discussion of cinema-thinking, worlding, cineworlding because the concept of the document has operated a reduction in thought. The documentation paradigm makes it appear that there is nothing in the shots worth thinking about beyond their contents. Carry on, nothing to think here. The concepts brought to the documentation paradigm are unfit for thinking-feeling audio-vision. The document is not a being, is not alive, does not affect its collectors or is affected by its associates. The task for cineworlding is to raise awareness of the livingness of cinema-thinking. To propose a new image of thought that is capable of intimacy with the four ecologies (concept, social, technics, environment). An important aspect of this is to develop a healthy suspicion of the explanatory power of forms.

John Wort Hannam Is a Poor Man

When I completed *John Wort Hannam Is a Poor Man* (JWH), I said out loud to myself: 'I have finally made a film!' I had been making films and music videos for many years already but JWH is still an important film for me because it was the first time I was able to make something that was coherent from beginning to end. It has bumpy bits and issues with colour and sound but it holds together. My instinct was correct. The film went on to win a Best Documentary Short Award, my first award as a filmmaker, and was used by the American Songwriters Association at a couple of conferences. That the film was able to be successful outside academia was important to me. It broke in me the idea that an academic filmmaker needed to stay inside the academy, needed to limit one's expectations to classroom and academic conference screenings. It also opened up for me ways of thinking about what Simon Zagorski-Thomas calls practical musicology (2022). JWH can be a scholarly film about music culture, an entertaining documentary film and a practical film for songwriters and touring artists. Fundamentally, I believe the success of the film is its openness for interpretation. Formally, it is a road film but aside from that there is nothing about the film that sets out to determine itself, to ground itself disciplinarily, so it can be approached from multiple locations.

Prelude: 'Honestly where did we park?'

The audio-image enters first. It is a jumble of voices at a distance that suggests a closed space. A visual-image of a jean-jacketed figure walking through sliding door out into a bright parking lot. The first line of the film is JWH saying, 'don't say anything rude Bob' to tour accompanist Bob Hamilton. JWH points to the camera 'I actually forgot he was coming. Till I walked down the stairs I forgot' and we both laugh, the filmmaker and John laugh together at this ridiculous situation being filmed. I was waiting by the front door of the hotel with the camera to get a shot of them leaving. The event of not finding their car mixed with my struggle to get John in focus perfectly captured for me the image of the not yet. This short exchange sets a mood that is emphasized immediately after when John looks back at the camera and laughs admitting he has no idea where the car is parked suggesting that 'we'll look like the two stooges'.

I always film before I am ready. I just jump into the middle with the camera. There is a lightness to the improvisation that works for me. It is evident in this opening scene that I am not ready. I have a terribly difficult time getting John in focus, the camera bobs and weaves everywhere, clearly distracted by the amount of light I am attempting to deal with. The trouble with focus is a technical issue that has to do with light. I love lots of light and open the aperture of my lens as wide as I can nearly all the time. This allows lots of light into the camera lens but also introduces technical challenges because I use a 50mm prime lens and the open aperture reduces the focal plane quite dramatically. Not as much as an 85 mm lens, my other option but certainly much more than my third 24 mm prime lens. The massive wash of light has to do with using a faster lens than I was accustomed to. A fast lens means that it allows more light through it than a slow lens. The lens speed is indicated on the lens as an F marking. F2.8 is slower than F1.4. More light getting through the lens means that there is more opportunity to shape the depth of field. Depth of field is when the subject is in focus but the background is blurry or out of focus. Before iPhone 12, you required enough light and a wide aperture to create a depth of field. The iPhone portrait mode uses a depth of field algorithm.

The aperture in this case was far too open and the light threatened to overwhelm any image coming into formation. The appropriate response to so much light is to close up the aperture but because I was not using a cinema lens I did not have access to a smooth manual control of the aperture. When I filmed JWH I was using fast photography lens, the Sigma Art series lens. The aperture control for the lens was by increments and clicked closed by steps, not smoothly like a manual aperture that all cinema lenses have. So I decided to just ride through the shot with it open and try to get the shot in focus. The trouble getting John in focus is because photography lenses are not designed to be focused on the run. Their throw is very short, the amount of turning distance to adjust focus, which is great for setting up still shots, but terrible for trying to match the changes of moving objects in process. You can easily pass right by focus, back and forth, focusing past John and then in front. It created a feeling of John not quite coming into focus. When I first shot this, aside from its comedy potential, I expected that the scene was garbage. But there was something quite beautiful visually about the fuzziness created by the lack of focus and the overwhelming white light. I was drawn to it and began trying to justify it. Perhaps it was a metaphor about a JWH coming into focus for us the viewer (as I have said in a number of interviews about the film). But I really don't believe this. It's a useful way of putting this into language. The beauty of the shot and its comedy is really why I kept it. Making sense of its beauty required some deeper thinking for me about the intensive space of cinema images. The light and movement, lens, sensor and focus that bring extensive coordinates into the cinematic plane of materiality.

'Superabstract invention'

Concepts are forms that operate on thinking, give the extensive space of thinking its coordinates. Innovations are structured by a language of forms. As Deleuze and Guattari point out content and expression undergo the forces of the form of content and form of expression. Orienting to the diagrammatic provides an opportunity to operate in the molecular, in the inside of a forms-becoming. To attune oneself to the minor gestures of a forms-becoming opens up what is previously automatic, to make space for imagination. Imagination 'is a pragmatic, synthetic mode of thought which takes the body not as an "object" but as a realm of virtuality, not as a site for the application of an abstract model or prefabricated general idea but as a site for superabstract invention' (Massumi 1992: 100). When my thinking stilled into a form, I believed I had accomplished something.[3] The stillness of form was the destination of thinking. If the film communicated a discrete unit of knowledge it was scholarly. However, I kept getting drawn back to Agnes Varda, Les Blank and Werner Herzog's documentaries. These films were not really documentaries, or at least did not possess the aesthetic of truth, the staged interview, the title cards, names, narration so often the form of the documentary. Documentary's portraiture. Most importantly, they did not provide a stable graspable object. Deleuze and Guattari's distinction between the molar and the molecular is useful here. The molar and molecular are not distinguished by size or scale but by their solidness. For instance, a film about a musician takes *musician* as a molar. It is a solid graspable entity. But it often goes by little noticed that this identity or industrial category is habituated in bodies and as bodies surfing forces generated by a constellation of technologies, spaces and many forms of human and more-than-human relations. There is becoming-musician where a body habituates itself to the rhythms and flows of all that is hidden by the identity musician, of all the spaces that are maintained by the habits of countless people in order for this becoming-musician to continue becoming. Its becoming is partially visible and partially kept out of sight. *Musician* is a form of expression that operates on the organic body as its content. The becoming-musician, its bodying occurs diagrammatically, operated on by a diversity of forces. There is always an existential dramaturgy of becoming-musician, a unique vector that comes to visuality as a semblance. This is the storytelling that inspires me most.

Lens choices

As soon as I could afford to buy cinema lenses I jumped at the chance. I had been using still photography lenses for many years but had had an early experience of operating an early Canon HDV camera with a telephoto cinema lens and absolutely fell in love with it. Choosing a lens or lenses is important of course because it is an essential part of the character formation of images. It is not just a piece of glass with focus and aperture controls. A lens squeezes and stretches images, contributes to texture and its coloration. Each lens has characteristics that are compositional. Perhaps there is an easy way to avoid the years of playing with lenses but I would not want to. Playing with lenses, microphones, cameras is an important part of my creative process. No different than it was when I was a full-time musician. Every instrument helped me make certain kinds of sounds come into being, so too do cameras allow certain visual-images, and microphones, certain sound-images come into the world.

In the beginning, I spent a lot of time reading books, manuals, user blogs and industry magazines about lenses. I have spent much more time thinking about lenses than thinking about cameras. Over and over again, I read that documentary filmmakers should have wide angle, normal perspective and close-up lenses. These are all numbered by millimetre. Wide angle are between 14 and 24 mm (lower than that is fisheye). Normal perception is usually considered 35 mm but some people (like me) use 50 mm. Close-up or portrait lenses are above this. My first set of Sigma lenses were 24, 50 and 85. I also had a 70–200 mm Canon telephoto lens which I rarely ever use in my cinema work. When I finally purchased my Canon cinema lenses, I got the same focal lengths with the CN-E prime lenses. It turns out that I use the 50 mm almost exclusively. If I was to do it over again, I would get a 50 mm only. Just one lens. Shoot everything with one lens until there are images that you can imagine in your mind that you just cannot get and then try to figure out what lens you need for that shot. While my current lenses cost about $5k CAD each I am now thinking about purchasing a new 50mm Canon prime lens that will be well above $10k CAD. Why would I spend this kind of money on a lens? I cannot tell you. I cannot put into words what a lens does, because I do not have the words exactly, I can see the difference, however, as a feeling. The first moment I put my eye to a lens my perception was populated by virtualities that operated intensively. The sensitivity of the lens is directly related to its ability to affect my body, to activate intensive force. A lens choice is not determined by its size or price but in its ability to affect you. Every lens will not affect you the same, some will not affect you at all, others will affect you strongly. When you choose a lens, let your body choose for you.

Intimate equipment

The hours spent pouring over lens options, cameras, lighting and developing framing and editing techniques. The endless conversations about new editing software, new camera hardware, the relationships with other filmmakers near and far away. The social media sharing between filmmakers around the world, the thrill of having films accepted into film festivals, the frustration of not, the joy of seeing work on a massive screen with your friends and being interviewed along with the other artists at the post-screening Q&A. The sheer horror of seeing your film projected on a massive screen and in that moment learning that the colour temperature (white) of a projector bulb is different from that of a computer screen. These are all aspects of cineworlding for me and nothing on this list corresponds to academic research. This is not to say that there is not an academic side to this that I also cherish. I love doing the hard work of conceptualizing my art practice, to do the deep work of thinking through the ethics of academic filmmaking, of reading ethnographic film and film studies literature. To be introduced to a world of filmmaking and be inspired in my craft. Reading philosophy and thinking about what tools are on offer. This is the two sideness of research-creation. It is not a choice between being an artist or a scholar but instead to innovate on a space between both. Risking never quite fitting in with either world completely because, in my case, I am always thinking about who is not present in the room, what perspectives are not included. When academics say this, they typically mean community people in the university, as if the university is the centre of something to anyone but themselves. I mean the other way primarily, the commons outside the university where all manner of social and cultural innovations are constantly taking place and so rarely is there a researcher around to chip in. A researcher is useful if they are available and oriented to becoming, even more so if they are oriented to queering the university: 'queering produces becomings that go beyond normative couplings to invent new connections be it with humans, animals, vegetals or machines' (Conley 2009: 25). It is perhaps useful to think about how the hyphen, what I called the enotikon, queers research and creativity, and to add on this another social layer, to think the way cinematic research-creation queers the human. As Conley notes: 'Deleuze and Guattari's queerings function at the level of singularity and collectivity, of aesthetics and ethics' (25) they are not content to limit queer to an identity because 'what can be called queering in the texts of Deleuze and Guattari is predicated on a queer revolution – sexual and social – and the becoming-revolutionary of the queer' (25). Queering for Deleuze and Guattari, the way I will use it in this chapter, gives some direction to the tension caused by artist and research identities, in the becoming-with of camera technology, the becoming-with of artists, of spaces, of refrains. Cineworlding is not about documenting, or about being unchanged, it is about constant becoming-with and queering, and in doing so of innovating on ways to make fugitive relations that burrow underneath identity, class, race, occupation, gender, sex, ability, nationality to make family. But that also burrow under the Human to get at the more-than-human relations. This can be at a small scale like the relations between perceptive faculties of the see-hear-music-image-camera becoming of chromesthesia, the social level of body-group-space-movement becoming of *bodying*, and the temporal level of action in the present seeding the future of the becoming of *anarchive*.

Title sequence 'I am a poor man' music video opening

The title sequence for JWH utilizes a music video-style montage that draws shots from across the short three-day tour. The audio recording of the performance comes directly off the camera and was recorded using a single shotgun microphone. John and Bob had used this song in sound check a number of times and from the first time they played it there was a suggestive intensity. Due to the limitations I put on the film, to only record the first fifteen seconds of taking the stage and the last fifteen seconds before coming off the stage, I relied on soundchecks and behind-the-scenes (BTS) musical moments for the soundtrack. The limitations were not randomly imposed nor imposed by John. I wanted to limit myself in order to focus on what audiences do not see. I also wanted to explore the possibility of using a BTS documentary with only song segments to encourage those new to John to purchase his music and attend a live performance. I did not want the audience to feel satisfied with having seen John perform, but to feel that they have seen the energy that will be more fully realized on stage and to be moved to see it for themselves.

Recording with a single shotgun microphone is a tricky affair. It requires that you listen very carefully and mix the performance with your body. Moving a microphone attached to a camera means that your entire body must flow according to what is happening in the sound. It requires knowing the arrangement and moving in advance of the event as quickly as necessary by the arrangement. It also requires that you think audiovisually in the future, to the future editing that will happen. As you think about the unfolding of the arrangement you think also about the in-folding of the film, constantly thinking-feeling for the shots that you can use and choosing carefully when to move knowing that you will need to find shots later to replace the shots that you know you will not be able to use. In this kind of improvisational production, there is a lot that can go wrong, but also a lot that can surprise and delight. Following the flows of energy is what is most important and since it is all happening so quickly and at multiple locations in time-space, both here and now, at the editing desk and in the future cinema constructed in your mind, it is not conceptual thinking that occurs but cinema-thinking.

Chromesthesia

In interviews when Les Blank was asked about being a documentarian, he would quite often reply that he was not one. That his music films were to him 'little operas'. The notion of little opera stayed with me. The components checked out. There were indeed sections of spoken dialogue that were expanded upon with music either performed or in proto music video format where clips were cut against music. The relationship between the shots and the audio was found through a practice that Blank only alludes to, which is already more than most. Blank says that he sifts through his clips to find the one that connects. That moment of connection for him emerges 'as a new chord', a kind of uncanniness in the experience of semblance. Oriented towards the semblance instead of the document, the opera instead of the documentary, opens up conceptual thinking to audio-vision's *chromesthesia*, its sound to colour, shape and movement relations that entangle perception. *Chromesthesia* is a way of conceptualizing the artistic thinking of sound-movement-light-image relationality in Blanks 'new chord', the eventness of the *perceptual coupling* of music and sound that leads to the emergence of the music-image.

Chromesthesia conceptually attunes perception to the field effects immanent in the dance of attention. As a practice it is allied in aim to Michel Chion's idea that reduced listening is a technique that 'disrupt established lazy habits and opens up a world of previously unimaged questions for those who try it' (2019: 26). Reduced listening proposes that one take sounds separate from their context and attempt a description. The goal is to focus attention to sound and in the process of trying to describe them, to open attention to the details of the sounds. As a thinking-feeling practice, it 'has the enormous advantage of opening up our ears and sharpening our power of listening' (28). In the same way as I turned to Manning's *dance of attention* as a field effect so too does Chion's reduced listening 'explore a field of audition that is given or even imposed on the ear, and this aural field is much less limited or confined, its contours uncertain and changing' (34). The interstices between visual-image and sound-image come alive in the making of Blank's new chords when we recognize that 'sound interprets the meaning of the image and makes us see in the image what we would not otherwise see or would see differently' (34). If the visual-image and sound-image fields are approached relationally, there is a metastability to chromesthesia where the sound-image operates on the visual-image and the visual-image operates on the sound-image. There is a risk here that thinking is stopped by dialectically reducing chromesthesia to an audiovisual image, a single unified image. But this does not occur in audio-vision; the chromesthesia is full of virtuality that populates the interstices of the visual and sound-images that cannot be rendered down into a verifiable relationship. The reason for this is that the viewer is acted on by these field forces just as the viewer applies their force of perception. Chromesthesia conceptually attunes us to virtualities, where thinking in terms of the documentary closes off these potentialities or at the very least invites a production process that attempts a reduction or disciplining of audio-vision.

Colouring: Hot and cold variation and LUTS

In digital cinema, in contrast with videography, colouring is essential. In videography, with a camcorder or phone, the shots have an existing colour that is baked into the shot. This means that there is coding work being done to collect data that has luminance, intensity, white balance and colour that is included in the image already. In digital cinema, more information is collected to allow and require you to make processing adjustments after shooting. The amount of metadata that is included in the shots is determined by camera settings. With a Canon camera, which I used to film JWH, I used a C-Log setting which preserves much more information than a camera shooting Rec-709 images. Rec-709 is a colour space. It is the colour space for TV, tablet, phone and computer screens. It is the colour space that you are used to seeing on digital devices, but it is not the colour space in a theatre as I would learn when I first screened JWH at a film festival. The image on the cinema screen was not what I saw on my studio monitors when I was editing and colouring. It was different. Not bad, but not correct. It did not fit the colour intensity that I had spent hours crafting. The reason, I would later learn, is because the white light of a cinema projector is not the same white light on a computer screen. And as a consequence, there is a shift in all of the colours. Colour space also has to do with the potentiality of the colours to come to expression. If you look at colour space graphs, you will see that they take up more or less space on a chart, which is a way of graphically representing the expression of colour in a colour space. When I was editing and colouring JWH, my timeline colour space was defaulted to Rec-709. So I was colouring based on that setting. But the colour space for a cinema is DCI-P3. When I learned this, I began making decisions about where the film was most likely to be screened. Any film that I was colouring for a festival I would set my timeline colour space to DCI-P3 and anything that was going direct to Vimeo or YouTube, I would colour in Rec-709. Newer computers and phones are increasingly using DCI-P3 colour space because it provides more colour potential, so in the last couple of years I colour everything in this colour space.

When you need to colour your images, there are two ways to do it. The best place to start is to use LUTs, which stand for *Look Up Tables*. If you are a social media user, you are already familiar with LUTs, it is what gets applied to your images when you choose a filter. But it is important to not think of it as a filter when you are colouring. There are filter effects but these do not impact colour exactly. A LUT is designed to transform the colour information in a shot according to a table that shifts white according to a set of characteristics of a historic film media (like Kodak ektachrome film) or by mood (Intense, Archive, Warm). LUTs are a great way to start colouring your film without having to know a great deal about doing colour correction. The experience of investigating LUTs will inspire you to think more deeply about colour extensively and about light intensively. The extensive space of colour is built, as I have explained earlier, on the intensive space of the colour information that is at play. These are not general characteristics, but specific to the shot that you have taken. The extensive space of colour is informed (not quite determined) by actions that have already been taken. In the editing suite when colouring, you will be guided in your choices by the intensive forces that you recall from the experience. Finding a match between the feelings for the shot and the realized colour is what guides the work at this stage, thinking-feeling chromesthesia.

This means of course that when you apply a LUT, it is going to bring out characteristics of your shot based on what is there. If there is a lot of colour information, because you shot in C-Log, Blackmagic Film, BMRaw or Raw, then you can expect more variation from source to coloured image than if you shot your original footage in Rec-709. There is just less colour information available. Rec-709 footage is not meant to be coloured. You can do it, but it is designed to be shot and used. That is the benefit of shooting in Rec-709. There is no processing required. But digital cinema requires processing and before you begin colouring you need to make sure you begin with the proper image. To do this means that the first step of colouring is to set the black and whites of your image to make sure your image is balanced. Check the white balance and correct it if necessary. This point should always be made in advance, but is always learned later. I spent quite a bit of time not thinking much about white balance until I began having to correct it in post and realized that there was only so much room to move the white balance. If it was shot with too high a kelvin temperature (the measure for white) and everything was orange, there was only so much blue one can add to make it look white. And vice versa. In JWH you can see this throughout the film; I shot it much too warm.

There is a great deal that can be talked about in terms of colouring images and the above quick description is meant to highlight the intensive forces of colour energy and its relationship to the camera sensor when shooting. In the opening music video sequence of JWH I move between live warm shots of John and Bob performing, the warmth holds the sequence together and the desaturated shots taken during the tour, stick out as virtualities, images for the future that give the opening a forward momentum, it pulls towards a future that is in-folding. The oscillation back and forth serves compositionally to give a sense of direction and technically to hide the necessary cuts that were made in the recording of the live performance. This kind of cinema-thinking is what I am interested in exploring throughout this book. It is not just a matter of developing theory to think about cinema, but to do so that one can make cinema and participate in its production. There are no books that I am aware of that cross back and forth between the technical practices of cinema production and theory about what cinema is. I believe this is an important space for investigation given the increasing universality of audio-vision in contemporary life.

Titles and graphical energy

Typeface is not casual. As any designer or semiotician will tell you, typeface speaks. It is not just a way of displaying words but it also communicates something else about those words. Typeface can work metaphorically, to make reference to a time, place, genre or historical period and it can also do less conceptual tasks, working intensively inside the words on the screen. A great deal of time gets spent trying and revising typefaces for title sequences. It is time well spent because when the film is finished you will use these typefaces on posters, advertising, thumbnails and so on. It is an important part of developing the concept of your film and should be done with care and input.

Introduction: The hotel lobby and the musician photographs

Documentaries tend to do boring introduction and include needless title information to identify characters. I am inspired by Les Blanks films who rarely ever provide names for people on the screen. People call each other by name over the course of the film and the viewer can take the name if they wish. The naming convention is kind of like wearing a name tag at a conference where no one talks to each other. I absolutely do not see the point of it. It is not the name of the body that is important but their character. The opening scene in JWH is a conversation between him and Bob about photos on the wall of a hotel where they are staying. This sequence tells us a lot without writing anything on the screen. It is a hotel that entertainers use when they are in town. It is clearly not a big city because they have photos of entertainers on their wall. John jokingly complains that his photo is not on the wall, which situates him relative to the mostly black-and-white signed headshots that populate this corner wall of fame next to the cash-dispensing machine. John launches into a story about 'the push-up man' that is quite funny. As we listen to the story, there is an invitation for intimacy that the proximity provides. The scene introduces the relationship between John and Bob and puts them in a necessary larger context without the use of an establishing shot, introduction paragraph or sit-down interview. Here we are together – John, Bob and the viewer on a journey. Let us start here in the middle of their relationship and in the middle of this action whatever it will be, and let ourselves be open to what is to come. This introduction is an invitation to intimacy, it is entirely up to the viewer whether they will open themselves to it.

Exit into light

At the end of the story, John walks out the sliding doors and we follow. The camera is once again overtaken by the white light that hit us earlier. But this time instead of stumbling around in the light the camera moves intentionally towards it. The full flash of white light provides a natural cut point to get us from exiting this scene to the introduction of the next scene where we find ourselves looking down an empty hallway. We hear a click and Hamilton comes through the side door and looks at us for a second before heading the other way. John follows Bob and looks at us with a kind of withering, not you again look. The intensity of the sharing is a non-verbal gesture of playful enthusiasm. We have crossed over from passive observers in the introduction to participants. We have been seen.

Act 1: The basement

John's music fades in as they walk down the hall; there is a diegetic shift from non-diegetic to diegetic as we find that John is now on stage playing the song that we are listening to in the soundtrack. A diegetic shift is when music from the soundtrack is actually music that is happening in the profilmic space. A shift from non-diegetic (soundtrack) to diegetic (profilmic). This is a continuity technique that allows perspective to move through cinematic time-space where we hear the future and then catch up to it as we turn the corner. This moment is interrupted by another song 'Blue Blood'. The image makes a sharp cut to an exterior driving shot of farm fields in southern Alberta. The song's refrain 'I wasn't born blue blood, I was born blue collar. Like my dad and granddad I'm going to follow. There's no money here you've got to earn every dollar' says something about JWH's connection to this land, further context that deepens our understanding of JWH. We then cut back to applause as JWH finishes the show at the club. The short music video cut makes a connection between playing music at clubs and blue-collar work. That continues after the show as John collects his unsold CDs and merch and packs up and discusses with the promoters the lack of attendance. John jokes, 'once people come see me once they don't want to come back'; the process of packing, setting up, packing up and moving establishes a refrain for the film.

Cinewolding is about establishing a world. Sound-images are important aspects of cinematic world-building. It is necessary to pay close attention to any music that you think might be useful for the later soundcheck. This is to film with the attention of yourself as future editor. An instrumental interlude that Bob plays during soundcheck becomes the soundtrack for him walking down the same hallway he entered, but this time he carries three instruments and a small case, the hall is bright but muted, the vibrancy is gone. This was achieved by colouring the hallways differently to engage the audience intensively. Colouring is compositional; it allows the editor to play with the energy of the bodying. The audience will probably not notice the colour shift or go back to compare the colour of the hallway from an earlier shot. But as you develop chromesthetic attention, your perception becomes more attuned to these shifts in what you see-hear and in doing so you begin to feel for the bodying that is not just Hamilton's lonely walk down the hallway, but that the afterness of the concert is itself a kind of intensive space.

Bodying

If we return to Jean Rouch's idea of the cineportrait with chromesthesia as a practice, we have what Erin Manning calls *bodying*. The Spinoza-Bergson-Vertov proposition asks what can a camera-image-body-editing-screening assemblage do? What can cineworlding do? What can an event do? One of the things that it can do is bodying. For Manning, 'one cannot separate the question of what a body can do from the milieu in which it dwells in relation with others' (2016: 190). Bodies that are in relation produce their relations. Not all bodies are in relations, are bodying, at the same time. When they are bodying there is an event that takes place, a kind of constellation of bodies that is worlding. Manning's concept of bodying brings out what a body is able to do in an event. Not from the perspective of the agency of the individual body, the 'volition-intentionality-agency triad' (Manning 2016: 195) that is the definition of the Human, but instead, what role the event plays in what bodies can do. Bodying recognizes field affects of the event, 'how the event accommodates' (195). Cineworlding is attuning perception to worlding events 'the relationscape of bodying . . . [that] invents worlds' (Manning 2016: 191). A worlding will have a form but it will always be a form in the making that will also have a moving on into another form. What is being proposed is not a formless process but an attention to the in-forming of process, the processes of world-becoming, worldings. Cineworlding uses chromesthetic techniques that 'allow for that dance of attention to be awakened or energized, to be made possible' (Manning 2016: 193). Cineworlding's attention to bodying will not be oriented to making a document of an event but instead be attentive to the bodying of events, what bodies are able to do: bodies of flesh and blood, bodies of grains and pixels. Instead of documenting the form of the event, cineworlding will allow bodying to become a conversation oriented to futurity. What can we learn about the possibilities of bodying in alternative event models, to the impacts of capitalism and the entertainment industry on bodying, to the effects of non-capitalist or anti-capitalist social formations and the bodying these events allow. And also the more monstrous posthuman bodying of becoming-camera, becoming-editor, becoming-audience.

Posthuman bodying: Technology and techniques

When I began making research-creation films, I was using HDV tapes. HDV was a significant jump from the DV tapes that had been used for some time. I was amazed by the beautiful twenty-four frames per second film look that was possible with these cameras. Now of course I look back at the cute diamond-shaped pixels and the slightly odd-shaped bokeh with delight. The switch from tape-based media to digital files happened quite quickly, but not as fast as the increases in sensor capability and size over the last few years. To put this into perspective, shooting on 35 mm film is closely equivalent to a 6k sensor for fidelity. There is plenty of dispute about this because of course film photography is a chemical reaction and not a digital image made up of pixels. They are completely different processes. But just for the sake of understanding the transformation of the technology. Let's say that 35 mm film is roughly 6k. When I began shooting digitally, we were working with a maximum fidelity of less than 1k. By the time I was able to afford a decent camera, a C-100, it was closer to 2k. After five or so years of working with this camera and making a lot of films, some of which were screened at film festivals and in large cinema, the image was quite good. When I finally was able to make the next jump I purchased my current camera, a Blackmagic Ursa mini-pro 4.6k. I was one of the first in Canada to get this camera when it was released but in less than a year and Blackmagic had released a 6k and then a 12k camera. Astonishing. I have yet to see footage shot at 12k, and I am certain my computer would absolutely melt down if I tried to play a clip at that resolution (and file size!). I have only worked on one music video project that used a resolution higher than 2k, because of the file sizes that get generated. Shooting at 4.6k in BMRaw is an absolute delight. There is so much that can be done with the shots afterwards, but you pay for that in file size. What makes that file so large is how much information is being stored in the image as a virtuality. Something that we will come back to later.

The real struggle with tape-based media was the tape ingestion into the computer. In tape-based media, every hour of footage required at least an hour of ingestion. You hooked the camera up to the computer, preferably to a high-quality digital I/O (in and out) and digitized the media. The medium of the tape and camera player into the I/O never worked the way you wanted. There were constant 'dropped frames' that would stop the ingestion process. The tape technology was never consistent enough to let the tape play all the way through the hour-long mini DV tape. So inevitably you would sit there and monitor the ingestion for dropped frames, set the ingestion up again and hit record on the computer. The benefit of this process was that it provided an opportunity to watch all of the media from start to finish. I always conceived of this time as an opportunity to watch the rushes, the daily quickly processed film footage from the film production days. The switch to SD cards, CF cards and now SSD drives built into the cameras massively decreases production time. It is now almost instantaneous. The downside of this is that watching all the footage is now a necessary practice, a self-imposed technique and not a requirement.

Act 2: Lyric theatre

The second act opens when John introduces Bob to the promoter of tonight's concert as he passes her something to carry into the hall. We follow John from the back alley of the hall, up a set of stairs that we first saw as a cutaway in the opening music video montage. The virtuality of the pastness coming into the present in this moment, its actualization gives the moment forward movement. The transition from daylight to a dark hallway to the bright stage presents a technical choice. If I was using a cinema lens, I could swiftly open the aperture to let much more light hit the camera's sensor to balance the image from outside to poorly lit inside, operating a transition, the adjustment that occurs in the eye reflexively, that balances differing visual visual-images. As we reach the stage, more and more light greets the camera and I would gradually close the aperture to make the opposite adjustments. But in this case, using a photographic lens I decide to leave the aperture where it is and lose the visual information in the dark hallway and risk an overexposed entrance to the stage. Which is precisely what occurred. On the stage I looked for something to use as a cutaway and then adjusted my aperture in time for JWH's soundcheck.

JWH begins playing 'A Quiet Life' and once again the microphone, lens, camera bodying assemblage takes the lead. Perhaps because I was a live and recording sound engineer before I began making films, I am used to listening to a sound system and used to listening to an empty room with all its strange resonances and vibrations. There is a process in live sound when the room is tuned. Tuning the room is about getting the sound system, artist, room acoustic relationship sorted out. It is an important practice that requires a good deal of experience with the virtualities of space. Soundchecks are done in an empty room but a full room puts a *lot* of sound absorbing organic matter in play. These are of course the bodies of the audience which 'eat up' lots of sound. Experienced sound engineers are accustomed to predicting the virtualities of the room and plan not for this moment but for the time to come. The sound-image in this shot provides an opportunity to think about JWH's bodying with the room, the microphone, sound system, sound engineer and Hamilton. 'A Quiet Place' continues.

Once again the overly cool (grey) clips of John and Bob walking down a nearly deserted western street until they enter a restaurant with a return to the saturated colouring that has become a refrain for present-ness as the music cuts. Bob asks John if there is a tab at this restaurant. These kinds of transitions do not bring any attention from non-filmmakers because they seem seamless, like a continuity or flow that is natural. But there is nothing natural about the flow, there are precise cuts and timings that need to be ordered to create the cinematic experience of a seamless flow. The editing room is about interstices, the gaps between visual-image and sound-image and also the interstices between sound-image and sound-image, visual-image and visual-image. The timing between the end of the soundcheck instrumental and Hamilton's question is an event that makes an enormous difference. If it is too rushed or too slow, there are consequences. The words get cut off or there is a loss of forward momentum. But the placement of the sound-image is related to the visual-image in this case because Hamilton's physicality, his facial gestures as he speaks, needs to line up with the sound-image of him speaking. This is not always the case. It is possible to move sound-images around if there are not obvious gestures in the visual-image, to take speaking from some location and put it in another location, even if we are only speaking about a fraction of a second dislocation. But this is not possible in this event so the editing needs to move back from this event to prepare all of the events from the soundcheck to this moment in the restaurant as one envelope and all of the shots that make up this envelope need to make sense with each other relationally because I decided to avoid jump cuts in the audio and visual-images. Jump cuts are obvious cuts in what would have been a longer shot. The jump cut suppresses duration and allows the viewer to fill in what is missing, so that there is a jump from one point in space to another that disregards the duration of the movement. When it was first used, as in the famous jump cuts in Jean-Luc Godard's *Breathless*, they must have been quite a shock to an audience. Experienced as a break in continuity that must have been quick technological feeling and inauthentic. Today, however, jump cuts are very normal and are likely not even noticed.

Filmmaker bodying: There's a guy in the backseat with a chainsaw for an arm

John talks to the waiter about seating option and he is asked how many for lunch. He looks back at the camera and says, 'three'. This is a minor moment but one that reminds the audience of the existence of the camera filmmaker assemblage. The conceptual reason for me to include this scene is to remind the audience of this event, and to include them in this moment, to be included into the eventness of the in-folding of the film. Three he says. But I am only looking at two so that includes me. We are three. Or at least, I as the filmmaker make up three. But is this not also the body of the viewer in all of their individually, geographic and temporal locations. This minor event of three, both makes reference to camera unsettling the anonymity of the camera but also, and this is much less discussed in theory, includes into the bodying the crowd behind the lens, which I will discuss in more detail in a later chapter. For the time being, the crowd behind the lens is the metastability of camera operator and audience. During the making of films, I am usually asked how to treat my existence. Do I exist in the profilmic world or am I, as a filmmaker, a ghostly presence that is somehow magically haunting the action? The proverbial fly on the wall. But isn't this just a conceptual game that we play before the camera begins bodying. There is no escape from the camera more-than-human perception, no escape from the multitudes of perspectives that exist as virtualities in each shot, the virtualities of bodying in the future events of each shot. It is this quivering dense virtuality that produces in me the uncanny feeling of semblance. The event of the naming of the camera in the shot brings these virtualities into awareness perhaps, for the viewer that takes note. But for the camera operator, you are always both there and elsewhere. You are physically in the room standing behind John and Bob in a crowded restaurant. Your presence is not as a fly that few will notice, but as a cybernetic entity called filmmaker that everyone in the room understands. This is an *event*! Who are these two men being followed by a camera. In a capitalist attention economy this is already a statement of value, and this valuing changes everything in the room. Capital courses through the bodying informing each gesture. Eyes turn towards the camera shyly, brazenly, curiously. Those eyes are not on a camera with no awareness, they are on the filmmaker who is always conscious of their presence. A fly indeed! What utter nonsense. Jean Rouch often suggested that the camera is not passive but is an instigator, a disturber. I resonate with the suggestion that the camera is an operator in the virtualities of experience. It is important, I think, to resist the idea that the camera is an intruder, taints the action, obscures authenticity. Which is to suggest that there is some other authentic worlding that should have been in-folding had the camera not been present. In a post-film Q&A for one of my films, the band was asked about my cinematic approach. He asked the band if I was a 'fly on the wall' and the leader of the band laughed and said, 'It's kind of like there's this monster with a chainsaw for an arm sitting in the backseat. In the beginning it's a bit weird but eventually it's just: oh it's the guy with a chainsaw for an arm'. Certainly, in another timeline in the multiverse, if I went for lunch with John and Bob without a camera, it would have been a different event. So what! Why is that of any interest at all. It is such an obvious statement in the form of a critique. What is interesting to me is, on the contrary, what monstrous bodying event does the camera produce? What kind of cineworlding does the camera perhaps make possible? The camera is not just a provocateur, we are collectively cinematic world builders, cineworlding. Let us start there and ask what kinds of worlding events can we make together, instead of worrying about the way a camera taints some kind of constructed authenticity.

There is, in my experience, a moment when each person finally accepts the monster with a chainsaw for an arm. For Bob, it was immediately after lunch. When we leave the restaurant together, Hamilton unexpectedly turns to the camera and says: 'John's a pretty awesome walk racer . . . you should see him do his walk racing.' John takes Bob's prompt and charges off down the street impersonating a walk racer. He stops and charges back directly at the camera set to a soundtrack of cars passing and my laughter. There is a quick cut to later that night and John walking down the hallways towards the camera as other guests of the hotel walk between John, and the camera say, 'Hey there's guy with a camera there' where John responds, 'He's coming with you guys!' We walk together out of the hotel catching up, talking briefly about getting some rest before the show. As we walk out of the hotel into the night, the sounds of cars driving by, the street lights bouncing off the parked cars. John begins to confide to us about needing quiet time during the day to prepare for the show. It is the first moment of intimacy in the film and it changes the relationship to the audience. John is no longer being followed by the camera; we are now co-composing the film. I keep the camera running as John puts his guitar into the now familiar van and I ask, 'Do you feel touring a big emotional strain' and he takes a few moments and walks towards the camera and tells us a deeply personal story about how his ongoing desire to be playing music and touring made it increasingly difficult to be at home with his wife. He admitted that 'I was gone so much that when I got home I didn't know how to transition to being home again . . . I didn't know how to step out of the role of musician and performer into the role of husband and house owner . . . dishwasher and partner and all of those things.' Bodying is not about identity. JWH is not a single entity, he struggled with finding a way to adjust to the bodying that occurs on the road. The intensive forces that are organized into musician are different than the intensive forces organized into husband/homeowner. I think when *musician* gets treated as an identity, it misses important forces that are at play in the bodying of the touring musician.

These forces are not visualized directly and are not structural, they are intensive. John recognizes in this moment that he must find a way to navigate across intensive space, to move between bodying, the bodying of the touring musician and the bodying of the husband/homeowner/father/dishwasher. The extensive space of JWH does not change; what changes is his ability to connect with the affects of domestic life after being on the road so much. This suggests that extensive space is habitual, not structural. That what is called identity is a way of labelling extensive space, which is coursed through by intensive forces organizing in relation to an environment, bodying. John struggled with JWH to move between habits: 'It's still stressful but I don't have the anxiety about the transition the way I used to.' Hearing that it was a painful process, and remains a difficult process prepares us for the rest of the film with an awareness of the organization of intensive forces at work. What is it that JWH is shaped into while on the road that makes John's home life difficult? What is the extensive space called musician and how do intensives forces get shaped within these ecologies of practices and environments?

Conclusion: Fumbling into the Anarchive

Moving between scenes, technique and theory are conceptual excursions written to give some insight and background into the techne of cinematic research-creation. This allows access into the extensive emerging from intensives space and blends techne into the posthuman episteme of cinema-thinking. This avoids the way technology is often separated from the proper business of teaching and research spatially, and most problematically, by making it a space of technicians and not professors, craft and trade, not art and research. In an attempt to write against these separations I move between bodying John Wort Hannam, and the bodying of camera technology. Cineworlding operates in perceptual, conceptual, technological turbulence because it is always about movement and becoming, and in movement there are always forces coming in contact with forces. I believe one strategy to get beyond the documentation paradigm is to pay attention to what forces populate the abstract machine, the diagram we label musician, and we label filmmaker. In musicology, it is common to treat great composers as a diagram. In fact that is what the canon is, a collection of diagrams for how to apply compositional, or performance force to sound. In music studies, it is common to think about the becoming of a musician learning to play a musical form.[4] The becoming of their body, their bodying is shaped by the force of a diagram, often called style, genre, tradition. But, of course, one does not embody these exactly; one is active in bodying, to prepare their body for the application of the appropriate forces, at the appropriate times, for the appropriate conceptual, social and environmental reasons. In this we can see bodying is about psycho-social-environmental formations.

Each film in my practice is not meant to be a final testament or a definitive document of, in this case JWH, but instead to be a practice of becoming-with in this moment. It shares with the documentation paradigm an interest in sharing beyond the moment of the event, but differs with it in what matters most. Cineworlding is not oriented to scientific conclusion of the functions of culture, but is instead interested in seeding future events. It enacts what Erin Manning calls anarchive 'never in creating an account of our activities ... but in generating techniques for sharing the work's potential, the speculative edge of its pragmatic proposition. Our hope was to find a practice that would allow action traces that would become mobilized across other environment of collective experimentation' (2020: 76). Can JWH seed compositional practice, community music events, other films? This is the orientation of the anarchive. Its anarchival value is probably why JWH was selected to be used at American Songwriters Association meetings in the year after its release.

Cineworlding is anarchivist in that it provides an opportunity to follow the becoming of multiple diagrams simultaneously seeing JWH as both a becoming diagram and a component of a becoming diagram. The entanglement we begin to see is that becoming-musician is both a diagram and a content for another diagram. This begins to sketch out the intensive forces of becoming that JWH will be composing with, bringing the social into his compositional practice, being composed by the social, and in the intimate spaces on the road seeing the way the intimate works through the social. This focus on becoming allows viewers to follow along with the moment-to-moment innovations between people, provides accounts of the abstract machines at work, the more-than-human bodying that swarms through the world, attempting to get us beyond the documentary paradigm, and the humanist mode of thought that contributed to its formation.

7

Quartet 2 and affect vectoring

In Chapter 3, we followed Togni's beauty affect from the soundtrack of an old movie, the reterritorialization of four notes in a score, whose virtualities were deterritorialized and reterritorialized into the body of the conductor, the gestures that produced an assemblage of choir, accordionist, harpist, audience. The beauty affect vectored across the media of TV, score, Pro Coro Canada assemblage and ended with the question: Will the audience become vectored by the beauty affect? There is a second question that was also not answered: Does the cinema assemblage also become vectored by the beauty affect? To ask about the role of cinema as a vector of affect challenges the common idea of so-called observational cinema. As Grimshaw and Ravetz have noted: 'despite its frequent use as a general description, the meaning of observation within specific contexts of filmmaking practice has yet to be closely scrutinized' (2009: 26). In this chapter, I want to turn my attention to the audience. As Deleuze and Guattari note: 'The territorializing factor, must be sought elsewhere: precisely in the becoming-expressive of rhythm or melody, in other words, in the emergence or proper qualities (color, odor, sound, silhouette . . .). Can this becoming, this emergence, be called Art?' (1987: 316). An audience in this view is not a consumer of a performance but is instead reterritorialized within the growing machinic assemblage that 'hooks up' the audience as it machines mobile blocks of sound-colour-movement as percept that machines affect.

Paying attention to the place of an audience allows us to understand cinema-thinking and its artfulness: '*cinema itself is a new practice of images and signs, whose theory philosophy must produce as conceptual practice*' (Deleuze 1989: 280). In this way, we are continuing our interest in cinema production as practical musicology. What happens when we encounter a film? We are suspended together in a sensation-place between beginning and end: 'before a film image is anything, it is a physical presence. It is not knowledge. It is not enunciation. It is not a translation. It is not even a code. It is, in Deleuze's terms, an *utterable* but not yet an *utterance*' (MacDougall 2006: 270). As an alternative to film studies where a critic produces an analysis, the object of analysis in this chapter is a nooshock that made itself known quite dramatically. The nooschock was utterable, a desperate cry for the conclusion of an event as expression of intensive forces, but not yet an utterance of conceptually formation that signifies referential meaning. I believe the vocalizing of the intensive nooshock was the sound of the vectoring of affect.

The pub screening

The student pub is crowded and noisy. A cacophonous clinking melody of glass on glass, and rhythm of heavy glass bottoms on scuffed wood tabletops. The organizers for this graduate student event did not plan to have a private event. This is a room more full of Friday night sociality than academic intention. Exactly the kind of pedagogical environment that I cherish.

A screen stands tall, white and ignored at the end of the crowded room. Its dull white is silent still, not yet lit up, not yet speaking to anyone. The white square comes alive with a quavering violin note without warning, a harmonic above the noisy glassware. Black-and-white images of digital code over a calligraphy brush on grey paper. The title card reads *Dan Brophy: Quartet 2*. Some beer drinkers turn around to acknowledge the screen and then turn back to conversation. Others begin to recognize that something must be planned and look around for some clue as to what is beginning.

Twelve minutes later, a table full of frat boys will be standing up, some on chairs, hollering at the screen 'finish it, finish it!!' bodies riddled with tension, affected by audio-vision, desiring a conclusion and fulfilment that will not be given. This audio-vision event holds back on the edge of satisfaction, making the edge sharper, a consequence of an affect field that vectors through attentive bodies in the room. *Quartet 2* never reaches climax, never falls into the body's expected cadence. The desire for cadence is a desire for completeness. A completeness that disperses the preacceleration. Instead, *Quartet 2* avoids becoming complete, signified on the white wall of cadence, it bends instead towards the black hole. The bending sends shockwaves of affect through the audience. Each shock wave is the consequence of the awakening of 700 years of Western tonal music. The denial is both a holding back and a gift. It is not a negation but a proliferation, drawing out hordes of dancing dead composers who rise in the body like Michael Jackson's thrilling zombies. Each zombie demands a cadence in its own way, to write on the white wall a proper name. The audience attentively awaiting the audiovisual closure that must be coming. It MUST be coming. It MUST FINISH!

The vocal urges to 'finish it' testify to the presence of virtualities. The filmmaker, actors and composer share the same urge for completion, can feel the audience's desperation as their own. These rules are not the privilege of musicologist nor music theorists, this motley audience of engineers, sociologists, geologists, business and management students know very well the rules of tonal music. They know the faciality of refrains, they are musicologists enough. The visual incompletion does not require a semiotic analysis to be understood, the audience are film scholars enough, as the white wall black hole tensions are played out on screen. They express their joyful displeasure with incompletion, the breaking of rules. To break a rule is a denial—a rule itself living virtually as a circuit in the body-social worlding desiring its own form of consummation—that is not a lack or gap, but an explosive nooshock vectoring bodies.

The audience does not see the screen and then hear the music, there is no simple division. Audio-vision is a heterogeneous event, a refrain of rhythmic flows unfolding and folding in time-space. It is hard to say where it begins or if it ends. *Quartet 2* is not a film about music, it is music. It is constituted by sonic-visual-affective *events* in excess of what is usually characterized as music,[1] a territorializing *refrain* that is constituted by bodies, technologies, environments, actualities and virtualities. The relationship between events and refrains is full of potentialities. *Quartet 2* is a music video and a laboratory. It provides an opportunity for video production to become music, and for music to become vision.[2]

Cineworlding refrains

For the last fifteen years, I have been using generations of visual technologies, new and old, to study refrains. There are no longer any technological obstacles in the way of cinematic research-creation. All the necessary technology is currently available. But there does seem to be an obstacle. Cinematic research methods traditionally, because of expense, difficulty in peer review and lack of institutional support, have not been widely embraced by the academy. Anthropology has done the most to develop cinematic research methods in the form of ethnographic film (Barbash and Taylor 1997; Crawford and Turton 1992; Grimshaw and Ravetz 2009; Heider 2006). New developments in the digital cinema ecosystem, however, have so far been little examined. The digital cinema ecosystem, emerging since 2009, is comprised of relatively inexpensive digital cameras and audiovisually enabled smart phones, free professional-level digital editing platforms, a worldwide network of film festivals, and the transformation of most art house cinemas to digital projection. This means that digital cinema produced on a laptop can be screened anywhere.[3] There has never been a better time to make scholarly informed cinema, so why is cinema so rarely produced by scholars?[4]

Since the 2009 emergence of the digital cinema ecosystem, there has not yet been a method book on digital cinema production methods in research. In 2018, Benjamin Harbert published *American Music Documentary: Five Case-Studies in Cine-ethnomusicology*. His focus was on documentary filmmakers working primarily in the film medium. This has been a significant contribution to blurring the separation between music researchers and music filmmakers. However positive its contribution, it remained historical with no section examining the possibilities of digital cinema ecology, and while it looked towards film studies, it remained located in ethnomusicology.

In 2019, a pre-conference symposium was held at the Society for Ethnomusicology. It was an exciting day of papers and panels on activist and community engagement using cinema, but the technology itself remained separate from theory. There were no papers or presentations that examined the specificities and opportunities of digital production methods and only one activity focused on the materials of digital production. This setting aside of the technological from the knowledge production paper sessions plays out the separation between techne and episteme. So while social science cinema is slowly emerging, it is perhaps necessary to reflect on Nietzsche's warning that 'some values are born old and from the time of their birth exhibit their conformity, their conformism, their inability to upset any established order' (Deleuze 2001: 81), that the potentials of digital cinema production for social science study may treat digital cinema as if it was film production, with all of its forms and limits.

There is a second important issue. There were no music videos. Cine-ethnomusicology remains inside the ethnographic/observational documentary form because perhaps it has been legitimated. However, a great deal has been done by scholars working in new materialism, process philosophy, posthumanism, and the multispecies feminism of Donna Haraway that have challenged the very subject of humanist documentary and ethnography. The work challenges both the tempocentrism (privileging the past and ethnographic present) and anthropocentrism (human exceptionalism) as a consequence of privileging the ethnos. It is not enough to use digital cinema for scholarship, it is necessary to think the emergence of posthumanography, to realize that the social science researcher has always been a pen and paper cyborg and it is now emerging as a cyborg with an externally networked memory of audio-vision.

I do not want to apply cinematic research-creation to music by basing it on old ideas and limitations, the emergence of a new idea being born old. 'Posthumanographer' is the term I propose for a cinematic researcher that has a technic self-awareness that reaches beyond the Ethnos, beyond the Anthropos, that also has as its goal a contribution to knowledge about making a life and a life in art. These ecological and technological questions are pressing.

Towards technocultural ecological studies

The emergence of cinematic research-creation is occurring at the same time as posthuman scholarship (Berardi 2011, 2015; Braidotti 2013; Brier 2008; Fiol 2010), what does that offer? It seems at the very least that we are challenged to develop a cinematic process that move beyond discourse, beyond the subject, beyond the objectivity of functionalism and the subjectivity of phenomenology. My intention with this book is to begin to lay a foundation for an approach to digital cinema production for social science-art entanglement that is framed neither by older ideas of culture nor by the textual analysis of critical theory, but by a production orientation to 'worlding' (Heidegger 1962; Haraway 2016), inclusive of the worlding of technics, what I have begun calling *cineworlding*.

New concepts allow researchers to move forward while also re-reading the past. My notion of cineworlding was born of my desire to understand the cinematic research-creation model that I have been developing (see, MacDonald 2020a,b,c). Cineworlding, as I have shown, is constituted by three assemblages (territorial assemblage, production assemblage, screen assemblage). This provides a posthuman ecological (techno-eco-subjective-cultural) model for screen production that is engaged in thinking-feeling the many traditional binaries and new hyphenations.

Worlding, from Heidegger to Haraway, has moved through a variety of stages. First, an ecological model was presented that was concerned about an organism in its environment (Bateson 1972a,b, 1979, 1987). This model was followed by a second-order cybernetic model which recognizes that the subject constructs models of itself within a system, it was not just understanding, but understanding-understanding (VonForester 2003, 2014; Maturana and Varela 1987). It was concerned with autopoiesis, the self-making of the being, self-organization in an ecology of other systems. These models were ecological and oriented to an analysis of the individual subject, fitting well with the inherited models of individual subjecthood, the volitional-intentionality-agency triad. New approaches suggest that the idea of *being* and *subject* have always been immersed and cut through by other systems, that thinking about the human individual makes little sense. We are never truly alone. Sympoiesis (Haraway 2016: 58), the recognition that nothing makes itself, allows us to rethink the discourse-ideology-hegemony model that has long informed cultural studies. Sympoiesis 'is a word proper to complex, dynamic, responsive, situated, historical systems. It is a word for worlding-with' (Haraway 2016: 58). Haraway suggests *holobiont* as a word that signifies symbiotic assemblages 'at whatever scale of space or time' (Haraway 2016: 60). Taking this kind of ecological orientation to music studies may propose many new kinds of interactions as we begin to let go of 'possessive individuals and zero-sum games' (60). Sympoiesis goes beyond the *command and control* ideas implicit in cybernetic systems to embrace distributed systems and collectively producing that 'do not have self-defined spatial or temporal boundaries' (60). These distributive becoming-with are not determinant and fixed but are open to evolutionary change. Sympoiesis is challenging and exciting because it produces all sort of assemblages, entanglements and knots, and moves by transmission, infection, ingestion and gestation. Cineworlding suggests that we are not documenting, but becoming-with: vectoring, machining.

Cineworlding is inspired by Donna Haraway's exuberant entangled worldings, 'finished once and for all with Kantian globalizing cosmopolitics and grumpy human-exceptionalist Heideggerian worlding' (Haraway 2016: 11). Worlding is 'a particular blending of the material and the semiotic that removes the boundaries between subject and environment, between persona and topos. Worlding affords the opportunity for the cessation of habitual temporalities and modes of being' (Palmer and Hunter 2018). Cineworlding follows flows and becomes part of the flow dissolving its distance. The music video, fiction film or documentary film become part of the scene it sought to analyse. The flow of the research-creation event extends analysis becoming part of the musicking it set out to understand, moving through a technosphere like a tagged salmon, making technosphere technocultural ecological studies possible.

We have always been worlding cyborgs

Cineworlding is not new,[5] it is as old as sound cinema. We may recognize that our 'new' innovations are the intentional entangling of social science with art – called research-creation in Canada – but we must also recognize that this has been around for quite a long time. In music studies, questions about what ethnomusicological film *is* are just the type of question that researchers have long grappled (Feld 1976). MacDougall has identified 'a shift from word-and-sentence-based anthropological thought to image-and-sequence-based anthropological thought' (1998: 292) as being an important observation for the difference in method. And while there is a history to be followed, these scholarly films have generally kept to themselves. They circulated in established 'ethnographic film festivals' remained committed to scholarly territorialization (university-as-settlement) and have ignored or kept a distance from developments in documentary cinema and cinema more generally.

Over the last fifteen years of making films, my approach has been, like MacDougall's before me, to 'develop alternative objectives and methodologies' (MacDougall 1998: 293) that pay attention to challenges posed to disciplinary borders (Russell 1999, 2018). I once believed that an ethnomusicological film is a film that an ethnomusicologist makes. But I have abandoned this naïve position recognizing that a 'critical cinema of music' (Harbert 2018: 246) requires a specific engagement with the articulation of methodology, the elaboration of an appropriate method that realizes an appropriate form of cinema that can either stand as a document, or to use a Deleuzian term, a machine of expression. I agree with Pink's suggestion that there is no essential hierarchy between mediums (print, film, photography), but only questions of appropriateness of methods (2013: 10). Centrally, the question is when is it best to use cinematic research-creation to study music?

Cinematic research-creation

Research-creation recognizes that making art is already research, and the outcomes of research are creative objects. Cinematic research-creation focuses on research entanglements with a film's planning, making and sharing. Each film becomes a collection of events, produces refrains for the exploration of cinematic-thinking-feeling of music to 'question anew the relation between technics and sense, and to reassess this difference for the age of the technological condition' (Hörl 2017: 5). Popular music and the youth cultures, for instance, have always been entwined with audiovisual technology (MacDonald 2022). Cinematic research-creation embraces fiction film, music video and documentary film forms as research processes and outcomes. This opens technological creative processes, technics and technocultures, to something more than participant observation. Making films and music videos is not a documentation approach (as illustrated in the last previous chapters) that attempts to keep distance but instead transforms research into creative works that flow through both the creative industries and the artistic undercommons. As Erin Manning has pointed out, the undercommons is 'a field of relation fabulated at the interstices of the now and the not-yet' (Manning 2016: 221), the *event*, (2013, 2014) and the *minor gesture* (2016) that can provide cinematic research-creation a way of thinking-feeling music. The relation between the undercommons, capitalism and the university is an ethical and political question as much as an ecological one. Perhaps cinematic research-creation can provide a useful method for these studies?

CineWorlding is therefore not about documenting music in order to understand what it is, but instead, it is about following music as it makes audiovisual technology a territorial refrain, constituted with its vibratory flows. It is about following these flows and becoming-with them, a cartography of the pathways along which music flows, and the assemblages that are constituted by its refrains. What does music do when it grabs hold of a refrain, when it flows out to initiate an event that once again, or continuously, constitutes refrains? Does a refrain move like a forest fire sending out audiovisual spark-signs that catch in fertile bio-technological spaces? Does it move along vectors as an infection?

Infectious vectors

Let us take a moment to reflect on the opening example from Chapter 1. A person walking home from a voting station on election day hears a person on the other side of the street obsessively yelling, 'We don't need no education'. These coded vibrations emanate from a living source at some distance producing a sound field.

A second person walks into that field and is vibrated, the vibrations unfold a memory of a song. It is incorrect, however, to say that there is a single memory. In this case, there is a rushing to the surface of a complexity of past events that exist inert in the body, like a multisided crystal that shows on each facet a chain of past events that emerge as a consequence of the nooshock of hearing. The memories are virtual and real and the affect shocked into existence by the vibrational field unfolds Pink Floyd's signature guitar riff from *The Wall* and the pace of the walker falls in time, not with the person yelling, but with the full thrust of the song.

As the walker continues along the street, their metabolism is adjusted by *The Wall*, its beats per minute constitute a territoriality in the body. All the way home, the walker grooves to the music. The walker is worn by the music, it is not their music but a territory that is shaping their metabolism. As Deleuze and Guattari remind us: 'These qualities are signatures . . . not the constituted mark of a subject, but the constituting mark of a domain' (1987: 316). *The Wall* grooves down the street and finds its way out onto the home stereo system filling up the apartment, the house. Extending the territoriality of the refrain. The next day it fills up a music classroom as a discussion of an event, and now onto this page, perhaps you are now worn by *The Wall*. *The Wall* is resonant for those who have heard it, but it is not for those who have not. For those who have been infected, it lives in the body. The infection is not a given, the power does not live in the music itself, but in the refrain that gets territorialized in the body.

In this example, the refrain illustrates three aspects or sides: a centre of expression, a territoriality, and an openness to the future (Deleuze and Guattari 1987: 310–23). Each of these sides is constituted by virtual and actual resources that blur a distinction between a pure event and a pure refrain. The event is constituted by extensions, by intensive qualities, and by self-enjoyment (Deleuze 1993: 86–9). Each event vibrating virtual grains of experience and adding grains of experience, a vibratory fluxing reterritoriality of becoming-wall.

Undercommons of the enlightenment

Back in the beery bar room that opened this chapter, the temperature continues to increase. The voices increase in both amplitude and desire, a collection of tables becoming swept up in the heat generated by *Quartet 2*'s continual denial of cadence. The painter looks over their shoulder playfully at the camera, at the audience, at you. She goes back to work painting a white canvas black.

She continues to paint around the thickening square of black paint that frames the smallest white square, indifferent to your desire for it to be completed. Denying your desire for completion, each stroke an affective force that stirs your body. In a kitchen, the painter sits on a countertop applying make-up and smoking a cigarette. She never finishes. The kitchen filling up with other people drinking cocktails and getting more and more in our way, filling up the frame except for the small square, the frame within the frame, that we must strain to see if the make-up application will ever end. Back and forth, two black-and-white scenes of painting never find completion. The sonic lines of the music never meeting up to find closure. They get so very close and then the cadence falls apart and an instrument breaks out on its own line of flight. And with its departure goes any chance that this time there will be closure. Each gathering of rhythm suggests a cadence is coming, a tingling heaviness that signals the rush of a cadence, the gravity of cadence, the final signifiance of the white wall. Suddenly an instrument rushes off along a line of flight dispersing the thickening tension, the denial sends a shock wave through the audience. The energy of its departure is the energy of its lack of completion. 'Finish IT!!', a young man yells. Despite the micro-fascism for closure that erupts in this beer hall putsch, completion continues to be denied. Beer is spilled and voices raised, struggling with the screen and already deeply drawn into its refrain.

They do not, as Kant's audience does, take a step back to critically reflect on what is occurring. This is a full-bodied participation, being vectored by a refrain, perhaps even against their will. In disregard for its unplanning, an event erupts. What joy if this could be done in a classroom. But Kant's ghost is always standing at the door maintaining/policing this social/passional order that is always kept at a safe distance, intellectualized/an-aesthetized. But not at this moment. We are in the 'undercommons of the enlightenment' (Harney and Moten 2013: 26) celebrating the strange vectoring of *Quartet 2*'s audiovisual non-completion, enacting a pedagogy beyond teaching space, celebrating our entrainment with audio-vision, the event of becoming swept away into a refrain.

Study

In the underground of the enlightenment, *study* is exuberant and unruly. *Quartet 2* was a study of music's visuality, and visuality's musicking and audio-vision's affects. Spinoza defines affect as being the power to affect and be affected.

Massumi explains that the so-called affective turn should not be understood to move beyond language, or image, or gesture or whatever to focus on affect as a thing in itself, but instead, to recognize that affect is already on the table (2015: 150), already at work in language, image, gesture and that affect 'is a way of focusing on the germinal modes of activity that factor into events as they are just beginning . . . to think through the implications of relational fields, and the potential we might find there' (Massumi 2015: 151). What is this potential we might find in the research-creation event? Is this entertainment or a laboratory of affect? Is this beery barroom screening scholarship? Is this research-creation study? Does this act of writing rescue the event for scholarship, absolve me of my sins as an artist? Do I need your absolution?

I feel I need to confess to believing that I have been continually infected by the affect vectors of what we call music. Perhaps it is best to not say believe. One does not believe something when one has a visitation. The visitation is the proof, it is the event that lays the foundation for a testament. Critics may suggest that one believes, but the so-called believer has seen-felt the possession with their own bodies. And as a consequence of the visitation of the vectoring of affect, I can no longer publicly support the claim that music is 'a work'. It is not a lineage of proper names nor genres. These do not explain why music seems to have no beginning, no boundaries, no borders. Music moves not by pathways or lines but by vectors and its spread can be mapped only after it has moved on. It cannot be captured and stilled, it is not a thing, it is more than a verb, it is not linguistic. Music is neither a social/cultural function nor a phenomenological experience, but both and neither. Its eventness, for it is a being, gathers and draws together semiotic resources into territorial refrains. Vibrating pools left behind as music moves by vectors through bodies and technologies, creating halobionts on many scales from a single person in their living room to massive events. These resources can be of any kind because music-as-refrain is a pre-signifying semiotic and the refrain uses other regimes of signs, bodies and technologies as its host. Music-as-refrain is rhythmic-movement-as-life. Its appearance is an in-folding of materials that comes into form but its form is constantly shifting, sending off sparks of particle-signs. Music did not invent the refrain but it grabs onto it.

The event of screening *Quartet 2* was at the end of a series of events, of studies with affect. The noisy response from a table of students was a kind of proof that *Quartet 2* was dealing in something that was yet unaccounted for. Affect vectored from the composer through the recording ensemble, through the music video composition, to the filming, through the editing suite, through the projector and surfaced in the bodies of the spectators. It is not a function of culture, an expression of socialization, but a vectoring of affect that indeed uses these as its resources.

Perhaps we do not need affect theory to legitimate it. In an interview somewhere Billy Corgan of the Smashing Pumpkins noted that his job is to emanate energy off of the performance stage, and then receive energy back from the audience so that the band can take that returned energy and blow it up. Perhaps affect theory recognizes what performers become enthralled by, perhaps addicted to. Being a dramatic conduit for the vectoring of affect, turning over one's life to the refrain is a powerful experience of becoming something beyond human. Or perhaps realizing that one's reality is not as subject but as relationality. Music-as-refrain has been called mystical, cosmic, perfect.

Study of becoming-node and vectoring

Quartet 2 infected me. On my first listen, there was an event of deciding that it must live another life as a music video. The refrain installed itself in a seed of audio-vision, not fully realized, but becoming, sprouting rhizomatic connections. Deleuze and Guattari describing how early twentieth-century psychiatry defined delusion as a

> decisive external occurrence, by a relation with the outside that is expressed more as an emotion than an idea and more as effort or action than imagination; by a limited constellation operating in a single sector; by a 'postulate' or 'concise formula' serving as the point of departure for a linear series or proceeding that runs its course, at which point a new proceeding begins. (1987: 120)

This description of delusion expressed for me a precise example of the power of the experience of the becoming of a film, how music refrained audio-vision, and transformed me into a node, through the technical process of filmmaking, in-folding light and sound, to vector through the bodies of the audience: 'Finish It!'

Herzog recognizes this process when he says that film ideas arrive fully formed struggling to overcome other virtual films. The virtual film that wins the battle over the other virtual films is the one that demands to be made. Federico Fellini described his entanglement with the virtual in relation to his experience with LSD, an experience that for him was unremarkable compared to living artfully inside cinema. Is the experience of visionary seeing-hearing expressed in cinema closely linked to hallucination, or delusion? Is the becoming of audio-vision a type of trance, a cinema trance as Jean Rouch describes it? A cinema trance that is the becoming of a type of possession? Is it possible to call oneself an author when one is possessed? The possession/infection/affect vectors through production, into the screening, into subsequent viewings, into other works, onto this digital sheet of paper, printed onto this piece of paper sometime in my future, your past, vectoring affect of an open reader's present.

This process, full of questions, is what I am calling cineworlding, a visionary possession of virtualities where the world-in-becoming moves through intuition and artfulness entangled with the development of techniques, expressed through a technological medium of digital cinema, film, music or writing. Where subjectivation is inseparable from media, what Bernard Stiegler calls *technics*. Something that Washboard Hank describes in the opening of a film we made together, as being like religion but many tens of thousands of years older.[6] Making art is to develop techniques to immerse oneself with immanence, biosphere-technics simultaneously, to see-hear worldings through and with a technical extension. The flow and flux of worlding the world. This is what I mean by cineworlding; it is not only a technique of cinematic research-creation, a posthumanography, but a way of living study artfully.

Cinematic research-creation as study

So what of *study*? I use this term in two senses. The first is musical. A study is a composition that is focused on developing a technique. In the process of learning the study, itself already fully musical/refrain, in the outflowing of the refrain and in-folding of technique becomes more developed. The study has two sides. One that is oriented to an audience and one side that is oriented to the bodying of the pianist. In music, the study is not inferior aesthetically, but it is also never divorced from its complicity of developing technique. A study is about technique, and technique is about study. A study vectors bodying.

The second sense of study is developed by Erin Manning who brings Moten and Harney's idea of study as 'the crafting of problems' (2016: 11) together with research-creation's 'inherent transversality' (2016: 27). Challenging the theory-practice split, Manning focusing on the hyphenation between research-creation, thinking the hyphen as 'a way' (2016: 47), that 'proposes singular forms of knowledge which may not be intelligible within current understandings of what knowledge might look like' (2016: 27). Research-creation as *a way of study* 'creates an opening for what Moten and Harney conceptualize as the undercommons' (2016: 27). The study dissolves the distinction between theory and practice, research and creation, in-folding these into the refrain as it moves/lives. Study has the character of what Deleuze and Guattari call the white wall and the black hole. The white wall is a surface upon which the study is inscribed in audio-vision and the black hole is the subjectivation that is developing. Practising study is to embrace *a way* that disregards the policing of discipline and focuses instead on becoming. What can study do? What can music do? What can the body do? What can the audiovisually enabled body do?

The enunciation of 'Finish it!' affected me in two ways. The first was the realization that affect continued its movement from Dan Brophy, through me, through the audiovisual process and through the bodies of the audience. It was the vectoring of affect. But perhaps, more important, the event recalled the joy of study before the classroom, before the graduate seminar, before the journal essay and harkened back to the 2 am sci-fi reading group. This is an event and is fresh and alive. But I did not have the language then to even begin to deal with it. It continued resonating in my body, instigating more study, more films, more reading, more thinking. It vectored a path to Massumi and Manning, to Harney and Moten. 'Study' is a word that captures both the development of technique and 'the way', the becoming of an artist-scholar, the becoming of a research-creation practitioner, a posthumanographer interested in following vectors of affect and all that constitutes these in-folding nodes.

To say 'a way' is to recognize the convergence of artistic techniques and one's life in becoming. Deleuze theorized 'a life' as immanence/creativity. A life is the becoming of living, the constant differentiation and change that is the energy of forces that is the in-event of living. Study is folded into 'a life' as Foucault recognized with the techniques of self. Technics, as Bernard Stiegler recognized, are not separate from a life either. Technology is a definitional component of human life. There is no human without technics. Recognizing the cybernetic condition of humanness sees mnemonic technologies like graphic and literary traces – now audio and visual recording – as setting up conditions for the emergence of subjectivation, sociality, psychology and environmental relational nodes. Guattari proposed thinking transversally along the three ecologies psychic, social, environmental. Stiegler adds technology as a fourth ecology.

This is the refrain that we had begun to construct in the first chapters. Our study with Pro Coro and now with *Quartet 2* has allowed us to sketch out aspects of the refrain which were only a horizon in Chapter 1. Now we can see much more precisely in our reality what was only social science fiction in Chapter 1.

This way (only *a way* and never *the* way) is the development of an assemblage/agencement of techniques working transversally entangling four ecologies, a point where four vectors cross. The cybernetic entity called the filmmaker always already populated by virtualities stretching out into a past and the future will be considered in upcoming chapters. Virtuality, in a Deleuzian sense, is the pastness and futurity of an event. There is a great deal to this. Virtuality is also influenced by Whitehead's potentiality and prehension, and Donna Haraway's more-than-human entanglements. Each cinematic study is audio-vision's becoming – a becoming-as-event that always constitutes and is constituting an entanglement of ecologies. The audio-vision event does not require writing to make it legitimate, to rescue it from its degradation as entertainment or art. The artist think-acts philo-technologically, *a way* is artistic praxis. Thinking audio-vision is research already. Research-creation is not a rubric to be thrown over this work to capture it for scholarly circulation. Rather, we are sneaking into the hyphenation between research and creation, and inspired by Moten and Harney constituting an undercommons, a joyful late-night pedagogical adventure far away from the deadening an-aesthetics of conference, class and seminar. The writing is called forth by its unfolding, written in spite of not having time. Not to explain something but to continue vibrational life, a rhythmic existential ongoingness. Each written study is a continuation of a way, philosophically unfolding of the layers of technique-subjectivation-composition. *A way* is cinematic research-creation, cineworlding music.

8

Crystal image in cinematic research-creation

Pimachihowan

Prologue

'No', he said in his characteristically deep voice, as he continued to show me the way to the outhouse nestled at the edge of a stand of birch trees. 'You can't separate music from the rest of what you are here to film.' Characteristic of Nehiyaw lifeways, and Indigenous lifeways more generally, methods that seek to separate out one activity from its relationality to others is frowned upon. Insistently I followed up, 'What about telling me about Cree aesthetics?' Thinking that maybe from this angle I could get an ethnomusicological foothold. Without missing a beat Conroy said with a soft chuckle, 'Take off your shoes and walk around in the woods for two weeks.' I felt disheartened. How am I going to make a film that will be meaningful for ethnomusicologists if we are not able to talk about music directly? He was blocking my learned attempts at separating out music from the world, a practice of bracketing. He was encouraging instead that I open myself to the relational thinking of the land: 'It's like this, iskotew (fire), it doesn't start on itself, it needs you and I.' Like the fire that is central to the scene from *Pimachihowan* that will be the focus of this chapter, music emerges from a set of relations.

Thinking relationally is not owned, is not identitarian, is itself open to sets of relations of relations. My interest is not to document Cree thought, but instead to enact a treaty ethnomusicology, a research-creation practice of *Etuaptmumk* or 'two-eyed seeing',[1] Western and Nehiyaw modes of relational thinking, that engender thinking-relationality-together in the ecotone of process philosophy and *Pimachihowan*. Conroy's initial gentle prohibitions and his invitation for thinking together encouraged an opening up of a thinking-feeling space for research-creation practice which have seeded techniques of 'artfulness' (Manning 2016: 46–63), cineworlding.

The approach that I am developing does not intend to convince the viewer of something but is instead an invitation to enter into a thinking-feeling space. It is not possible to work relationally and have the cinematic form remain unchanged, remaining in the 'perspicuous mode, favoring clarity over experience. Sensation often explained rather than felt' (Harbert 2018: 5). As reviewers have noted on previous versions of this chapter, the location of music in the film is not at all clear, nor is the film's relationship to ethnomusicology, as there are only three pieces of music in the entire film, no discussion with musicians and no music performance. Feedback from readers has helped me clarify the thinking-feeling in duration of *Pimachihowan*, a research-creation process that began by taking serious intuition (Manning 2016: 47): 'Intuition is rather the movement by which we emerge from our own duration, by which we make use of our own duration to affirm and immediately to recognize the existence of other durations' (Deleuze 1991: 33). This chapter will seek to clarify, or perhaps better, to explain and defend a 'cinematic way of theorizing music' (Harbert 2018: 5).

From documentary production to research-creation

We sat together drinking coffee at the Sewepagaham family home at Little Red River Cree Nation in what settler Canadians call northern Alberta. Conroy Sewepagaham, Dr David Lertzman and I had been struggling for over a year to make some progress on our film. The initial plan was to make an instructional film for the University of Calgary's Haskayne School of Business, to provide an opportunity for MBA students destined for work in the Alberta Oil and Gas industry to understand the perspective of Indigenous people in northern Alberta. Over the previous months we had attempted to film Conroy in an interview style, to make a conventional documentary about David's research on sustainability in the Oil and Gas sector. Each attempt at an interview fell apart. It was starting to feel that a direct interview about Pimachihowan, the Nehiyaw existential practice for living-well, was not possible. Over hours of conversation, and months of meetings, we were getting no closer. On this morning we decided that instead of controlling the filming situation Conroy would author the situation.

A day later, finishing our coffee and conversation in the late morning sun that characterizes northern Alberta winters, Conroy said we are ready. Without any explanation or discussion, we collected our gear and jumped into the truck. Not knowing what was coming was not unusual to my filmmaking practice. I had already been used to making road films, following musical groups and filming long segments that I was drawn to, following my intuition. This observational documentary approach is always exciting because it opens an improvisational field less oriented to an outcome, because you rarely know what is happening, and as a consequence one is more open to the play of the world through the viewfinder and microphone.

Conroy pulled off the snow-packed dirt road and parked the truck. Without explanation he walked into the woods with David close to his heels. As Conroy and David crossed the snowy threshold of clearing-becoming-Boreal Forest, I began to feel that Conroy was introducing us – an us that is quite virtual as a consequence of the audiovisual recording – to the relational thinking that he had introduced to David, and then later to me when I joined the project, which I will discuss in detail later. We held back with the camera to watch the event of Conroy and David disappear into the canopy. It would be an image of transition, perhaps, even as it risks falling into cliché. A force began to gather in the audiovisual field, something was happening, and just like a musical improvisation, it was necessary to relax into it, let it move one's technologically enhanced body. This is the 'ciné-trance' (Rouch 2003).

When we caught up to them, Conroy was telling David about the moose tracks in the snow. Where the moose came from, where he had gone, how big he was. David was an impatient student eager to share what he knew and letting us know that 'we are in nursery school right now'. Once again this 'us'. Who is this 'us' that I am compelled to call into existence? Surely it is the 'us' who are all gathered in this snowy forest, but the camera equipment is also there. The camera equipment is a stand-in for others, a portal that enhances the virtuality of this moment, not a passive recording technology but an 'instigating camera' (Rouch 2003).

Deleuze and Guattari provide a way of thinking about the relation between the actual and the virtual. The virtual is the pastness and futureness of the actual, 'a thing's destiny and condition of existence' (Massumi 1992: 37). Not a duality but a heterogeneous relation. The actual is surrounded by a cloud of virtual. Perhaps what is instigated by the camera is both the multiplication of the virtual, and the collapsing of the actual-virtual into a circuit.

In Jeff Todd Titon's discussion (1992) of his film *Powerhouse of God*, he describes a scene where the film crew shows up at the house of the preacher planning to film him mowing the lawn (93). But when they arrive, he is dressed in fancy clothes and the camera crew decide that this is not an authentic shot.

When I first read this passage, I felt a sadness that they had not shot the scene of John mowing the lawn in a suit and tie. Not only would it have been cinematically glorious but it would have also inverted the gaze, subverting what I call the ethnographic law of simple correspondence, a correspondence preserved in the observational documentary. Don't look at the camera, because this camera isn't supposed to be here. We are preserving the audience's anonymity, preserving your authenticity, an illusion to ourselves that we are a fly on the wall, that no one knows living is performing. We cannot allow our ethnographic science to be polluted with performance, we want to maintain the unified distant and authoritative gaze of the Dēmos surveilling the Ethnos.

But wearing fancy clothes is an 'event' (Deleuze 1993: 86) where John-of-the-future will be there with you, in the theatre dressed as you are now, mowing the lawn on the cinematic plane,[2] the event of John-of-the-past-who-saw-the-future. The virtuality of the scene, had Titon filmed the event, would have unleashed significant forces of disruptive creativity. The virtuality of the image of the John as time-travelling-lawn-mowing-protagonist, both in the here and now while the camera rolls, and in a future theatre when the projector rolls, would tear apart the ethnographic law of simple correspondence. John splits into parts: John-of-the-future, John-of-the-past-prepared for-the-future, John-meeting-you-in-the-future he prepared for. Perhaps this is why Titon could not film this scene. It is not a lack of authenticity, but an excess of creativity. The virtuality of John's performance would have critically disrupted the logic of the ethnographic gaze. But is there indeed any ethnographic law of simple correspondence? or is this another way of maintaining the machinery of whiteness, the policing of complexity and virtuality, the need to ensure that John remain an informant, to not become a protagonist in this, his existential dramaturgy of which the film team is part but not author?

Conroy breaks branches off of fallen trees as David follows behind him commenting about the oils that make these branches good fire starter. The crunch of the snow at −40° Celsius and the sharp snap of breaking branches fill the cold air. Conroy settles in a space and lays the collected branches in a pile. He takes off a glove and pulls out some pieces of the glove's synthetic fur lining. He stuffs the small bunches deep into the small pile of branches. David asks, 'Conroy, while you're doing this can you say something about Pimachihowan?' Conroy rubs his cold hands together and without looking up replies: 'We're doing it right now.'

With this statement, Conroy opens up a space for thinking-feeling cinematic research-creation and poses a wordless question: Will you, the filmmaking team, watch and listen, and be open to what you are about to experience? Will you notice that the lesson I want to share with you is about duration and patience? To enter into Conroy's space means to move from ethnographic film to research-creation.

Research-creation

Research-creation is not a theory or a methodology (Manning 2016: 40). It was introduced in Canada as a funding-category[3] but 'research-creation does much more than what the funding agencies had in store for it' (Manning 2016: 27), it is 'more dynamic than method, open to the shift caused by repetition, engaged by the ways in which bodies change, environments are modulated and modulating, and ecologies are composed' (Manning 2016: 40). It is becoming oriented to thinking-feeling the techniques and technics of the four ecologies (conceptual, social, technological, environmental), where the environment is always imbricated in the social, conceptual and technological, and where each works transversally on the others. Research-creation blurs its founding terms and recognizes that 'technique is necessary to the art of thought – thought in the act – but it is not art in itself' (40). It is the 'conjunction', the hyphen between research and creation where 'modes of knowledge are always at cross-currents with one another, actively reorienting themselves in transversal operations of difference, emphasizing the deflection at the heart of each conjunction . . . asking how the thinking in the act can be articulated, and what kind of analogous experience it can be coupled with, asking how a making is a thinking in its own right, asking *what else that thinking can do*' (41, italics added), because 'what is at stake is the very redefinition of knowledge' (41). Thinking cine-ethnomusicology through research-creation threatens the disciplinary borders of ethnomusicology, not from the outside by a power attempting to collapse it but from inside, a creative force that may bring about new ways of thinking music through cinema. It is also not the imposition of art practice on ethnomusicology but an expansion of what counts as ethnomusicology, by 'rethinking how artistic practice reopens the question of what disciplines can do' (27).

For a number of years after finishing *Pimachihowan*, I treated it as a special film that I made, but not an example of cine-ethnomusicology. Research-creation practice has convinced me, however, that I have been trying to avoid facing its consequences for ethnomusicology. Research-creation occurs in the hyphen, not as the binding of two objects, but as thinking-feeling that lives in the interstices between the practices. Cineworlding and then posthumanography emerged out of the vibrating enotikon between research and creation.

While Conroy lights the fire, he begins speaking in Nêhiyawêwin and, then switching to English, says:

> We take care of things, we respect things. One of the biggest teachings of Pimachihowan is that when you respect the environment, you respect yourself, and when you respect yourself, you respect the environment. It's not like that very much these days . . . we forgot . . . we forgot . . . we forgot to respect ourselves. So that's one of the biggest things we can do, come out to the land. Pimachihowan will always be there. It's not about you, it's not about you or I. That's what Pimachihowan is. It's about everything around us. It's not something that you can learn overnight. It's all about patience, and the time that it takes. If it takes longer than usual, then you wait. Patience is the greatest teacher and with Pimachihowan, you can't rush things. [trees creaking] It's like these trees around us. It's one of those things that the old ones always taught us, that over time . . . things will go their way.

The kind of thinking in Conroy's fire resonates with Eduardo Kohn's *How Forests Think* (2013) where he proposes 'a kind of thinking that grows' (14) a thinking that is beyond the human 'learning to think with images' (222) with those who look and look back, living lives that cross over each other if only for a moment, worlds that are each an 'open whole' (27) that 'begins with the likeness of thought-at-rest' (67). Conroy's Fire Lesson is that duration (dureé) is a mode of knowing, productively expands, not contradicts, Kohn's Peircean commitment. Deleuze's reading of Peirce through Bergson (Bogue 2003: 35) shows that for a spatial open whole there is also the open whole of dureé always present (44): 'within every framed image dureé "insists" and "subsists", manifesting in a disquieting way, a more radical Elsewhere, outside homogeneous space-time' (44). It begins not with thought-at-rest but the always mobile creative force of living-thinking.

Conroy's lesson occurs in multiple registers, I will deal with three. The first is the event of Conroy's Fire; the second is the filming and editing of the event, which Conroy had prepared for and prepared me for, though not to my knowledge at the time. This is also part of Conroy's Fire Lesson as he says about Pimachihowan: 'It can't start on itself. It always has to be something. You and I are that something. It's like a child. You take care of a child and eventually that child will take care of you.'

The event of Conroy's fire stretches into the past, as a virtuality, long before he led David into the fire-making scene. I will consider this in section two:

'Conroy's Lessons'. The filming also has a virtuality oriented towards the future, *Pimachihowan* as a film. This third force of Conroy's Fire Lesson moves into the future on small and large screens. In 'Conroy's Cinematic Event Still Burns', I will consider a number of diverse responses to the film to illustrate the variety of ways the filmic event of Pimachihowan splits off and moves into the future along divergent lines of flight.

The goal of this chapter is to think about research-creation within cine-ethnomusicological meaning as a 'process of translation' (Massumi 1992: 14) of an event, and the production of a crystal image (Deleuze 1989: 127), that is, an element of cinema-thinking but has been all but outlawed in research. The notion of the crystal image, to which I alluded above with the Titon example, will help illustrate that the filming of Conroy's fire, from which a Cree Tea Dance emerges as a sound-image, needs to be understood as a crystal image made up of: (a) an event happening in the territorial flux, (b) the vectoring of its affects that draw me backwards in time to link the sound-image of the Tea Dance to this moment in the territorial flux, that will be vectored through the editing room, and (c) vector into the future, realized as a heterogeneous film image (crystal image/hyalosign) made up of audio-image, sound-image and textual-image, separated by interstices which reserve a creative force capable of stimulating ethnomusicological thinking in bodies not yet gathered. The crystal image needs an introduction and so we must turn back to Conroy's Fire.

Conroy's fire

The sound of crunching snow at very low temperatures is at once completely familiar and otherworldly. It is a heterogeneous mix of a rumble that teases the edge of perception, the packing of popcorn foam, and a high-pitched tearing of a tiny ice plane by cold rubber. All around us frozen trees creak a warning of the cold in case we did not recognize its danger. Moving with intentionality, Conroy snaps branches off of fallen trees. Each snap is an event. A sharp wooden punctuation that moves out from each branch as a small explosion of air molecules. Small reflections of even spaced birch trees produce a pointillist sonic portrait of the energy of separating wood at −40° Celsius. There is an unromantic music in Conroy's wordless movement through the bush. Low rumbles of footsteps and the sharp attack of breaking branches. David, in a voice that is somewhere between explaining and asking, comments on the oils inside the branches. David is obviously not explaining this to Conroy, nor to the film crew occupied with dealing with framing and shockingly fast battery depletion. David is already in the future thinking about the viewer, concerned that the viewer has no idea what is happening. Perhaps his explanation gets in the way of the music of the forest, the event of Conroy's fire, or perhaps his facile explanation is not even heard.

Conroy settles a small pile of branches on the snow. With bare hands he pulls out a lighter and begins the process of catching the collection of twigs and fur on fire. Soon small wisps of smoke dance. Conroy begins to explain the importance of relations. Conroy's lesson is almost complete by the time we recognize what is happening. With the skill of an expert composer, we reach the climax of the song to recognize finally the connections that have been laid out for the listener. We are drawn backwards through time actively reorganizing our fresh experiences now made meaningful. Suddenly so many images (of sound, colour, movement, texture and time) become thought. Thinking becomes lively in the recognition that we are sitting around a hearth, and Conroy is gifting a teaching. The fire grows in step with our understanding that this moment is thick with becoming.

Minutes earlier we walked across a smooth space, now the hearth striates, lays out an orientation for us. We now sit around a fire in the centre of a small clearing that orients us according to the cardinal directions, and moves us back into the time of growing and dying trees, the season of the falling snow, the history of the Little Red River Cree, colonization, Canada. A force moves out from the hearth that has the power of vibrating consciousness of the first hearths of humans and awakens dancing shadows of a million years of human history, of early humans who we only know by the names of their species. While also awakening our skin to the sudden shock of warmth that comes with the sudden shock of thought. The skin comes alive in the glow of the fire. A thermal perimeter is recognized by the skin. It is with mild distress that I recognize moving through the invisible screen that separates us from the cold. A body response that says go back, you are going in the wrong direction. But it is necessary to get some distance from the event of the fire, because in the future, I want us to have a memory of David and Conroy sitting down together by the fire. This will be the poster for the film. It is obvious now. This is the film. This is where there will be music, because music, the Tea Dance, is welling up in me. The old cassette tape that we listened to around the kitchen table, the Tea Dance that Conroy's father shared with us. It is about being together, it is the sound of being together, it is right now.

Just as the snap of the twigs moved out through the forest in multiple directions, including at me, so too does the force of Conroy's fire. The emergence of the Tea Dance in my thinking is not magical or accidental, it was called into being by the force of the fire composition. I recognize that this way of thinking music does not align with the ethnomusicological and anthropological film literature (Baily 2009; Feld 1976; Hockings 1975; MacDougall 1998; Rouch 2003; Ruby 2000; Russell 1999, 2018; Saunders 2007; Titon 1992; Young 1975; Zemp 1988) but it does find resonance in Deleuze's work in cinema, in research-creation (Loveless 2019, 2020; Manning 2016), and Harbert's thinking about the role of aesthetics in cine-ethnomusicology (2018).

If we begin by recognizing that Conroy is more than an informant, that he is instead an existential dramaturge of a research-creation event, then it is possible to think the unfolding of the event as the activation of a kind of thinking that Conroy prepared. Conroy's Fire put into motion thoughts that were laid in place as separate thoughts that, when ignited, formed constellations of relations that moved into the past and future. It is also necessary to recognize that there is not a moment, an explosive instant where it all comes together, but a stacking of events, separated by interstices where a potential comes alive, where a not-yet-thought-sensation grows into thought. In Conroy's dramaturgical practice, we can see that 'cinema is a matter of a neuro-physical vibration, and that the image must produce a shock, a nerve-wave which gives rise to thought' (Deleuze 1989: 165). The image brings me to thought, and the thought brings me back to the image, in a continuous circuit moving through time as thoughts multiply in their heterogeneity 'bringing together critical and conscious thought and the unconscious in thought' (Deleuze 1989: 165). Thoughts producing more thoughts, activating past and future virtualities that tumble over each other like excited puppies. This is the realm of the crystal image.

Crystal image

'The cinema does not just present images, it surrounds them with a world' (Deleuze 1989: 68) and with these words Deleuze introduces, in 'Cinema 2: The Time-Image', the first of the time-images, the hyalosign (Deamer 2016: 145), in his chapter 'The Crystals of Time'. Its worlding is why the cinema from 'very early on looked for bigger and bigger circuits which would unite an actual image with recollection-images, dream-images and world-images' (Deleuze 1989: 68). The hyalosign brings together optical (opsign) and sound (sonsigns) situations and, in this case, also text. The hyalosign 'links the actual image to a virtual correlate' (Deamer 2016: 145) that destabilizes the ethnographic correspondence mentioned earlier. The hyalosign is a cinematic technique that delinks, by virtual of the entrance of the sonsign, the actual image relation on the ethnographic plane, that simultaneously relinks it to a virtual image, or images. The hyalosign is a time-image, composed of interstices of creative power between the opsign, sonsign and sign. In the case of Conroy's Fire, the ethnographic correspondence between the image of Conroy, David, fire, smoke, trees, and snow (the becoming of the opsign) is disrupted by the entrance of the Tea Dance, a disruption between the opsign's ethnographic continuity and the emerging sonsign and accompanying text. The correspondence is cut off and the virtual imminent in the image is released: 'The hyalosign is a crystal image because the indiscernibility of the real and the imaginary, or of the present and the past, of the actual and the virtual, is definitely not produced in the head or the mind, it is the objective characteristic of certain existing images which are by nature double' (Deleuze 1989: 69). The image of Conroy and David by the fire is a continuation of the ethnographic image, but it also becomes something else, something released from the common sense observation of observational documentary, an image of dureé, a time-image.

Is the crystal image, the hyalosign, out of bounds in ethnographic filmmaking? Or is it often unnoticed and little discussed? Is it possible that the hyalosign, because it works at the level of aesthetics and not science (Harbert 2018: 5), risks undermining the science of ethnography? That it contributes to undermining ethnography because, as this example plainly illustrates, there is a thinking-feeling force in the hyalosign that does not favour 'clarity over experience' (Harbert 2018: 5). Perhaps it is research-creation that allows the hyalosign to take a dominant place at the metaphorical and literal centre of *Pimachihowan*? The rest of the film, all that which leads up to Conroy's Fire, and all that which follows, moves out from the hyalosign, from the crystal image as if it were shards of that crystal. The film was not written front to back, Conroy authored a research-creation event that brought the crystal image into being and the rest of the film was written through the crystal. It is not that the rest of the film and voice-overs and music, commissioned by David and composed by southern Alberta musician-rancher Bill Cody Shearer, are unimportant, as no facet of a crystal would be unimportant, or possible to cut out. The crystal image/hyalosign makes a contribution to thinking about developing cinematic techniques for cine-ethnomusicology in its relationship with research-creation. As all of this was made possible by Conroy's Lessons, so it is to these that I now will turn.

Conroy's lessons

Initially, my role was to make a short documentary for Dr David Lertzman's developing Petroleum Education Learning Tool (PELT) that was intended to be a web-based platform to communicate with oil and gas industry workers who find themselves engaged in resource-based cross-cultural communication for which they are not prepared. While David's main focus with Conroy was to explore the interface between industry and Traditional Ecological Knowledge for the PELT site, my job was to produce a film. My filmic skills, the limits of ethnographic film theory, and my understandings of ecology were all put to the test in the first week of filming with the collapse of a 'typical' observational approach to ethnographic film (Young 1975).

My first assignment was to meet Conroy at his home, twelve hours north of Edmonton, Alberta. David had developed a short list and a series of interview questions he wanted me to ask.[4] I arrived at Conroy's home with my gear and he put me up in the family hunting cabin featured in the film. While he went to do some work, he left me to get settled in. I spent a few hours with my audio gear recording ambient sounds of the Boreal Forest. The hunting cabin is at the western edge of the Wood Buffalo National Park, established in 1922 to protect the habitat of the last remaining herd of bison in northern Canada. I remarked to David as we were planning this trip that, at the time, this territory was off the edge of Google Maps.

The air was heavy with the sounds of bees buzzing through the heavy grass. The rustling of leaves from thick stands of birch trees filled the air even in the slightest of breezes. My ears were sensitive to every cracking branch, because there are moose, deer, bear and caribou in the area as well as large numbers of rabbits and squirrels. The forest is so alive that at night Conroy asked me to lay large square wooden planks on the ground in front of each of the two cabin windows. Each wooden square was poked through with large construction nails: 'It's to keep the bears from climbing in the window,' he said with a soft deep chuckle. He was not laughing about the threat of bears, but the look on my face. I spent the afternoon seeing how far I could extend my hearing through my microphones and field recorder. Through my headphones, I began to explore the flow of forest sounds, reflecting on Steven Feld's complex observations about Acoustemology (2003). My training in Néhiyaw Traditional Ecological Knowledge had begun.

We spent the next few days driving around the dirt roads of the Little Red River Cree Nation. We spent the first evening discussing David's wish list for video and interviews over moose meat and potatoes. We were sitting in the living room of his father's home, children running around, TV blaring, cousins playing music and his father sitting at the table watching it all.

Over these days, I came to realize that David's wish list was impossible. Besides, Conroy had his own plan. I had heard David talk about Conroy's pedagogy in some of our preparatory meetings. I began to feel that I was losing the focus that I had arrived with. We were not just driving around the territory, I was seeing with my own eyes all of the places that David and Conroy had discussed. We visited the river, Conroy explaining the way it freezes in the winter, the ice roads that connect the community, literally roads made of ice. He showed me how to notice changes in the river, how to look for tracks in the mud, where to look for moose in swamps. Now the river ice was melted and the water level was high. The little five-vehicle ferry was having trouble with the swift current. We crossed over on the ferry and I filmed the journey standing in the flatbed of the truck, holding onto the side rails, hoping that my tripod would not tip over. He taught me to read the transformation of the environment at the river crossing, to see process in the details of the homes and forest.

We visited the place where his great-grandfather Sewepagaham set out to sign Treaty 8, he told me about how Sewepagaham had established peace with the neighbouring Dene some years before. The treaty was signed in 1899. In Canadian history classes, the treaties are made to sound ancient, but in conversation with Conroy it felt so recent. I filmed these locations and jotted down the stories. Each location had a story, and each story a location. It is the Néhiyaw concept of *Kack'skee'so'go'ya'man* 'seeing with your own eyes,' it is a spatially located process necessary to Néhiyaw Traditional Ecological Knowledge (TEK). But we were not observing *nature*, I was being drawn into a process, a *matrix that embeds*, with a digital cinema camera in my hands.

'A matrix that embeds'

Gregory Bateson worked to bring aesthetics, environment and sacredness together, into what he called *the pattern that connects*. Small developed this into *Musicking* (Small 1998). Bateson's goal was an interdisciplinary ecological scholarship that he characterized as a study of the organism in its environment. This interdisciplinary interest has become consolidated in biosemiotics

(Hoffmeyer 2008), and are being further developed as an ethnography beyond the human (Kohn 2013). At the core of these approaches is an interest in an ecological approach based upon the study of productive biological semiotic systems that may be characterized as a shift from *Skei* to *Syn*.

In the short educational film *The Matrix that Embeds*, Humberto Maturana and Heinz von Foerster explain that the form of the described universe is shaped by the tools used to do the describing,[5] what might be called enframing, worlding the world. In other words, the method taken to describe the universe is, therefore, not just one method among many that will lead to the same end, but is a *choice*, made often with little foreknowledge of the consequences the method will have for the model. As Deleuze notes, 'when the problem concerns existential determinations . . . we see clearly that choice is increasingly identified with living thoughts, and with an unfathomable decision. Choice no longer concerns a particular term, but the mode of existence of the one who choses' (Deleuze 177). Choice is existential, but first there must be an opportunity to choose, a selection from which to choose. Perhaps Conroy's Lessons are an invitation to choose? But to choose between what?

Von Foerster explained that the root word of science (skei) means to take things apart as in schism and schizophrenia. Taking apart in the act of naming, produces a perceptual field entrained, and a universe of parts made utilitarian by its itemization. An understanding of ecological becoming requires a perceptual field entertained by the overflowing relations of a universe becoming.

The opposite of skei is the root syn, to connect, to put together, as in the root of system. In *Steps to an Ecology of Mind* (1972) and *Mind in Nature* (1979), Gregory Bateson presented systems of interconnected 'minds' established upon *the pattern that connects*. In his later work *Where Angels Fear* (1987), he along with his anthropologist daughter Mary Catherine Bateson explore aesthetics and sacredness as the experience of being embedded in human-animal-planet matrix (Charlton 2008). Bateson's ecological view was of the whole, and had to 'accommodate aesthetics to the question of consciousness' (Harries-Jones 1995: 212). He argued aesthetics and consciousness were two parts of a necessary triad with the sacred. Harries-Jones, summing up Bateson, wrote: 'The sacred (whatever that means) is surely related (somehow) to the beautiful (whatever that means) in that the sacred is a sort of surface, or topology, on which both terms, beauty and consciousness could be mapped' (212). Following Bateson, it is possible to inquire after questions of aesthetics through the sacred, as the pattern that connects, provided that these patterns are seen in process.

Heinz von Foerster, however, did not feel that the paternal association of pattern, from the root *pater* meaning father, was the correct metaphor. Pattern presupposes a master form, a maker, a platonic form, capable of being the standard for its parts. Instead of father (pater/pattern), Foerster suggested mother, mater or matris, from which a system emerges as wholes, built of relations-of-difference that embed. Instead of a pattern (pater), von Foerster suggests matrix (mater), and substitutes *the pattern that connects*, for *the matrix that embeds*. The change of metaphor from father science to mother matrix introduces a new metaphor that finds more resonance with traditional ecological knowledge of Indigenous peoples in Canada, and maybe more broadly.[6] For instance, when Sewepagaham talks about *Kimaamanow*,[7] there is some hesitancy with the often-used translation *mother earth*. I believe the hesitancy comes from the fact that the English words do not quite capture what is being expressed. Matrix with its root in *matris* brings us closer than the English word 'mother'. The process of engaging with the *matrix that embeds* is part of the practice of living Pimachihowan, experienced as process and sacredness. A choice emerges between choosing to make a film about Nêhiyaw culture that may stand in for the culture or taking an approach that is oriented towards process, relations and becoming.

'Making good tea takes time'

Over the two weeks I spent with Conroy on that first visit, everything was duration.

Conroy explains:

With our teachings, it is subtle. If it's walking down through a boreal forest or tracking down a game animal it's soothing. It's totally opposite to what youth are now being engaged on. It's not 'bam' right in your face, here's a frag grenade, 'boom' you have instant reaction. With our teachings it's calm, it's soothing, it's *pah'pe'ya'ht'ik*, slow, it's like steeping your tea. You don't rush it because it doesn't taste good. It's like that, our teaching needs to steep nice and slow. It takes time. So when you ask how can we teach that to non-indigenous folks or even with our people who are not able to be granted that kind of teaching, how do we do that, at the end of the day we have to teach them patience. You don't get an instant reaction, you're not going to get instant gratification. When you go out and walk on the land and say 'here it is', you're not going to go out there and say 'wow I'm changed'. You have to do it repetitively, you have to do it over the years. It's slow healing and without the slow healing it's not true healing.

Towards the end of the visit, we took his big truck to the end of the road and then turned off on a very rough side road that went north directly into the mountain from which you can see the entire territory. This space was particularly important and I was very excited to film it. I had heard David talk for some years about this hike and I was very excited to be making it. But I was to be disappointed, this time.

Not far into the trail, the truck bogged down in the soft mud. A massive truck, now useless, listed into the very deep soft mud. Conroy jumped out and walked around the truck a few times before grabbing the rifle that was always in the cab with him. 'Let's go . . . time to start walking,' he said. To get home was going to take hours. We began walking. Night was coming on quickly. It never gets dark this far north in the spring, less than 100 kilometres from the Northwest Territories, at the very end of the northern Boreal Forest before tundra stretches all the way to the Arctic. Soon it was after midnight, though the light made it feel like 9 p.m. The dirt and then gravel road stretched out in front of us winding through the forest. Deep Boreal Forest on both sides of us. No vehicles, no houses, no street lights. Just us, our footsteps in the gravel, nothing but time to talk together. To reflect on what we have seen. The stories, the rivers, fields, streams. The swamps where moose like to hang out, the horse flies larger than any I've ever seen, and the dragonflies, even larger, that swoop down with a heavy low buzzing sound. I felt the soft landing of a horse fly on my left shoulder, it distracted me. Its body was the size of a quarter. In a flash, a massive dragonfly picked up the horse fly and bit its head off. Here we are. This is the Boreal Forest, a massive swirling ecosystem on an order and scale that I cannot conceptualize, but can feel. I can feel the complexity stretch out. And I have been slowly opening to the feelings of complex networks of inter-relations, systems and systems and systems in layers and layers and layers. I was beginning to experience the process that I think Conroy had laid out for me, the way he laid it out for David, and for oil industry visitors before him. I was beginning to 'see with my own eyes', and I was given a choice to release into a *matrix that embeds.*

Years later when reflecting back on this story with Conroy, he began chuckling. He looked at me very soberly and in his characteristically deep and quiet voice said, 'Brother, do you really think I would get my truck stuck?' I had told the story of Conroy's truck getting stuck over and over again never recognizing that it was not ever stuck, it was an existential situation (Freire), a lesson in Indigenous Critical Pedagogy. Conroy was the teacher and this long slow walk, a lesson.

Conroy guided me through a series of these existential pedagogical situations that provided opportunities to (directly) experience time as duration. Over that time together, I learned about the prohibition of talking about 'nature' or 'the land', why it was necessary to understand the problems with the English language in regards to ecological systems. Duration became a manner of living, an ontogenetic practice that allowed new worldings of the world. Duration had the impact of reducing conscious entrainment, promoting ecological entertainment. As Bateson said of aesthetics, which I can now read as an encouragement for neurodiverse modes of thinking-feeling: 'increasing aesthetic sensibility to pattern and modulation of natural pattern: this is the material for dream and poetry' (1991: 256). Metaphors are ways of seeing and choices. Sacredness is a metaphor for embeddedness. One can choose the metaphor of the matrix that embeds. Conroy helped me witness that 'ecological aesthetics creates a series of settings which verify participation. It registers a relation between the parts and the whole, in a manner very different from an observer pretending to be outside the setting, engaged in an exercise of eco-management' (Harries-Jones 2005: 67–8). With Conroy, I became a witness to the epistemological 'chunking' (Manning 2016) of modernity, and set out to find an approach to cine-ethnomusicology that would stay true to Conroy's initial prohibition to not separate music from Pimachihowan. The approach found me. It welled up in my body, in my mind, during the event of Conroy's fire. I cannot say if the idea is mine, Conroy's, the forest's or a little bit of all three. But I know I did not author this moment, it does not bear my name and perhaps it does not require a name beyond the event of Pimachihowan.

'Seeing with your own eyes'

We didn't speak much about Pimachihowan on the first trip to Little Red River. It became a later focus based on the transformative ecological aesthetics pedagogy that Conroy utilized in our preparation. We decided that oil and gas workers, and the general public, needed to understand by seeing with their own eyes.

This, as the above description sought to make clear, was never just about seeing but always about the matrix that embeds. To 'see with your own eyes' meant that one needed to be in that place, to be immersed in this ecology, where systemic knowledge emerges from experience.

Cineworlding can utilize the tools of digital cinema to assist *seeing with your own eyes*, but first it requires that filmmakers learn how not to objectify/entrain perception, and to do this I believe we might have to break away from the history of anthropological cinema and the fantasies of observational documentary style. The 'humanized camera' (Grimshaw 2001) operates in a primarily realist film model which is a 'golden standard' of ethnographic cinema worldwide (Suhr and Willerslev 2012). But because of Conroy's teaching, the film we set out to make had to have immersion in the environment as the standard, but not necessarily the ethnographic law of correspondence. Places hold stories (Feld and Basso 1996) and while this is better accepted in print, it is less well understood cinematically. In ethnographic film circles it is acknowledged that 'implicit in a camera style there is a theory of knowledge' (MacDougall 1998: 202), but that theory of knowledge is rarely made explicit:

> Visual anthropology with its contemporary theory of knowledge has reached the stage when the initial motivations, be it a struggle against lecture films, the 'all-knowing' cinematic eye, and a human-centered focus, have slowly exhausted themselves. Coinciding with the success of hybrid genres of docufiction and mockumentary – implying the increasing film literacy among the audience – are new questions and challenges that ethnographic filmmakers need to face. (Borecky 2016: 119)

Conroy provided a choice between worlds, and the consequences of this choice pushed me into thinking about cine-ethnomusicology differently.

Conroy's cinematic event still burns

This film has been shown many times since it was released in 2015, the virtuality of Pimachihowan is now an actuality and has inaugurated virtualities, or cinematic offerings that have become actualized over a number of projects that I have finished since 2015. I have used Pimachihowan in countless classes and workshops, always using Conroy's Fire as the beginning of a conversation about techniques. But it is truly only in the writing of this chapter, a chapter I have written and re-written so many times that I have lost count, that I am beginning to clarify my thinking. What I have written here, that which will bear my name, is not truly mine. I have not come up with these ideas alone, as I have learned long ago from Conroy; it emerges from bringing things together. Showing this film brings the film in contact with new audience, invites new viewers to engage in circuits of thinking cine-ethnomusicology with Conroy. Sometimes the audience response is magic and other times downright depressing. In one dramatic event in an anthropology class, half the class walked out during the screening. There is power in the interstices between the opsigns and sonsigns, but this power is immanent to the film experience, it can be released when a receptive and generous mind chooses to think along with the interstices in the film. It remains a virtual force until a mind allows thoughts unthought to be thought. I am interested, of course, in the event of incompletion, what limits the work of the film, but this is a difficult subject that is hard to research because it is pointless perhaps to ask: Why did you not get anything out of the film? So I will have to focus on just a few instances where the virtuality of the film becomes actual.

1. Sometimes the viewer experiences duration negatively. One viewer remarked that during the film she worried that she would have to tell me how boring and slow the film was, until she became absorbed, drawn into the matrix. When at the end of the film Conroy explains that people need to operate slowly to have certain forms of experience, she realized that what Conroy was saying had already been incorporated into the film, and she had spent the entire 30 minutes struggling under the weight of an unfamiliar duration. The form of the film expressed the content before the content was expressed conceptually. I see this as a contribution towards cineworlding, where duration has an ontogenetic dimension. Once the unthought of the power of duration became thought, the filmic experience, the entire filmic experience, both the recognition, the 29-minute gap of recognition and concern constitutes the thinking-feeling of Conroy's Fire.
2. *Pimachihowan* began being used at the University of Calgary and was screened at festivals and environmental events in and around Calgary, Alberta. It was screened by a climate change organization at Vancouver Island University and drew a large crowd. During the post-film Q&A, a faculty member was concerned about the scene of Conroy walking

into the forest. He suggested that it looked too much like we were constructing a romantic image of cliché *Indians*. I explained to him that Conroy himself decided on that particular scene and that it was decided to keep much of that scene in the middle of the film. For us it was an important moment of exploration, but for him, it seems too heavy in romanticism, too much cliché. The conversation lasted for some time and the audience member felt it necessary to press on with the critique. I tried another time to explain that it was Conroy's initiative and choice to present himself and his teachings that way. It became clear that there was no way to get to a shared understanding of the scene. It impressed upon me the ongoing becoming of the film. The conversation was rich and for a time I was left absolutely unsure of how to read this scene. The important observation here was how a forceful and informed critique reopened my thinking. The critique illustrated the gap, the interstices between the opsign and sonsigns, these interstices can reopen an event, reopen thinking. The discussion was the event and it was made possible when the critic thought the film through their deconstructive lens.

3. In 2019, I received a surprise email from a Mining and Tailings Technology director from SunCor Energy:

I use the video a lot when people ask me about it. It is so great. The first thing is it challenges our western way of thinking. Pimachihowan: Living with the Land; the definition of the word is right in the title. You have learned it in 5 seconds. However if you want a deeper understanding of the word (or better the concept) watch the 40 minute video. I like it so much because it reflects my own growing understanding of traditional knowledge. Much of it (to me) represents depth rather than breadth. Once we have defined a word, a thing, a feeling we think we know it in a western context but there is great depth to many words, things and feelings we miss. In addition the concept of Pimachihowan is such an interesting concept to initiate a dialoged around how we show up work (every day on the 28th floor in downtown Calgary) as well as our own concept of sustainability. I absolutely love using this video as an example of how much more there is for us to learn.[8]

This email was tremendously interesting to us because the film had started being used in an initiative called 'Team Spirit to Spirit' initiative where the purpose is to 'facilitate a leadership cultural shift in the space of sustainability, reconciliation and innovation by drawing from Indigenous wisdom and awareness while fostering a connection and appreciation for nature and cultures within and across Suncor' (personal correspondence). This is an interesting example of the kind of ongoingness of the life that a film project may live, crossing into a highly political space and doing the intercultural work that we hoped for, deep within the networks of a global oil and gas company. It is our hope that our film can play a small role in new kinds of decolonial becomings. We so often present our work for communities that are onside with our objectives, so it is fascinating to see research-creation work cross over into corporate spaces that I might (maybe too hastily) characterize as hostile to the work that we are doing in the world.

4. At the very first screening of the film at MacEwan University, a Nehiyaw elder stood up and addressed the room. She explained the powerful experience of watching the film. In particular the part that had untranslated Nêhiyawêwin. She felt like Conroy was speaking to her. And as she looked around the room she recognized how few people understood what Conroy had said, and that, it was spoken to her, to those who carry the language. There are parts of Pimachihowan that are not for those who do not speak Nêhiyawêwin. To not translate was a choice to create a situation for Nêhiyawêwin speakers to have their own space with the film. She also resonated deeply with the embodiment of traditional practices that drew her into her memories of her kokum (grandmother) and nimosom (grandfather). In her body, the opsigns and sonsigns initiated a generational thinking-feeling that helped her connect to the land, to Pimachihowan. As she spoke about Nehiyaw traditional life, the language that Conroy used, the care and attention Conroy paid to everything, the duration of the experience, she continued Conroy's lessons into the bodies of the settler audience, closing the gap between the screen and the auditorium. In this way, the power of Conroy's fire continues to burn.

Epilogue

Pimachihowan is now also a monument to the hopes and dreams that we all shared during the planning, making and screening of the film. In the early summer of 2021, David was killed in a grizzly bear attack near his home in the foothills of the Rocky Mountains in southern Alberta. The time we spent working and living together making this film was an important personal and professional experience for us all. Conroy is now Chief of Little Red River Cree Nation and is leading his nation into a postcolonial future. As was evident at David's memorial celebration, his teaching and leadership will have a lasting impact on many students and faculty at the University of Calgary, as well as the wide network of activists, elders, teachers and students he walked beside. Pimachihowan is a monument to our time together at that point in our lives and Conroy's Fire will continue to inspire me to continue exploring 'cinema of modes of existence' (Deleuze 1989: 177) because 'we need an ethic or a faith, which makes fools laugh; it is not a need to believe in something else, but a need to believe in this world' (Deleuze 1989: 173). Cineworlding starts from a faith in worlds. From a belief that as we do cinematic research-creation and forward our profession we can add something, perhaps cultivate a thinking-feeling-knowing together that makes worlds.

9

The crowd behind the lens, *WE'RE TOO LOUD*

At a conference of audiovisual ethnomusicologists, a new group that had been established only two years before, I was going have my first opportunity to screen one of my films to ethnomusicologists and visual anthropologists. *WE'RE TOO LOUD* (WTL) is a film about a rock band on Hornby Island, a small island in the chain of gulf islands in the Canadian Pacific Northwest. During the back to the land movement in the 1970s, Hornby became a destination for hippies. My interest in making the film emerged from my dissertation research (MacDonald 2016b) that attempted to document the cultural impact that music festivals, often created by back-to-the-landers, have had on western Canadian communities. While much has been written about the ideas of this movement, often framing them in terms of white flight, little had been written about what happened to these idealistic youth, what did they accomplish? WTL was conceptualized as one part of a two-part series; the companion film *Ark: Return to Robson Valley* (2022) is a nonfiction film set in the interior of British Columbia.

The main character of WTL is Breagan Smith, the now-adult child of one of those hippie families. As discussed in earlier chapters, Breagan is struggling to remain on the island where he grew up. Hornby is now marketed as 'Hawaiian of the North' and houses that were built by hand in the 1970s with locally milled wood are now being sold for half a million dollars. Because it is a vacation island, there is not much in the way of an economy and little opportunity for Breagan's generation. While the community dropped out of capitalism, it turns out that capitalism is not far behind. This film allowed me to explore this idea, one that I think is very contemporary.

These films are made in an existential context that I am trying to grasp. If there is a future for humans on earth then humanity, more-than-human worlds and technics will need to be interwoven sustainably. Outlines of two potential futures can be discerned at this moment. One future may be called posthuman and the other transhuman. I believe that Smith is composing, or dreaming, a posthuman futurity. The posthuman future begins with a critique of the whiteness, classicism and chauvinism of the human, the transhuman conversely seeks eternal life for the human. For the transhuman, technology is added to the human to extend its power, its vitality, its endurance. For the posthuman conversely, technology was already at work with the emergence of *Homo sapiens*. In my opinion, the transhuman escalates the divisions and errors of the humanities that posthumanism tries to address. The transhuman project is characterized by cryogenics, private space exploration, the metaverse, robot dogs on the US-Mexican border, university education made to serve industries (to call it neoliberal is no longer enough), platform capitalism, the escalation of the attention economy, political echo chambers that produce rapid escalation in populist anti-democratic tendencies. Perhaps, unsurprisingly, transhumanists describe themselves in much more positive terms,[1] but humanists did not see the impacts of their universalisms and chauvinisms either. In order not to make these positions too facile, too black and white, in the next chapter I will sketch out a posthuman self-analysis of the still-colonial haunting that remains to be dealt with in my body, and the surprise I felt when seen as a monster.

Politics of purity

As a consequence of the vacation economy, there is a desire to 'keep' the island pure. But, of course, Breagan didn't grow up on an idyllic island in the Pacific; he grew up making rock music and partying, something that he intends to keep doing. The film picks up with Breagan setting up for a show and then follows him as the rest of his shows get cancelled over the summer because the community hall wasn't cleaned well enough. The central tension of the film revolves around whether the provided mop was broken or not, but the subtext of the film is the concern that Breagan feels about being 'too loud' for the vacation culture that he feels is making it impossible for him to stay. Being 'too loud' becomes a metaphor for freedom. But Smith continually constructs a connection between making rock and roll and growing gardens. What drew me to telling Breagan's story was his ecological idea of freedom, of autonomy, that was about living in relationship with the ecology of the island, not the idea of the island, but actually the earth and sea. The subtitle of the film was 'an ecomusicological love story', though as you will see this part of the story seems to have been too subdued to get the attention of some of my fellow scholars.

I was excited to screen the film to an audience of ethnomusicologists and visual anthropologists for a few reasons. I was excited to get feedback from an informed audience and eager to engage in a discussion of film technique. As a self-taught filmmaker this was a professional debut. The first question came from a visual anthropologist who asked, 'How is this an ethnography?' I was stunned. This is not so much a question as an accusation that says *what do you think you are doing and why was this film screened?* I honestly don't know how I responded. I think I said something about experimenting with ethnographic form or something. The discussion about whether or not this was ethnography spilled out into the post-conference discussion. I was lovingly supported by Harbert and Gubner and a group of scholars with whom I had a great conversation about the differences between scientific ethnography and the impure form that I was attempting.

As I have discussed earlier, my experience of the conference and my subsequent work has been informed significantly by this experience. What I expected to be an exploration of new ways of doing ethnomusicology turned into something much less exploratory and profound, much more disciplinary. I also felt that I was incapable of expressing the impure form that I was experimenting with clearly enough to my fellow ethnographers. In the years following this little conflict, my films have been successes at film festivals and a much broader sharing of my work than ever before. My films, at the time of writing, have been screened at almost fifty festivals around the world, have won awards, have been screened at universities, in classrooms, have been used by cultural organizations. In other words, they have done more work that I initially hoped. In this chapter, I want to articulate the response that I wished I could have had for the question: 'How is this ethnography?' In short, the answer is that WTL is posthumanography. It is an impure form because it is constituted by art/ethnography/philosophy/critical theory. The impurity of the form is a statement of its heterogeneity, the kinds valued by posthumanism. The posthumanographer does not escape this heterogeneity either. The posthuman is not a unified subject characterized by the volition-intentionality-agency triad. Cinematic posthumanography, cineworlding, is constituted by a crowd behind the lens.

Becoming-posthumanographer

I do not think that we have fully grasped what happens when students become ethnographers, artists, philosophers and critical theorists. Sure this is an identity, but there is a transformation of subjectivity or at least additional subjectivities that begin to live in the body. I believe that universities are machinic and that they produce us according to a disciplinary diagram. In the process of becoming a filmmaker, I think something shorted out in my ethnographic programming. The short was a consequence of the transdisciplinarity of research-creation. I began to read philosophy and critical theory to try to make sense of this tension. This only further exacerbated the tensions. I tried to settle all of this tension one way or another. I was reading Erin Manning and Brian Massumi when I realized that I was holding on to a very Hegelian (post-Kantian) idea of myself. That I was looking to try to resolve the tension between irresolvable fields. Art, ethnography, philosophy and critical theory will not resolve into some kind of dialectical unity. Once I began to accept that I could not get resolution my subjectivation as research-creation practitioner started to become clearer. I constantly shift between perspectives. It is as if I have internalized a bus load of personae that see and approach the world differently. My experience of the world is constantly in flux. Not situation to situation, but IN the flow of situations functioning at intensive speeds much faster than my consciousness can follow. What is left behind are complex multisided affective formations that get vectored in the editing suite, in the film, in the Q&A, in the writing. It is in the vectoring that the thinking happens.

Social and environmental intimacy as critical public pedagogy

WE'RE TOO LOUD was a film I made just after finishing *Pimachihowan*. The more I thought about the work I was trying to do with this film the more I realized that my interest in process was primarily an interest in technocultural ecological assemblages and their productivity. The subtitle for the film is 'An Ecomusicological Love Story', which was meant to signify its location as scholarship and its 1960s handheld aesthetics was a none-too-subtle nod to Jean Rouch, to the heyday of observational rock documentaries like *Woodstock* and *Sympathy for the Devil*, shot at the period when Smith's parents moved to Hornby. The eco-love story is not about romance, but intimacy. It is about the intimacy of writing songs, tending gardens, sharing (tending?) music with friends. It is about the way Breagan sees music and gardening as being transversal to each other. Cineworlding connects these two activities by cutting gardening scenes next to music scenes and situates them in a context of gentrification and precarity. To do this I make extensive use of quotes from Wendell Berry's[2] 'The Unsettling of America' as intertitles.[3]

WTL was informed by posthumanography's critical pedagogy: 'traversing the traditional disciplines of the Humanities, offers new potential to expand contemporary discussion about the decomposition of the human as an enhanced and revised subject in the posthuman era, and of human-actioned systems as complex arenas of heterogeneous ethnical concern and accountability' (Bignall and Braidotti 2019: 3). Music is a kind of gardening and gardening a kind of composing. For Breagan, the transversality of these practices is foundation to his well-being and well-becoming. Both contribute to the formation of a diagram that contributed to successful life on a small island in Canada's Pacific Northwest. The question of posthuman ecology is not just about environmental ecology. The film is about sustainability of four ecologies – conceptual, social, technological, environmental – and the way gentrification was threatening a minor diagram that hippie back-to-the-landers had produced over a generation. Minor in this sense refers to an alternative mode of existence.

The crowd behind the lens

The crowd behind the lens: artist, social scientist, philosopher/critical theorist. A filmmakers bodying is the act of in-folding flows of audio-vision. The digital cinema camera's viewfinder is populated by images and indicators communicating layers of information, data, readings, all functions. Beyond this other sets of relations, other planes occupy attention. Attention darts around the visual-images, the relations between the sound-images and visual-images, the relations beyond these images (outside the frame), all changing according to a camera consciousness emerging virtually within events. Each shot and scene is an expression of audio-vision's 'event-triggering tension' (Massumi 2011: 17), a vectoring of affects. The event in Breagan's worlding is one half of the process. The other half of the process is what is going on behind the lens. The event-triggering tension happens at the meeting place of Breagan's worlding and my worlding. Virtualities flowing through my body are actualized in relation with Breagan's. Flows of forces in two direction whose meeting place is the event of the shot. Somehow, buffeted by these forces, or more specifically, in spite of the overflow of perception a decision is made to hit record. The decision is more felt than known, a triggering in the double sense of the triggering of the event that is 'perceptually felt, not so much "in" vision as *with* vision or *through* vision' (Massumi 2011: 17) an audio-vision effect that moves through the body-camera-microphone assemblage. Asking what a techno-embodied assemblage can do finds confluence with posthumanism's interest 'to build on the generative potential of the critiques of humanism developed by radical epistemologies that aim at a more inclusive practice of becoming-human . . . toward becoming-world' (Bignall and Braidotti 2019: 1) what they call thinking in zoe/geo/techno-oriented frames.

Cinema-thinking contributes to posthuman knowledge formation. Bignall and Briadotti ask: 'What is a posthuman system of language, or of perception and subjectivity?' All of the previous chapters have explored various aspects of this question. In early chapters, we followed the vectoring of music through bodies to see what assemblages were composed. These assemblages or halobionts operating on many geographical and temporal scales, from the very small to the quite large. In Chapter 5, we focused our attention on the ways that cinematic production can bring out the subjective assemblage, showing subjectivity to be more fractal-like than unified. The white wall and black hole recursion moved in two directions simultaneously, into the black hole of subjectivity and out into the machinic assemblage of artist-director-camera-lights-music video assemblage. And then further out into the technosphere and capitalsphere.

Artistic vectors

A red light appears onscreen and on the body of the camera, potentiality actualizing. The overflow of information does not subside, but something nonetheless changes, virtualities shaping actuality of audio-vision event begin to proliferate virtualities like sparks flying off sound-images, particles of potentialities forming circuits, some small, some large, circulating, orbiting, populating images with layers and layers, more possibilities, more connections, more layers of thought-feeling, audio-vision reaching well outside the frame and returning enriching relations. The past and future occurring in the flow of present-ness: audio-vision effect is cinema-thinking.

The perception working through the camera is not of the order of 'natural' perception. It is already trained to see virtualities, trained to see-hear the 'lived abstraction an effective virtual vision of the shape of the event, including in its arc the unseen dimensions of its immediate past and immediate future' (Massumi

2011: 17) including its future in the edit suite and on the cinema screen. This cinema-thinking entangles with the world as an artist, entertained by the plane of material as it moves across an interstice to a plane of composition. But also as a social scientist scanning virtualities as functions. Artistic perception draws aesthetic personae, ways of composing that have been learned through watching films,[4] while sociological perception enacts the reports of other researchers, these other partial observers. In cineworlding, there is never one person behind the camera, but three groups. The artist, the scientist and the philosopher that will, since the writing cultures debate, use artistic techniques to produce concepts and no longer write reports. The emergence of cineworlding with its necessary pedagogy, requires the exploration of the three parts of the cinematic researcher-artist (artist, scientist, philosopher) before we can return to the viewfinder. These three each have their own subjectivation, their processes of becoming, their own interests. They are not harmoniously developed and often refute or deny each other. Sometimes they criticize each other or feign superiority. It is time to give up the false pretence that an ethnographer is a single uncomplicated, unfractured entity. The posthumanographer knows they emerge from flux and are attentive to what can be learned through the fluxing.

Artist

For the next number of years, I continued to make observational documentary films and more than once ran into the critique that sections or drafts of my films were too artistic to be included in the documentary I was editing. The cinematic techniques I was developing were becoming hemisphered into creative practice and scholarly practice. Soon I found myself spending more and more time hanging out with the video technicians who worked in the basement of the old arts building. We discussed equipment and techniques but never talked art nor research methods. I was living in a world that was split along two poles. One pole had art (music videos and fiction films) on one side and on the other, research (observational documentary). The other pole had creative practice on one side (episteme) and technology (techne) on the other. Reading Foucault I could not help shake the feeling that these two poles had something to tell me about the way the humanities understood cinema.

As I began to read more and more film studies, I began to see another pole develop. Film studies and music and the moving image studied what Michel

Chion called audio-vision, where the object of analysis was always a finished film. There were no studies on producing audio-vision; that was left to a separate non-academic literature where filmmakers talked about the technical aspects of cinema. There were only a few exceptions to this and it was here that I began to gravitate.[5] The more I read about these filmmakers, read interviews, articles, books, the more and more I could not tell them apart, or perhaps keep them apart. They should perhaps be separated into scholars and artist but I could see scholarship and artistic techniques in all of them. Perhaps most specifically I began to discern the outline of a kind of technology-thinking rumbling under the surface. I would love to say that it was looking for a way out, but in fact, it was not going to get out. It was already in its place. Ethnographic film had established itself in anthropology, separate from neorealism. Cine-ethnomusicology was developing and I was playing some small role in that. Everything was in its place. Until I read Deleuze.

Packets of affects in audiovisual thinking

How many times today have I picked up my phone flipped through platforms and scrolled? How many stories and video clips have I viewed? I have absolutely no idea. I do know, however, that when I pick up my phone there is a series of swipes and taps that I do not have to think about. The phone is part of my body. I can justify it by saying that it is about communication, staying *in touch* with the world, but it is also the world staying *in touch* with me. I use the idea of touch in two senses. To be in communication with and to be physically touched. We do not often think of the phone as a being that is touching us, but this is quite actually what happens through the percepts and affects of audio-vision. Consider the process of scrolling through content. It is a kind of sifting for a connection, moving through large quantities of audio-vision until something *catches* your attention, *hits* you. The use of these tactile terms is not an error. When you get caught by a short video you are affected. There is the capture of attention that coincides with a release of affect. Consider Roland Barthes's description of looking at photos of his recently deceased mother, the punctum, the piercing of livingness, nostalgia and loss, that welled up in him while looking at the photo of his mother. As Brian Massumi notes, 'the punctum is the appearance through the photo of an affective afterlife. It is the strike of a life as a force, beyond an actual life' (Massumi 2013: 57). In this sense, the photo has a two-sidedness 'the simultaneous participation of the virtual in the actual and the actual in the virtual, as one arises from and returns to the other' (Massumi 2002: 35). For Barthes, the virtual was the livingness in the photo and the actual was the image in the photo. The photo is a percept; it is grasped by Barthes's perception. The grasping of it as a percept releases affects, virtualities, that stir Barthes's flows of livingness. Barthes is impacted by precept and affect. It is not just a photo but a combination of virtuality and actuality that is the experience of being pierced or grabbed. It is a kind of shock that occurs as a microperception, 'felt without registering consciously' (Massumi 2015: 53). Affect then is 'synesthetic, implies a participation of the sense in each other; the measure of a living thing's potential interactions is its ability to transform the effects of one sensory mode into those of another. (Tactility and vision being the most obvious but by not mean the only example's; interoceptive senses, especially proprioception are crucial)' (Massumi 2002: 35). While we might not be Barthes looking at a photo of his mother, we are nonetheless experiencing the same operation, the circuit of percept and affect as we scroll through social media.

The mass production of digital images and audiovisual images made possible by audiovisually enabled smartphones has increased the reach and variety of these experiences. They have gone from being notable to being habitual (are they now like coffee?). I have begun to think of these hits as sugar packets, a little hit that keeps my mood up. Let us call them *packets of affects*. These packets are bite-sized visual or audiovisual content that are focused for maximum affective engagement. There is no straightforward answer to what social media does. Facebook, for instance, has been the leading platform for

> self-presentation, communication, and manically showing off one's life, in addition to being a hotspot of future social media bubbles, in addition to being a tool for Facebook and Twitter revolutions, in addition to being an indelible memory of millions, it is also a medium of confession, indeed a compulsion to confession, and in this sense it is a medium not just of communication, but also of self-division. (Raunig 2016: 115)

To read and write confessions! A feast of packets of affects, short quick hits. The division here is two-fold. The first and perhaps most obvious is the division from oneself, the confession is not a secret and ephemeral act with a confident or priest, but is a published affair. The confession is performative and constructs an online self. The second and more pernicious is the voluntary giving away of personal details and data to the capitalists who control the platforms and peddle in information. As is widely known, the moment-to-moment events of one's life online are organized algorithmically for the benefit of capital that now moves much faster than human thought. In the early twentieth century, capital utilized psychoanalysis to satisfy drives and get past defences, now algorithmic processes do this job but at a much finer grain that was ever possible before.

TikTok has sped up the packet delivery. There is now no longer any need to prepare text, to pour over the spelling. The audiovisual capability of the smartphone, now with more than 4 billion in use on the planet makes the production and delivery of audiovisual affect packets blindingly fast. In this context, it is perhaps no surprise that what was once called art is now being called *content*. But *content* obscures what is happening here, audio-vision has become the central modality for the affective grab. Modality and not language. Audio-vision must not be reduced to a language, to fall back into linguistic signifiers; it is much more than this. Peirce described semiosis as being composed of three parts: firstness (affect) secondness (percept), thirdness (concept). In the foregoing discussion, we have discussed affect and percept, without recourse to concept, to the name of Barthes's mother. Audio-vision's indexicality is slippery, that is to say, it operates microperceptually. Additionally, as Gilles Deleuze has pointed out, audio-vision is made up of movement-images and time-images that extend Pierce's semiosis into a variety of other signs all bearing duration and change, a semiosis that was more free of capitalisms capture than social media. Social media is a machine for the production of capitalist value both for its operators and its users, and is transforming art practice. Users produce content in the hopes for likes, shares and followers. Users trade their information, or perhaps speculate might be better, in the hopes of generating social and cultural capital. This capital becomes an important aspect of their digital as well as their biological lives. The trade between digital hardware and human wetware has wide-ranging implications for the human. From the perspective of art production, this has led to the transformation of art into content.

DIY+ and the micropolitics of capitalist audio-vision

What began as a digital disruption of cinema has solidified into platform capitalism and is having a wide-ranging impact on the people who were once called aspiring artists. They are now more likely to be identified or self-identify as aspiring content creators. Content creators operate in what once was called

DIY production, more closely identified with anti-capitalist tendencies, like Breagan. DIY is different now. Digital tools have been proliferating. There has been a fascinating array of digital tools that have developed to help creators increase the speed, efficiency and impact of their creative practices all while reducing the cost and time associated with their production. DIY used to require long periods of practice, an acceptance of lo-fi aesthetic sensibilities and difficult distribution obstacles, dirtbag artfulnes. Today's emerging DIY rarely associates it with punk rock or any kind of underground; it aspires to global markets and capitalist values. Punk rock's DIY artists have given way to DIY+ content creators, parallel transhumanism's Human+. Platform capitalism values the proliferation of apps (digital applications) that speed up the production of audio-vision in the technological environment of Instagram, Facebook stories and TikTok just to name the most prevalent. Influencers are able to trade their accumulated cultural and social capital for economic capital. Early adopters of time-saving apps are promised an economic advantage on this marketplace of DIY+ content creators. App market places proliferate with tools to reduce time spent on production. This reduces the gap between content production and dissemination, allowing high-speed production of audio-vision.

As I was writing this, I came across an advertisement of a music video production app that promised me the ability to make a music video in a minute! I laughed to myself and downloaded the app. I uploaded random videos (that the app sifted from my photo stream) and chose a song that was included in the app based on a list of style or mood preferences. A minute later, I was adding effects and giggling at this silly music video of my dog Barley (affect packet!). Two minutes later, I downloaded the final video clip. Seconds later, I sent the video clip via IG to my partner for their chuckle (the vectoring of affect packets). They wrote back seconds later on IG (vectoring affect packet). We had a chuckle and a short text chat about Franco 'Bifo' Berardi and the end of the world (vectoring affect packet). The music video vectoring of affects was startling, not because it was good, but because it was affective and was made and shared in minutes. I may never watch it again; it is disposable audio-vision. But it was affective and provided an opportunity for creativity and communication. This app could quickly be adapted to make Instagram-ready advertisements for a local company or local band in short order and with very little training. And this sort of app responds to the increasing pressure for musicians to have audiovisual 'content' available to be shared on social media. Is this an automation of audio-vision? Is the skill-set that I have developed over the last fifteen years being outsourced to very basic AI?

Automation of the politics of audio-vision

But what did this app allow me to skip over? In other words, what was automated in this process? Is this tool just a straightforward time-saving device or should music studies scholars be taking moments like this to think more deeply about content creators and DIY+ and transhuman aspirations? This book is an exploration of audio-vision, its affects, percepts and concepts, about the events of production, and the kinds of thinking that I call cinema-thinking. Apps do not just 'save time' but automate artistic thinking, a kind of thinking that as of yet humanities scholars understand very little. One of the central reasons for this is a long-standing and very limited view of what constitutes thinking. This leads to a view that sees the app as having very little consequence on thinking. This separation obscures the politics of automation and the deleterious effects of losing audio-vision thinking to capitalist automation even before we know what we are at threat of losing. As I have tried to show throughout the book, there is bio-technological thinking that occurs in digital cinema production, in the production of audio-vision, and that the automation made possible by capitalist-oriented apps hasten the emergence of transhumanism, an ethico-aesthetic paradigm (Guattari 1995) that will exaggerate the problems of whiteness and classicism already present in the humanities. Just as the humanities begins a process of self-critique and the development of creative alternatives to the human, the transhuman is being mobilized, shaping a future out of reach of these critiques.

Social scientist: Ethnography

Making a contribution to the social sciences does not mean tying audio-vision to scientism or the universalizing that has characterized humanism. It also does not mean that audio-vision must become what Deleuze and Guattari would call a major science, working in allegiance with powers of domination, colonization and discipline. Though it is all too easy today to see the ways that scientific ethnography has done this. It is necessary to ask what the scientific value of ethnography might be. Deleuze and Guattari argue that the difference between these three approaches (art, science, philosophy) is their orientation to chaos. Chaos is not defined as disorder but by the 'infinite speed with which every form taking shape in it vanishes' (Deleuze and Guattari 1994: 118). This void is pure virtuality, not a lack of order but 'containing all possible particles and drawing out all possible forms'. Science approaches virtuality by slowing it down, turning speed into a function. We can see the way the concept of culture is used by ethnographers to slow down the virtuality of social becomings, and then transcribe upon this a specific type of concept, a function, that can explain social order. The function can then become a subject for analysis, dispute and the production of discipline-specific knowledge. One might think of the organization of instruments into classes, ritual, tradition, identity, race, economy, hybridity, space, psychology, medicine, acoustics, technology, culture, indigeneity, colonization as functions that give shape to analysis.

Ethnographers operate as partial observers producing ethnographies that develop or replace functions. According to Deleuze and Guattari, the 'role of a partial observer is *to perceive* and *to experience*' (1994: 130), but they are quick to note that the perceptions and affects do not belong to the human but instead belong to 'the thing studied'. Of course the human who is also the ethnographer does indeed experience the perceptions and affects of music, but their point is that the ethnographer, within the human, is an 'ideal observer' who has been internalized by the person who sets out to do ethnography.[6] The ethnographer as partial observer is a force, or perhaps, as ethnographers multiply they become forces that perceive and experience. The percepts and affects of music are music's own. They operate on the ethnographer as the ethnographer operates on them, attempting to discern functions that explain their operations and their vectoring. Ethnographers are instituted, shaped or formed, in the body of the student and researcher. They are constituted by approaches or by proper names. There is, for instance, a collection of ethnographers in my body that all respond to a music event. Over the years their numbers have grown. Each appreciative reading of an ethnography instates a new force, a new partial observer, with the power to enrich observation and experience.

The ethnography is a report that seeks to illuminate the functions of a culture. The identification of these functions is the central motivator for the social scientific approach in ethnomusicology; it produces, as science does, a plane of reference (Deleuze and Guattari 1994: 118). The plane of reference is constituted by functions that describe relationships between bodies as objects moving through space. Functions are constituted by endoreference and exoreference, coordinates on the plane of reference. The plane of reference begins to take form in the training of ethnomusicology students. World music survey courses lay out initial coordinates especially as they are laid out against popular music and Western art music history courses. Conversations are underway in many universities about the value and appropriateness of this pedagogical formation. Many critics have clearly argued that they maintain a colonial framework and should therefore be reconsidered. And while this position gains traction, there are few alternatives emerging. The reason perhaps can be identified in the colonial history of the university and its disciplines, the university-as-settlement. The endocoordinates of humanism, the human, and its exocoordinates, technology and nature must be rethought as posthumanography.

The plane of reference for music ethnography, as the plane of reference complexifies, has continuously transformed over the history of ethnomusicology. If one compares the focus of comparative musicology to that of phenomenological or Marxist ethnomusicology, for instance, the differences are quite profound. The former focused very closely on the organization of notes that differ between cultures in the search for universalizing principles for human music production. The endoreference were the notes and cultures, set across two axis that could be compared and contrasted, that is, produced functions. Phenomenological ethnomusicology on the other hand focuses very closely on the phenomenological or sensual data of the ethnographer where a Marxist ethnomusicology will examine systems, both technological and social, that give shape to a social field of music making that especially will include economic and social systems of power and exclusion. Both phenomenological and Marxist approaches (though many more can be named) added two more sets of coordinates to ethnomusicology's plane of reference. Ethnography populated as it is with living beings required the introduction of the internal states of bodies, endoreference, as well as the positions of those bodies in space-time, exoreference. The coordinates of music and culture remained and ethnomusicology can be said to become more complex. In the 1990s, during the period lightly called ethNOmusicology, the sets of references moved again. Music cultures were treated as bodies and their endoreferences were plotted against the exoreferences of political, economic and media systems.

These examples illustrate only the very beginning of a wide diversity of functions that an ethnomusicologist can take 'to the field' (exoreference). The point here is not to weigh in on their various strengths but instead to point out that the starting methodology brings to the world a set of coordinates, references, functions and partial observers. And that over time the sets of coordinates that populate the plane of reference called ethnomusicology have become more complex. The speed of complexity shows no sign of slowing down.

Conceptual personae, plane of immanence, concepts

The ethnographer is constituted by partial observers, the force of perception and experience. The proliferation of partial observers discussed above is a consequence of both ruptures in ethnographic practice and a confluence of the humanities and social sciences. With some of the ruptures discussed above, it is necessary to look to the philosophical stream that joins ethnography. Philosophy does not populate the body with partial observers but instead introduces conceptual personae, a force to think-feel along with. The conceptual personae's role is to 'show thought's territories, its absolute deterritorializations and reterritorialization' (Deleuze and Guattari 1994: 69). The work that it does is to be a friend to thinking, to be a critic of thinking. It exists entangled with concepts and planes of immanence upon which concepts and conceptual personae are organized. Phenomenological ethnomusicology perhaps most clearly illustrates the role of the conceptual personae. Merleau-Ponty as a conceptual personae works through phenomenological concepts for the reader, feels along the contours of sensual thought, shaping a phenomenological plane of immanence: 'Conceptual personae constitute points of view according to which planes of immanence are distinguished from one another or brought together, but they also constitute the conditions under which each pane finds itself filled with concepts of the same group' (Deleuze and Guattari 1994: 75). Moving from the plane of reference to the plane of immanence, from partial observers to conceptual personae introduces the second subjectivity behind the camera. But more needs to be said about concepts if they are going to help secure the ethnographic plane of reference, or perhaps, rupture it so badly that something other than ethnography will be required as a concept and function.

There are relationships between concepts and functions, between planes of reference and immanence, between partial observers and conceptual personae. These relationships are not structural, they are not supplied, not evident, nor are they foreshadowed. They are events. The functions of partial observers slow down a process and in doing so inaugurates a line of flight that connects to a conceptual personae and to a concept or constellation of concepts. The plane of immanence, formed and forming, resonates in the concept, calls forward an event setting thinking-feeling off in one or more directions.

Worlding as activist cine-ethnomusicology

The confluence of ethnography and digital cinema does not require giving up on the aims of ethnomusicology but it does require their rethinking. In Feld's classic 'Ethnomusicology and Visual Communication' (1976), he identified a confusion that stems from an 'inability to disentangle' (293) the manner in which one deals with disentangling the humanistic or social scientific from its role as entertainment. While he suggests that some ethnomusicologists recognize that film production is as important for students as writing, we can now recognize almost fifty years later how minor this orientation was. There has always been ethnomusicological film but it has remained in potential. The few articles in the *Journal for Ethnomusicology* on film production prove this point as does the 2019 pre-conference symposium on film production. Benjamin Harbert's 2018 *American Music Documentary: Five Case-Studies in Cine-Ethnomusicology* similarly illustrates that so far there has been little development of an ethnomusicological orientation to film production methods. Harbert focus on documentary filmmakers as the basis for cine-ethnomusicology suggests that there are not enough established ethnomusicological filmmakers to constitute of stand-alone volume on disciplinary methods not a uniquely ethnomusicological film theory. It might be said that the confusion that Feld identified is still causing problems. The filmmakers in Harbert's text provide excellent examples for the use of films to think about music, but because they are not social scientists, they have their own interests and preoccupations. The films can be read as music films that contribute to the understanding of music, and Harbert does this with great effect. The films included in American Music Documentary, however, as the title suggests, are working out issues in another discipline, documentary theory and practice. This is not a critique of Harbert's work, but an observation of the lack of development in ethnomusicology. We might once again ask as Feld did, 'And where is ethnomusicology in all of this?' (Feld 1976: 316). Feld concluded optimistically that perhaps 'it is at the best possible point, because it has the opportunity to tap directly into the foundation being built in the anthropology of visual communication'. Visual anthropology has continued to develop and so too has ethnographic film but not necessarily in the same directions. Ethnographic film festivals are no longer, if they ever were, oriented to social science cinema by nature. They are often dominated by nonfiction films made by filmmakers. This is not a weakness but an observation that is in line with Harbert's orientation.

The most significant limit placed on the development of ethnomusicological film has been the orientation, shared with anthropology, to see films as a way of making records for later analysis (MacDougall 2006: 264). To use a film or digital camera as a field recorder for interviews is a sensible option. But it is not the basis of filmmaking of either the social scientific or documentary variety. To do this is to ignore, as I will explore later, the unique contribution that digital cinema can offer ethnomusicology, the study of music as an event. It also radically misses cinema technology. In much the same way that writing ethnography seemed transparent until the writing cultures debate that recognized ethnography as a form of writing, so too does ethnomusicological film need this level of meta-analysis.[7] In Karl Heider's *Ethnographic Film*, for instance, there is both a 'neutralness' of methodology combined with a simple binary between ethnographic truthfulness and aesthetic pleasure (MacDougall 2006: 265). This binary is only possibly maintained by ignoring the process of cinematic production. This leaves Heider to require an evaluation mechanism 'ethnographicness', instead of a direct analysis of production practices in ethnomusicological film. The focus on the product of the film is to miss the process and potential avenues for ethnomusicological analysis. Paraphrasing David MacDougall, if we were to start from scratch, unhindered by the legacy of arguments in ethnomusicology, we would likely come up with a very different approach to the study of music in society. Neither filmmaking nor digital cinema production has been seen to constitute an aspect of the film. Production processes have been treated as technological practices held at a distance from the episteme of ethnography.

Philosophy

Critical posthumanism, for instance, informed by science and technology studies, nomadic, cyborg and critical intersectional feminism, critical race theory and postcolonial studies returns to the central question of the humanities, what is the human, to recompose it. After more than a century of critique of the exclusionist, human endocoordinates (set out across the four axes of whiteness: heterosexual, able-bodied maleness, economic exchange and family ownership) the critical posthumanities attempt to rethink these coordinates. The process is in two related parts. The first is to set difference and not sameness at the heart of the project. This is a radical reworking of humanism. Instead of the human as a universal valued form, the human is emergent and entangled. Philosophies of difference and of process are contributing to this development. Process philosophy makes a break with platonic philosophical systems that characterized the dominant mode of philosophical and scientific thought over the preceding centuries. Activist philosophy seeks to sketch out the political valences of process philosophy and creativity.

The second move is to include that which has been externalized, technology and nature, into relations. This works against modernity/coloniality in the universal human that has been used as the marker of value in all of its militaristic and epistemological adventures. It also promotes a critical evaluation of the entangled biosphere, complete with technologically enhanced external memories, adapted ecologies and negative ecological, social and psychological impacts. The radical reworking of the plane of reference is producing new coordinates and new functions. Ethnographies of technoculture and of natureculture are introducing new ways to think ethnography. In the process, the prefix 'ethnos' is once again under attack. Often the critique of the term has to do with its relationship to colonialism. Often in defence it is pointed out that Ethnos means people. And while this is true, it does not mean all the people, it means those people who are not the Dēmos. The Dēmos, the unified body of citizens that constitute the democracy of free bodies, is imagined to have a shared set of endocoordinates for which the Ethnos is the term that marks the exocoordinates. Ethnography, writing about people, is a function between the Ethnos and the Dēmos. The ethnography's function is to help the Dēmos understand the Ethnos, and to constitute themselves in the mirror of Otherness. Beginning with a colonial gaze, whether the individual ethnographers shared that perspective or not, they nonetheless had no difficultly traversing the ethnographic bridge, as it were, the direction from Dēmos to Ethnos clearly established in established areas studies.

Critical Black thought and postcolonial theory has shown that on two levels the supposed Ethnos had always internalized the Dēmos. The internalization of the coordinates of the Dēmos inside the Ethnos functioned at the level of structural power differentials as well as psychic differentials. These might also be considered functions, of a very special sort that required a high degree of care. The Dēmos, whiteness in this case, but it could be a nation-state, a class, or any territorialized group who wields power, presents for itself sets of coordinates that protect its self-consciousness. It constructs a plane of reference with a set of functions that perpetuate a world of privilege, writing colonial difference into the logic of its functions. The one-directional logic of the ethnography is a good example of this. W. E. B Dubois and Franz Fanon blazingly analysed the double consciousness that emerges within this colonial system of power. Walter Mignolo has given a name to this function: the colonial difference. The colonial difference is a function of power and of resistance. It is an exoreference that contributes to the production of a doubling of consciousness, the endoreference of coloniality. Power moves across four ecologies (conceptual, social, technological, environmental) shaping their relations in each event. This radical conceptual of the doubling of consciousness internalizes the worlding of the world of a community with its processes of subjectivation, as well as the worlding of the colonial world, and its subjectivations.

What happens when the Dēmos becomes aware that the Ethnos has always been looking back? When the Dēmos internalizes that they, the Dēmos, have caused the double consciousness? Perhaps many things. The most obvious are two possibilities that seem to be playing out. The first, which is playing out in news headlines around the world, a doubling down on the humanist plane of reference. Nationalisms and fascism have been emerging in an attempt to retain the old order, to keep the coordinates and the bodies that have been kept under those coordinates in place and the direction of view policed. The second is a move to radically rework the exclusionary humanism; this is the role being played by posthumanism, an attempt to remake a plane of reference that internalizes the lessons learned.

Perhaps one outcome is a dissolving of the Ethnos-Dēmos binary in three senses. First, as described above, following the struggle against the colonial difference, which is ultimately to struggle against coloniality and to find a way towards decoloniality. The second is to recognize that the Dēmos has already been dissolved. The impacts of global capitalism have transformed citizens into consumers, students into customers, elected officials into brands and political action into purchasing practices. Neoliberalism and now platform (cybernetic) capitalism have transformed a world populated by citizens who share (supposedly thought this may have always been a fiction of nationalism) a view of the world, into an explosion of interconnected worlds. I am not necessarily taking a moral position on this at this moment. From the perspective of the plane of reference, it is first necessary to set out the endo- and exoreferences for this field. The Marxist class divisions, while useful until perhaps the 1980s, have lost their connection to the field. Capitalism powers radical multiplications of identities, a proliferation of subjectivities, that Deleuze and Guattari characterized as schizophrenic. The third approach, which is perhaps more actively productive than the other two, is to participate in the health of the undercommons.

Critical theory

It may be desirable to understand global capitalism as a new form of colonization, and certainly it has characteristics of coloniality, built as it is from these foundations. But that would be to miss a crucial detail, the transformation of power. Foucault clearly outlined the disciplinary society that emerged alongside of capitalism. Advances in the second half of the twentieth century, however, transformed capitalism as it became an integrated world system. There is no longer an outside, the third reason to dissolve the Dēmos-Ethnos binary. The integrated world system of capitalism requires a rethinking of the logic of ethnography that can make sense out of the integrated and cybernetic reality of capitalism, the role of the smartphone in your hand from waking till sleeping. The constant surveillance by business, the human body as GPS tracked consumer in a world under existential threat. The global connections across privately owned platforms that promote personal broadcasting of the most intimate details of one's life in exchange for social and cultural capital. Where successful environmental activism brings together an understanding of the biosphere on illuminated screens made of metals whose mining is destabilizing countries. The role that these technologies play in the production of subjectivities and, ultimately, the emergence of a society characterized not by discipline but by control. Ethnomusicology has developed two responses to this context: reflexivity and relationality.

Reflexivity in ethnography begins as a rupture that sets up another set of coordinates on the plane of reference. Reflexivity is the emergence of a form of relationality that moves ethnography into the body of the ethnographer drawing the ethnographer into the plane of reference. Emerging as a cybernetic notion that recognizes a change in the observer while a system is being observed, the observer is no longer a fixed form, a neutral instrument observing the operations of a system, but is now part of the system.

Becoming and observing an observer and becoming slowly slip inside each other multiplying the coordinates on the ethnographic plane of reference. Giving this two axes relationality coordinates upon the ethnographic plane of reference required new functions in the form of applied, shared and activist ethnographies. As the ethnographer transforms, they begin recognizing their positionality, their access to institutional power which becomes a circuit. First shared, then applied and then activist modes of ethnography might be seen as increasingly the reversal of the institutional power, attempting to reverse the flows which at the beginning were established to extract from the field.

This proliferation of coordinates on the plane of reference threatens to return the plane of reference to chaos. Ethnographers engineer a confluence with philosophy, turning to concepts formed on a plane of immanence before returning a new stream to ethnography. Where ethnography located functions on a plane of reference, philosophy works by creating concepts on a plane of immanence. The coordinates of science are characterized by an intense slowing of speed in order to make functions appear. Concepts, however, attempt to retain the speed of thought.

The death of ethnography?

The twentieth century is marked by the transformation of community in a profound way. Empires of imagined communities held together by print media in the nineteenth century were replaced by the cultural imperialism of the United States, Hollywood, American popular music, television. American media propagandize the 'American Dream' and the United States entered into a neocolonial relationship with the world, where popular culture worked alongside official economic, industrial and diplomatic policy. American neocoloniality has hidden its military interventions behind a choice for freedom, making it possible to simultaneously take distance from European coloniality while taking over its aims and its techniques. Americanization is a public pedagogy, a culturally informed teaching and learning practice that has as its aim the cantering of American-styled consumption. The transformation of economic policy from production to consumption created a fertile ground for the digital disruption that has further transformed 'culture', liquidating from it any lingering pre-modern characteristics, putting every previous meaning of culture to work in the global economy.

The UK government of Tony Blair made culture an industry in the 1990s. New concepts not only provide new ways of thinking about the present but also work on the organization of the past. The cultural industries, while present and important throughout the twentieth century, came under closer governmental analysis, while also being absorbed, after a period of technological disruption, into increasingly centralizing digital platforms, which centralize dissemination (and therefore power) while radically decentralizing the content. What marks this new period is the integration of digital technology into the intimate lives of users, the global use of these digital audiovisual technologies, and more than ever before, the way users' every activity shapes the outcome of the information that they are provided. In this way, each user curates a world that appears to them as 'the' world, and this world is populated by other users like them who have been brought together by algorithmic cybernetic interaction – a system – that to the user appears to be chance. Because these digital worlds appear to the users as autonomous creations there has been little push back even after much publicized cases of manipulation, surveillance and even common observation. Targeted advertising, targeted news feeds, targeted lifestyle support, we all see ourselves in our feeds that we casually call echo chambers. What does the emergence of these corporately administered and surveilled spaces mean for those of us who study humanity? And what kinds of skills are necessary to develop within the humanities for this study. Empirically oriented cultural studies, which I want to distinguish from semiotic, psychoanalytic and philosophical orientations require a new kind of work that at its base requires new language and new methods: posthumanography.

To date, the focus on globalization, imagined communities has been philosophically oriented to unification, to nationalism, to global consciousness. And while this may have been occurring in the twentieth century through the domination of global media, the emergence of digital media in the twenty-first century has moved in the opposite direction. Unification and belonging, the nationalist projects of modernity, are being destroyed. The hegemony of master narratives is losing its power and in its place emerge echo chambers (worldings) that encourage the emergence of new kinds of belonging, new kinds of hegemony which threaten the nationalist myths without also challenging the political and military power of the state. In fact, as we have seen with the transition of power from Trump to Biden, this emergence aims to take over the state's monopoly on violence. The nation, and its institutions, are becoming sites of internal struggle. But at the same time economic authority of the nation is being challenged by a growing technocratic elite whose wealth comes from digital platforms which contribute to the disruption of cultural authority and introduce opportunities and challenges, the emergences of progressive and radical movements equally with anti-government, anti-science conspiracy theory and regressive white supremacist movements. Platforms have no ethics and make possible both the emergence of Black Lives Matter and Q'anon. The concern that media culture would become homogenous within mass media needs to be replaced with ways of understanding how it is becoming possible to live in the same geographical space, even the same family unit, but in different and sometimes incompatible lifeworlds.

The obstacle to this work is a lack of audiovisual production capacity. It is no longer a question of literacy in the sense of being able to 'read' media, we have all been taught to read media by capitalist power, the question is how to 'hack' media, to create alternative lifeworlds, and this requires a knowledge of how to produce media and in learning to do so to discover how media hacks the users. In the process of learning how to produce media, we can learn how to spot locations of power and how to identify pedagogical resources for a posthumanities of technocultures. And perhaps, more importantly, as we identify the cultural power of digital media, do not we also develop a responsibility to actively engage in the production of future-looking alternative lifeworlds, lifeworld futurity?

Globalization and corpocultures

Since the collapse of the Soviet Union and the emergence of China as an economic superpower, it is impossible to think about globalization apart from economic control, control societies, digital communications and automation. This was not always the case. The creation of the Communist Internationale in the nineteenth century and the International Workers of the World in America ushered in an opportunity to briefly think about globalization separate from coloniality. These alternative international groups imagined a world of unified workers able to exert pressure on international companies, limiting their power by controlling their ability to take advantage of labour. Unfortunately, labour and trade unions became bound by national logic and with the success of the Bolshevik Revolution, internationalism was replaced by state communism. This would have the effect of producing different lifeworlds. A lifeworld of commerce and a lifeworld of labour. The industrial and then financial (though this might as easily be reversed) lifeworld had already established a global perspective in the age of European colonialism. Labour's international lifeworld would only begin in the nineteenth century and would be dimmed before the Second World War. By the time America and the Soviet Union were fighting over the moon, trade unions would briefly enjoy successes and would seem to leave the question of internationalism behind, a cause taken up by activists. Since the early 1970s when American moved their currency off of the gold standard, truly virtualizing it, only capital was global. American industrial production, one of two areas of work to be successfully unionized, began an irreversible migration that would have destabilizing effects on American life that by the beginning of the twenty-first century would begin to emerge into public consciousness. The late twentieth century marked a short-lived series of large public demonstrations against financialization that would come to a head with the Occupy movement, which was universally ridiculed by mainstream media for having no focus, no point, no central demands, ignoring that the main point was an attempt to resuscitate internationalism around issues of economic, civic and environmental insecurity. It seemed that the Dēmos was trying to regain its place in the nation-state, feeling perhaps that it was being replaced by capital. It is my thesis that the Dēmos no longer signifies the people, but is instead, the capital in both the financial and geographical sense, the merger of political and economic power has been increasingly privatized. Two immediate features of this division are the corpoculture takeover of space exploration, which has a shocking parallel to the early stages of colonization, this time with its focus on a new world, the moon and mars. As well as the widespread automation of work which has the potential to reduce the opportunities of employment with no guaranteed living wage in its place. There exists only minimal resistance to these new expressions of power because I believe there is little space for discourse outside of corpocutlures about what is coming. Evidence once again of the dissolution of the Dēmos.

Both the terms 'Dēmos' and 'Ethos' need to be replaced as they no longer have any theoretical value. In its place I am suggesting that the term 'worlding' can provide an orientation for posthumanographic scholarship oriented to both understanding and resisting transhumanism.

Conclusion: Research-creation's transversality

There must be a reason, an appropriateness, to choose cinema-thinking. To define cinema-thinking through the critique of writing operates in the reactive mode at the very beginning, and remains, through negation, tied to writing-thinking as the major thus subordinating the very thing that must be understood for itself and on its own terms. Cinema-thinking does not fill in gaps in writing-thinking; it operates differently and for itself. It is obvious that cinema-thinking was only possible with the advent of the cinema technology, but this does not mean that a completely new mode of thought was introduced into the world. It is possible to consider the invention of cinema as setting free a force that has always been immanent to thought, that was virtual in thought, and that was actualized in the invention of cinema. That cinema was captured by entertainment and capitalism does not on its own push cinema-thinking out of the university. Though as Steven Feld recognized in the 1970s, it does present a challenge to overcome, how do researchers disentangle social science cinema from entertainment?

I do not, however, think that this is a useful starting point. This approach avoids understanding cinema-thinking moving directly past what it can offer to a determination of what the correct object looks like, a belief that there exists purity of form that can be found. There is plenty of evidence to suggest that there is an aesthetics of truth, or what Jill Godmillow calls a 'pornography of the real'[8] in documentary and cinema vérité. It is not the consequence of Feld's question but an assumption that there needs to be a separation between social science film form and entertainment film form. Must we retain purity? However, as Feld knew or would come to know in his translation of Jean Rouch's writings on filmmaking, ethnofiction uses cinematic storytelling to communicate ethnographic content. Cinematic ethnography is, therefore, already not a pure form.

It is necessary to define cinema-thinking from within practice in order to make space in scholarly discourse for the mess of cineworlding. This book is in response to a number of situations that have illustrated the need for this approach, written for those who make cinema, for those who want to think about the impurities of cinema-thinking, for those who are interested in expanding modes of scholarly discourse, and for those who might be interested in cinema because of the opportunities for sharing that are being developed. In order to open space for a conversation about cinema-thinking, we must first clear out of the way some preconceptions that have hindered the development of a scholarly analysis of film production.

As some universities move to expand the kinds of outcomes that constitute objects of knowledge, like a thesis or dissertation, there has not been a matching expansion of media-thinking. It is assumed that making a film is working in a grammar of images instead of words and because scholars can write then they can make a film. This is never stated but implied. It is implied in the lack of cinema production classes offered to students and in the lack of opportunity to think about thinking in different media. To act in a medium is to think in a medium. When the entire curriculum is composed of reading and writing and then a student is offered an opportunity to work in a different medium, without thinking about thinking in a different medium then the scholarly work is impoverished. Cinema-thinking is thinking differently than print in profound ways. We cannot be expected to have original thoughts in a medium that we know little about, have little capacity in and do not understand technically. It is also necessary to recognize that while we are surrounded by audio-vision, we do not necessarily understand its relation to thought. I believe taking the time to work through the consequences of cinema-thinking can be a small step towards decoloniality in knowledge production.

10

Elders' Room

The opportunities and challenges of decoloniality

If the body is populated with aesthetic and conceptual personae, as I argued in the last chapter, perhaps settler scholars are also composed of colonial personae, colonial diagrams. If solidarity with the commons is central to ethical futurity, its building is fraught with risk. There are power differentials between the settlement and the commons, the settlement and Indigenous nations, racially Othered communities that are also run through by class-based differences. The risk is not for technocrats of settlement, but for those who have already borne the brunt of enclosure. If there will be solidarity between the university-as-settlement and the commons, it will require engaging with truth and reconciliation. In Canada, *Truth and Reconciliation* refers to the Truth and Reconciliation Commission of Canada that was established in 2008 as part of the 'Indian Residential Schools Settlement Agreement' (TRC 2015: 23) with a mandate to

> Reveal to Canadian the complex truth about the history and the ongoing legacy of the church-run residential schools, in a manner that fully documents the individual and collective harms perpetrated against Aboriginal peoples, and honors the resilience and courage of former students, their families, and communities; and
>
> Guide and inspire a process of truth and healing, leading toward reconciliation within Aboriginal families, and between Aboriginal peoples and non-Aboriginal communities, churches, governments, and Canadians generally. The process was to work to renew relationships on a basis of inclusion, mutual understanding, and respect. (TRC 2015: 23)

In order to begin reconciliation there has to first be truth telling. The settlement needs to face its complicity in coloniality. As I have been suggesting over this book, it means seeing European and American scholarship as *regional* cultural studies that presented itself as universal knowledge. Recognizing this is meant to encourage and empower the localization of knowledge production. Local knowledge production can be a way of building solidarity. As bell hooks writes:

> Those of us who truly believe racism can end, that white supremacist thought and action can be challenged and changed, understand that there is an element of risk as we work to build community across difference. The effort to build community in a social context of racial inequality (much of which is class based) requires an ethic of relational reciprocity, one that is anti-domination. With reciprocity all things do not need to be equal in order for acceptance and mutuality to thrive. If equality is evoked as the only standard by which it is deemed acceptable for people to meet across boundaries and create community, then there is little hope. Fortunately, mutuality is a more constructive and positive foundation for the building of ties that allow for differences in status, position, power, and privilege whether determined by race, class, sexuality, religion, or nationality. (hooks 2009: 87)

Mutuality is a form of social intimacy, a relation in the encounter. Social knowledge production that is built on mutualism has the potential to be transformative to move towards reconciliation: 'reconciliation's non-representational pull of resolution . . . [where] reconciliation takes the form of feeling a transformative experience' (Robinson 2020: 203). Robinson's discussion about the affect of reconciliation shares much with the vectoring of affect discussed in earlier chapters. But I wonder how else this affect might be experienced. Is it an affect of reconciliation as Robinson suggests when settler audiences are drawn to their feet in acclaim of Indigenous artistic performance, or an *affect of relief* to have avoided the truth of a history and continuity of Indigenous oppression?[1] I'm perhaps going to be a buzzkill in this chapter because I believe that in music and sound studies, as is the case in much of colonial society globally, settlers have not yet faced the truth of the truth and reconciliation process.

This is evident in my experience every time committees get together to discuss entrance requirements and curriculum in music school. The conservatory is taken for granted and its preservation is universally agreed upon without discussion. I have never been in a room with music scholars discussing equity, diversity and inclusion, and colonization, and truth and reconciliation where the question has been asked: is this idea/structure of the conservatory morally and politically salvageable? Conversation skips over this and moves directly to tinkering with the organization and incorporation of the commons into the conservatory. We seem to operate as if the survival of the conservatory is unquestionable and universal. Doesn't this sound colonial? I wonder if this lack of discussion is a prohibition, resisting a critical decolonial interrogation. I do not think either a yes or no answer is good enough. I also want to begin this discussion with the point that I am not suggesting that the conservatory be dismantled to be replaced by the research university, they are both the settlement. I am interested in this penultimate chapter to contribute to a discussion that comes out of my proposition for cinema-thinking and my personal experience making *Pimachihowan* and *Elders' Room*. Pedagogically we need to have a far-reaching conversations that we have yet to have. If, as I have tried to show, that bodying is diagrammatic and works across four ecologies (conceptual, social, technological, environmental), then there is perhaps posthuman vectors and transhuman vectors, vectors of decoloniality and vectors of neocoloniality. And from what we have seen in these previous studies, these vectors undoubtable move through each other contributing to in-foldings along their trajectories. The aesthetic-political question for me as I look through a camera is which vectors are being in-folded into this shot and how might we think of these expressive in-folding to tease out when they are complicit with coloniality and contributing to decoloniality. As is probably evident by now, I believe that research-creation has much to contribute to decoloniality of music and sound studies. I also think we can go further than Stevance and Lacasse's *interdiscipline*. But to do this, I think, requires that settler scholars begin to publicly examine their own complicity with coloniality, moments of coming into awareness what Paulo Freire calls *conscientização*, and give up on the purity[2] that is often evident in critical work. Alexis Shotwell notes: 'If we took seriously a notion of real interdependence of self with social world and ecologies, those worlds and those environments would need substantial redress. It is hard to conceive of what healing in this broader sense could be' (2016: 34) and as Shotwell notes it is difficult to work towards this healing when

> the forms – the structures and technologies of sorting and managing identity – were developed in the work of colonization, and those are still the modes the state uses in its partial and incomplete attempts at righting those wrongs . . . we ought to consider how might we pursue, in [Taiaiake] Alfred's words, a response to the *whole context of the situation and all of the factors involved* in order to resist, shift, and reconfigure the available classificatory frameworks toward true, complexly interdependent, flourishing. (Shotwell 2016: 35)

Coloniality holds both the settler-colonizer and the Indigenous colonized in place, the oppressor and the oppressed. In Paulo Freire's critical pedagogy, he urges the dissolving of the bonds that hold the oppressor-oppressed identities to their place. The question of how to do this is related to Harney and Moten's undercommons of the enlightenment, the cultivation of the undercommons, and the outside of teaching. These proposals are, I think, different yet related to the aspiration of an *interdiscipline* in music and sound studies. I do not think, following Shotwell, that we can produce a classificatory system for musicology and sound studies that can be decolonial, it will remain mired in coloniality. The alternative is to let go. Let go of both the traditional conservatory and the research university, to open space for research-creation's social and cultural futurity, for dreaming the future and creating it in the present. What about grades and curriculum. Let it go. Why do we need to hold onto such things in art school anyway? What about evaluation? Let it go. Replace it with conversation about practice and materials, about sharing ideas in community space. What about grad school acceptance? Let's figure it out. Perhaps we can forget grades and focus on the art portfolio (in whatever medium including writing) that students create.

The proposition to let go comes out of the struggle of writing about *Pimachihowan*, from an experience during the making of *Pimachihowan*, and the filming of *Elders' Room*. The chapter on Pimachihowan was the first completed chapter in this book and the hardest to write. The experience of its writing produced the seed for cineworlding. Chief Sewepagaham's pedagogy and his resistance to separating music from the livingness and in-act of Pimachihowan forced me to think differently. In the process of trying to write about the film as ethnomusicology, I was constantly facing a challenge of fitting it into the discipline. Draft after draft (almost ten versions) moved slowly. In each draft I would feel the pressure to conform it to a discipline, to try to make an argument for why this is an example of audiovisual ethnomusicology. I then met Erin Manning and shared a draft with her and her comments began to open up my thinking. She was not bound to audiovisual ethnomusicology and admitted to knowing little about ethnographic film. She asked me why I felt so obliged to fit the film into a disciplinary box. I had no good answer. There is no one sitting next to my desk making sure I fit into ethnomusicology. So why am I twisting and turning to try to make it fit? Why not let it be my teacher. Let it tell me what it is that it can be.

The proposal to let go comes from this experience. To let go of my need to only work on music topics, to let go of my practice of not writing about non-music-centric films. *Pimachihowan* and *Elders' Room* make contributions to decoloniality in the oil and gas industry and in education. Why not make these films central to what I am doing as a research-creation practitioner? I believe the answer to this has to do with a need for a belonging into audiovisual ethnomusicology, the need to belong to a discipline. But what of another kind of belonging might I aspire? The kind that is belonging to this place, this province and its issues. In *Belonging: A Culture of Place* (2009), bell hooks writes about her return to Kentucky, to the challenges of leaving a city, to return to where she was born. I do not have the opportunity yet to return to Cape Breton, the small island where I was born. But I can do the work of making Alberta home, the place where I live and work. To do this, as bell hooks suggests, requires that I 'use my resources not only to recover and protect damaged green space but to engage in a process of hilltop healing' (68). The hilltop healing in Alberta is coloniality. Filmmaking is the art practice that I can use to enact healing:[3] 'art and artifice, resides in that space where art and life come together' (hook 2009: 160). The goal of my practice should not be about endearing myself to discipline, to settlement, but to community, the commons. There still remains in the previous chapter, where I explore the crowd behind the camera, residual energy of disciplinarity, the truth of the enduring coloniality that haunts my body.

Colonialities vectoring and becoming-wintigo

There is a story that I withheld from Chapter 8 that I feel needs to be included here. The story picks up on the long walk back to Chief Sewepagaham's house. The truck had been performatively stuck in the mud and we began the long late-night walk back. Hours into the walk, a pickup truck zooms by. It returns sometime later coming up behind us very quickly. The driver pulls off to the side of the road and begins loudly speaking towards us in *Nêhiyawêwin* (Cree). Chief Sewepagaham chuckles and replies. There is a collective laughing that was not explained to me as we get into the back of the truck and make our way home. The shared joke is that his cousin thought that Sewepagaham was walking with or being followed by wintigo. Wintigo[4] are terrifying white-skinned cannibalistic creatures who have an insatiable hunger. Being confused for a wintigo was fraught for me. When it happened I quite honestly did not know how to respond but to chuckle. But in time I began to think of it more processually. My body is a white screen after all, why not project wintigo onto it? But the more I began to think about it, the more I began to wonder about the ways that coloniality can be understood as a wintigo, a possession, a haunting. It could be that the haunting that Erin Manning noticed was also noticed during the making of *Pimachihowan*. That my relationship to the haunting of colonialism, to the livingness of coloniality in my body is something that I must consider, that I must face. Can the wintigo explain something of the terrors of coloniality that as a society we cannot yet face?

Wintigo's reflection

I catch my reflection on the glass wall encasing a large pile of buffalo skulls. A bearded white face that probably looks quite a lot like any of the faces of the colonial murderers who I see stand gloatingly next to this mountains of buffalo bones. The cacophony and madness of rifle shots out of the window of a moving train floods my mind. A scene from Jim Jarmusch's *Dead Man*. Don't we all want to be guiltless like Johnny Depp's William Blake, or Leonardo DiCaprio's Hugh Glass? Doing that, however, means leaving this slaughter unexplained, the souls of murderers unexamined. What kind of madness is colonization? It is not just the capture of land, but the identification and systematic eradication of a keystone species of a nation, and the attempted cultural genocide that followed. Mountains of buffalo dead, bones that testify to darkness and madness, and the horrors of the residential school system dedicated to assimilation to 'kill the Indian in the child' (Shotwell 2016: 24). Treaties were signed between the Canadian government and Indigenous nations, promising partnership as Treaty Commissioner Alexander Morris did in 1876: 'What I trust and hope we will do is not for to-day and tomorrow only; what I will promise, and what I believe and hope you will take, is to last as long as the sun shines and yonder river flow' (TRC 2015: 53). The official position by the government, however, was always conceived to be an agreement to 'cede, release, surrender, and yield' their land (TRC 2015: 53). This is by definition bad-faith actors. What produced these bad-faith actors, these colonialists? Sartre suggested in his analysis of colonialism that 'violence and destruction were an integral part of the desired objective . . . for the child of the colonialist, violence was present in the situation itself, and was a social force which produced him . . . this is because it used to be violence-*praxis* when the system was in the process of being installed' (Sartre 2004: 718). Coloniality is *violence-praxis* that is not just an operation but works as a machinic operation, a component of the diagram, the bodying and vectoring of coloniality. A vectoring that was recognized when my body became a white wall upon which wintigo was projected. I saw the way I was being seen and it shook me deeply. It was a lesson that remained intensive until I visited Head-Smashed-In Buffalo Jump and saw the photos of the white-skinned murderers, liars and monsters who looked just like me. It was wintigo's reflection.

Surveillance and witnessing

Head-Smashed-In Buffalo Jump is a UNESCO World Heritage Site located in Blackfoot traditional territory in what settler Canadians call southern Alberta. It is an interpretive centre dedicated to educating visitors about the central role buffalo played in the lives of the Blackfoot Confederacy, a collection of Indigenous nations that live on the western plains of Turtle Island (North America). It is also a monument to the madness of colonization, the machinery of whiteness that by 1881 completed a 'near extinction'[5] of the once massive buffalo herds that roamed the short grasslands here.

I hesitate in front of the exhibitions. I explained when I arrived that I was in pre-production for a film about an educational initiative called *Elders' Room* at the Kainai Highschool on the Kainai (Blood) Nation. I asked if I could film some of the exhibitions for use in the film. The management agreed easily with little in the way of restrictions. I had been filming the ridges of bones, the dark emptiness of empty eye sockets, the soft light pooling gently on broad foreheads. Playing with the reflection of myself in the glass I began to think about the surveillance implicit in observational documentary. Is it possible to make an observational documentary that short-circuits the surveillance function? To find another way to think about observation?

The lights dimmed in the air-conditioned viewing room and the screen lit up with an interpretive documentary film about how Blackfoot since time immemorial used Head-Smashed-In Buffalo Jump as a hunting ground. Reenactments were elaborated with archaeological interpretation. It was hard to shake the feeling that this film intended to distance me, my whiteness, from my complicity. I shared the room with a small number of other tourists. There was such a distance from my lesson at Conroy's fire. The temperature-controlled room shut out the sharp wind that cut across the plains and bent the tall grass. Details about the overwhelming number of buffalo and their annihilation, the arrival of the Royal Canadian Mounted Police, colonization, the 'opening' of the west, as if it were closed. How can we image that the fences of farmers and ranchers, the steel lines of train tracks, the human enclosures called reservations that penned in Blackfoot peoples separating them and their descendants from their land and lifeways can be called an opening? Nowhere was there a character study of murderers. Nowhere was there an explanation of what drove white people to such incivility. I was left cold, not by what I learned, but instead, by what I did not. What I could not learn here. Conroy's fire continued to burn in my imagination. I needed to see the land with my own eyes and so did everyone who was going to understand the importance of what Kainai youth, elders, teachers and guidance counsellors built in the Kainai High School. It was a small room that was transformed when students reached out to elders to build a learning lodge. A place where elders could practice traditional pedagogy. To make sense of the lodge, of the act of decoloniality that emanates from the lodge it was necessary to not start with death and madness, that was something that I had to deal with. I needed to start with seeing the land with my own eyes.

That evening I downloaded a Blackfoot welcome song that was recorded by Kainai drummers. For two days I drove around the traditional territory listening to the welcome song and filming scenes of the land. Following the approach that we had learned with Conroy, I began to find myself becoming transformed through the lens of my camera. Reaching out, not to steal images, but to share a journey of seeing the land with my own eyes, to witness the beauty and openness of the land. These two days began my land acknowledgement.

Land acknowledgements[6] are intended to recognize the traditional territories and treaty obligations – treaty is a formal relationship between colonial forces (Britain and then Canada) and sovereign Indigenous nations – that settler colonialism has historically attempted to erase and undermine. Land acknowledgements are a public response to the outcome of the Canadian Truth and Reconciliation Royal Commission that confirmed that the Canadian government attempted to wipe out Indigenous language, culture and identity. One of the most public weapons was the Indian Residential School, the use of colonial pedagogy as a genocidal weapon. Long before post-structuralists theorized the production of subjectivity, coloniality used police and education to operationalize epistemological warfare upon subjectivities. Subjectification operated by forced assimilation.

Many colonial organizations currently use land acknowledgements though its use is not without critique.[7] Some argue its performativity stops short of real transformation. Land acknowledgements alone risk falling short of a truly engaged relationship with the land and the Indigenous nations that have lived on this land since time immemorial. As I travelled through the Blackfoot nation, listening to the welcome song, I felt that the opening of the film needed to become a critical land acknowledge in audio-vision, an act of critical pedagogy. While the central topic of the film is *Elders' Room*, its founding is inseparable from the ongoing struggle with coloniality expressed through intergenerational trauma, of murdered and missing Indigenous women and girls, disproportionate imprisonment of Indigenous people, unequal access to infrastructure including education, industrial development and even clean water.

Elders' Room as critical pedagogy is not made for Indigenous people, though the story of *Elders' Room* can be of value to many high schools in Indigenous nations around the world. The critical pedagogical orientation to *Elders' Room* is for settler Canadians. It is a film about Indigeneous cultural renaissance and the work that elders, teachers and youth are doing together to challenge coloniality. The film's director Dr Shirley Steinberg helped realize a story featuring Kainai elder Peter Weasel Moccasin, a residential school survivor, and his granddaughter Karsen Black Water, who is also one of the youths who led the creation of *Elders' Room*. As a white settler filmmaker, I found myself telling two stories to two different audiences. It is a story about Indigenous resistance but also an act of witnessing[8] as a critical pedagogy of whiteness.

Cineworlding witnessing as critical pedagogy of whiteness/coloniality

Cineworlding witnessing is an inversion of Paul Freire's existential situation. It is not about providing literacy education to Indigenous people but instead as a critical pedagogy of whiteness/coloniality. In Freire's *Education for Critical Consciousness* (2008), he proposed a form of political literacy education while providing literacy education to non-literate Brazilians. He noted, however, that Portuguese was a colonial language and that contributing to universal literacy in Portuguese would make a contribution to the ongoing colonial project (because colonization is not a historical period but a process). But he also understood that participation in the developing economy in Brazil meant that it was essential to be literate in Portuguese. This presented an ethical dilemma. Not providing literacy education in order to struggle against colonialism meant that people not literate in Portuguese would be left out of the economy and further marginalized.

Economic participation is necessary because equity cannot happen without access to employment. However, conventional literacy education would do cultural and social damage to an already marginalized and colonized population further separating them from language and culture. His starting point, the foundation for critical pedagogy, was a politicized literacy education.

The first step was to work with a visual artist to create a series of twelve sketches about the daily life of the community. Community members would come together with a teacher/facilitator in what Freire called a culture circle. The culture circle is different from the classroom for two reasons. First, the teacher is not in a position of authority as the only individual in the room with knowledge. Second, the student is not an empty disciplined body waiting to be filled with factoids. In the culture circle, the teacher can be recognized as having a method, and their experience and knowledge in delivering a method can be respected but only when the community agrees about a project. This method addresses ethical as well as political questions, what Felix Guattari calls an ethico-aesthetic paradigm. Art, however, is a complex object with a history tightly bound with coloniality, it is necessary to do three things before returning to audio-vision witnessing: (a) situate Art in its Western context, (b) discuss Art in its relationship to modernity/coloniality, (c) introduce decoloniality.

Art in modernity

Aesthetics is a branch of philosophy that studies Art. It emerged in modernity. 'Modernity' is a difficult term because while it is often used to suggest a time period between that of premodern and postmodern, the 'idea and feeling of it can be traced back to the Renaissance and the sense of *newness*' (Mignolo and Walsh 2018: 118). For some, modernity begins in the European Enlightenment, while for others it is the European Renaissance. As Walter Mignolo points out, its dominant meaning of 'growth, development and advancement to higher stages' is in use by 1600 (119). As I will discuss later, 'modernity' was a term that is used as the opposite of tradition, but both 'modernity and tradition are two modern concept' (119), not concepts that point to different periods. On first notice this is quite counter-intuitive and requires that we think about collective and social fiction, the stories we tell ourselves about ourselves to make sense of the world. This is what Donna Haraway means by 'stories that story'.

Let us start with the idea of creation stories. Creation stories tell 'us' about where we come from. These stories make sense out of the world and provide an orientation to our thinking. In Christianity, for instance, a singular God created the Garden of Eden and populated it with everything including two humans, who as you may know, broke the rules and began human histories search for a way of making it right with God for messing up and leaving paradise. This story provides a beginning (In the beginning was the word), a conflict (eating the apple from the tree of knowledge), and a teleology, a through line that point the direction to the end (salvation or rapture or the end times depending on your interpretation). Having been raised Christian, it was a very strange experience for me to discover that Confucius and Plato, for instance, wrote long before the development of the Christian Bible, and that the Mi'kmaq stories of Unamaki, what settlers call Cape Breton Nova Scotia, were much older than that even. From Mi'kmaq stories I learned about keeping balance, from Christian stories I learned about progress. Modernity is a creation myth that Western society tells itself about itself and its place and role in the world. And like the Christian story, and unlike the Mi'kmaq story, it is a story that sees itself to be universal, concerning all people everywhere at all times.

Art has a creation story. I use a capital Art to designate a historical period (eighteenth century) of the emergence of Art in Western society. The concept of Art emerged as expressive practices become separate from their useful place in community practices. Once the concept took hold for the moderns, it changed how they viewed the place of expressive practices in all society everywhere. By the early twentieth century, Cubist artist works like that of Picasso could be presented in the same exhibit as 'primitive African art'. Modern audiences were invited to marvel at these art works often rarely reflecting on the social process of modernity that allowed this kind of middle-class paid viewing to occur.

Archaeologists and museums showed art works of ancient civilizations and religious art of preceding modern societies side by side. But the artisans/craftspeople who made these historic objects did not think of themselves as artists, nor as the objects as artworks. The artisans would be dismayed by this new situation. But the audiences were not. How did this massive social change occur that produced the moderns? To understand this we have to think historically, about the rise of modernity, the emergence of colonization, the global spread of capitalism, and the transformational impacts this had both on the colonizers and the colonized. And since, as postcolonial theorists have clearly illustrated, colonization is not just a historical period, it is an ongoing process entwined with modernity that is itself entwined with capitalism. Walter Mignolo calls this ongoing process *coloniality* and thinking about *modernity/coloniality* a process of a developing *decoloniality*, a way of thinking-feeling against modernity/colonialities ongoingness.

Aesthetics created the art work for the moderns. When aesthetics developed, there were two competing ideas. The first by Baumgarten that aesthetics is the study of sensation in relation to art, the second by Kant that aesthetics is the study of aesthetic judgement. Both of these approaches accepted as a starting point the relationship between individuals and the art object, as an object of disinterested contemplation. Moderns believed art objects were 'useless' but in a very positive way. The work of art is not supposed to do any work, it is meant to be appreciated alone. It is helpful to situate these thinkers in the broader period of humanism where Art begins to become a kind of secular religion and artists became more like priests and philosophers than artisans and craft persons. Before this period, artisans created works of spiritual usefulness, for certain, but their work was not about them. Artisans did not sign their work, while they did cultivate personal styles it was not about their creativity but about their devotion to their spiritual practice (their study) or to facilitate community rituals. After the eighteenth-century art historians began to produce histories of these artists, and the ones that were genre defining were talked about as being a genius. The genius is a creation of the nineteenth century and along with the bohemian, the starving artist of the Romantic period, has continued to have an impact on contemporary understandings of art and artists, even for the artists themselves.

This is all made possible by radical economic changes characterized by the rise of the moderns. The period of royalty and divine rule was challenged by an entrepreneurial class that began to take advantage of commerce. Economic exchange itself became transformed with the centralization of wealth in the hands of capitalists. Craftspeople were displaced as industry-centralized production of all kinds and modern urban life emerged, the moderns. This was accelerated by global trade made possible by colonization and the centralized wealth of European countries transformed how these societies operated internally. Eventually, an artist class emerged but only after it became possible for artists to make their own money, or in many cases to not make much money. No longer servants or craftspeople working for those with wealth and power, artists began to sell their works for money, not just their services. The emerging European middle class began to become involved in art works and over time this led to the formation of what is called the art world, where artists were economic actors working with agents, ticket sellers, promoters and media. The art world is not static; however, it changes over time and in response to technological, social, economic changes in the society more generally.

In *The Death of the Artist* (2019), William Deresiewicz proposes four periods for thinking about artists over time: artisans, artists, professionals and producers. Artisans produce expressive works within a larger system of often religious/spiritual practice. It is also necessary to note here that it is necessary to recognize that the spiritual system is also the cultural system within which they lived. There was no separation between religion and life that developed with the separation of church and state in modernity. It was part of this transformation that the artist emerged as a quasi-religious figure of modernity. In the twentieth century, with the flourishing of universities and fine arts programmes, artists of all kinds become professionals, they worked and taught in schools, conservatories and universities. The professional artist created and showed art and for the most part made their living teaching. In recent years, with the financial cutbacks to universities, the increasingly tenuous contract-to-contract realities facing university sessionals (professors that are hired a semester at a time on a part-time basis with no job security), and with the expansion of digital platforms which has changed the working life of artists in extreme ways, Deresiewicz argues that artists are emerging as producers, that a large amount of their professional life is now spent marketing themselves on social media platforms. The artist, which in the earlier three periods was expected to have time to work and develop, now is expected to produce 'content' constantly.

On a personal note, as a contemporary creative, I was given advice recently that suggested that my Instagram (IG) story should begin each day with a photo of myself followed by ten-story posts about my work. I have been using IG stories as part of my creative practice but have used it to show behind-the-scenes clips during production, when I am on set. Four years ago, this was enough to have me invited to speak on a panel about the use of social media in the arts. Four years later, I am no longer doing the minimum. I am currently living my life as a professional artist because I was able to get a full-time job at a university, I lived part of my life as an artist selling my works on the open market. I find myself now being pressured to become a producer, to market myself daily on social media to create interest in my 'content'. Content and no longer art.

As a professional artist, I have the privilege and perhaps responsibility to think about what has happened with the art world. Do I accept this new status as producer and focus my creative energies competing in the art world or do I perhaps try to find another path? Now that I have sketched out the economic cultural history of the transformation of expressive practices, I can now suggest the following: I want to contribute to the revitalization of the political and ethical usefulness of scholarly creative practice.

Art and coloniality

We have begun to think about art's supposed separation from society, the discourse of disinterested contemplation and the way this was a fiction. I say fiction because disinterested contemplation already presupposed that the art work had become an economic object. Kant assumed that the aesthetic judgement was strictly aesthetic, but it was already economic as well entwined with forms of capital (social, cultural, institutional, economic, libidinal etc.) that are all exchanged.

The modern period began with the global expansion of Western colonial-capitalist powers. Technological developments led to the ability to travel further, to expand military power, to expand communications systems, systems of art and religion, and economic systems. These technological innovations gave Western imperial powers an advantage in the world. As Western imperial powers dominated bodies (or attempted to), they simultaneously developed a philosophy of knowledge, an episteme, that justified their dominance. Where they could have created a knowledge system that recognized their unique contribution as one cultural contribution in a world of many, they instead began to see themselves as the most advanced people in the world. As their economic activity increased, their wealth increased, and so did their capacity for even more military and administrative force. The Western episteme was a predatory worlding that used its pretention of universality as its justification. The Western episteme innovated in the sciences, the arts, philosophy and technologies of all kinds, its place in the universe changed. No longer was the God of the bible the centre of the universe. It was now the time of Man, and this modern Man was the white male who wielded the power of modernity. These philosophers of Man created a self-justifying episteme that put everything else below them. Everything (material as well as spiritual) was at the disposal of the moderns and if one did not accept the moderns narrative it was because of an inherent inferiority or inability.

When art separated from religion and craft, a hierarchy was produced. Art was valued more highly than craft in European culture. European 'modern' urban culture was valued more highly than 'traditional' European cultures, and far superior to 'primitive' cultures (take note of two different names for rural society). Walter Mignolo has called this the colonial difference. This term allows us to see the way that moderns coloniality is connected to value differentiation, where we can see in an abstract way that urban sociality and village sociality are two different forms of sociality that both make sense for their particular locals, the colonial difference constructed a narrative that valued urban sociality and looked down upon village sociality as backward and outside of history. This led to the joint construction of urban life and folk life. Folk traditions were regarded as quaint, but even in the connotation of this word we can see that there is a diminution of 'folk' traditions. These practices are not seen as the practices of citizens in a rural town, but instead, as folk traditions, old and out of place in modernity. Perhaps worthy of collection and preservation but not of daily use and value. These practices have nothing to teach the moderns about their lives on the land. This led to a view of rural people as out-of-touch with cultural practices that are less valuable than those of urban society, unless they are determined to suit a narrative of nationality.

The colonial difference is even more extreme in the colonial and neocolonial context. In the colonial context, Indigenous cultural practices were outlawed, institutions were created to study and effectively surveil Indigenous communities, and Indigenous people in many colonial countries effectively became prisoners in their own territories, separated from their traditional lands and lifeways and restricted from travel even across their own territories. Colonial administrations set up schools to 'educate' and 'modernize' Indigenous people. These processes established a colonial difference, entire ecological knowledge systems developed over millennia were deemed primitive and obsolete. Attempts were made to eradicate cultural practices, ecological knowledge and language systems, and entire ways of life.

Modern art was taught to be worthy and Indigenous cultural practices were taught to be primitive and underdeveloped. The colonial difference made modern and primitive opposites, where modern was always valuable and primitive was a historical curio virtually obsolete. But of course Western pharmaceutical companies, museums and resource companies generate massive wealth for themselves trading in goods that were stolen from Indigenous communities. And when colonial powers reflected on the value of these stolen lifeways, they would assure themselves that 'primitive' people did not have the capacity to make these resources market ready and therefore valuable. It was up to the moderns to realize the wealth of the world (that God gave them?).

Colonialities most obvious power is its violence through military conquest and enforced economic control, its most enduring power is epistemological violence. Epistemology is the study of ways of knowing, and Freire's interest in literacy is informed by the politics of knowing, not just how we learn but the political consequences of learning. Let us call, after Michel Foucault, the collection of what is thought and said, modernity is an episteme with two other sides: coloniality and the cultural difference. After Mignolo we can no longer separate modernity/coloniality. But as Mignolo teaches, as soon as you recognize that modernity and coloniality are two sides of the same practice, we open a path towards decoloniality as a resistant episteme.

Knowledge is not separate from lives, cultures and bodies of learners; it is inseparable from them, but also does not define them exclusively. Further, a dominant episteme does not operate without resistance. In a literate society like the one Freire was working in the colonial episteme understands non-literacy not as oral/aural cultural, but as illiteracy, as a deficit, a literary delinquency. Oral/aural culture becomes illiteracy, and the illiterate are delinquents that need to be fixed. The oral/aural culture is non-literate but not illiterate. But this conversion from non-literate to illiterate is understood to be a symptom of underdevelopment and poverty. The colonial difference meant that literacy was a sign of knowledge and non-literacy a type of lack, and a sign of inferiority and underdevelopment. The value of oral/aural culture and all of its complexity was ignored or perhaps from the dominant side of the colonial difference, invisible.

In this context, it becomes difficult to distinguish the well-meaning educator from the openly supremacist because in both cases they begin from the same perspective, seeing non-literacy as a problem, a deficit that needs to be fixed. In no cases, and sadly this often remains true today, is there an awareness of the uniqueness and value of oral cultures within systems of Western education. It is important to note that even *non-literate* is a differential of literacy. Like non-modern a term that means lack. I prefer Vivien de Castro's concept of extramodern. Of course, today non-literate cultures are more often valued for their 'traditional' cultural values, but let us take a moment to think about what this seemingly passive word, 'traditional' suggests.

One of the ways of thinking that I want to encourage as we move forward is to think about language through the colonial difference. 'Traditional' is a word that distinguishes itself from modern. Traditional culture can be valued, like traditional art, traditional law, traditional lifeways but does it hold equal significant to Art, Law, Modernity? Often the answer is no. That it is valued as a curio, a tourist experience, or valued through a romantic lens but it is not valued as a legitimate contemporary and ecological way of living. Coloniality remains as long as the colonial difference remains intact. To identify the colonial difference, Walter Mignolo explains, is to practice decoloniality already, because it is the first step in recognizing the ongoing impacts of modernity/coloniality. Tradition and primitive are inventions of modernity, they do not point to an outside of modernity, and it is the moderns way of naming and controlling difference.

Decoloniality

To understand Nehiway aesthetics means to take off your shoes and walk around the woods for two weeks.
Chief Conroy Sewepagaham, Little Red River Cree Nation

I had four introductions to decoloniality before I began to understand what I was being invited to realize. The first introduction was not one moment but a series of visits to my MacDonald relatives in a small village called Loch Lomond, Cape Breton. In Loch Lomond, my relatives all spoke Gaelic as their first language. Their accents, different from mine, seemed as alien as the sharp cheese and black boiled tea that punctuated our trips. Neither my father nor I spoke a word of Gaelic beyond hello, *Ciamar a tha sibh*, and my distance from the language of my family was always a curiosity to me. At that time, there was still a Gaelic language newspaper and a radio show on the local Canadian Broadcasting Corporation, but beyond that I had no access to it. While I was provided opportunities to learn French in school, because Canada has two official languages, Gaelic instruction was rarely accessible. As the years moved on and those relatives passed away, so did the Gaelic language in our family. I experienced the end of Gaelic in my family, an ancient language that my grandfather was discouraged to learn and speak in public because it marked him as backward, out of modernity. But also the language of my ancestors, a language that had survived among native speakers in Loch Lomond well into the 1980s. Fortunately, a language revival did occur and Gaelic is still spoken.

In the 1990s, I was an avid hiker and I took part in protesting planned rock extraction from a coastal part of Cape Breton that I and my friends hiked a lot. When I arrived I was surprised to find a large number of Mi'kmaq protesters which included elders and drummers. During the Mi'kmaq-led gathering, I learned that the land that I had been hiking for years was a sacred site and I was invited along with everyone present to bring a small rock to the location and put them all together as a way of celebrating our togetherness. The gathering introduced me to Unamaki, the Mi'kmaq name for Cape Breton, one of seven regions in Mi'kmaqi, the homeland of the Mi'kmaq people. I was introduced to the idea that I was a settler on Unamaki and that I was part of a treaty between the English crown and the Mi'kmaq nation. These were all new concepts to me.

In the early 2000s, I was a hired researcher in a project called Native Dance. My task was to travel across Canada and interview Indigenous dancers for the project. I decided to begin in Unamaki and contacted elder Joel Denny. At the end of three days of discussion he said to me that he understood what I thought I was doing, but that Indigenous people do not need settlers to document their cultural practices. Indigenous people already know and understand what they do. He suggested that what I was doing was looking for something that settler Canadians have lost and that I, or perhaps we, were not going to find it in the lifeways of Indigenous people. That we have to look into settler history in order to discover what was lost and then once we do that we will no longer have to ask Indigenous people why they do what they do, because according to Elder Denny, settlers will already know.

I began to wonder about what was lost and embarked on a study of folk and traditional music which culminated in my dissertation about music festivals in western Canada. I still felt lost in the discourse of tradition seeing deep conflicting narratives about folklore and traditional music, where urban musicians make 'traditional' music often with acoustic instruments for sale in the music market. I did not feel closer to finding what was lost. I followed that project with a five-year project on hip-hop culture in Edmonton, Alberta, not in an attempt to continue my previous inquiry but because I was invited to contribute to thinking about urban culture education by a couple of leading Hiphoppas (MacDonald 2016a). It was during this project that I began to think about the role of filmmaking more deeply.

It was during these years that I was invited to join a project to make a film on the topic of cultural sustainability that was intended to be a training film for MBA students at the University of Calgary, a programme that had deep ties with the oil and gas industry. The film, *Pimachihowan*, was the result, which was the focus of the last chapter. But it was the process of making the film that was my fourth introduction to decoloniality.

Early in the pre-production I inquired about Nehiyaw (Cree) aesthetics. Chief Sewepagaham replied that I would need to take off my shoes and walk around in the woods for two weeks, that Nehiyaw aesthetics are not separate from everything else. Perhaps it was because I was finally ready to hear this, that I understood what I had been missing for decades, that I had been asking questions that were always contextualized by divisions, questions about art, religion, history, governance and that the question was always preloaded by the idea that these practices are separate and distinct aspects. The thing that Elder Denny was trying to show me was that I had lost the idea of relations, that I was living in a world of objects, that was the lesson Conroy's fire.

The colonial matrix of power

Perhaps the first critique of coloniality is challenging the universality embedded in the ethnocentrism of so-called Western thought. We have begun to do this already by illustrating the way that Art, a way of thinking about expressive practices that emerged during modernity/coloniality, elevated the expressive practices of some European 'creatives' and diminished others with the names of 'traditional', 'folkloric', 'primitive'. But of course this was not applied evenly, where traditional expressive practices were incorporated into the narratives of nationhood, many 'primitive' expressive practices were outlawed, or treated as objects of interest by anthropologists, museums and galleries separated or out rightly stolen from the cultures of which they formed part of the existential relations. I am using existential relations instead of cultures because culture has come to mean so many things that it is sometimes hard to know how any individual reader will understand it. Existential relation, therefore, is an attempt at thinking decoloniality. And since, as Walter Mignolo and Catherine Walsh have illustrated in *On Decoloniality*, decoloniality is about knowledge, it is necessary to theorize, and to think about theorizing as a practice of 'vision' (2018: 138). The practice of decoloniality recognizes that coloniality is a shorthand for the *colonial matrix of power*, an 'apparatus that was built by a selected community of humans of a given religion (Christianity), in a continent called Europe and around the fifteenth century, in the process of defining themselves as human'

(153). The colonial matrix of power is predatory worlding. I believe this is the root of my wintigo haunting. To exorcise the wintigo, I believe I have to cultivate relationality across the four ecologies, what I have been calling worlding.

Conclusion: Witnessing and friendship

I am writing this book as an act of friendship towards you and to chaos. I do not mean chaos in the sense of Mathew Arnold's 'Civilization and Anarchy', where in order to fight chaos we must choose 'the best of what has been thought and said' and stick to it in order to shield ourselves. I do not know what is the best in this sense, but I do know that this line of thinking has contributed to domination, misery, power struggles and suspicion of institutions. And I do not mean friendship that seeks any means necessary in order to not cause discomfort in some readers. I mean friendship in two senses. In the first sense I mean friendship in the way Deleuze and Guattari (1994) meant, by presenting a bridge over chaos that you can choose to cross if what I present in these pages works for you. I am not writing for everyone and I am not trying to persuade you that what I have come up with is right for you. *CineWorlding* is a consequence of my personal, professional and technical experiences. It is a provisional answer to questions that have come from my engagement with the world and the way that filmmaking has continued to provide me joy and sometimes therapy. Chaos in the Deleuzian sense is not the absence of order but an order that works on time scales and by rules that do not make any 'sense' to humans of this period.

I also mean friendship as an act of decoloniality. While not always successful I have been inspired by personal experiences of witnessing Indigenous people in Canada while they have fought, and sometimes won, greater recognition and control over their nations. I have witnessed firsthand the resurgence of traditional ecological knowledge and have been inspired by this fight against coloniality. I am writing this as a settler to Canada with a family tradition that is informed by Gaelic and Acadian ancestry on Cape Breton Island. I have had the privilege of becoming cosmopolitan in Derrida's sense. And as a consequence of this I feel that I have no home territory but a responsibility to develop a deep respect for hospitality. Perhaps because it is central to my life in both material and psychological senses I have been welcomed into many territories and have joined many families. I have seen others for whom a similar nomadic sensibility has wiped out territoriality, however. As a Portuguese friend expressed it: 'it's the difference between being a tourist and being a traveler'. A traveller becomes part of a community, contributes what one can, and opens oneself to collective worlding and the consequences it may have on you. A tourist extracts value for themselves and moves on. The moderns, their modernity/coloniality has acted like a greedy, murderous tourist. Extracting resources as it endlessly travels the earth feeding on the planet (wintigo?). I think we can see this as we watch Elon Musk and others investing billions into space exploration and plans to colonize the moon and Mars. Modernity/coloniality has no plans to put down roots anywhere. We can also see that modernity/coloniality is transmuting into transhumanism, the continued haunting of the wintigo weaponized in algorithms and control society.

A traveller, on the other hand, has an ethical responsibility to its hosts. As a traveller I do not have a say over my host's rules or priorities, and I do not want any. The privilege of a traveller is that you get to choose the places where you rest, and the consequence is that you are always a little bit uncomfortable and are required to extend relationality. That is the trade-off. Plato did not like travellers who told stories that entertained audiences. But cineworlding is not just about entertaining, it is about witnessing and friendship.

One of the outcomes of being a traveller, I think, is the development of an ethics of mutual respect. And this brings us back to decoloniality. When Ojibway people met Europeans they treated them with hospitality, as travellers. They made an agreement that was documented in a two-row wampum. This is the first treaty between Indigenous people and European colonial powers. Tourism, it turns out, is not an Indigenous concept. The two-row wampum spells out something that I understand as a call for a traveller's ethics. Each row of shells represents a worlding. They run parallel. They run parallel because the Ojibway knew that it was possible for different worldings to coexist in the same space-time. But tourists do not. Tourists take their worlding with them and are chauvinistic about it. Their worlding becomes an epistemological weapon. For instance, while living in France, I cannot tell you how many times I heard tourists, often American, complain that the restaurant servers only spoke French: 'How can they run a business like this?' This is the kind of everyday evidence of the tourist culture, the wintigo haunting, that I am attempting to theorize as a way to explain the manifestation of the vectoring of the colonial matrix of power. If tourists understood the ethics of the two-row wampum, they would attempt to learn everything they could about the culture they were visiting so that they could fit into this worlding and see what they would become in the process.

Travelling changes the youth, as they say in France. Sure it does. But youthful travel, and I do not mean age, is tourism. Travel requires repetition, becoming, solidarity, witnessing. It takes time and effort and often costs emotionally, economically and physically.

I do not want to extend this metaphor too far, but I want to point out that understanding the two-row wampum, and understanding why that treaty is still not lived up to, needs to be central to the settler side of a decoloniality. I am a settler, and a settler is a traveller. I am not separate from the power dynamics of modernity, quite the opposite. I am very close to its centre. I enjoy institutional, racial, gender, class, mobility and technological privilege. I also believe that privilege can, and perhaps must, be invested. And this book is an attempt to invest in a research-creation method that can work towards decoloniality. My hope is that decoloniality can be part of every subject as we posthumans develop new ways to live, ways that can contribute to the healing of the moderns murderous history on our shared planet. Through cineworlding, I am attempting to develop a practice that will help me become something other than Dylan Robinson's *Hungry Listener*.

11

Activist minor cinema

In the one time I had an opportunity to give an award speech at a film festival, I said to the audience: 'Shh, don't tell anyone this film is research.' At the time I thought I was making a joke. But as the years passed and my film practice has become even more oriented to film festivals and public screenings, my joke has taken on a different dimension. I am increasingly interested in passing between the university and the commons. In Chapter One I reflected on Moten and Harney's discussion of coloniality, of the university-as-settlement and the commons. Cinematic research-creation can be in, but not of the university when it is oriented not to building a discipline of research-creation but to developing research-creation techniques for the commons. Making films to reach out to film festivals and public screenings plays a supporting role for communities and artists with whom I work. It is true though that I also feel the desire for film festival success. The competitive thoughts that flicker in the dark corners of my ego that perhaps I could make films that were more entertaining, more conventional and more popular. This is a feeling that I am trying to resist because my films are not about fitting into a common film form, but instead, as I have tried to make clear throughout this book, about developing a decolonial practice of cinematic technics. I resonate with Wim Wender's idea of *Inventing Peace* where 'we explore how to create conditions for peace by thinking together *with* technology: how technology and its creative use can change our habitual ways of looking at the world' (2013: 133). The contemplation of peace with and through the digital cinema ecosystem is to open thinking to the possibility that digital cinema production can be a form of collective decolonial therapeutics. I concluded the last chapter by thinking about traveller's ethics as a way of distancing and healing the wintigo of colonialism that I find in myself, in tourists and transhumans alike. Wender's and Zournzai's peace is a process; it is active and, as process, activist. An important question for cineworlding is: 'how does cinema restore our belief in the world?' (Deleuze 1989: 182). A belief that the world can be beautiful and loving. A belief in the world means making the world something worth struggling for. Cinematic research-creation can play a role in restoring belief as a way of working for peace. Telling research-creation stories with trust that belief in the world can come from a 'darkened auditorium, [where] something strange can happen but only if participations are willing to play the game, to become players. For cinema offers itself as a primary site for disruption and transformation' (Grimshaw 2001:120). And perhaps this disruption and transformation can contribute to peace.

Activism in two forms

Activist for Brian Massumi has two related meanings, political activism and process philosophy. There are currently over 4 billion smartphones on the planet and this number is growing. Never before in human history has audiovisual recording capacity been this accessible and with it a proliferation of social media sites enabling the immediate sharing of self-produced media. We are witnessing and contributing to an emergence of a new way of seeing ourselves, each other and the world. For many, the lights of a bedside lamp are replaced more often than not by the light of streaming audiovisual images. From waking to sleeping, we carry our screens with us. They reach out to us, little sounds to let us know that we are missing something, need to remember something, want to remember something. They witness the world with us and have become an intimate part of us. This intimacy is remarkable and characterizes our collective becoming as digitally enhanced humans. There is an ethical and, therefore, political element to this. We are now the cyborg of mid-twentieth-century sci-fi, and what we do with our technology is political. It is undeniable that the utopian hopes of the early days of the digital have been replaced by its nearly total capture by capitalism. The wide-open expanses of the early days of the cyberspace have been enclosed and difficult to even remember. Platforms and paywalls close off information access and segment the internet into echo chambers that have deleterious effects on democratic life. Engaging in producing local and creative audio-vision is political. It keeps Felix Guattari's dream of a postmedia ecological activism alive, one oriented to sharing the unique and renegade 'crystallizations of individual and collective subjectivities' (1995: 130) that continue to proliferate beyond the corporatized media conglomerates and their streaming services.

Through our digital audiovisual enhancements, we can track climate activists, changes in weather patterns, mass migrations and political instabilities. We also watch cute pet videos and become more and more aware of our relations beyond the human. We broadcast our meals, our feelings, our sexualities, our identities, and as we do these categories proliferate with possibilities. Humanity is posthuman-becoming. We are no longer even bothering with a critique of humanism and are actively moving past it. We are also no longer content with anthropocentrism, the human species is one among many and learning to live alongside each other is essential. We are living in the posthuman condition (Braidotti 2019), 'the philosophy we need to make sense of the particular condition we are in',[1] thinking-feeling-acting at the confluence of posthumanism and post-anthropocentrism. In this context, cineworlding might be activist, not as surveillance but as an embedded and embodied grounded posthumanography.

Guattari's postmedia ecological activism and Braidotti's posthuman condition have much to say to each other. As Gary Genosko reflects on Guattari's use of the prefix post and its distance from postmodernism: 'a hallmark of Guattari's thought is the refusal of phasal developmental schemas and an insistence on simultaneous elaboration and a co-mingling polyphony. And Guattari vigorously protected his post- from association with postmodernism in order to avoid any suggestion that it might be apolitical' (Genosko 2018: 15). For Guattari, the idea of a post-mass-media age would 'provide tools for resingularising otherwise passive and alienated audiences' (15). This has indeed occurred and with it the developing of even more dynamic methods of capitalist capture and algorithmic intelligences that individually tailors a semiosphere for each human component of its system with its emphasis on influence of all kinds. It is now impossible to tell the difference between a customer and a citizen as politics has become about brand management and accumulation of capital of all kinds. This of course is not new and is, as Guattari would point out, a mutation in the methods of capture. Guattari's hope for the production of subjectivity lay in the potential development of 'minoritarian becomings linking local and regional upheavals to planetary problematics' (Genosko 2018: 19) and it is this that marks the joining of aesthetics and politics with the minor.

The second meaning of *Activist* for Massumi is its engagement with process philosophy where the event is central: 'To begin to think life, we must begin in the middle with an activist sense of life at no remove: in the middling immediacy of its always "going on"' (Massumi 2011: 1), an event is 'a vibration with an infinity number of harmonics or submultiples' (Deleuze 1993: 86), where there is a self-enjoyment. When I worked with Chief Sewepagaham editing *Pimachihowan*, each time I would edit a new version of the film he would ask that it be slowed down. Over and over I worked on slowing down the tempo of the film until finally, when re-listening to an interview I realized that he was trying to get me to understand that slowness was not an OBJECT LESSON in the film, but THE EVENT of the film. Editing the film with the affects of duration would provide an opportunity for settler audiences to realize, by the end of the film, that duration and tempo is deeply embedded in culture, and that dominant Western culture is characterized by fast tempos and high intensity. Nehiyaw Traditional Ecological Knowledge on the other hand is characterized by a sensitivity to duration. Fast tempos and high intensity make you less attentive because the media is constantly reaching out for your attention. A consciousness of the transformational capacity of duration, however, requires more patience and concentration which will help you develop an awareness that is more alert to small variations in the natural world. It is these small variations that Chief Sewepagaham wanted the audience to experience. As he says to Dr Lertzman: 'As you know David, you need to take your time to make good tea.'

Following Isabelle Stengers, I am not interested in arguing for the 'value' of audio-vision in scholarship but the 'ecological question of what "counts" and "could count" for that practice' (2010: 37) and to pose 'an immanent question of the way in which each practice defines its relationship to others, that is to say, "presents itself" to others' (2010: 37). This is an ecological question that brings to the fore a relationship between cinematic research-creation and the posthumanities. But also in another direction, social and cultural theory's relationship to cinematic technology, the emergence of the digital cinema ecosystem, to ecologies of practice in film, to film studies, to a history of amateur cinema, to film festivals, to academic film screenings, to educational film distribution, and their relationship to university libraries and public access television, and to ethnomusicology's own histories of practices with cinema in both its recognized practitioners (Baily, Titon, Zemp etc.) and 'neglected peers' (Seeger). But to think activism only in terms of fighting for value misses activism as process, the transformation that Sewepagaham and Massumi are articulating. A practice that is not political, but ethico-aesthetic. It is a practice of decoloniality, of engaging in the undercommons. Of doing cinema that is transformative, therapeutic and builds community.

Individual self-enjoyment is a process that

> involves the notion of a creative activity belonging to the very essence of each occasion. It is the process of eliciting into actual being factors in the universe which antecedently to that process exit only in the mode of unrealized potentiality. The process of self-creation is the transformation of the potential into the actual, and the fact of such transformation includes the immediacy of self-enjoyment. (Whitehead 1966: 151)

Massumi identifies the 'paradox of an immediate self-enjoyment belonging to the very essence of its every occasion' as the 'complicating knot' that activist philosophy engages (2011: 2). 'Technically speaking, for activist philosophy, the *end* of the experience knows its *beginning*' (Massumi 2011: 9) and 'the "what" of an experience is only fully definite at its culmination. The knower, according to James, is the end of the experience's becoming. What it "knows" is its own beginning, retroactively. An experience determinately knows what it's been only as it peaks – which is also the instant of its perishing' (Massumi 2011: 9). Only when Sewegagaham points out that slowness is healing do we recognize that we have been struggling against healing the entire time. I believe that this points to cinematic research-creation's minor cinema.

Minor cinema

Embracing the cinematic form in research-creation as a search for peace recognizes that

> critical race, decolonial, and feminist theory have each, in overlapping ways, asked us to attend to the *forms* we mobilize our research – with writerly vocality understood here as form – and to understand these as devices through which we craft our research towards certain values, politics and ideologies. Research-creation contributes to this by asking us to pay rigorous attention too 'non-writerly' forms as challenges to conventional knowledge production as inherited within the settler colonial spaces of the Canadian university. (Loveless 2020: 230)

As I have tried to suggest, it is not only to work in cinema that characterizes cinematic research-creation, but a commitment to invent new cinematic forms. To not speak in a major cinematic language but, instead, to be oriented to the minor. The minor throughout this book has been drawn from Manning's

Minor Gesture (2016). With the help of this concept we have inquired after the relationships between intensive space and extensive space, and the virtual and actual. We have seen that these relationships take temporary and habitual forms that we have called the diagram. And that each diagram is a collection of techniques and practices that connect transversally conceptual, social, technological and environmental ecologies. The diagram operates within the four ecologies as an ecology and contributes to an ecology of practices that are intensive to the extensive space of the larger form. Cineworlding represents the ecologies of practices that I have discussed throughout the book. In reference to each, my films work a kind of minor operation, using the language of the major form but trying to do something else: 'the major is a structural tendency that organizes itself according to predetermined definitions of value. The minor is a force that courses through it, unmooring its structural integrity, problematizing its normative standards' (Manning 2016: 1). Cinematic research-creation, in my view, should not be organized into scholarly cinema, hived off from the popular cinema of our time. Instead, it can be oriented to working as a minor cinema to problematize the normative standards of cinematic storytelling, to strive towards becoming minor cinema.

The term 'minor cinema' is well known in film studies, but not with the 'greatest amount of precision' (White 2018: 357). White suggests that minor cinema can be understood in four ways: sub-national, sub-state, small-country and Indigenous cinema. Szymanski, however, suggests that to connect minor cinema to identities and states necessarily looks at subjectivity 'through the lens of identity' (2012: 93) and that while there is value in seeing the relationship between subjectivity and identity 'there is nothing inherent in identity – no matter how oppositional – that prevents its co-opted reification; nothing that prevents even the most seemingly radical identity from turning into a new standardization of subjectivity' (2012: 93). Minor cinema, in Szymanski's view, is one oriented to breaking up conservative models of subjectivity, models that it must be said, will always end up being conservative. This has to be handled carefully. This is not to say that tradition is bad and traditional subjectivities need to be broken up, to be opened to progress. This is haplessly colonial and capitalistic. Instead, it is about breaking up the subjectivities *in* cinema, the extremely limited number of models that make it to the screen. To bring the subjectivities of the most devote religious conservatives, for instance, to the screen so that others can understand them with compassion. The outcomes of these films do not have to be acceptance of practices, but at least a humanizing of these perspectives. When I leave documentary film festivals, I often feel like I have compiled a list of enemies and enemy practices. What I am proposing instead with minor cinema is a preference of complexifying each other to each other. In an era of increasing political polarity, catastrophic ecological collapse, a preference for digital cancelling over complex discussion, this proposition may seem naïve. Perhaps instead of considering this naïve, we may see in its enthusiasm an affirmation towards livingness, towards peace, towards the cultivation of understandings and belongings across difference.

Guattari writes in his essay 'Cinema of Desire' that

> cinema, television and the press have become fundamental instruments of forming and imposing a dominant reality and dominant significations. Beyond being means of communication, of transmitting information, they are instruments of power . . . because they participate in the elaboration and transmission of subjective models. Presently, the media, for the most part, functions in the service of repression. But they could become instruments of liberation of great importance. (2009: 238)

I want to propose the idea that minor cinema is oriented to innovating on subjective models. So far I have not discussed any of my fiction films. I decided early on in this project that the fiction films would await a next book after the groundwork of the cinematic research-creation techniques and questions have been posed. This will allow me to begin with posthumanography's poetics within improvisational fiction films that I have been making as minor cinema. Orienting to posthuman poetics and posthumanography is perhaps the most dramatic troubling of the ethnographic method. Instead of making films that attempt to solidify subjective forms within a formed culture, posthumanography as minor cinema can be oriented to innovations in posthuman future building, anarchiving futurity. In this way, cineworlding and posthumanography may be allied to decolonial, feminist futurity and can struggle against the neocolonial surveillance of emerging transhumanism.

Notes

Introduction

1 This book covers only the music videos and observational documentaries that I have made over the last fifteen years. I had to leave the ethnofiction films, like *Unspittable* (2018), *Waiting to Connect* (2019), *And, And, And . . .* (2021), *Ark: A Return to Robson Valley* (2022), that have become the center of my research-creation practice for the next book tentatively titled *Free Radicals*.
2 I am thinking here about Frano 'Bifo' Berardi's work on poetry.
3 You can do as much or as little as you want of these exercises. The experiences that come out of the assignments will give access to the complex language in the text which will begin to feel explanatory of the logic of sensation. What is often thought to be most simple in art may indeed, when taken seriously, open up a universe for contemplation and theory.
4 https://thesocialplatforms.wordpress.com/2017/02/15/the-philosophers-of-technique/

Chapter 1

1 I am thinking here of William Deresiewicz's *The Death of the Artist: How Creators Are Struggling to Survive in the Age of Billionaires and Big Tech* (2020).
2 Andy Bennett and Paula Guerra's KISMIF (Keep It Simple, Make It Fast), an international network of academics, artists, artivists and students who meet every two years at the University of Porto, Portugal, is a good example of the kind of alternative networks that I am thinking about here.
3 Cineworlding is not oriented to scientific conclusion of the functions of culture, but is instead interested in seeding future events. It enacts what Erin Manning calls anarchive 'never in creating an account of our activities . . . but in generating techniques for sharing the work's potential, the speculative edge of its pragmatic proposition. Our hope was to find a practice that would allow action traces that would become mobilized across other environment of collective experimentation' (2020: 76).
4 Lone Bertelsen writes in the Introduction to *Incalculable Experience*, issue 30 of *The Fibreculture Journal*, about Erin Manning's use of *interstices*: In 'Fugitively,

Approximately', Erin Manning encounters the statement 'all black life is neurodiverse life', made by Fred Moten in a manuscript review of her book The Minor Gesture. Manning suggests that '[w]hat is produced in the interstices is not an account of how black life is neurodiverse, or how neurodiversity is black'. Rather, it is 'the being of the relation itself that is prodded, not to create a count, but to better account for the incalculability at its core'. Manning emphasizes that Black life and neurodiverse life, as experiences of what Moten terms 'minor social life', are devalued and violently excluded when neurotypical whiteness – aligned with 'executive function' – is taken as the measure for what counts as human (Moten 2018 in Manning). For Manning 'neurotypicality is nothing else than an articulation of whiteness at work'. In 'Fugitively, Approximately', then, neurodiverse scholarship and black studies meet as Manning shows us the incalculable value of 'minor sociality'. For her minor sociality is 'a way of thinking' and living 'beyond rehabilitation, beyond a logic of reparations'.

5 Erin Manning writes about preacceleration in *Relationscapes*: There are always at least two bodies. These two stand close, facing one another, reaching towards an embrace that will signal an acceleration of the movement that has always already begun. The movement within becomes a movement without, not internal-external but folding and bridging in an intensity of preacceleration. This means: you are never stopped. To move is to engage the potential inherent in the preacceleration that embodies you. Preaccelerated because there can be no beginning or end to movement. Movement is one with the world, not body/world but body-worlding. We move not to populate space, not to extend it or to embody it, but to create it. Our preacceleration already colours space, vibrates it. Movement quantifies it, qualitatively. Space is duration with a difference. The difference is my body-worlding, always more than one. Our embrace quickens the molecules that compose us. An adaptation occurs – we begin to recompose. Volumes, always more-than-one, emerge from surfaces, recombining with lines, folding, bridging, knotting. This coming together proposes a combination of form-forces where preacceleration potentially finds passage. The passage flows not in a pre-inscribed direction: this is an intensive flow. Preacceleration: a movement of the not-yet that composes the more-than-one that is my body. Call it incipient action (2012: 13).

6 Anti-Copyright! Reprint freely, in *any* manner desired, even without naming the source. Inspired by Woody Guthrie's example: 'This song is Copyrighted in U.S., under Seal of Copyright # 154085, for a period of 28 years, and anybody caught singin it without our permission, will be mighty good friends of ourn, cause we don't give a dern. Publish it. Write it. Sing it. Swing to it. Yodel it. We wrote it, that's all we wanted to do.'

7 As an example, George E. Marcus wrote in 1998 that 'there is renewed interest among anthropologists in such topics as ethnicity, race, nationality, and colonialism. While such primordial phenomena as traditions, communities, kinship systems, rituals, and power structures continue to be documented, they can no longer in and of themselves serve as the grounding tropes which organize ethnographic description and explanation. The most venturesome works in the trend of ethnographies are profoundly concerned with the shaping and transformation of identities (of one's subjects, of their social systems, of the nation-state with which they are associated, of the ethnographer and the ethnographic project itself). These are the most radically questioning of analytic and descriptive frameworks which rest on, and privilege, a particular "solidity that does not melt into the air" – that is, exclusive identities, emergent from an authoritative cultural structure, which can always be discovered and modelled. The modernist problematics of ethnography, outlined in the next section, instead emerge from a systematic *disqualification* of the various structuring devices on which ethnographic realism has depended' (59).

8 In Picturing Culture (2000) Jay Ruby writes: 'When French "New Wave" filmmaker Jean-Luc Godard decided in the late 1960s to make nonbourgeois films because he wished to radicalize his audience's vision of the world, critics assumed he had somehow lost his ability to produce comprehensible work . . . Such a radical departure is only feasible or even understandable if there is a rationale to support a new practice – once that makes it possible to visualize culture and to see behavior as an embodiment of culture so that it can be filmed, and to create film styles that transmit anthropological knowledge to a desired audience while at the same time making the theoretical position of the maker clear and the method employed explicit' (240).

9 I should, however, say that research-creation in sound studies has been significantly more embraced by composers than it has by ethnomusicologists where disciplinary norms of ethnographic paper writing seem resistant to change, even though leaders in the field like Steven Feld have long supported innovations in photography, audio, and audiovisual methods.

10 I am indebted to Governor General Award–winning playwright Kim Senklip Harvey for the model of embracing 'dirtbag' as a self-descriptor. It is very liberating to embrace the complex and unsettled aesthetics of rural-urban working-class expressive practice that is a punk without the punk formalities. Please see her website: kimsenklipharvey.com

11 When I began making films with my PhD supervisor Federico Spinetti, they were framed by ethnomusicological and anthropological ideas: observational documentary and ethnographic cinema. These paradigms centred on

documentation and while there was plenty of critical writing about the colonial history, the Othering of ethnographic film (often framed as a past period), there was little discussion of its artfulness. Discussion often circled around fieldwork techniques, ways of 'properly' doing ethnography, ways of collecting documentation.

12 In his landmark essay 'Ethnomusicology and Visual Communication' (1976), Steve Feld wrote that 'the interest seems due to the explosive fascination with audio-visual media in both the humanities and the social sciences. The confusion, it seems, is due to several forms of inability to disentangle the manner in which one deals with audio-visual media in a humanistic or social scientific context from the popular roles these media play in our larger cultural milieu' (293). Feld discusses major theorists in ethnomusicology that are interested in cinematic forms of research noting that 'we find an abrupt shift from no statements on film at all, to a full blown discussion of film production (Hood 1971: chapter 5) as a *basic* skill, and film analysis (Lomax 1968: chapters 10 and 12) as a basic means for data retrieval. Hood and Lomax treat the making and analysis of film as a principled and central ethnomusicological concern, like the writing of research monographs or preparation of transcriptions' (294–5). It is interesting to read about an 'explosive fascination' nearly fifty years later when there is finally the technological capacity to found an audiovisual ethnomusicology journal. At the time of this writing, the very first edition of AVJEM journal (audiovisual ethnomusicology journal) is in publication with Benjamin Harbert and Frank Gunderson as editors. The central question that Feld asks here, how to disentangle, still has not been achieved, nor has the explosive fascination resulted in much of a development of audiovisual ethnomusicology. In 2018 Frank Gunderson remarked in a keynote address at the Society of Ethnomusicology pre-conference symposium that audiovisual ethnomusicology has remained, since the 1970s, in a near constant state of 'potential'. The time I am taking in this book to theorize cinema-thinking is to help get past this basic question that Feld is asking. I believe if we remain focused on the film as object, we miss the significant differences between monographs and films, risk putting them in competition with one another, and risk missing an opportunity to theorize posthuman thinking in audiovisual practice. The relationship between written monographs and films becomes a productive one when we can turn back to print monographs to rethink them as an already acceptable form of posthuman thinking. What critical tools can we take from a deep analysis of film production that can then enable researchers to re-examine the foundations of cultural research?

13 For instance, why does humanities scholarship need to be written in a book to be of scholarly value? Thinking in audio and audiovisual media is an increasingly accepted form of documentation, but rarely recognized as more-than human thinking. Cinema-thinking challenges normative models of thinking in the

humanities. It takes seriously the claim made by Deleuze and Guattari that thinking, and the subject that thinks, is both greater and less than the still too prevalent singular rational human that does the thinking. The original sin of the Humanities, Deleuze points out, was Descartes' smuggling in of two unthought precepts into his famous cogito. The first is that in order to say *I think*, even before the existential claim of *I am*, there has to be what Deleuze calls an 'image of thought'. What is it that the thinker recognizes as thinking. There already has to be an image of thought in the possession of the one who thinks in order to recognize it as thinking.

Chapter 2

1. In *Cinema 2*, Deleuze writes: 'Time simultaneously makes the present pass and preserves the past in itself. There are, therefore, already, two possible time-images, one grounded in the past, the other in the present . . . the past is not to be confused with the mental existence of recollection-images which actualize in us. It is preserved in time: it is the virtual element into which we penetrate to look for the "pure recollection" which will become actual in a "recollection-image"' (98).
2. Erin Manning in *The Minor Gesture* (2016) discusses autistic perception and artistic perception using the terms entertainment and entrainment. I am deeply impacted by this way of thinking about artistic perception, and audio-vision, in relation to neurotypicality enforced by social science and humanities disciplines. The neurotypicality of ethnography for instance that has little room for the virtualities that overpopulate my cinematic practice.
3. I am interested here in thinking the enotikon and the slur non-dialectically and in a way that allows the space between the two terms for creative emergence. For Brian Massumi 'relation in activist philosophical sense is *not connective*' (Massumi 2011: 21).
4. As Brian Massumi writes: 'It might not sound political, at least in the way it's usually meant. But it is, because the virtuality is of an event to come, and as we say before the event always has the potential to affectively attune a multiplicity of bodies to its happening, differentially. Aesthetic politics brings the collectivity of shared events to the fore, as differential, multiple, bodily potential for what might come' (2015: 68).
5. While studies of musical memory have been oriented to memory systems, I believe it is possible to pose questions from a radical empirical orientation. For a review of studies on music and memory see: Berz (1995).

6   Quoted from 'Watch This: Fellini on LSD', Austin Film Society. https://www.austinfilm.org/2020/11/watch-this-fellini-on-lsd/ (accessed 19 December 2021).

7   Can we not see a visual clip of *Saturday Night Fever* (which still exists in this alternate reality but the storyline is quite different!) as just this sort of in-folded into the forming . . . what should one calls this. Deleuze's notion of the crystal image is useful perhaps, as long as it is a crystal with light passing through it so that the colours, intensities, and reflections on its facets are constantly changing. Perhaps this clip comes to mind because music erupts from the sounds of the city as if it were the refrain of the city. It would be a metaphor in the Batesonian sense, where a metaphor *is* connection, not a simile (like the) which can only ever be a description of the connection. Perhaps a second connection, that the groove of the music is evident in the world only through the body of the walker, that the soundtrack is a virtuality circulating in and motivating the walker's body. Music regulating the pulse of the body as it moved through space, John Travolta becoming-music, becoming-disco. Cinema brings an audience into the body's intensities allowing us to see-hear its physicality, its groove. We become witnesses to the groove, to the assemblage of body-city-style-music. In the seeing-hearing of the groove, we are also grooved, entertained and entrained to the beat as we enter into the assemblage. An audience moves between the objectivity of the walker's body and joins the subjective intensity of the walker's feelings of themselves alive in the groove of the music. There is no subjective objective divisions, they are blurred in relationality.

8   As Erin Manning and Brian Massumi's *para-institutional 3 Ecologies Initiative*, my own *Cypher 5* discussed in my book *Remix and Life Hack*, and music festivals as discussed in my book *Playing for Change* are only a couple of examples.

9   I intend to follow this book with a short educational primer called *Make your own damn films! (and do it with your friends)* and a second part of this book that focuses on the fiction-nonfiction improvisational films that I have been making called *Free Radicals&Posthumanography's poetics: Improvising, Anarchiving, & Minor Cinema*.

Chapter 3

1   This approach might be seen as oriented to art-based research, what can be learned about creative practice, about cinematic-thinking, through the production of works. The artistic thinking is drawn out through the application of auto-ethnography. The auto-ethnographic exploration moved into another register, more fiction than report. This kind of writing has much in common with anthropologist Michael Jackson's existential anthropology that seeks to works with creative writing practices transversally with ethnography.

2   It might be suggested that transversality sounds like bricolage, a concept already well known in ethnography. But transversality and bricolage are not the same. Bricolage is the connections of different methodologies working interdisciplinarily.
3   This focus on *what a machinic assemblage can do* moves the discussion away from cybernetics. To make an overgeneralization, cybernetics focus on structure and systems of control. Take two examples. The first is Nikolas Luhmann's *Art as a Social System*. While the premise is important the process of art worlds does not become any clearer. Perhaps because Luhmann sees the social system produced by a system of communication about art and aesthetics. In reducing the social system of art to statements, to discourse, it misses an opportunity to explore the more-than-human dimensions of making in art worlds.
4   Christopher Small applied Gregory Bateson's *Steps to an Ecology of Mind* to the *ritual* of orchestral music. Small takes an important first step to understand music as process by describing music's reality as a verb: musicking. But then this powerful observation moves away from process, emergences, autopoiesis, sympoiesis to contemplate the structuring components of the systems, called ritual, of an abstract symphonic orchestra. The problem with the analysis is on the one hand Small is interested in process, but in practice, the symphony orchestra is abstracted. He states that it does not matter where it is happening because the structure occurs anywhere. But as Whitehead asserts, to abstract is to already make an error, a fallacy of misplaced concreteness. To deal with the processes of the symphonic orchestra is to deal with the real, not the abstract process. It is to understand how the events of the orchestra hold together. Is not the idea of coherence, of holding together, precisely what Deleuze and Guattari were asking with the notion of machinic territoriality?

Chapter 4

1   From the Idle No More website (idlenomore.ca): 'Idle No More started in November 2012, among Treaty People in Manitoba, Saskatchewan, and Alberta protesting the Canadian government's dismantling of environmental protection laws, endangering First Nations who live on the land. Born out of face-to-face organizing and popular education, but fluent in social media and new technologies, Idle No More has connected the most remote reserves to each other, to urbanized Indigenous people, and to the non-Indigenous population. Led by women, and with a call for refounded nation-to-nation relations based on mutual respect, Idle No More rapidly grew into an inclusive, continent-wide network of urban and rural Indigenous working hand in hand with non-Indigenous allies to build a movement for Indigenous rights and the protection of land, water, and sky.'

2   The famous Canadian news broadcaster Peter Mansbridge, who retired in 2017.
3   Christopher Small introduced process ontology into ethnomusicology in *Musicking* (1986). Small introduced Gregory Bateson's cybernetic view of the world as complex nested ecologies or minds. His ideas were developed further in two other directions. Deleuze and Guattari introduced Bateson's ideas into continental philosophy, now an important strand of new materialism. The second less well-known development is biosemiotics, noted by Deleuze scholar Ronald Bogue (2003: 58–76), but still in need of explicating. In this work Small began to nudge towards research findings as emergent properties of process, developed further by Charles Keil and Stephen Feld (2005) in their studies of groove. While Keil's approach to participatory discrepancies has had perhaps limited value, the orientation to attending to the particularities of flows and their subsequent emergent properties continues to have a minor impact on the field. I expect, however, that the real impacts of the introduction of process ontology into ethnomusicology have only just begun.
4   The most powerful critique that I received about this film is the lack of personhood, that is, the lack of backstory for each of the featured Hiphoppas. The critique was that not enough information was provided to give the sense of their lives, that somehow, they became abstracted forms. I took this critique very seriously and it led to my break with observational documentary as a necessary starting point for cineworlding.

Chapter 5

1   Rosi Braidotti discusses two sides of the multi-versity in *The Posthuman* (2013) where there is a conservative and progressive vision. The multi-versity that is oriented to cognitive production for the marketplace and the one that is locally oriented to the well-becoming of the city space in which it is located. See *The Posthuman*, pp. 178–81.
2   I think of cineworlding as three assemblages using the original French term, 'agencement', which includes a sense of individuality and style, which assemblage does not. The envelope or agencement of the three assemblages of cineworlding is akin to the attack decay sustain release envelope that define the agencement of a sound. It is a useful concept to help consider the nodes that shape an instrument's sound, to feel for the event of a sound's becoming, but then in discussion of the characteristics or uses of the sound the ADSR envelope surprisingly does not come to the surface as much as you had expected. The ADSR is a way of conceptualizing the intensive space that allow for the emergence of the extensive space of the sound, its identity, but its identity is not a form but a becoming. The three assemblages

are everywhere present and play an exceptionally important role in the becoming of a film. In filmmaking, there is a constant diagrammatic process that it intensive in a film. The diagram is concept that points to what Deleuze and Guattari call an abstract machine, the way of doing a work that operates between content and expression.

3   For more on post-anthropocentrism see Braidotti *The Posthuman*, pp. 55–104.
4   'Technics' is the word Bernard Stiegler uses for the technical object. Stiegler makes the point that technics have an evolutionary life of their own (1994) and that cinema, or what Michel Chion calls audio-vision (2009), is radically altering human life for the good and the bad.
5   There is an interesting discussion in Heider's *Ethnographic Film* (2006: 78–82) where he discusses the close up in ethnographic cinema. In this discussion he focuses on the information that is shared by the body and considers a close up on the face as useful but a limitation of the whole body shot. He does not go so far as to condemn a closeup of the face but certainly warns about its limitations and its conventionality in entertainment cinema. What is find most interesting in his discussion is that he does not mention subjectivity a single time.
6   For more on this please see: Arnold et al. (2017).
7   For more on mediation, ideology, and affect see *Politics and Affect* (Massumi 2015: 83–97).
8   Certainly the sciences have. For the sciences, including the social sciences, expression is functions. The sciences use functions to explain the world. It is without question that this has been very successful. Artists use percepts and affects but these are considered less socially valuable as forms of knowing and are relegated to entertainment and not philosophy or science.
9   In cineworlding, there is no methodology but only an orientation to the event, and in the event, creativity. The previous discussion of diagramming becomes central as the becoming cinematic body of the filmmaker is diagrammatic. The body is constituted both by actuality and virtuality: 'Diagramming is the procedure of abstraction when it is not concerned with reducing the world to an aggregate of objects but, quite the opposite, when it is attending to their genesis' (Massumi 2011: 14–15). In filmmaking the shot is teaming with virtuality on both sides of the camera, as I will explore in throughout the book. Often in my filmmaking there are music video-style montages that some critics have found less than scholarly. But here I different fundamentally with those who see no place for artistic expression in scholarly work. Artistic expression is a way of unfolding the virtuality within perception: 'We never just register what's actually in front of our eyes. With every sight we see imperceptible qualities, we abstractly see potential, we implicitly see a life dynamic, we virtually live relation. It's just a kind of shorthand to call it an object. It's an *event* . . . we just don't look, we sense ourselves alive. Every perception

comes with its own "vitality affect"' (Massumi 2011: 43). A scholarship of movement and duration, of becoming, is a scholarship of livingness. I believe that orienting scholarship to posthuman livingness is a step towards decoloniality as it both upsets the humanist image of thought and speculates upon alternative futurity.

Chapter 6

1 https://www.mickeyhartfineart.com/music-1
2 Consider the difference between proximity and intimacy. Proximity does not define intimacy, as one can be intimate with someone without proximity, though proximity does provide a great opportunity for intimacy. It is possible to watch a film, to be separate but connected in extensive space in both geographical and temporal ways, and experience an intensive space called intimacy. This intimacy is not with something on the other side of the screen; it is with the screen, and it is machinic intimacy. It is the affect of being impacted by a flow of intensity that is the opening of an intensive space that we call Intimacy. Intimacy draws attention to intensive space; it does not define it, but points to its existence.
3 Jean Rouch's cineportraits, for instance, have inspired me for some time. I really liked the cineportrait concept' it operated a deterritorializing of my thinking about the documentation paradigm, but it had limitations. The portrait, like the document, caused a kind of stillness in my thinking. A stillness that I once valued and that was valued in my education. It operated a structuring of artistic expression with a dominating form, the portrait, that even the cine could not really destabilize. It sent me back into the dirtbag artfulness of my own entertainment certain that I had little to share. This was the experience of the power difference in my thinking that valued portraiture as a real art and cinema as Plato's dancing shadow. Cinema shares with portraiture a love of light. But cinema is an art of light and movement, of time and duration. I had to break with Rouch's cineportrait in order to love movement's becoming. Not a portrait of a body, but the cineworlding of bodying.
4 Disciplines in music studies each have a perspective on this:

Musicology perspective: sound is the content and music is the expression, JWH is the diagram.
Ethno perspective: JWH, promoters, audience is the content and folk music is the expression, becoming-concert tour is the diagram.
Cineworlding perspective: images in movement is the content and the film is the expression, the becoming-film form is the diagram.

Research-creation perspective: the film is the content and the cinematic experience is the expression, becoming-knowledge mobilization is the diagram.

This collection of diagrams does not attempt to fix anything in its place as every diagram offers strategies for ways of becoming.

Chapter 7

1. The relations between bodies in the frame and the out-of-frame move with the harmonic and melodic developments of the music. The music video provides a way to think video and music, to get perhaps get beyond the soundtrack visual track binary, the subservience of music to visuality so common in film studies. The music video provides musicologists a way to study the movement of affects, to think affects as vectors that continue to travel through technologies and bodies.
2. 'The poetic of aesthetics becomes the aesthetic of poetics'. That these metaphors take us back to the whole of relatedness and experience recalls dynamic sociological and musicological versions of getting into the groove provided by Alfred Shultz and Victor Zuckerkandl: 'sharing of the other's flux of experiences in inner time, thus living through a vivid present in common constitutes . . . the mutual tuning-in relationship, the experience of the we' (Feld 1988: 89).
3. While many of the traditional obstacles to scholarly film have been quickly overcome, peer review remains a challenge. The *Journal of Visual Ethnography* was a first example of a peer review digital cinema platform but at the time of this writing (November 2021), it seems to be offline.
4. The emergence of ethnographic film (Grimshaw 2008; Hocking 1975; Loizos 1993) and cine-ethnomusicology (Harbert 2018; Feld 1976; Zemp 1988) have been slow to have much of an impact on their respective disciplines. Cine-cultural studies will no doubt also be embraced by a small number of researchers with the vast majority relying on traditional forms of print scholarship. While scholars like Sarah Pink (2013) have led the way, in recent years, in showing the way visual ethnography and sensual ethnography can enhance research work, there certainly is not a large amount of cinematic scholarship being produced.
5. Sarah Pink connects ethnography and art practice in *Writing Cultures* (1986), where Clifford recognizes that ethnography is a literary style and a social science method. But as I will show later it is much older than this. Pink argues quite correctly, that visual ethnography must deal with embodiment and the senses and that reflexivity and institutional languages of visual ethnography are being impacted by digital media. One may get the sense that non-representational theories that diverge from cultural studies and youth studies methods are 'part of

this move towards a more engaged, participatory, collaborative and public form of visual scholarship' (Pink 2013: 5). I want to frustrate the idea that there is a teleos from positivist to non-representational music cinema because, as I will show, these newer non-representational methods (Del Rio 2008; Vannini 2015), including the cineworlding that I am forwarding, are emerging perspectives that allow us to see-hear older works in a new way.

6   Washboard Hank is the Paganini of the Washboard (MacDonald 2022).

Chapter 8

1   Institute for Integrative Sciences and Health. Guiding Principles (Two-Eyed Seeing). In: Cape Breton University [Internet]. 2004 (cited 25 August 2021). http://www.integrativescience.ca/Principles/TwoEyedSeeing/
2   In 'The Fold', Deleuze talks about a 'formless elastic membrane' that separates chaos of the multiple from one of the events: 'the screen makes something issue from chaos' (Deleuze 1991: 86). Though he does not mean a cinema screen in this discussion of the event, the connection is intriguing.
3   In chapter 1 of *Minor Gesture,* Erin Manning provides a history of the development of research-creation. For other accounts of this development please see Owen Chapman's Family Resemblances, Stevance and Lacasse Research-creation as a interdiscipline, Natalie Loveless Making art at the end of the world, and Loveless et al. Knowings & Knots.
4   Before I would be able to travel into Treaty 8 territory, David and I met with their leadership to discuss our project, to get approval and feedback. We met at the Treaty 8 office in the north part of Edmonton, Canada. David explained our project and our history together and the types of questions we are exploring. There was interest in us contributing educational material, something David and I were both very interested in attempting. I had no idea how much of an impact this request would eventually have and how difficult.
5   'The Matrix that Embeds' Humberto Manturana and Heinz von Foerster, American Society for Cybernetics and Change Management Systems. Directed by Pile Bunnell 1998. https://www.youtube.com/watch?v=acx-GiTyoNk (accessed 19 March 2017).
6   Because of the colonial history of Western rationality, in both science and the humanities, meta-questions for researchers in post Truth and Reconciliation Canada is of great ethical, epistemological and methodological importance. Indigenous writers have long recognized the negative impacts of skei, the tearing apart of 'things' in Western rationality. In 'Custer Died for Your Sins' Vine Deloria Jr. (1969) critiqued

colonial scholarship when he wrote: 'Into each life, it is said, some rain must fall, some people have bad horoscopes, others take tips on the stock market, but Indians have been cursed above all other people in history. Indians have anthropologists' (78). Although Treaty 6 and 8 were signed between Indigenous peoples and the Canadian government as an agreement to share the land and to provide western education, these treaties were systematically ignored. The promised education was delivered in the form of a system of residential schools dedicated to 'kill the Indian in the child,' European aesthetic education was used as an epistemological weapon. The federal government apologized in 2008. Soon after, the Truth and Reconciliation Commission of Canada traveled across the country to hear and record testimony of the impact of residential schools. Concluding in 2015, it is now public record that Indigenous people were physically, psychologically and sexually abused in a government-supported system of cultural genocide. However, while the government says 'we are sorry', treaty obligations as of 2017, are still rarely lived up to. What's more, the epistemological operation of colonization remains opaque. It is this field that I am seeking to theorize aesthetic education not in the hopes of explaining Traditional Ecological Knowledge but instead of contributing to an allied ecological aesthetic education.

7   This is not a Cree word but instead is *Michif*, a complex language comprised of Cree and French. It is not a patois that mixes and reduces the complexity of two languages into one hybrid but is instead a language that was built by expert speakers of both Cree and French and therefore has very complex grammar structures.

8   Personal Correspondence, 6 November 2019.

Chapter 9

1   A leading transhuman think tank Humanity Plus describes itself in this way: 'Technologies that support longevity and mitigate the disease of aging by curing disease and repairing injury have accelerated to a point in which they also can increase human performance outside the realms of what is considered to be "normal" for humans. These technologies are referred to as emerging and exponential and include artificial intelligence, nanotechnology, nanomedicine, biotechnology, stem cells, and gene therapy, for example. Other technologies that could extend and expand human capabilities outside physiology include AI, robotics, and brain-computer integration, which form the domain of bionics, memory transfer, and could be used for developing whole body prosthetics. Because these technologies, and their respective sciences and strategic models, such as blockchain, would take the human beyond the historical (normal) state of existence, society, including bioethicists and others who advocate the safe use of technology, have shown concern and uncertainties about the downside of these technologies and possible problematic

and dangerous outcomes for our species. We aim to impact change. We have the knowledge to equip you with the tools, resources and mindset to navigate your own transformative journey into the future. This is Humanity+'s network of members, advisors, associates and partners. Areas include entrepreneurs and innovators in the fields of science, technology, philosophy, and the arts.' Cited from humanityplus.org. For a further articulation of the transhumanist position please see: *Transhumanism: What Is It?* (Vita-More 2018).

2   I was introduced to this work while reading bell hooks. hooks-Berry-Freire form a critical ecological triad that continues to inform my work in critical pedagogy (MacDonald 2016b, 2020b).

3   *We're Too Loud*: An ecological love story
    Fade in
    [1] 'One of the peculiarities of the white race's presence in America is how little intention has been applied to it' (35):

    1. Aerial Hornby Island
    2. We're too loud – graphic (haley) – Breagan's track
    3. Some people say don't feed the deer
    4. Set up and sound check
    5. Live performance at soundcheck
    6. First visit

    [2] 'In the loss of skill, we lose stewardship; in losing stewardship we lose fellowship; we become outcasts from the great neighborhood of Creation.'

    1. Show – Breagan's track
    2. My camp morning
    3. Veggies and home visit
    4. Andrew comes to Hornby
    5. Getting payment back shows may be canceled

    [3] 'Generation after generation, those who intended to remain and prosper where they were have been dispossessed and driven out by those who were carrying out some version of the search for El Dorado' (36).

    1. Andrew at home
    2. Larger garden
    3. Breagan Water
    4. Fertilizer
    5. Bone tree – Breagan's track

[4] 'A change of heart or of values without an environmental practice is only another pointless luxury of a passively consumptive way of life.'

1. cancelled show
2. angry Andrew
3. Bregan family story
4. Silas' interview
5. Breagan's conclusions
6. final explanations
7. pineapple at home
8. we're too loud music and credits

4   It is without question that early German filmmakers were directly impacted by Wagnerian ideas evident in both their writing and their films. There is a history of films that might be classified as music-image films. To go beyond music and the moving image, to follow music into cinematic movement. One might begin this history with Anna Belle Serpentine Dance (1895 Thomas Edison dir) and Danse Serpentine (1896. Lumiere brother dir.) and continue it into Ballet Machanique, Black and Tan Fantasy, the great (and lesser) Hollywood musicals, Ozu's domestic films, Wender's road films, independent music-image films of Les Blank, Agnes Varda, of NFB experimental animations and stopmotion films, perhaps nowave films like Downtown 81, hip-hop films like Beat Street, the Qatsi series, Tony Gatlif's films and many more.

5   Jean Rouch, Adriy Tarkovsky, Sergei Eisenstein, Federico Fellini, Dzigo Vertov, Hugo Zemp, Michel Brault, Agnes Varda, Werner Herzog, David MacDougall, Jean-Luc Godard a collection of filmmakers and ethnographic filmmakers who wrote about making cinema.

6   It is interesting to note that ethnomusicology because of its blurry inheritance of anthropology and musicology that students who enter graduate school from a music programme may have a different level of comfort with the idea of science than students with an anthropology background. Further, in the context of the development and proliferation of studies and the expansion of ethnomusicology into a very diverse collection of subfields that from my perspective it is no longer possible to speak authoritatively about what ethnomusicology does. But certainly, ethnography defines an important social scientific contribution to all of these subfields. Ethnography is a function, and it is to this that we must turn.

7   It is interesting to note, as Jay Ruby has, that Writing Culture ignored developments in visual anthropology at the time. It is further interesting that the reboot of the work continues to omit cinema production from analysis.

8 WHAT'S WRONG WITH THE LIBERAL DOCUMENTARY, Jill Godmilow available online: https://www3.nd.edu/~jgodmilo/liberal.html

Chapter 10

1. I am thinking here of the Wet'suwet'en blockades of Coastal Gas Link construction that is occurring as I write this book. The Royal Canadian Mounted Police, Canada's federal police agency has been mobilized to break up the Wet'suwet'en blockage of their traditional territory while the Canadian state accepts and enforces an injunction from the oil and gas company against the sovereign nation of the Wet'suwet'en.
2. Alexis Shotwell explores the issue of purity in *Against Purity: Living Ethnically in Compromised Times* (2016).
3. This quote is from bell hook's discussion of her grandmother's quilt-making practice and I love the idea of thinking about filmmaking as a craft of weaving stories. In this chapter titled *Aesthetic Inheritances*, hooks focuses on the craft of quilt making and its role in cultural memory. Filmmaking does, or can, have this quality when it is separated from its role as entertainment or document. Jonas Mekas went a long way in making this connection in his diary films and I think this emphasis is also found in John Baily's fieldwork films.
4. Wintigo, sometimes spelled Wendigo, is sometimes dealt with as folkore, as ghost story, as psychological phenomena. For an example in contemporary public media see the Lake Land newspaper article: The Haunting of the Lakeland: The Legend of the Fort Kent Wendigo by Chris Lapointe, 31 October 2020.
5. https://headsmashedin.ca/about-head-smashed-buffalo-jump-world-heritage-site (accessed November 2021).
6. [Welcome to the University of Calgary]. I would like to take this opportunity to acknowledge the traditional territories of the people of the Treaty 7 region in Southern Alberta, which includes the Blackfoot Confederacy (comprising the Siksika, Piikani and Kainai First Nations), as well as the Tsuut'ina First Nation, and the Stoney Nakoda (including the Chiniki, Bearspaw and Wesley First Nations). The city of Calgary is also home to Métis Nation of Alberta, Region 3. I would also like to note that the University of Calgary is situated on land adjacent to where the Bow River meets the Elbow River, and that the traditional Blackfoot name of this place is 'Moh'kins'tsis', which we now call the City of Calgary. https://www.ucalgary.ca/indigenous/cultural-protocol (accessed November 2021).
7. https://www.cbc.ca/news/indigenous/land-acknowledgments-what-s-wrong-with-them-1.6217931 (accessed November 2021).

8   I would like to thank *Elders' Room* reviewer Adrian Huysman for the idea of my filmmaking practice as 'swwitnessing'. This is a powerful observation that has inspired the thinking-feeling of this chapter. The review can be read here: https://abdn.pure.elsevier.com/en/publications/elders-room (accessed September 2021).

Chapter 11

1   Rosi Braidotti's discussion of the posthuman condition. Available: https://rosibraidotti.com/2019/01/28/the-posthuman-condition-and-the-critical-posthumanities/ (accessed 29 September 2021).

Bibliography

Ames, Eric. 2012. *Ferocious Reality: Documentary According to Werner Herzog*. Minneapolis, MN: University of Minnesota Press.

Arnold, Gina, Daniel Cookney, Kristy Fairclough and Michael Goddard. 2017. *Music/Video: Histories, Aesthetics, Media*. New York: Bloomsbury.

Attas, Robin and Margaret Walker. 2019. 'Decolonizing Music Pedagogies'. *Intersections* 39 (1): 3–20

Baily, John. 2009. 'The Art of the "Fieldwork Movie": 35 Years of Making Ethnomusicological Films'. *Ethnomusicology Forum* 18 (1): 55–64.

Barad, Karen. 2014. 'Diffracting Diffraction: Cutting Together-Apart'. *Parallax* 20 (3): 168–87.

Barbash, Ilisa and Lucien Taylor. 1997. *Cross-Cultural Filmmaking: A Handbook for Making Documentary and Ethnographic Films and Videos*. Los Angeles, CA: University of California Press.

Barla, Josef. 2018. "Technology/Technicity/Techné. New Materialism". In New Materialism: Networking European Scholarship on 'How Matter Comes to Matter'. online resource. https://newmaterialism.eu/almanac/t/technology-technicity-techne.html.

Bateson, Gregory. 1972a. *Steps to an Ecology of Mind: Collected Essays in Anthropology, Psychiatry, Evolution, and Epistemology*. Chicago, IL: The University of Chicago Press.

Bateson, Gregory. 1979. *Mind and Nature: A Necessary Unity*. New York: Bantam Books.

Bateson, Gregory. 1991. *Further Steps to an Ecology of Mind*. New York: Cornelia & Michael Bessie Books.

Bateson, Gregory and Mary Catherine Bateson. 1987. *Angels Fear: Towards and Epistemology of the sacred*. New York: MacMillan Publishing.

Bateson, Gregory, Don D. Jackson, Jay Haley and John Weakland. 1978. 'Toward a Theory of Schizophrenia'. In Milton M. Berger (ed.), *Beyond the Double Bind: Communication and Family Systems, Theories, and Techniques with Schizophrenics* New York: Brunner/Mazel Publishers.

Bateson, Mary Catherine. 1972b. *Our Own Metaphor: A Personal Account of a Conference on the Effects of Conscious Purpose on Human Adaptation*. New York: Alfred A. Knopf.

Batty, Craig. 2015. 'A Screenwriter's Journey into Theme, and How Creative Writing Research Might Help us to Define Screen Production Research'. *Studies in Australasian Cinema* 9 (2): 110–21.

Batty, Craig. 2016. 'Screenwriting Studies, Screenwriting Practice and the Screenwriting Manual'. *New Writing* 13 (1): 59–70.

Batty, Craig. 2016. 'Writing With/On/For the Screen'. *Journal of Writing in Creative Practice* 9 (1/2): 3–6.

Batty, Craig and Susan Kerrigan. 2018. *Screen Production Research: Creative Practice as a Mode of Enquiry*. London: Palgrave MacMillan.

Bennett, Andy and Keith Kahn-Harris, eds 2004. *After Subculture: Critical Studies in Contemporary Youth Culture*, New York: Palgrave MacMillan.

Berardi, Franco 'Bifo'. 2011. *After the Future*. Oakland, CA: AK Press.

Berardi, Franco 'Bifo'. 2008. *Félix Guattari: Thought, Friendship, and Visionary Cartography*. New York: Palgrave MacMillan.

Berardi, Franco 'Bifo'. 2015. *And: Phenomenology of the End*. New York: Semiotext(e).

Berardi, Frano 'Bifo'. 2018. *Chaos and Poetry*. New York: Semiotext(e).

Berardi, Franco 'Bifo'. 2021. *The Third Unconscious*. New York: Verso.

Berger, Sally June 24. 2011. 'Ultimate Insider: An Interview with Les Blank'. https://www.moma.org/explore/inside_out/2011/06/24/ultimate-insider-an-interview-with-les-blank/.

Berz, William L. 1995. 'Working Memory in Music: A Theoretical Model'. *Music Perception: An Interdisciplinary Journal* 12 (3): 353–64. doi:10.2307/40286188.

Blank, Les. 2013. *Interview with Ben Harbert*. Unpublished.

Blank, Les. 2014. *Criterion Collection: Les Blank, Always for Pleasure*. New York: The Criterion Collection.

Bogue, Ronald. 2003a. *Deleuze on Cinema*. New York: Routledge.

Bogue, Ronald. 2003b. *Deleuze on Music, Painting, and the Arts*. New York: Routledge.

Böhme, Gernot. 2012. *Invasive Technification: Critical Essays in the Philosophy of Technology*. New York: Bloomsbury.

Bonta, Mark and John Protevi. 2004. *Deleuze and Geophilosophy: A Guide and Glossary*. Edinburgh: Edinburgh University Press.

Borecky, Pavel. 2016. 'Tuning Solaris: From the Darkness of a Shopping Mall Towards Post-Humanist Cinema'. *Visual Ethnography* 5 (2): 109–37.

Boulé, Jean-Pierre and Ursula Tidd, eds (2012), *Existentialism and Contemporary Cinema: A Beauvoirian Perspective*. New York: Berghahn Books.

Braidotti, Rosi. 2006. *Transpositions: On Nomadic Ethics*. Boston, MA: Polity Press.

Braidotti, Rosi. 2013. *The Posthuman*. Cambridge and Malden: Polity.

Braidotti, Rosi. 2019. *Posthuman Knowledge*. Cambridge: Polity Press.

Braidotti, Rosi and Simone Bignall. 2018. *Posthuman Ecologies: Complexity and Process after Deleuze*. New York: Roman & Littlefield.

Braidoti, Rosi and Maria Hlavajova. 2018. *Posthuman Glossary*. New York: Bloomsbury.

Brier, Soren. 2008. *Cybersemiotics: Why Information is Not Enough*. Toronto, ON: University of Toronto Press.

Brody, Richard. 2008. *Everything Is Cinema: The Working Life of Jean-Luc Godard*. New York: Metropolitan Books.

Buchanan, Ian and Marcel Swiboda. 2004. *Deleuze and Music*. Edinburgh: Edinburgh University Press.

Canet, Fernando and Hector J. Pérez. 2016. 'Character Engagement as Central to the Filmmaker Subject Relationship: *En Construcción* (José Luis Guerin, 2001) as a Case Study'. *Studies in Documentary Film* 10 (3): 215–32.

Cassirer, Ernst. 2012 [1930]. 'Form and Technology'. In A. S. Hoel and I. Folkvord (eds), *Ernst Cassirer on Form and Technology: Contemporary Readings*, 15–53. Basingstoke: Palgrave Macmillan.

Chapman, Owen and Kim Sawchuk. 2012. 'Research-Creation: Interventino, Analysis and "Family Resemblances"'. *Canadian Journal of Communications* 37: 5–26.

Charlton, Noel G. 2008. *Understanding Gregory Bateson: Mind, Beauty, and the Sacred Earth*. Albany, NY: State University of New York Press.

Chion, Michel. 2003. *Film, A Sound Art*. New York: Columbia University Press.

Chion, Michel. 2019. *Audio-vision: Sound on Screen* (2nd edn). New York: Columbia University Press.

Clayton, Martin. 2008. 'Toward an Ethnomusicology of Sound Experience'. In Henry Stobart (ed.), *The New (Ethno)musicologies*, 135–69. Plymouth: Scarecrow Press.

Clifford, James and George E. Marcus. 1986. *Writing Culture: The Poetics and Politics of Ethnography*, Berkeley, CA: University of California Press.

Cohen, Thomas F. 2012. *Playing to the Camera: Musicians and Musical Performance in Documentary Cinema*. New York: Columbia University Press.

Conley, Verena Andermatt. 2009. 'Thirty-six Thousand Form of Love: The Queering of Deleuze and Guattari'. In Chrysanthi Nigianni and Merl Storr (eds), *Deleuze and Queer Theory*, 24–36. Edinburgh: Edinburgh University Press.

Crawford, Peter Ian and David Turton. 1992. *Film as Ethnography*. Manchester: Manchester University Press.

Cumming, Gabriel and Carla Norwood. 2012. 'The Community Voice Method: Using Participatory Research and Filmmaking to Foster Dialogue about Changing Landscapes'. *Landscape and Urban Planning* 105: 434–44.

Damasio, Antonio. 2018. *The Strange Order of Things: Life, Feeling, and the Making of Cultures*. New York: Pantheon Press.

Deamer, David. 2016. *Deleuze's Cinema Books: Three Introductions to the Taxonomy of Images*. Edinburgh: Edinburgh University Press.

Decherney, Peter. 2008. 'Dudley Murphy: Hollywood Will Card'. (review). *Modernism/Modernity* 15 (3): 578–80.

DeLanda, Manuel. 2002. *Intensive Science and Virtual Philosophy*. Lonodon: Continuum.

Del Rio, Elena. 2008. *Deleuze and the Cinemas of Performance: Powers of Affection*. Edinburgh: Edinburgh University Press.

Deleuze, Gilles. 1984. *Francis Bacon: The Logic of Sensation*. Minneapolis, MN: University of Minnesota Press.
Deleuze, Gilles. 1986. *The Movement-Image: Cinema 1*. Minneapolis: University of Minnesota Press.
Deleuze, Gilles. 1989. *The Time-Image: Cinema 2*. Minneapolis: University of Minnesota Press.
Deleuze, Gilles. 1990. *The Logic of Sense*. Columbia, NJ: Columbia University Press.
Deleuze, Gilles. 1991. *Bergsonsim*. New York: Zone Books.
Deleuze, Gilles. 1993. *The Fold*. Minneapolis: University of Minnesota Press.
Deleuze, Gilles. 2001. 'Nietzsche'. In *Pure Immanence: Essays on A Life*, trans. Anne Boyman, 53–102. New York: Zone Books.
Deleuze, Gilles. 2003. *Fracis Bacon: The Logic of Sensation*. New York: Contiuum.
Deleuze, Gilles. 2005. *Pure Immanence: Essays on A Life*. New York: Zone Books.
Deleuze, Gilles. 2007. *Two Regimes of Madness – Texts and Interviews, 1975–1995*. Edited by David Lapoujade. New York: Semiotext(e).
Deleuze, Gilles and Felix Guattari. 1983. *Anti-Oediups: Capitalism and Schizophrenia*. Minneapolis, MN: University of Minnesota Press.
Deleuze, Gilles and Felix Guattari. 1986. *Kafka: Toward a Minor Literature*. Minneapolis, MN: University of Minnesota Press.
Deleuze, Gilles and Felix Guattari. 1987. *A Thousand Plateaus: Capitalism and Schizophrenia*. Minneapolis, MN: University of Minnesota Press
Deleuze, Gilles and Félix Guattari. 1994. *What is Philosophy?* New York: Columbia University Press.
Deleuze, Gilles and Claire Parnet. 2007. *Dialogues II*. New York: Columbia University Press.
Deloria, Vine. 1988. *Custer Died For Your Sins*. Norman, OK: University of Oklahoma Press.
Delson, Susan. 2006. 'Dudley Murphy: Hollywood Wild Card'. (review), *Library Journal* 73: 578–80.
Derrida, Jacques. 1995. *Points. . . Interviews, 1974–1994*. Edited by Elisabeth Weber. Stanford: Stanford University Press.
Donald, James. 2009. 'Jazz Modernism and Film Art: Dudley Murphy and *Ballet mécanique*'. *Modernism/modernity* 16 (1): 24–49.
Dornfeld, Barry. 1992. 'Representation and Authority in Ethnographic Film/Video: Reception'. *Ethnomusicology* 36 (1): 95–8.
Feld, Steve. 1976. 'Ethnomusicology and Visual Communication'. *Ethnomusicology* 20 (2): 293–325.
Feld, Steven. 1988. 'Aesthetics as Iconicity of Style, or "Lift-up-over Sounding": Getting into the Kaluli Groove'. *Yearbook for Traditional Music* 20: 74–113. https://doi.org/10.2307/768167.
Feld, Steven. 2003. 'A Rainforest Acoustemology'. In Michael Bull and Les Back (eds), *The Auditory Culture Reader*, 223–39. New York: Berg.

Feld, Steven and Keith H. Basso. 1996. *Sense of Place*. Sante Fe: School for Advanced Research Press.

Fiol, Stefan. 2010. 'Dual Framing: Locating Authenticities in the Music Videos of Himalayan Possession Rituals'. *Ethnomusicology* 54 (1): 28–53.

Flaxman, Gregory. 2000. *The Brain is the Screen: Deleuze and the Philosophy of Cinema*. Minneapolis: University of Minnesota Press.

Foucault, Michel. 1988. *Technologies of the Self: A Seminar with Michel Foucault*. Boston, MA: University of Massachusetts Press.

Freire, Paulo. 2010. *Education for Critical Consciousness*. New York: Continuum.

Genosko, Gary. 2009. *Félix Guattari: A Critical Introduction*. New York: Pluto Press.

Genosko, Gary. 2011. 'Guattari's Contributions to the Theory of Semiocapitalism'. In Eric Alliez and Andrew Goffey (eds), *The Guattari Effect*, 115–33. New York: Continuum.

Genosko, Gary. 2018. *The Reinvention of Social Practices: Essays on Félix Guattari*. London, UK: Rowman and Littlefield International.

Gorksi, Paul. 2000. 'Filming You Filming Me: Highlighting a Multicultural, Self-Reflective Approach in Ethnographic Educational Filmmaking'. *Multicultural Perspectives* 2 (2): 41–4.

Grimshaw, Anna. 2001. *The Ethnographer's Eye: Ways of Seeing in Modern Anthropology*. New York: Cambridge University Press.

Grimshaw, Anna. 2011. 'The Bellwether Ewe: Recent Developments in Ethnographic Filmmaking and the Aesthetics of Anthropological Inquiry'. *Cultural Anthropology* 26 (2): 247–62.

Grimshaw, Anna and Amanda Ravetz. 2009. *Observational Cinema: Anthropology, Film, and the Exploration of Social Life*. Bloomington, IN: Indiana University Press.

Guattari, Felix. 2000. *The Three Ecologies*. New York: Bloomsbury.

Guattari, Félix. 1995. *Chaosmosis: An Ethico-Aesthetic Paradigm*. Sydney, Australia: Power Publications.

Guattari, Felix. 2009. *Chaosophy: Texts and Interviews 1972–1977*. Los Angeles: Semiotext(e).

Guattari, Felix. 2011. *The Machinic Unconscious: Essay in Schizoanalysis*. Los Angeles: Semiotext(e).

Guattari, Félix. 2013. *Schizoanalytic Cartographies*. New York: Bloomsbury.

Gullion, Jessica Smartt. 2018. *Diffractive Ethnography: Social Sciences and the Ontological Turn*. New York: Routledge.

Haraway, Donna. 2008. *When Species Meet*. Minneapolis: University of Minnesota Press.

Haraway, Donna. 2016. *Staying with the Trouble: Making Kin in the Chthulucene*, Durham, NC: Duke University Press.

Harbert, Benjamin J. 2018. *American Music Documentary: Five Case Studies of Cine-Ethnomusicology*. Middletown, CT: Wesleyan University Press.

Harries-Jones, Peter. 2005. "Understanding Ecological Aesthetics: The Challenge of Bateson." *Cybernetics and Human Knowing (Special Issue)* 12 (1–2): 61–74.

Harney, Stefano and Fred Moten. 2013. *The Undercommons: Fugitive Planning & Black Study*. New York: Minor Compositions.

Harper, Graeme, Ruth Doughty and Jochen Eisentraut, eds 2009. *Sound and Music in Film and Visual Media: An Overview*. New York: Continuum.

Harries-Jones, Peter. 1995. *A Recursive Vision: Ecological Understanding and Gregory Bateson*. Toronto, ON: University of Toronto Press.

Hebdige, Dick. 1979. *Subculture the Meaning of Style*. New York: Routledge.

Heidegger, Martin. 1962. *Being and Time*. San Francisco: Harper San Francisco.

Heidegger, Martin. 1977. *The Question Concerning Technology and Other Essays*. New York and London: Garland Publishing.

Heidegger, Martin. 1992/1943. *Parmenides*. Bloomington and Indianapolis: Indiana University Press.

Heider, Karl G. 2006. *Ethnographic Film: Revised Edition*. Austin, TX: University of Texas Press.

Henley, Paul. 2009. *The Adventure of the Real: Jean Rouch and the Craft of Ethnographic Cinema*. Chicago, IL: University of Chicago Press.

Herzog, Werner April 30 1999. 'Werner Herzog Reads his Minnesota Declaration: Truth and Fact in Documentary Cinema'. https://walkerart.org/magazine/minnesota-declaration-truth-documentary-cinema.

Hockings, Paul. 1975. *Principles of Visual Anthropology*. Paris: Mouton Publishers.

Hodkinson, Paul and Wolfgang Deicke. 2007. *Youth Cultures: Scenes, Subcultures and Tribes*. New York: Routledge.

Hoel, Aud Sissel and Iris van der Tuin. 2013. 'The Ontological Force of Technicity: Reading Cassirer and Simondon Diffractively'. *Philosophy & Technology* 26 (2): 187–202.

Hoffmeyer, Jesper. 2008. *Biosemiotics: An Examination into the Signs of Life and the Life of Signs*. London: University of Scranton Press.

hooks, bell. 1990. *Yearning: Race, Gender, and Cultural Politics*. Boston, MA: South End Press.

hooks, bell. 2009. *Belonging: A Culture of Place*. New York: Routledge.

Hörl, Erich. 2017. *General Ecology: The New Ecological Paradigm*. New York: Bloomsbury.

Ikoniadou, Eleni. 2014. *The Rhythmic Event: Art, Media, and the Sonic*, Cambridge, MA: The MIT Press.

Jackson, Michael. 2005. *Existential Anthropology: Events, Exigencies and Effects*. New York: Bergahn Books.

Jackson, Michael. 2013. *Lifeworlds: Essays in Existential Anthropology*. Chicago, IL: The University of Chicago Press.

Jackson, Michael. 2017. *What is Existential Anthropology?* New York: Berghahn books.
Jackson, Michael. 2018. *The Varieties of Temporal Experience: Travels in Philosophical, Historical, and Ethnographic Time.* New York: Columbia University Press.
Jenssen, Toril. 2009. *Behind the Eye: Reflexive Methods in Culture Studies, Ethnographic Film, and Visual Media.* Translated and edited by Peter I. Crawford. Denmark: Intervention Press.
Jonathan, Kahana, ed. 2016. *The Documentary Film Reader: History, Theory, Criticism.* Foreword by Charles Musser. New York: Oxford University Press.
Keil, Charles and Seven Feld. 2005. *Music Grooves.* Tucson, AZ: Wheatmark.
Kennedy, Barbara M. 2000. *Deleuze and Cinema: The Aesthetics of Sensation*, Edinburgh: Edinburgh University Press.
Kerrigan, Susan, Berkeley, Leo, Maher, Sean, Sergi, Michael and Wotherspoon, Alison. 2015. Screen production enquiry: A study of five Australian doctorates. *Studies in Australasian Cinema* 9: 1–17.
Kohn, Eduardo. 2013. *How Forets Think: Toward an Anthropoloogy Beyond the Human.* Oakland, CA: University of California Press.
Kun, Josh. 2005. *Audiotopia: Music, Race, and America*, Berkeley, CA: University of California Press.
Kunzru, Hari. 1997. 'You Are Cyborg'. *Wired* 5 (2 February). https://www.wired.com/1997/02/ffharaway/.
Lambert, Gregg. 2012. *In Search of a New Image of Thought: Gilles Deleuze and Philosophical Expressionism.* Minneapolis: University of Minnesota Press.
Latour, Bruno. 2000. *Pandora's Hope. Essays on the Reality of Science Studies.* Cambridge, MA and London: Harvard University Press.
Latour, Bruno. 2002. 'Morality and Technology: The End of the Means'. *Theory, Culture and Society* 19 (5–6): 247–60.
Loizos, Peter. 1993. *Innovation in Ethnographic Film: From Innocence to Self-Consciousness, 1955–1985.* Chicago, IL: University of Chicago Press.
Loveless, Natalie. 2019. *How to Make Art at the End of the World: A Manifesto for Research-Creation.* Durham, NC: Duke University Press.
Loveless, Natalie. 2020. *Knowings & Knots: Methodologies and Ecologies in Research-Creation.* Edmonton, Alberta: University of Alberta Press.
Lundy, Craig. 2018. *Deleuze's Bergsonism.* Edinburgh: University of Edinburgh Press.
MacDonald, Michael. 2016a. *Remix and Life Hack in Hip Hop: Towards a Critical Pedagogy of Music.* The Netherlands: Springer.
MacDonald, Michael. 2016b. *Playing for Change: Music Festivals as Community Learning and Development.* New York: Peter Lang.
MacDonald, Michael B. 2020a. 'Thanks for Being Local: CineMusicking as a Critical Pedagogy of Popular Music'. In Shirley Steinberg and Barry Down (eds), *Handbook for Critical Pedagogy*, 1242–54. Sage Press.

MacDonald, Michael B. 2020b. 'CineMusicking: Ecological Ethnographic Film as Critical Pedagogy'. In Cutter-Mackenzie (ed.), *Research Handbook on Childhoodnature*, 1735–52. New York: Springer.

MacDonald, Michael B. 2020c. 'Unspittable: Long-form Ethnographic Music Video as Cine-Ethnomusicology Research-Creation'. *Visual Ethnography Journal* IX (1): 114–37.

MacDonald, Michael B. 2022. 'Should We Call It Cine-Culturual Studies?: Cineworlding Popular Music and Youth Studies'. In Andy Bennett (ed.), *Bloomsbury Handboook for Popular Music and Youth Studies*. In press.

MacDougall, David. 1998. *Transcultural Cinema*. Princeton, NJ: Princeton University Press.

MacDougall, David. 2006. *The Corporeal Image: Film Ethnography, and the Senses*. Princeton, NJ: Princeton University Press.

Madden, Raymond. 2010. *Being Ethnographic: A Guide to the Theory and Practice of Ethnography*. New York. Sage.

Manning, Erin. 2009. *Relationscapes: Movement, Art, Philosophy*. Cambridge, MA: The MIT Press.

Manning, Erin. 2013. *Always More Than One: Individuation's Dance*. Durham, NC: Duke University Press.

Manning, Erin. 2016. *The Minor Gesture*. Durham, NC: Duke University Press.

Manning, Erin. 2020. *For a Pragmatics of the Useless*. Durham, NC: Duke University Press.

Manning, Erin and Brian Massumi. 2014. *Thought in the Act: Passages in the Ecology of Experience*. Minneapolis: University of Minnesota Press.

Marcus, George. 1998. *Ethnography through Thick and Thin*. Princeton, NJ: Princeton University Press.

Marks, Laura U. 2000. *The Skin of Film: Intercultural Cinema, Embodiments, and the Senses*, Durham, NC: Duke University Press.

Marrati, Paola. 2008. *Gilles Deleuze: Cinema and Philosophy*. Baltimore, MA: The John Hopkins University Press.

Massumi, Brian. 1992. *A user's guide to Capitalism and Schizophrenia: Deviations from Deleuze and Guattari*. Boston, MA: The MIT Press.

Massumi, Brian. 2002. *Parables for the Virtual: Movement, Affect, Sensation*. Durham, NC: Duke University Press.

Massumi, Brian. 2011. *Semblance and Event: Activist Philosophy and the Occurrent Arts*. Cambridge, MA: MIT Press.

Massumi, Brian. 2013. 'Becoming Architectual: Affirmative Critique, Creative Incompletion'. In Special Issue: *The Innoovatioon Imperative: Architectures Vitality. Architectual Design* 83 (1): 50–5.

Massumi, Brian. 2015. *Politics of Affect*. Boston, CA: Polity.

Maturana, Humberto and Francisco Varela. 1987. *The Tree of Knowledge: The Biological Roots of Human Understanding*. Boston, MA: Shambhala Press.

McIntosh, Jonathan. 2006. 'How Dancing, Singing, and Playing Shape the Ethnographer: Research with Children in a Balinese Dance Studio'. *Anthropology Matters* 8 (2): 1–17.

Mignolo, Walter. 1995. *The Darker Side of the Renaissance: Literacy, Territoriality, & Colonization*. Ann Arbor, MI: University of Michigan Press.

Mignolo, Walter D. and Catherine E. Walsh. 2018. *On Decoloniality: Concepts, Analytics, Praxis*. Durham, NC: Duke University Press.

Møhl, Perle. 2011. '*Mise en Scène*, Knowledge and Participation: Considerations of a Filming Anthropologist'. *Visual Anthropology* 24 (3): 227–45.

Moten, Fred. 2018. *Stolen Life*. Durham, NC: Duke University Press.

Muggleton, David and Rupert Weinzierl, eds 2003. *The Post-Subcultures Reader*, New York: Berg.

Nayar, Pramod K. 2014. *Posthumanism*. New York: Polity.

Norton, Barley. 2021. 'Ethnomusicology and Filmmaking'. In Stephen Cottrell (ed.), *Music, Dance, and Anthropology*, 121–43. Hertfordshire: Sean Kingston Publishing.

Palmer, Helen and Vicky, Hunter. 2018. 'Worlding'. In *New Materialism: Networking European Scholarship on 'How Matter Comes to Matter'*. online resource. https://newmaterialism.eu/almanac/w/worlding.html.

Pink, Sarah. 2009. *Doing Sensory Ethnography*. New York: Sage.

Pink, Sarah. 2013. *Doing Visual Ethnography*. New York: Sage.

Pisters, Patricia. 2012. *The Neuro-Image: A Deleuzian Film-Philosophy of Digital Screen Culture*. Stanford, CA: Stanford University Press.

Pitts, Virginia. 2013. 'Writing from the Body: Kinesthetics and Entrainment in Collaborative Screenplay Development'. *Journal of Media Practice* 14 (1): 61–78.

Powell, Anna. 2012. *Deleuze, Altered States and Film*. Edinburgh: Edinburgh University Press.

Prager, Brad. 2011. *The Cinema of Werner Herzog: Aesthetic Ecstasy and Truth*. New York: Wallflower Press.

Protevi, Jon. 2018. '*Geo-hydro-solar-bio-techno-politics*'. In Rosi Braidotti and Maria Hlavajova, *Posthuman Glossary*. London: Bloomsbury Press.

Raunig, Gerald. 2016. *Dividuum: Machinic Capitalism and Molecular Revolution*. Boston, MA: MIT Press.

Redner, Gregg. 2011. *Deleuze and Film Music: Building a Methodological Bridge Between Film Theory and Music*. Bristol: intellect.

Rizzo, Teresa. 2012. *Deleuze and Film: A Feminist Introduction*. New York: Continuum. .

Robertson, Robert. 2009. *Eisenstein on the Audiovisual: The Montage of Music, Image and Sound in Cinema*. New York: I.B. Taurus.

Robinson, Dylan. 2020. *Hungry Listening: Resonant Theory for Indigenous Sound Studies*. Minneapolis: Duke University Press.

Rodowick, David. 1997. *Gilles Deleuze's Time Machine*. Durham, NC: Duke University Press.

Rony, Fatimah Tobing. 1996. *The Third Eye: Race, Cinema, and Ethnographic Spectacle*. London: Duke University Press.

Rouch, Jean. 2003. *Ciné-ethnography*. Minneapolis, MN: University of Minnesota Press.

Rouch, Jean, John Marshall and John W. Adams. 1978. 'Jean Rouch Talks about His Films to John Marshall and John W. Adams'. *American Anthropologist* 80 (4): 1005–20.

Ruby, Jay. 2000. *Picturing Culture: Explorations of Film & Anthropology*. Chicago, IL: The University of Chicago Press.

Ruesch, Jurgan and Gregory Bateson. 1951/1987. *Communication: The Social Matrix of Psychiatry*. New York: W.W. Norton and Company, Inc.

Rushton, Richard. *Cinema after Deleuze*. New York: Continuum.

Russell, Catherine. 1999. *Experimental Ethnography: The work of film in the age of video*. Durham, NC: Duke University Press.

Russell, Catherine. 2018. *Archiveology: Walter Benjamin and Archival Film Practices*. Durham, NC: Duke University Press.

Sartre, Jean-Paul. 1956. *Being and Nothingness*. New York: Washington Square Press.

Sartre, Jean-Paul. 1976/2004. *Critique of Dialectical Reason: Theory of Practical Ensembles*. New York: Verso.

Saunders, Dave. 2007. *Direct Cinema: Observational Documentary and the politics of the sixties*. London: Wallflower Press.

Schrader, Paul. 2018. *Transcendental Style in Film: Ozu, Bresson, Dreyer*. Oakland, CA: University of California Press.

Seeger, Charles. 1977. *Studies in Musicology 1935–1975*. Berkeley, CA: University of California Press.

Shotwell, Alexis. 2016. *Against Purity: Living Ethically in Compromised Times*. Minneapolis, MN: Minnesota Press.

Shzr Ee, Tan. 2021. 'Special Issue: Decolonising Music and Music Studies'. *Ethnomusicology Forum* 30 (1): 4–8. DOI: 10.1080/17411912.2021.1938445

Simondon, Gilbert. 2016/1958. *On the Mode of Existence of Technical Objects*. Minneapolis, MN: Univocal -- Minnesota University Press.

Small, Christopher. 1998. *Musicking: The Meaning of Performing and Listening*, Middletown, CT: Wesleyan University Press.

Steinberg, Shirley R. and Awad Ibrahim, eds 2016. *Critically Researching Youth*, New York: Peter Lang.

Stengers, Isabelle. 2005. 'Introductory Notes on an Ecology of Practices'. *Cultural Studies Review* 11 (1): 183–96.

Stengers, Isabelle. 2010. *Cosmopolitics 1*. Minneapolis, MN: University of Minnesota Press.

Stévance, Sophie and Serge Lacasse. 2018. *Research-Creation in Music and the Arts: Toward a Collaborative Interdiscipline*. New York: Routledge.

Stiegler, Bernard. 1998. *Technics and Time 1: The Fault of Epimetheus*. Stanford: Stanford University Press.

Stiegler, Bernard. 2008. *Technics and Time 2: Disorientation*. Stanford: Stanford University Press.

Stiegler, Bernard. 2010. *Technics and Time 3: Cinematic Time and the Question of Malaise*. Stanford: Stanford University Press.

Stiegler, Bernard. 2019. *The Age of Disruption: Technology and Madness in Computational Capitalism*. Hoboken, New Jersey: Wiley.

Sullivan, Nikki. 2014. 'Somatechnics'. *Transgender Studies Quarterly* 1 (1–2): 187–90.

Suhr, C. and R. Willerslev. 2012. Can Film Show the Invisible?: The Work of Montage in Ethnographic Filmmaking'. *Current Anthropology* 53 (3): 282–302.

Szymanski, Adam. 20123. 'It's All About Love: Félix Guattari's Minor Cinema'. *Kinephanos* 3 (1): 92–109.

Tarkovsky, Andrey. 1986. *Sculpting in Time: Reflections on Cinema*. Austin, TX: University of Texas Press.

Titon, Jeff Todd. 1988. *Powerhouse for God: Speech, Chant, and Song in an Appalachian Baptist Church*. Austin, TX: University of Texas Press.

Titon, Jeff Todd. 1992. 'Representation and Authority in Ethnographic Film/Video Production'. *Ethnomusicology* 36 (1 winter): 89–94.

Truth and Reconciliation Commission of Canada. 2015. *Final Report of the Truth and Reconciliation Commission of Canada, Volume One: Summary*. Toronto, ON: Lorimer.

Turino, Thomas. 2014. 'Peircean Thought as Core Theory for a Phenomenological Ethnomusicology'. *Ethnomusicology* 58 (2): 185–221.

Vannini, Phillip. 2015. Non-Representational Ethnography: New Ways of Animating Lifeworlds, *Cultural Geographies,* 22 (2): 317–27.

Vita-More, Natasha. 2018. *Transhumanism: What Is It?* New York: Humanity+ Publication.

Von Foerster, Heinz. 2003. *Understanding Understanding: Essays on the Cybernetics and Cognition*. New York: Springer.

Von Foerster, Heinz. 2014. *The Beginning of Heaven and Earth Has No Name: Seven Days with Second-Order Cybernetics*. New York: Fordham University Press.

Walker, Margaret. 2020. 'Towards a Decolonized Music History Curriculum'. *Journal of Music History Pedagogy* 10 (1): 1–19.

Wenders, Wim and Mary Zournazi. 2013. *Inventing Peace: A Dialogue on Perception*. New York: Palgrave MacMillan.

White, Jerry. 2018. 'Introduction: Four Kinds of Minor Cinema (and Some Thoughts on a Fifth)'. *Canadian Review of Camparative Literature* 45 (3): 357–80.

Whitehead, Alfred North. 1966. *Modes of Thought*. New York: The Free Press.

Wolfe, Cary. 2010. *What is Posthumanism?* Minneapolis: University of Minnesota Press.

Yakir, Dan and Jean Rouch. 1978. '"Ciné-Transe": The Vision of Jean Rouch: An Interview'. *Film Quarterly* 31 (3): 2–11.

Young, Colin. 1975. 'Observational Documentary'. In Paul Hockings (ed.), *Principles of Visual Anthropology*, 65–82. Paris: Mouton Publishers.

Zagorski-Thomas, Simon. 2022. *Practical Musicology*. New York: Bloomsbury.

Zemp, Hugo. 1988. 'Filming Music and Looking at Music Films'. *Ethnomusicology* 32 (3 autumn): 393–427.

Zourabichvili, Fraçois. 2012. *Deleuze: A Philosophy of the Event*. Edinburgh: University of Edinburgh Press.

Index

Page numbers followed with "n" refer to endnotes.

abstract machines   18, 40–2, 142
activism, forms of   260–3
activist cine-ethnomusicology   226–7
activist philosophy   228
actual   100–2, 105, 110, 114, 119–20, 139, 147, 191
aerial cinematography as deterritorialization   86–7
aesthetics   201, 204, 247, 248
aesthetic sensibility   92
affects   13–14, 182–4, 218, 223, 275 n.9
  of relief   238
  vectoring of   183–6, 195
agencement   135, 141–2, 187, 274 n.2
Allegory of the Cave (Plato)   45
alternative reality   51–2
  cineworlding practice in   62–3
  research-creation   67–9
American Music Documentary: Five Case-Studies in Cine-Ethnomusicology (2018, Harbert)   226
Amplify   116–20
anarchive   157, 171
'An Ecomusicological Love Story' (MacDonald)   214
anthropocentrism   177, 261
Antwoord, Die   132
art
  and coloniality   250–3
  in modernity   246–50
artfulness   15–17, 19
artist   217–18
  emergence of   248
  professional life   249
artistic expression   276 n.10
artistic vectors   216–17
aspiring artists   220
assemblage of enunciation   58, 85, 129
  collective   131

audio-vision   45, 46, 48, 57, 58, 63, 64, 143, 144, 187, 218, 220
  automation of the politics of   222
  capitalist, micropolitics of   220–2
  effect   216, 218
  event-triggering tension   215
  high-speed production of   221
audiovisual affect packets   218–20
audiovisual culture   119
audiovisual images, mass production of   219
audiovisual machines   18
aural culture   252
automation   234
  of the politics of audio-vision   222

Barthes, Roland   218–19
Bateson, Gregory   200, 201, 204
beauty affect-vector   90
becoming-body   49, 50, 60, 65–7, 138, 157
becoming-posthumanographer   213–14
behind-the-scenes (BTS) documentary   157
Belonging: A Culture of Place (2009, hooks)   241
Berardi, Franco 'Bifo'   130
Bergson, Henri   46–8, 53, 106–7, 109, 110, 116, 145
Bignall, Simone   216
biogram   65–7, 142
Blackmagic Ursa   165
Black Water, Karsen   245
Blank, Les   158, 162
body
  defined   137–8
  in *Quartet 2* (2010)   102–4
body-camera-microphone assemblage   216

bodying   57–8, 65–7, 154, 164–5, 171
   filmmakers   168–70, 215
   posthuman   165–6
Body without Organs (BwO)   79
Bonta, Mark   38
Boreal Forest   203
Borecky, Pavel   205
Braidotti, Rosi   8, 216, 261
Breagan Smith (character)   211, 212, 214, 215, 221
Breagan Smith and the Good Times   82
BTS documentary. *See* behind-the-scenes (BTS) documentary
BwO. *See* Body without Organs (BwO)

cadence   181–2
camera lens
   aperture   152–3, 166
   choices   154–5
   depth of field   152
camera technology   165
Canon prime lens   155
capital   220
capitalism   229, 230
Cardinal, Andrew. *See* Amplify
The Century the Self (Curtis)   130
chaos   256
Chapman, Owen   68, 76
Chion, Michel   63, 158, 217–18
choral composition   85
choral music assemblage   94
chromesthesia   5, 45–6, 56–8, 126, 143, 156, 158–9
chromesthetic techniques   164
Chung, David   117
cine-ethnomusicology   9, 75–6, 81, 176, 193, 204
'Cinema of Desire' (Guattari)   265
cinema-thinking   19–20, 35–6, 98, 216–17, 235–6
   with the editor   16–17
   percepts and affects   13–15
   in using camera   13
cinematic ecology   25
cinematic machining   83
cinematic research-creation. *See* research-creation
cinematic research methods   175–6

cinematic techniques   63–5
cineportrait   164, 276 n.3
cineworlding
   assemblage   112
   as decolonial futurity   71–3
   music   56, 60, 62, 81, 98–9
   and posthumanography   97–100
   as practical musicology   93–5
   practice   62–3
   refrains   175–7
   screen assemblage and   120–1
   technocultural ecological studies   177–9
   Unspittable (2019, MacDonald) as   116–20
   witnessing   245–6
co-composition   132
collective assemblages of enunciation   131
colonial administrations   251
colonial difference   229, 251–3
colonial episteme   252
coloniality   30, 32, 37, 40, 72, 228–31, 239, 240, 255, 257
   art and   250–3
   moderns   251
   power   252
   vectoring   241–2
   as violence-praxis   242
colonial matrix of power   255–7
colonial murderers   242
colonization   242
colouring images   159–61, 163
colour space   159–60
commons   24, 29
   musical   26–7
concepts   225–6
   and functions   225
conceptual personae   225–6
Conley, Verena Andermatt   156
consciousness   46–7, 110, 201
content   142–4, 153, 220
content creators   220–1
Corgan, Billy   184
corpoculture   234
creation stories   247
creative commons   24
creativity   34

critical pedagogy of whiteness/
    coloniality   245–6
critical theory   71, 230–1
critique   30, 71–2
critique enthusiasm   71
crystal image   101, 195, 197–8
culture circle   246
Curtis, Adam   130
cybernetic capitalism   229
A Cyborg Manifesto (1991, Haraway)   6–7
cyborgrapher   7, 9
cyborgs   125, 179

Damasio, Antonio   36
dance of attention   134, 135, 158, 164
dancing virtualities   46
DCI-P3   159–60
Deamer, David   110
The Death of the Artist (2019,
    Deresiewicz)   249
de Castro, Vivien   252
decolonial futurity, cineworlding
    as   71–3
decoloniality   23–5, 29, 37, 40, 72, 229,
    239, 244, 253–7
    institutional   71
    music   23–5, 40
    practice of   255
    of undercommons   39
DeLanda, Manuel   90, 147, 148, 151
Deleuze, Gilles   13, 15, 18, 28, 35, 38–40,
    42, 43, 47, 48, 79, 80, 83, 84, 98,
    101–3, 105, 106, 109, 110, 115,
    119, 127–8, 130, 137, 138, 142,
    143, 145, 153, 154, 156, 173,
    179, 181, 184, 186, 187, 191,
    197, 201, 220, 222, 223
    movement-image   98, 115
    process ontology   99
    time-image   98, 115–16
delusion   184
Dēmos   125, 228–30, 234. *See also*
    Ethnos
Denny, Elder   254
Denny, Joel   42
Deresiewicz, William   249
deterritorialization   58, 80, 82–5, 90, 91
    aerial cinematography as   86–7

developing techniques   63–5
diagram   38–41, 53–5, 135, 139,
    142–3, 264
    between plane of material and
        composition   18–20
diagrammatic machine   142
diagrammatic music education   49
diagrammatic thinking   141–4
diagramming   276 n.10
digital audiovisual technologies   232
digital cinema
    camera   99
    ecosystem, emergence of   176–7
    ethnography and   226
    production   131, 176, 177, 222,
        259
digital images, mass production of
    219
dirtbag artfulness   32–3
DIY+ content creators   221
DIY production   221
documentary paradigm   150–1, 171
documentary production   190–2
documentation paradigm   26, 36, 39
double consciousness   229
Dubois, W. E. B   229
duration   109

ecological aesthetics   204
editing   139
    assemblage   136
Education for Critical Consciousness (2008,
    Freire)   245
Elders' Room (Steinberg)   239, 240,
    243, 245
    critical pedagogy   245
Ellington, Duke   39
enclosure   24, 29
enlightenment   24
    undercommons of   25, 33, 181–2
entertainment   51
episteme-techne   124–6
epistemological violence   252
ethico-aesthetic   1, 3, 5
ethnofiction   120–1
ethnographer   223, 225, 230
ethnographic film   130, 227
Ethnographic Film (Heider)   227

ethnography   3, 9, 31, 45–6, 66, 76–7, 98–100, 104, 198, 213, 227–9, 231, 235
  death of   231–3
  and digital cinema   226
  plane of reference   230–1
  reflexivity and relationality in   230
  social scientist   222–4
ethnomusicological film   179, 226–7
ethnomusicology   9, 31–2, 37, 193, 213, 223–6, 230, 281–2 n.6
  digital cinema for   227
'Ethnomusicology and Visual Communication' (1976, Feld)   226, 270 n.12
Ethnos   125, 228–30, 234
event   180
  of perception   145
  of a shot   138–9
existential relations   255
expression   142–4, 153
extensive space   140, 147–9, 153, 170, 264
  of colour   160
extramodern   252

Facebook   219
faciality in music videos   127–9
Fanon, Franz   31, 229
Feld, Steven   45, 113, 199, 226, 235
Fellini, Federico   58, 67, 184
fiction   121
fiction films   265
filmmakers bodying   215
Floyd, Pink   49, 55, 60–2, 181
The Fold (Deleuze)   15
folklore   254
folk traditions   251
Foucault, Michel   42, 186, 230, 252
frame   105–8
Freire, Paulo   239–40, 245, 246, 252
Freud, Sigmund   130

Gaelic   253
The Genius of the Violin (MacDonald)   38
Genosko, Gary   261
global capitalism   229
globalization   232–4

Grimshaw, Anna   173
Guattari, Felix   1, 5, 13, 18, 28, 35, 36, 38, 40, 42, 43, 79, 80, 83–5, 119, 128, 130, 142, 153, 154, 156, 173, 181, 184, 186, 191, 222, 223, 246, 260–1, 265

Hamilton, Andre   112, 113
Hank, Washboard   185
Haraway, Donna   6, 178, 187
Harbert, Benjamin   100, 176, 197, 226, 227
Harney, Stefano   23, 25, 27, 30, 68, 69, 71–2, 185–7, 240
HDV tapes   165
Head-Smashed-In Buffalo Jump   243
Heidegger, Martin   134, 177, 178
Heider, Karl G.   66, 67, 100, 227
Herzog, Werner   112, 184
holobiont   178
Homo sapiens   52, 125, 212
hooded image   140
hooks, bell   8, 31, 51, 141, 238, 241
humanist literacy   124
humanities   141–2, 144
  thinking   30, 35
Husserl, Edmund   46–7
hyalosign   197–8
hypermodernity   37, 40

Idle No More   104, 105, 108, 273 n.1
I Fink Ur Freeky (Antwoord)   132
illusions   46
image of thought   18–20, 26, 43, 106, 119, 141, 142
  modernity/coloniality   37
imagined communities   232
immanence, plane of   43, 44, 47, 48, 139, 142, 145, 225–6, 231
In Between (Cassidy)   126–7, 129, 132, 140–1
  posthumanography of   126–7
Indigenous communities   251, 254
in-folding   41, 43, 44, 50, 57, 59, 63–4, 67, 126, 239
institutional decoloniality   71
intensive space   57–9, 134, 140, 147–50, 171, 264

Index

intimacy 132–4, 142, 147, 149, 214–15
  vs. proximity 276 n.2
Intimate Encounters: Queer Entanglements in Ethnographic Fieldwork (Weiss) 133
intimate entanglements 133
intimate equipment 155–7
intimate temporality 88
intuition 15–16, 19, 41, 190

John Wort Hannam Is a Poor Man (JWH, MacDonald) 151–3, 171–2
  bodying of 164–5, 167
  camera bodying 166
  colouring images 159–61, 163
  diegetic shift from non-diegetic to diegetic 163
  end of the story 162
  filmmaker bodying 168–70
  lyric theatre 166–8
  opening scene 162
  'A Quiet Life' 166–7
  titles and graphical energy 161
  title sequence for 157
jump cut 167–8

Kant, Immanuel 41–2, 90, 92, 178, 182, 248, 250
  notion of thinking 36
  unconscious 40
kino-eye 112, 138
Krev, Niko 117
Krevenchuk, Colton. *See* Krev, Niko

Lacasse, Serge 37, 68, 118
Lambert, Gregg 40, 42, 144
land acknowledgements 244–5
landscape-face-music assemblage 87
Langer, Suzanne 140
Leibniz's critique of Descartes 15, 18
Lertzman, David 43, 190–2, 194–200, 203, 209
Linklater, Richard 1–3
literacy 124, 252
  education to Indigenous people 245, 246
Living Flame of Love (MacDonald) 77
  machinic case study 83–4
  aerial cinematography as deterritorialization 86–7
  beauty affect vectoring 89–91
  music icons painted in audio-vision 88–9
  Pro Coro Canada 91–3
  refrain, temporalization and micropolitics 87–8
  sound machines 91–3
  Togni's beauty 84–6
Look Up Tables (LUTs) 160
Loveless, Natalie 69, 134, 263
LUTs. *See* Look Up Tables (LUTs)

MacDougall, David 100, 103–4, 113, 179, 227
machine assemblage, of movement-images 145
machine-perception 18
machinic assemblage 79–80, 130, 145
  as process 81–2
machinic operation 53, 56
machinic process 53–4
machinic relations 40–3
machinic unconscious 40–1, 129–30
The Machinic Unconscious (2011, Guattari) 130
machining 52
Manning, Erin 15, 17, 28, 34, 35, 37, 41, 43, 65, 66, 69, 71, 72, 133–4, 138, 140, 158, 171, 180, 185, 186, 240
  concept of bodying 164
Margø (character)
  In Between (Cassidy) 126–7, 129, 132, 140–1
  monstrous faciality 136
Margolis, Cassidy 126–7, 132, 136, 140
Marrati, Paola 46–8
Marxist ethnomusicology 224
Massumi, Brian 25, 28, 34, 35, 43, 44, 53, 57, 81, 137, 139, 140, 143, 183, 186, 218, 260, 261, 263
The Matrix that Embeds (Humberto Maturana and von Foerster) 201–2
Matter and Memory (Bergson) 116
Maturana, Humberto 201

Megamorphosis (2016, MacDonald), territorial assemblage in 111–14
microperceptions 16
Mignolo, Walter 37, 71, 229, 246, 248, 251–3, 255
minor cinema 263–5
minor gesture 133, 135, 180
The Minor Gesture (2016, Manning) 264, 268 n.4, 271 n.2
modernity 30, 32, 37, 40, 252, 255, 257
    art in 246–50
molar 154
molecular 154
montage 106, 108, 109, 140
Morris, Alexander 242
Moten, Fred 23, 25, 27, 30, 68, 69, 71–2, 185–7, 240
movement 65–6, 137, 138
movement-images 64, 98, 115, 138–40
    machine assemblage of 145
Murch, Walter 16
musical commons 26–7, 30, 39
music-as-refrain 183, 184
musicking 27, 80, 82
music machines 54
music pedagogy 80
music video 5, 63
    aesthetics 45
    app 221
    digital production of 131
    faciality in 127–9
    as schizoanalysis 129–31
    vectoring of affects 221
mutuality 238

natureculture 138
Nehiyaw aesthetics 255
neocoloniality 37, 40
neoliberalism 229
neorealism 66, 67
neurotypicality 30, 33, 34, 138
Nietzsche, Friedrich 99, 103, 121, 176
non-literacy 252

objects 105–6
observational documentary 45, 46, 127, 130, 176, 191, 192, 205, 217, 243
obsessive refrain 56, 58

On Election Day 60, 63, 65
oral cultures 252
Ottawa Folklore Centre 78–9
out-of-field 106, 108, 109

packets of audiovisual affects 218–20
partial observers 223, 225
Peirce, Charles Sanders 106, 109, 194
    semiosis 220
PELT. *See* Petroleum Education Learning Tool (PELT)
percepts 13–14, 218, 222, 223, 275 n.9
Petric, Joseph 83, 84, 86, 91
Petroleum Education Learning Tool (PELT) 199
phenomenological ethnomusicology 224, 225
philosopher 217
philosophy 227–30
photo 218–19
Pimachihowan (MacDonald) 43–4, 189, 190, 193–4, 239, 240, 255
    crystal image/hyalosign 198
    hyalosign 198
    research-creation 193–5
    Sewepagaham, Conroy
        cinematic event 205–8
        filming of fire 194–8, 204, 206, 208, 209
        lessons/teachings 194–6, 199–200, 202, 205, 207
    virtuality of the film becoming actual 206–8
Pink, Sarah 179
pitch 148
plane
    of composition 13, 16, 18–19, 28, 41, 60, 64, 85, 135, 139, 217
    of immanence 43, 44, 47, 48, 139, 142, 145, 225–6, 231
    of material 13, 16, 18–19, 28, 41, 54, 57–60, 84, 85, 135, 217
    of reference 223–5, 228–31
platform capitalism 220–1
Plato 45, 46, 121, 247, 257
    forms 52, 149
    philosophical systems 228
    unconscious 40

universe 149
political activism 260–1
polyversity 54–5
  alternate reality 51–2
  worlding study in 55
  worlding *The Wall* (Floyd) 56
post-anthropocentrism 8, 125
posthuman 212, 216
  body 27–31, 165–6
  condition 8, 9, 261
  ecology 125, 177, 215
posthumanographer 110
posthumanography 9, 97–100, 102–4, 114, 125, 130
  of *In Between* (Cassidy) 126–7
  as minor cinema 265
posthumaographer 101–2
post-Kantian 41–3, 214
postmedia ecological activism 260, 261
power
  colonial matrix of 255–7
  Western imperial 250
Powerhouse of God (Titon) 191–2
practical cine-musicology 76–7
practical films 77–8
practical musicology 151
pre-acceleration 65, 174, 268 n.5
  towards record 135–6
primitive cultures 251
process ontology 99, 274 n.3
process philosophy 228, 260–3
Pro Coro Canada 83, 84
  sound machines 91–2
production assemblages 111, 118–20, 139
production process 62
Protevi, John 38
proximity 147
  vs. intimacy 276 n.2
pub screening 174–5
pure sensation 116

Quartet 2 (2010, MacDonald) 102–4, 174–5, 181–3
  affect vectoring 183–6
  my body, sensations, our bodies in 102–4
  study of becoming-node and vectoring 184–5

queering 156

racial inequality 238
Raunig, Gerald 219
Ravetz, Amanda 173
RAW Nation 116–17
Rec-709 159, 160
reconciliation 238
Redner, Gregg 110
refrains 19–20, 54, 63, 80–1, 84–5, 87–8, 180, 184
  cineworlding 175–7
  in grain/pixel/colour/sound 21
  obsessive 56, 58
  territorializing 175, 180, 181, 183
relational enlightenment 52–3
relation-of-nonrelation 143
Remix and Lifehack in Hiphop (2016, MacDonald) 112
Repression 117
research-creation 4–5, 26, 34–6, 39–40, 72, 76, 118, 179–80, 187, 193–5, 259
  as critical pedagogy 36–8
  from documentary production to 190–3
  drama in 144–5
  in-folding of 41, 43, 44, 50, 57, 59, 63–4, 67
  Pimachihowan (MacDonald) 193–5
  posthuman 125
  proposition 31–2
  as realization of alternate reality 67–9
  as study 185–7
  transversality 77, 234–6
'Research-Creation: Intervention, Analysis and "Family Resemblances"' (2012, Chapman) 34
reterritorialization 82, 83, 85, 87, 90, 91
  of the refrain 80, 88
Robinson, Dylan 150, 238
Rouch, Jean 112, 115, 117, 120, 121, 164, 169, 185, 235
Round Dance and Media (2013), frame and shot, virtual and actual in 104–11
Ruby, Jay 100
Rushton, Richard 120

Russell, Catherine 45

sacredness 201, 204
Sartre, Jean-Paul 242
Sawchuk, Kim 68
schizoanalysis 129–31
science-fiction (sci-fi) 51–2
  study in undercommons 69–71
scientific ethnography 222–5
scientist 217
sci-fi. *See* science-fiction (sci-fi)
screen 46–8, 139
screen assemblages 111, 115, 120, 139
  and cineworlding 120–1
screen production
  process 118
  research 119
scriptwriter 59–62
scriptwriting 59
self-enjoyment process 262, 263
semblance 139–40, 149
semiosis 220
  model 109
sensation 102–4, 110
sensory flow 57
settlement's enclosure 24, 29
Sewepagaham, Conroy 43–4, 190–2, 202, 203, 205, 209, 240, 241, 244, 255, 262, 263
  Pimachihowan (MacDonald)
    cinematic event 205–8
    filming of Conroy's fire 194–8, 204, 206, 208, 209
    lessons/teachings 194–6, 199–200, 202, 205, 207
shot 108–9, 138–9
  event of 138–9
Shotwell, Alexis 239, 240
silence as musical moment 28
Simondon, Gilbert 16
Small, Christopher 80, 81, 93, 200
snap shots 107
social and environmental
  intimacy 214–15
social science cinema 176
sonic/sound-images 44–6, 163, 215
sound field 56–7
sound-image field 158

space 109
speculative-pragmatics 143, 144
Spinetti, Federico 102
Spinoza, Baruch 27, 79, 137, 138, 182
Spinoza-Bergson-Vertov
  proposition 134, 136–40, 164
spirituality 86, 87
Steinberg, Shirley 245
Stengers, Isabelle 262
Stévance, Sophie 37, 68, 118
Stiegler, Bernard 123, 185, 186
superabstract invention 153–4
sympoiesis 178
Szymanski 264

tape technology 165–6
Tea Dance 195–7
'Team Spirit to Spirit' initiative 207–8
techne 124
technicity 15–17
technics 124–5, 185, 186, 275 n.4
technification of perception 125
technocultural ecological studies 177–9
technoculture 138
techno-embodied assemblage 216
technological machines 52
technology 123–4, 133, 134, 186, 279–80 n.1
TEK. *See* Traditional Ecological Knowledge (TEK)
tempocentrism 177
temporalization 87–8
territorial assemblage 111–14, 119, 139
territorial flux 111–13, 119, 195
territoriality 83
  of spirituality 87
territorializing factor 173
territorializing refrain 175, 180, 181, 183
thinking-feeling 25, 27, 30, 36, 42, 52, 64, 134
  decoloniality of 33
thinking-feeling of artfulness 141
The Third Unconscious (2021, Berardi) 130
TikTok 220
time-image 64, 98, 120
  films 115–16
Titon, Jeff Todd 191–2

Togni, Peter   83–93
tonal music   174, 175
traditional culture   252–3
Traditional Ecological Knowledge
    (TEK)   199, 200, 202, 256, 262
traditional music   254
transhuman   212
transversal art-ethnography of
    process   80–1
transversality   76–7
Truth and Reconciliation   237
Truth and Reconciliation Commission of
    Canada   237, 244, 279 n.6
Turino, Thomas   106
Twitter   219
two-row wampum   257
typeface   161

unconscious, machinic   40–1, 129–30
undercommons   180
    decoloniality   39
    of the enlightenment   25, 33, 181–2
    musics   26–7, 40
    sci-fi study in   69–71
undisciplined thinking   51
university-as-settlement   26, 30, 224,
    237, 259
Unspittable (2019, MacDonald), screen
    production assemblage in   115
    as cineworlding   116–20
urban sociality   251

Varda, Agnès   121
vectoring of affect   183–6, 215
vectoring of affect packet   221
Vertov, Dzigo   112
    kino-eye   112, 138
village sociality   251
violence   242
virtual   98, 100–2, 105, 110, 114, 119–20,
    139–40, 147, 187, 191, 192, 216.
    See also actual

virtual film   184
visual anthropology   205
visual ethnography   278 n.5
visual-image field   158
visual-images   44–6, 48, 215
vitality affect   137, 145, 276 n.10
volition-intentionality-agency
    triad   123–5, 134, 150, 164,
    178
von Foerster, Heinz   201–2

walking   65
The Wall (Floyd)   49, 50, 56, 60–2,
    66, 181
Walsh, Catherine   255
Weiss, Margot   133
WE'RE TOO LOUD (MacDonald)   75–7,
    82, 211
    critical public pedagogy   215
    posthumanography   213, 215
    sustainability of ecologies   215
Western episteme   250
Western imperial powers   250
Whitehead, Alfred North   143, 187, 263
whiteness   32, 37
white-supremacist capitalist patriarchy
    8
white wall/black hole   88–9, 91, 94, 128,
    174, 175, 186
    recursion   216
    system   128
wintigo   241–2
    reflection   242–3
Woodman, Charles. *See* Repression
worlding   43, 44, 52, 54–5, 177–8
    as activist cine-
        ethnomusicology   226–7
    study at polyversity   55

Zagorski-Thomas, Simon   77, 151
Zaugg, Michael   83, 84, 91–3
Zourabichvili, Francois   140, 145

www.ingramcontent.com/pod-product-compliance
Lightning Source LLC
Chambersburg PA
CBHW070750020526
44115CB00032B/1602